STUDIES ON VOLTAIRE AN

*SVEC*

2005:09

INDEX

A fully searchable index to over
fifty years of research published in *SVEC*
http://www.voltaire.ox.ac.uk/svec_index

Manuscripts should be prepared in accordance with the *SVEC* style sheet, available on request and at the Voltaire Foundation website (www.voltaire.ox.ac.uk) One paper copy should be submitted to the *SVEC* general editor at the Voltaire Foundation, 99 Banbury Road, Oxford OX2 6JX, UK; an electronic version, with a summary of about 750 words, should be sent to jonathan.mallinson@trinity.ox.ac.uk

# 'Seeing' speech:

## illusion and the transformation of dramatic writing in Diderot and Lessing

ROMIRA M. WORVILL

To Carolyn + Del,
from the author,
with love.
Dec. 30th, 2005
Thank you
for a
great
christmas!

**SVEC**

**2005:09**

VOLTAIRE FOUNDATION

OXFORD

2005

ISBN 0 7294 0864 7
ISSN 0435-2866


Voltaire Foundation
99 Banbury Road
Oxford OX2 6JX, UK

The correct reference for this volume is
*SVEC* 2005:09


This series is available on annual subscription

For further information about *SVEC*
and other Voltaire Foundation publications see
www.voltaire.ox.ac.uk, or email svec@voltaire.ox.ac.uk


This book is printed on acid-free paper

Typeset and printed in Europe by the Alden Group, Oxford

# Contents

# Acknowledgements

Throughout the preparation of my doctoral thesis and its subsequent transformation into this book, I have benefited greatly from the generous help and wise counsel of a number of people whom I would like to acknowledge and thank here. They are: Dr Peter Allan of Mount Allison University; Dr David Smith of the University of Toronto; Dr Nicholas Cronk of St Edmund Hall, Oxford, and the Voltaire Foundation; Dr Kate E. Tunstall of Worcester College, Oxford; Dr Barry Nisbet of Sidney Sussex College, Cambridge; Dr Jonathan Mallinson of Trinity College, Oxford, and of the Voltaire Foundation; Rebecca du Plessis, Publishing manager, Voltaire Foundation; the staff of the Taylorian Library in Oxford and of the Vaughan Memorial Library at Acadia University in Nova Scotia; my college, Linacre; the members of my family in Canada (Bob, Daisy and Emma) as well as my family in England (Carol and Mike, Charles and Gerry). However I would particularly like to thank my thesis supervisor and friend, Francis Lamport of Worcester College. I have learned so much from Francis, not only about German literature, about scholarship and about writing, but also about tolerance, about patience and about persistence. Thank you, Francis, for all that you have done.

Romira Worvill

# List of abbreviations

All these are given in full, with abbreviation on first mention, thereafter abbreviation only. Exception is *HD*, which is only used when a specific reference is being given (either in footnote or in brackets beside quotation or comment).

DPV   Denis Diderot, *Œuvres complètes*, ed. Herbert Dieckmann, Jacques Proust, Jean Varloot, *et al.* (Paris 1975-), 34 vols projected.

Göpfert   Gotthold Ephraim Lessing, *Werke*, ed. Herbert G. Göpfert, 8 vols (Munich 1970-1979).

*HD*   Lessing, *Hamburgische Dramaturgie* (1768).

LM   Lessing, *Sämtliche Schriften*, ed. Karl Lachmann, 23 vols (Stuttgart, Berlin and Leipzig 1886-1924).

*OC*   *The Complete works of Voltaire* (Geneva, Banbury, Oxford 1968-), 135 vols projected.

Petersen   *Lessings Werke*, ed. Julius Petersen, Waldemar von Olshausen, *et al.*, 25 vols (Berlin n.d.).

# Introduction

In the spring of 1760 Diderot's two plays, *Le Fils naturel* and *Le Père de famille*, together with the accompanying works of theory, *Les Entretiens sur 'Le Fils naturel'* and the *Discours de la poésie dramatique* appeared in German translation under the title *Das Theater des Herrn Diderot*. In the preface, the anonymous translator salutes the French dramatist as the new Aristotle, someone 'der die alten Wege weiter bahnet, und neue Pfade durch unbekannte Gegenden zeichnet'.[1] Lessing, the unidentified translator who hopes that a Frenchman's rejection of French neo-classical models in the name of nature and truth will help the German stage shake free of French influence, went on to create three highly successful plays, *Minna von Barnhelm* (1767), *Emilia Galotti* (1772) and *Nathan der Weise* (1779). These works, which are still performed today, helped found a national drama of international repute and bequeathed to German culture a gallery of unforgettable characters. Minna, Tellheim, Werner, Franziska, Marinelli, Orsina, Gonzaga, Conti, and, of course, Nathan have loomed as large in German consciousness as Le Cid, Chimène, M. Jourdain, Alceste, Hermione, Phèdre, or Figaro in the French. In 1780 (the year before his death, as it was to turn out) Lessing republished *Das Theater des Herrn Diderot* with minor modifications to the text, his name on the title page and a new preface. This second preface reiterates Lessing's convictions about the value of Diderot's theatre writings and contains an eloquent acknowledgement of his personal debt to his French contemporary. He welcomes the opportunity to thank a man who, he says, had contributed so much to the formation of his own taste, and he adds that without Diderot's theory and dramatic models, his own taste would have taken a completely different direction.[2] 'Vielleicht eine eigenere', he continues, 'aber doch schwerlich eine, mit der am Ende mein Verstand zufriedener gewesen wäre.'[3] These statements, which Lessing never chose to explain further, have tantalised Lessing scholars ever since, for whilst Lessing's sense of obligation leaves no room for doubt, the matter of how, exactly, Diderot's models and doctrine ('Muster und Lehren') helped shape Lessing's mature plays remains unresolved.

---

1. 'Who extends the old pathways and blazes new trails through unknown territories', Gotthold Ephraim Lessing, *Werke*, ed. Herbert G. Göpfert, 8 vols (Munich 1970-1979), iv.148. Future references will be to this edition (identified as Göpfert), unless otherwise stated. All translations are my own, unless otherwise stated.
2. Göpfert, iv.149.
3. 'Perhaps a more original one, but scarcely one with which, in the end, my mind would have been more satisfied.' Göpfert, iv.149.

The problem is easy to summarise. At a superficial glance, Lessing's words might seem merely to state the obvious. It is a fact that his finest dramas, those on which his reputation as a playwright principally rests, were all composed after he had immersed himself in the plays and theory Diderot published in the late 1750s.[4] It is therefore tempting to see Lessing's three major plays (a 'serious' comedy, a middle-class tragedy and a philosophical drama) as realisations of Diderot's theory of the *drame* in the context of the German theatre. Upon closer inspection, however, it becomes clear that various obstacles stand in the way of such a tidy account of the development of Lessing's mature style, since a number of the features generally considered hallmarks of Diderot's theatre aesthetic are also present in Lessing's thinking and dramatic style before 1757. In the *Theatralische Bibliothek* of 1754, Lessing's second theatrical periodical, he published translations of two essays on sentimental comedy (Chassiron against the genre and Gellert in favour), framed with an introduction and a conclusion of his own. In the introduction, Lessing points to the development of sentimental comedy in France and domestic tragedy in England as new dramatic forms modifying the traditional distinctions between comedy and tragedy and drawing them closer together.[5] In the conclusion, he rejects tearful comedy of the type favoured by La Chaussée, but defends plays that effectively combine moving scenes with humorous ones. He argues that 'true comedies' ('wahre Komödien') have never lacked touching scenes and defines them as plays which 'so wohl Tugenden als Laster, so wohl Anständigkeit als Ungereimtheit schildern, weil sie eben durch diese Vermischung ihrem Originale, dem menschlichen Leben, am nächsten kommen'.[6] Only this kind of comedy,

4. The scholarly consensus is that Lessing only came across Diderot's critique of French theatre in *Les Bijoux indiscrets* after he had translated the plays and theory of the late 1750s and that Erich Schmidt ('Diderot und Lessing', in *Die Gegenwart* 9, 1881, p.133-36 and p.153-55, [p.135]) was mistaken to suggest otherwise. The passage from Diderot's novel is reproduced, in Lessing's German translation, in numbers 84 and 85 of the *Hamburgische Dramaturgie* (1768), which is the only reference to this particular work in Lessing's writings. For discussion of this question, see *Lessings Werke*, ed. Julius Petersen and Waldemar von Olshausen *et al.*, 25 vols (Berlin and Vienna 1907; Hildesheim and New York 1970) ix.10 and n.1 (henceforward Petersen); Roland Mortier, *Diderot en Allemagne, 1750-1850* (Paris 1954), p.81; Francis Lamport, 'Lessing traducteur et critique de Diderot', in *Etudes sur 'Le Fils naturel' et les 'Entretiens sur le Fils naturel' de Diderot*, ed. Nicholas Cronk (Oxford 2000), p.171-80 (p.172). Apart from Schmidt, the only exception to the general view is Klaus-Detlef Müller, who simply asserts that Lessing read and translated the passage from *Les Bijoux indiscrets* in the late 1740s. He makes no reference to the critical discussion and provides no supporting evidence for his claim. See *Das Theater des Herrn Diderot: aus dem Französischen übersetzt von Gotthold Ephraim Lessing*, ed. Klaus-Detlef Müller (Stuttgart 1986), p.426-27. The findings of the present study tend, indirectly, to confirm the general view.

5. Göpfert, iv.13.

6. 'True comedies' are those which 'depict both virtue and vice, decency and folly, because it is through this very fusion that they most closely approach their original, human life.' Göpfert, iv.55.

asserts Lessing, can transcend the narrow tastes that characterise particular social classes and appeal to 'das Volk'. Thus, already by 1754, he is thinking in terms of a new kind of socially useful, true-to-life drama with universal appeal.

His interest in the evolving intermediate genres first came to fruition in 1755, not in the form of a *wahre Komödie* but as an extremely successful middle-class tragedy, *Miss Sara Sampson*, which established the type on the German stage.[7] The play is set in contemporary England, deals with non-heroic, fictional characters, is written in prose and was conceived for the new, so-called 'natural' acting style.[8] After this theatrical success, more theory. In a series of letters exchanged with Friedrich Nicolai and Moses Mendelssohn in 1756 and 1757, Lessing elaborates his theory of *Mitleid* (sympathetic identification) which he sees as the principal effect for which tragedy should strive, insisting (in opposition to his friends) that all drama must have a moral and social goal. Lessing also alludes to 'a mass of disorganised thoughts on middle-class tragedy', which he has set down on paper and proposes sending to Nicolai (this text no longer exists).[9] These explorations are all motivated by Lessing's aim of furthering the development of an authentically indigenous drama. To achieve this, he sees it as absolutely necessary to abandon the false model of French neo-classicism foisted on the public by Gottsched, a position vehemently expressed in the seventeenth *Literaturbrief* of 1759, where Lessing suggests that the Germans would have more to learn from Shakespeare, who is closer to the spirit of the Ancients.[10]

Finally, as I shall show in chapter 5 (p.117-44), there is evidence in the two completed tragedies of the 1750s (*Miss Sara* and *Philotas*) that Lessing was already writing into his plays *tableau*-like scenes, one of which is referred to in the dialogue itself as an *Anblick* (a 'spectacle'). The rejection of French neo-classicism in favour of other models, a theoretical and practical interest in intermediate genres, the exploitation of prose and mimetic acting, commitment to the moral and social role of drama and the incorporation of visually expressive scenes are considered defining elements of Diderot's dramatic theory, and they are all present in Lessing's own theory and/or practice before he came across the theatrical writings of his French contemporary. So what did Lessing mean?

This question, which a critic writing in the 1980s described as 'one of the unsolved riddles of literary history', has spawned quite a number of

7. Richard Daunicht, *Die Entstehung des bürgerlichen Trauerspiels in Deutschland*, 2nd edn (Berlin 1965), p.270.

8. Theodore Ziolkowski, 'Language and mimetic action in Lessing's *Miss Sara Sampson*', *The Germanic review* 40 (1965), p.261-76.

9. Gotthold Ephraim Lessing, Moses Mendelssohn and Friedrich Nicolai, *Briefwechsel über das Trauerspiel*, ed. Jochen Schulte-Sasse (Munich 1972), p.45. This letter (20 July 1756) is not in Göpfert's edition.

10. Göpfert, v.71-72.

thoughtful and thought-provoking articles.[11] There is still no critical consensus on the answer. Modern engagement with the problem can be dated from the appearance of three studies in the early 1950s: Robert R. Heitner's article entitled 'Concerning Lessing's indebtedness to Diderot' (1950), a chapter from Roland Mortier's well-known reception study, *Diderot en Allemagne* (1954), and an article by Theodorus van Stockum called simply 'Lessing und Diderot' (1955). These three scholars come at the issue from different angles, and subsequent critics have tended, on the whole, to follow one or other of the approaches charted in their treatments.[12]

Heitner's article was motivated by a desire to clarify the facts concerning the question of Diderot's influence on Lessing and to stem the swelling tide of claims that were either false or exaggerated. He identifies the principal source of such errors as the 'discrepancy between the words of Lessing's tribute and the evidence to be found in his writings'.[13] His own conclusions are carefully weighed, and although he insists that he does not want 'to minimize the significance which Diderot had for Lessing', he nevertheless arrives at the view that Lessing only 'wished to make use of Diderot's propaganda value in the popularisation of an attitude toward drama which he himself had conceived of previously, and in general *without* Diderot's influence'.[14] Heitner's position reflects the one taken earlier by Julius Petersen in the introduction to his edition of Lessing's translations of Diderot, to which Heitner refers. Petersen insists that what Diderot represented for Lessing was not so much a teacher as a stimulus, and that whilst Aristotle furnished Lessing with firm principles, Diderot simply provided ideas ('Einfälle') that do not always stand up under close scrutiny.[15] Heitner's view that Lessing's acknowledgement of the importance of Diderot's 'models and precepts' should not be taken too seriously is endorsed by Karl Guthke, in his 1973 survey of Lessing criticism.[16] Although Guthke finds Lessing's comparison of Diderot with Aristotle easy to understand in the light of Lessing's rejection of neoclassical tragedy, he adds: 'Weniger verständlich ist Lessings Behauptung in der Vorrede zur zweiten Auflage (1781 [*sic*]), Diderot habe an der Bildung seines Geschmacks maßgeblichen Anteil gehabt.'[17] A number of

11. Joseph Carroll, '*Minna von Barnhelm* and *le genre sérieux*: a reevaluation', *Lessing yearbook* 13 (1981), p.143-58 (p.143).

12. Robert R. Heitner, 'Concerning Lessing's indebtedness to Diderot', *Modern language notes* 65 (1950), p.82-88; Theodorus van Stockum, 'Lessing und Diderot', *Neophilologus* 39 (1955), p.191-202.

13. Heitner, 'Concerning Lessing's indebtedness to Diderot', p.84.

14. Heitner, 'Concerning Lessing's indebtedness to Diderot', p.87.

15. Petersen, ix.11.

16. Heitner, 'Concerning Lessing's indebtedness to Diderot', p.87.

17. 'Much less comprehensible is Lessing's assertion in the second edition (1781 [*sic*]) that Diderot exercised a measurable influence on the formation of his own taste.' Karl S. Guthke, *Gotthold Ephraim Lessing* (Stuttgart 1973), p.36.

the critics who have made more recent contributions to the debate reach conclusions similar to those of Heitner.[18] Whatever the specific focus of their study (Lessing's translations of Diderot, his interest in a middle genre, his possible application of Diderot's theory of *conditions*), scholars writing in the tradition established by Heitner tend, on the whole, to underplay the significance of the statements Lessing made in 1780, to limit Diderot's role in Lessing's development to that of an ally in the struggle against French neo-classicism, and to stress Lessing's originality and independence from French thought.[19]

Mortier, in his study of 1954, cites Heitner's article and appears to agree in some respects with his views. He, too, sees the Diderot translation as 'une œuvre de combat',[20] but he gives the facts a rather different emphasis. Mortier recognises the difficulty of explaining exactly what Lessing meant by his remarks in the second preface, but he nonetheless insists on the importance of taking the words at their face value. In his opinion, 'On ne saurait ignorer, ni même traiter à la légère, un témoignage aussi formel' even if its full significance remains unclear.[21] The main thrust of Mortier's study is to demonstrate the immense scope of German interest in Diderot's writings as a whole, and in the section on drama he traces allusions to Diderot's work in numerous German writers of the period.[22] Less concerned with the specifics of Diderot's impact on this or that individual, he nevertheless offers a few brief suggestions as to where

18. Lessing, *Das Theater des Herrn Diderot*, ed. Müller, p.428-30; Alison Scott-Prelorentzos, 'Diderot, Lessing and "Das wahre Lächerliche"', in *Momentum dramaticum. Festschrift for Eckehard Catholy*, ed. Linda Dietrick and David G. John (Waterloo 1990), p.135-48; Günter Saße, 'Das Besondere und das Allgemeine. Lessings Auseinandersetzung mit Diderot über Wahrheit and Wirkung des Dramas', in *Gesellige Vernunft: Zur Kultur der literarischen Aufklärung*, ed. Ortrud Gutjahr, Wilhelm Kühlman and Wolf Wucherpfennig (Würzburg 1993), p.263-76.

19. Scott-Prelorentzos explains Lessing's tribute to Diderot in the following way: 'One is tempted to think that in 1780 Lessing, re-reading the *Dramaturgie*, saw so many rifts in Diderot's theories that he opted to concentrate on praising *Le Père de famille* and its undoubted effect on German theatre' ('Diderot, Lessing and "Das wahre Lächerliche"', p.138). Saße concludes that Lessing considers Diderot 'mehr ein probates Mittel zum Zweck seiner antiklassisistischen Polemik, als daß er sich mit ihm als substantiellem Denker auseinandersetzt' ('more a proven means to be used in advancing his anti-classical polemic than a thinker of substance with whom to come to terms') ('Das Besondere und das Allgemeine', p.265).

20. Mortier, *Diderot en Allemagne*, p.60.

21. Mortier, *Diderot en Allemagne*, p.77.

22. Mortier sees the influence of Diderot on German drama of the second half of the century as extensive. He writes that Lessing's appeal to the German-speaking population to consider Diderot's (and therefore Lessing's) new ideas 'ne devait pas rester vain, toute l'histoire du théâtre allemand de 1760 à 1780 en fait foi' (*Diderot en Allemagne*, p.59), and again, 'Les contemporains de Lessing ne s'y sont pas trompés: l'année 1767, celle de *Minna* et de la *Dramaturgie*, consacre définitivement le prestige de Diderot homme de théâtre. Comme l'a très bien dit l'historien du drame bourgeois en Allemagne, M. Pinatel, de 1767 à 1774 aucune œuvre importante n'échappe à son influence' (p.84).

he sees potential evidence of Lessing's assimilation of Diderot's ideas. For Mortier, *Minna von Barnhelm*, with its contemporary subject matter, its particular tone ('une note en demi-teinte, comme un sourire attendri') and the representation of Tellheim as both an individual and a soldier (that is, from the perspective of his 'condition d'officier'), all suggest Diderot's theory.[23] He hints that similar evidence could be adduced from *Emilia Galotti*, and offers the view that *Nathan der Weise* represents a masterful application of Diderot's summarily presented concept of a philosophical play. Although not explored in detail, his essential argument is that Lessing's subsequent writing was principally affected by Diderot's ideas for broadening the range of dramatic genres to include different kinds of *genre sérieux* that would provide scope for the depiction of *conditions*.

Mortier's observations have given rise to several studies along these lines. Joseph Carroll and Günter Hartung follow his lead in examining how *Minna von Barnhelm* (Carroll) or, indeed all three of Lessing's mature plays (Hartung) may be seen to reflect Diderot's theorising about intermediate genres.[24] But their speculations remain inconclusive because, in the matter of genre, it is impossible to identify with certainty what Lessing may owe to Diderot and what may simply be the result either of his independent reflections (on Plautus and the *wahre Komödie* for example) or of the trends towards the blurring of the boundaries between genres that had been reshaping contemporary drama since the 1730s. Moreover, those arguing the case for seeing Diderot's influence in Lessing's choice of intermediate forms cannot cite any text where Lessing comments specifically on Diderot's genre scheme. None of the passages from Diderot that Lessing quotes or refers to in the *Literaturbriefe* and the *Hamburgische Dramaturgie* concern genre as such, and genre is not mentioned in the famous chapter from *Les Bijoux indiscrets*, which Lessing considers to be a succinct articulation of the essentials of Diderot's theory.[25]

It is true to claim, however, that the dramatic characters of Lessing's post-Diderot plays are more vividly portrayed and more convincing than those of his earlier works, and in suggesting here the influence of Diderot's theory of *conditions*, Mortier is taking up a theme that had already been raised by contemporaries of Lessing.[26] Since the appearance of Mortier's

23. Mortier, *Diderot en Allemagne*, p.77-78.

24. Carroll, '*Minna von Barnhelm* and *le genre sérieux*'; Günter Hartung, 'Diderots *Système dramatique* und der Dramatiker Lessing', *Beiträge zur Romanischen Philologie* 24:2 (1985), p.295-99.

25. Göpfert, iv.626.

26. See, for example, Herder's comments on *Emilia Galotti*: 'Er zeigt den Charakter des Prinzen in seinem Stande, den Stand in seinem Charakter – beide von mehreren Seiten, in mehreren Situationen' ('He shows the character of the Prince in his *condition*, and his *condition* in his character – both from several aspects and in several situations'): Johann

study, a number of critics have revisited this idea. Peter Demetz, in his edition of *Nathan der Weise*, finds that Tellheim 'inkarniert schon die erste interessante *condition* der deutschen Schaubühne', and he asserts elsewhere that 'Lessing mag der Vorherrschaft der Stände über den Charakter abgeneigt sein [...]; aber die Figuren seines späteren Werkes, sogar der Prinz und Marinelli in *Emilia Galotti*, sind konkrete Charaktere in einer spezifischen Welt.'[27] More recently, Richard Critchfield has examined the representation of Tellheim, Hettore Gonzaga and Odoardo as examples of the successful exploitation of Diderot's theory of *conditions* and he concurs with an opinion also held by Demetz, namely that in *Nathan der Weise*, even though the play does not depict contemporary life, Nathan's *condition* (as a merchant) is a vital force.[28] Francis Lamport notes that whilst Lessing's later achievements in terms of character portrayal are greatly superior to those of Diderot, 'la théorie des "Stände", telle que Lessing la comprenait, n'a pas été sans influencer sa propre œuvre'.[29]

At the same time, the proposal that Lessing's mature plays can be seen as embodying in some way Diderot's theory of *conditions* is hotly contested by other commentators who point to Lessing's critique of Diderot's views on this matter in numbers 86-96 of the *Hamburgische Dramaturgie*. They exploit Lessing's own analysis to show that his success in creating convincing dramatic characters is the direct result of his *not* applying Diderot's theories. Günter Saße argues that Diderot's concept of stage characters, which relies on the idea that *dramatis personae* function as models, is utterly at odds with Lessing's beliefs about how sympathetic identification between the characters and the audience is achieved.[30] Similarly, Elmar Buck attributes Lessing's major accomplishments to his

Gottfried Herder, *37. Humanitätsbrief*, in *Sämtliche Werke*, ed. Bernhard Suphan (Berlin 1877), xvii.183.

27. 'Tellheim embodies the first interesting *condition* on the German stage', Gotthold Ephraim Lessing, *Nathan der Weise*, ed. Peter Demetz, *Dichtung und Wirklichkeit* 25 (Frankfurt 1966), p.125; 'Lessing may be opposed to the predominance of condition over character [...] but the figures represented in his later works, including the Prince and Marinelli in *Emilia Galotti*, are concrete individuals in a specific world', Peter Demetz, 'Die Folgenlosigkeit Lessings', *Merkur. Deutsche Zeitschrift für europäischen Denkens* 25:8 (1971), p.727-41 (p.737-38).

28. Richard Critchfield, 'Lessing, Diderot, and the theatre', in *Eighteenth-century German authors and their aesthetic theories*, ed. Richard Critchfield and Wulf Koepke (Columbia, SC 1988), p.11-28 (p.19).

29. Lamport, 'Lessing traducteur et critique de Diderot', p.178-79.

30. 'Anders als bei Diderot, bei dem die den *conditions* inhärenten Normen das primäre sind, die das Drama im Handeln und Erleben der Protagonisten zu veranschaulichen hat, ist bei Lessing das Allgemeine das Sekundäre, das der Rezipient in der reflexiven Affektivität der *Furcht* als ihn betreffend erfährt. Daraus resultieren zwei unterschiedliche Rezeptionsbeziehungen', Saße, 'Das Besondere und das Allgemeine', p.275 ('With Diderot, the norms inherent in the *condition*, which the play makes apparent through the actions and experience of the protagonists, are the primary thing. With Lessing it is different. For him, what is general occurs at a secondary level, experienced by the spectator as personally relevant through the self-reflexive emotion of fear').

rejection of Diderot's theories of character and *conditions*, which, Buck insists, are fundamentally untheatrical.[31] Thus although there is general agreement that Lessing's portrayal of dramatic character develops significantly in the post-Diderot plays, the reasons for this are in dispute and those who oppose the idea that Lessing adopts Diderot's theory of *conditions* are able to support their position by reference to Lessing's criticism of Diderot in the *Hamburgische Dramaturgie*. Thus, the line of thinking initiated by Mortier's study has not yet resulted in critical agreement, and whilst explorations of Diderot's and Lessing's treatments of both genre and *conditions* have yielded some interesting insights, there is also much that they leave out. Being predominantly literary in emphasis, these studies focus on questions of subject matter and ethos, the kind of events (and characters) that Lessing chose to dramatise. But these analyses fail to explain the most striking transformation in Lessing's post-Diderot drama, namely the development of his skills as a playwright. Regardless of genre or theme, *Minna von Barnhelm*, *Emilia Galotti* and *Nathan der Weise* are vastly superior to Lessing's earlier plays in terms of their theatricality. They are much better adapted to stage representation and have a greater impact on the audience than the earlier ones. However this very striking development in Lessing's capacity to conceive and write stage-worthy dramas is not accounted for in the discussions of genres and *condition*.

Van Stockum's article, 'Lessing und Diderot', opens up this line of approach. Like Heitner, Van Stockum is keen to dispel unwarranted and exaggerated claims about Diderot's role in Lessing's development as a writer. Unlike Heitner, though, he believes that the impact of Diderot's ideas on Lessing can be traced. He begins by defining the areas worth examining from this perspective and he limits these strictly to dramaturgy and dramatic praxis.[32] He restricts the field further by drawing attention, as other critics do, to innovative dramatic ideas that Lessing and Diderot unconsciously shared before 1760 (use of prose, interest in contemporary life, exploitation of middle genres). For Van Stockum, this leaves only two other possible areas of thought for Lessing to draw on: Diderot's theory of dramatic imitation (what Van Stockum calls his 'dramaturgische Naturnachahmungslehre') and his emphasis on the moral purpose of drama. Other critics find Van Stockum's point about moral purpose puzzling, especially as Van Stockum asserts that in 1757, Lessing's concept of the pleasure proper to tragedy was not yet linked to its moral effect. In support of this statement, he cites a letter Lessing wrote to Mendelssohn in the context of their discussion of tragedy.[33] In fact, it is in these letters that Lessing is at great pains to argue, in opposition to

---

31. Elmar Buck, 'Lessing und Diderot – die Konditionen des Theaters', in *Schauspielkunst im 18. Jahrhundert: Grundlagen, Praxis, Autoren*, ed. Wolfgang F. Bender (Stuttgart 1992), p.205-19 (p.219).

32. Van Stockum, 'Lessing und Diderot', p.192.

33. Van Stockum, 'Lessing und Diderot', p.201.

Mendelssohn and Nicolai, that tragedy does and must have a moral purpose, and that this purpose is accomplished through the evocation of *Mitleid* in the spectator. Jochen Schulte-Sasse therefore rightly dismisses Van Stockum's statements about moral purpose as erroneous.[34] On the question of illusion, though, Van Stockum makes a valuable contribution to the discussion, not found in any of the other commentators mentioned so far. Furthermore, his claim is based on the positive statements concerning Diderot's achievements that Lessing makes in numbers 84 and 85 of the *Hamburgische Dramaturgie* where he reproduces his own translation of Diderot's commentary on drama from *Les Bijoux indiscrets* and highlights Diderot's repeated insistence on the fact that theatrical representation should be, above all, a lifelike imitation of nature. 'Den klaren lautern Diderot!' concludes Lessing, 'Aber alle diese Wahrheiten waren damals in den Wind gesagt.'[35] Van Stockum points out that 'Wir haben es hier mit einem der zentralen Grundsätze von Diderots Dramentheorie zu tun, den Lessing offenbar billigt; man het [*sic*] ihn dessen Verismus, Realismus, bzw. Naturalismus genannt, vielleicht aber wäre *Illusionismus* dafür die treffendste Bezeichnung.'[36] Van Stockum's emphasis on 'illusion', or 'illusionism', as central to the nature of Diderot's impact on Lessing seems to me to get to the heart of the matter. He says no more than this, however, and does not explore how Diderot's concept of illusion is absorbed into Lessing's theory or writing practice.

Very few scholars seem to have taken up this aspect of Van Stockum's study. The most interesting is a brief article (three pages) by Heidi Ritter, published in 1985. Ritter suggests that the commentary on acting in the early numbers of the *Hamburgische Dramaturgie* shows that Lessing's reading of Diderot had further stimulated his own interest in the efficacy of the new natural acting style.[37] In particular, she argues that Diderot's insistence on finding the proper balance between speech and gesture helped Lessing refine his own dramatic technique. She sees Diderot's influence emerging in the more extensive stage directions Lessing includes in *Minna von Barnhelm*, and in scenes, such as act II, scene viii, which conform to Diderot's definition of a 'scène composée'.[38] She adds that it is Lessing's more skilful handling of dialogue in *Minna von Barnhelm* that

34. Lessing *et al.*, *Briefwechsel über das Trauerspiel*, p.202.

35. 'How clear and how plain-speaking Diderot is! But at that time, all these truths were uttered to the wind.' Göpfert, iv.626.

36. 'We are dealing here with one of the central tenets of Diderot's dramatic theory, and one which Lessing clearly accepts; it has been called Diderot's doctrine of verisimilitude, his realism or rather naturalism, but perhaps "illusionism" would be the most accurate name for it.' Van Stockum, 'Lessing und Diderot', p.199.

37. Heidi Ritter, 'Zur Schauspielkunst bei Diderot und Lessing', *Beiträge zur Romanischen Philologie* 24:2 (1985), p.301-304 (p.301).

38. Ritter, 'Zur Schauspielkunst bei Diderot und Lessing', p.303. She notes, though, that these stage directions are not as detailed as Diderot's and that they are still often written into the dialogue.

allows what Lessing calls 'die individualisierenden Gestus' ('the individualising gestures') to achieve their most effective expression and thus make
the play more dramatically successful.[39] At the same time, she suggests that
Lessing does not seem to have accepted so readily Diderot's theory of the
*tableau*, citing as proof the fact that Lessing avoids the use of this device in
the place where one might have most expected to find it, namely at the
very end of *Minna*.[40] Ritter is right to draw attention to the role of acting
and performance in Lessing's mature comedy and by emphasising the
importance of the relationship between speech and gesture, her article
seems to me to bring us closer than any other to an understanding of what
Lessing found valuable in Diderot's theory. Yet her thinking on the
matter of stage *tableaux* is open to question. The fact that Lessing nowhere
comments on Diderot's observations concerning stage *tableaux* has surprised other commentators, particularly in view of the importance often
attached to this aspect of Diderot's theory, both by his contemporaries
and subsequently.[41] But to conclude as Ritter does that the omission
signifies Lessing's aversion to the concept seems to me untenable in the
light of Lessing's theatrical practice. *Emilia* and *Nathan* both end with a
*tableau* and visual scenes of this type are also to be found in some of his
pre-Diderot plays.

Neil Flax pursues the issue of stage *tableaux* in an article on Lessing's
second middle-class tragedy, *Emilia Galotti*. He argues that although
Diderot is Lessing's primary source for ideas concerning pictorial representation in the theatre, Lessing's use of the stage *tableau* differs from
Diderot's, in that Lessing exploits it simultaneously as a natural and an
arbitrary sign, not unlike metaphor in poetry.[42] Flax's argument hinges
on the claim that the scene in which Odoardo murders Emilia is 'an overt
quotation of a familiar pictorial motif', which would have been easily
recognisable to the audience.[43] But this interpretation does not seem to
conform to the facts, since a simple comparison shows that the *tableau*
called for in Lessing's stage directions does not visually resemble the
widely disseminated engraving by Gravelot that Flax uses to make his
case. The engraving depicts an open-air scene in a market square before an imposing building. The body of the murdered Virginia has just

39. Ritter, 'Zur Schauspielkunst bei Diderot und Lessing', p.302. In *HD* 4, Lessing
writes: 'ich merke nur an, daß es unter den bedeutenden Gesten eine Art gibt, die der
Schauspieler wohl zu beachten hat, und mit denen er allein der Moral Licht und Leben
erteilen kann. Es sind dieses, mit einem Worte, die individualisierenden Gestus' ('I simply
note that among the signifying gestures, there is one kind to which the actor must pay close
attention and which alone allows him to make the moral clear and lively. These, in a word,
are the individualising gestures'), Göpfert, iv.250.
40. Ritter, 'Zur Schauspielkunst bei Diderot und Lessing', p.303.
41. Lamport, 'Lessing traducteur et critique de Diderot', p.179.
42. Neil Flax, 'From portrait to *tableau vivant*: the pictures of *Emilia Galotti*', *Eighteenth-
century studies* 19 (1985), p.39-55 (p.49-50).
43. Flax, 'From portrait to *tableau* vivant', p.50.

collapsed to the ground in the bottom right-hand corner of the image, her father's hand still on her arm, but he has already turned his attention (and his body) towards the magistrate and officials positioned on the steps of the building, and the knife, seized from the nearby butcher's stand, points directly at them. Beneath his raised his arm, other citizens are stirring. The principal figures, Virginia, Virginius and the magistrate, are arranged along a diagonal running from the bottom right corner of the image to the upper left side, linked through the arms of Virginia and her father, and the raised knife, in a way that makes the causal sequence of the historical narrative perfectly intelligible. In Lessing's play, the setting is not an open forum but an antechamber in Gonzaga's well-protected summer palace, far from the public gaze. Emilia and Odoardo are alone, the two figures drawn close together by Odoardo's disarming of Emilia. After she provokes the fatal blow, Odoardo catches her in his arms and holds her for several moments before she dies, when he lays her gently on the floor. Gonzaga and Marinelli, the only witnesses, enter after the stabbing but in time to see her die.[44] The differences between Gravelot's conception of the subject and the stage *tableau* envisaged in Lessing's play illustrate well Lessing's declared purpose of creating 'eine modernisierte, von allem Staatsinteresse befreite Virginia'.[45] Visually, Lessing's stage *tableau* recalls much more closely a scene from La Noue's *Mahomet II*, described by Diderot in the *Entretiens* as a 'tableau frappant' ('ein rührendes Gemälde', in Lessing's translation) and cited as an example of the kind of simple action suitable for 'illusionistic' representation on the stage.[46] For these reasons, Flax's article is not ultimately persuasive, although his analysis, which highlights the transformation of Emilia from the subject of a portrait in the opening scenes of the play to that of a *tableau vivant* at the end, makes it clear that Lessing was very interested in these kinds of effect.

In my own efforts to come to grips with the Diderot–Lessing relationship, I have tried to draw on the strengths of all three approaches outlined here. Mindful of the warnings of Heitner and his disciples, I have made every effort to respect the facts and not to do Lessing the injustice of overstating the case for Diderot's role. At the same time, I agree with Mortier that we must take Lessing's tribute seriously, especially since we know him to be a writer who used language carefully and thoughtfully. But it is Van Stockum's emphasis on the importance of Diderot's 'dramaturgische

---

44. Göpfert, ii.203-204.

45. 'A modern Virginia, freed from any connection to the interests of the state', Göpfert, ii.707.

46. 'La vue de Mahomet tenant un poignard levé sur le sein d'Irène, incertain entre l'ambition qui le presse de l'enfoncer, et la passion qui retient son bras, est un tableau frappant', Denis Diderot, *Œuvres complètes*, ed. Herbert Dieckmann, Jacques Proust, Jean Varloot *et al.*, 34 vols projected (Paris 1975-), x.141. Future references to Diderot will be to this edition, using the abbreviation DPV, unless otherwise stated.

Naturnachahmungslehre' as formulated in the *Bijoux indiscrets* that represents for me a crucial starting point. I will try to show that this particular critique of neo-classical tragedy, together with the alternative approach to dramatic form that accompanies it, lies at the heart of what Lessing found so important in Diderot's concept of dramatic representation. Ritter – surprisingly to me – makes no mention of this passage from Diderot's novel, and she limits her discussion of Lessing's practice to *Minna von Barnhelm*. I will thus try to build on the insights of both Ritter and Van Stockum by showing how Lessing's reading of Diderot's theory, which unifies language and gesture by reference to the spectator who watches and listens to the performance, allowed him to develop a style of dramatic language that would better support the new acting styles and the creation of illusion.

Oblique support for this approach is provided by various currents in Lessing scholarship, which have long documented a reorientation of aesthetic positions and style in Lessing's post-1760 period. Thus, Victor Anthony Rudowski, analysing Lessing's statements in the letters on tragedy, comments 'On the one hand, the idea that theatrical performance is not an essential part of the dramatic method was to remain a permanent aspect of his critical system. On the other, his position in regard to the importance of illusion seems to have undergone considerable revision in his later thinking.'[47] Similarly, Frederick Burwick notes, 'In his answer to Mendelssohn (18 December 1756), Lessing claims that illusion is no matter of special concern for the playwright. Lessing will later change his mind and discriminate generic differences in the nature of illusion and in the ways in which it may be propagated.'[48] J. G. Robertson believes that despite Lessing's refusal, in the letters on tragedy, 'to countenance the idea that illusion is essential to the aesthetic effect', by the time of the *Laokoon* 'he had thought more deeply on the subject; and in the *Dramaturgie* he has plainly accepted Mendelssohn's views'.[49] Only Otto Hasselbeck links this shift to Lessing's reading of Diderot, in particular of the *Entretiens*, and he sees Lessing's comparison of Diderot with Aristotle (in the 1760 preface) as positive evidence of Lessing's interest in Diderot's theory of mimesis.[50]

Similarly, in relation to the treatment of speech in Lessing's tragedies, Emil Staiger and Jürgen Schröder both draw attention to the differences in Lessing's skill in the pre- and post-1760 works. Without going into

47. Victor Anthony Rudowski, *Lessing's 'aesthetica in nuce': an analysis of the May 26, 1769, letter to Nicolai* (Chapel Hill, NC 1971), p.51.

48. Frederick Burwick, *Illusion and the drama: critical theory of the Enlightenment and Romantic era* (University Park, PA 1991), p.88.

49. J. G. Robertson, *Lessing's dramatic theory, being an introduction to and commentary on his 'Hamburgische Dramaturgie'* (Cambridge 1939; New York 1965), p.430.

50. Otto Hasselbeck, *Illusion und Fiktion: Lessings Beitrag zur poetologischen Diskussion über das Verhältnis von Kunst und Wirklichkeit* (Munich 1979), p.107 and p.187, n.3.

detail, they point to the usual suspect, identifying parallels between statements Lessing makes in the *Hamburgische Dramaturgie* and ideas he would have come across in Diderot's theatrical writings.[51] As for the language of Lessing's comedies, Michael Metzger too, emphasises the superiority of technique in *Minna von Barnhelm*. Only this work truly displays 'Lessing's mastery of the language of comedy, his full use of the techniques acquired during his literary apprenticeship in Leipzig, and his penetration beyond these to a new conception of the expression of character'.[52] Finally, it is a fact that the first work in the field of aesthetics that Lessing would complete in the period following the Diderot translation was the *Laokoon*, a semiotic study proposing an account of how the effect named 'illusion' can best be achieved in different artistic media through the effective deployment of the signs proper to them.

In three areas then (the importance Lessing attaches to dramatic illusion, the effectiveness of his dramatic language, and his interest in sign theory), critics are well aware of developments that occur in Lessing's thought and writing after 1760. All of these elements are dimensions of drama as imitation, aspects of the *Naturnachahmungslehre* evoked by Van Stockum, since the nature of the aesthetic illusion achieved by a dramatic work is a function of its sign system, and language is one of its signs. Illusion, theatrical signs and dramatic speech are all explored in Diderot's dramatic theory, and the aim of this book is to show that it was through his study of Diderot's theoretical and practical treatment of these matters that Lessing came to a richer appreciation of the possibilities inherent in theatrical form.

As Marian Hobson and others have shown, 'illusion' was a central preoccupation of eighteenth-century aesthetics, not just in relation to drama but across all the arts.[53] Lessing's ambitious semiotic project which terminated as the *Laokoon* is itself an indication of this.[54] It would therefore not be surprising to find that the artistic nourishment Lessing drew from his French contemporary's work is related to this major trend in the aesthetics of the time. Moreover, viewed from this perspective, the question of Lessing's debt to Diderot becomes more than just an unsolved 'riddle' from literary history, a leftover 'curiosity'; it emerges as a case-study in the transmission and assimilation of mainstream aesthetic ideas of the day. Lessing's theatrical *œuvre*, from the early comedies to *Nathan*,

---

51. Emil Staiger, 'Rasende Weiber in der deutschen Tragödie des achtzehnten Jahrhunderts', in *Stilwandel. Studien zur Vorgeschichte der Goethezeit* (Zürich 1965), p.25-74 (p.56); Jürgen Schröder, *Gotthold Ephraim Lessing: Sprache und Drama* (Munich 1972), p.143 and p.145.

52. Michael M. Metzger, *Lessing and the language of comedy* (The Hague, Paris 1966), p.239.

53. Marian Hobson, *The Object of art: the theory of illusion in eighteenth-century France* (Cambridge 1982).

54. David E. Wellbery, *Lessing's Laocoon: semiotics and aesthetics in the Age of Reason* (Cambridge 1984).

offers the opportunity to examine a general shift that occurred in the eighteenth century from a dramatic aesthetic still rooted in the neo-classical mindset to a coherent and aesthetically viable alternative result-ing from the re-evaluation of illusion.

Not surprisingly, in view of Lessing's own interest in semiology, it is helpful to approach this transformation in conceptions of dramatic form from the perspective of the semiotics of theatrical representation. Theatre generates meanings in the way that is unique to it as an art form when an actor performs (acts and speaks) for an observer who looks on and interprets what he or she sees and hears.[55] Dramatic performance can involve the use of a wide range of signs: linguistic signs, other vocal signs (shouts, sighs), facial expressions, gestural signs, movement about the stage, signs associated with the actor's appearance (including mask, hairstyle and costume), spatial signs (stage space, décor, props, lighting) and non-verbal acoustic signs (sounds, music).[56] Successful theatrical performance can be said to rely on the effective interplay of a network of sign systems, functioning in harmony. Strictly speaking, theatrical signs are signs of signs, that is, they tend to be drawn from primary sign systems that exist within the surrounding culture such as those regulating dress, gesture, interior decoration, music, codes of writing, and so on.[57] Spec-tators watching a performance spontaneously relate the artistic signs generated by a play to the sign systems outside the theatre from which they derive. Clearly, not all plays or genres exploit all the possible sign systems that are available to theatrical representation: for example, only some plays use masks; many plays make no use of music; linguistic signs can take the form of verse or prose and can be spoken or sung. The theatre of a particular culture, epoch, social stratum, or genre therefore represents a selection from among all the conceivable possibilities, and this choice of elements constitutes the theatrical code governing the play(s) in question.[58] In addition, the aesthetic sign systems that are put to use in a particular play may be accorded equal status, or they may be deployed according to a hierarchical structure. Different genres are often characterised by the dominance of a particular sign system, such as language or music, and the different codes or sets of norms that have come into being at different points in time can be envisaged as the result of changes taking place in the formation of such dominants.[59]

55. Erika Fischer-Lichte, *The Semiotics of theater*, translated by Jeremy Gaines and Doris L. Jones (Bloomington and Indianapolis, IN 1992), p.7. This is an abridged version in English translation of Fischer-Lichte's original text, *Semiotik des Theaters*, 3 vols (Tübingen 1983).
56. Fischer-Lichte, *The Semiotics of theater*, p. 13-17.
57. Fischer-Lichte, *The Semiotics of theater*, p. 9.
58. Fischer-Lichte, *The Semiotics of theater*, p. 11.
59. Fischer-Lichte, *The Semiotics of theater*, p.135.

Although theatre makes use of signs drawn from other cultural sign systems, there are different ways of combining these theatrical signs in terms of their overall effect. They may be deployed in such a way that anyone familiar with the signs of the surrounding culture will be easily able to interpret them when they are recruited as artistic signs. On the other hand, the artistic signs may be such that it is necessary for the spectator to be familiar with the theatrical code as an artistic code in order to interpret them successfully and to experience their full impact. Stage representation that strives to create the illusion of scenes drawn from human life (illusionistic theatre) does not rely upon special knowledge of a particular theatrical code, but presupposes only that the members of the audience belong to the same cultural domain and are therefore able to interpret the theatrical signs by reference to their own experience of sign use in the surrounding culture. Other forms of theatre, for example No theatre, classical ballet or Italian opera, exploit a more sophisticated theatrical code which is most effective when the spectators have some familiarity with the aesthetic sign systems at work and know how to interpret them.[60] In other words, whilst all theatrical codes rely on artistic signs and the conventions associated with them, some codes overtly proclaim themselves to be artistic or aesthetic codes, whilst others utilise theatrical signs that have the same form as the primary signs of the culture in question and thus obfuscate the gap between the theatrical code and other cultural codes. In the eighteenth century, dramatists such as Diderot and Lessing, who reject French neo-classical tragedy in favour of domestic drama and middle-class tragedy, are opting for an illusionistic type of theatrical code over a more formalistic one.

The contrast between self-evident artistry and its concealment that characterises different kinds of theatrical code is reflected at the level of dramatic language in the form of the linguistic signs that plays exploit. In some respects, the words of a play have the same function as words in other literary works: they serve to constitute, for the recipient, the world represented by the work. At the same time though, the words of a play share this role with other sign systems, both visual and acoustic, and this, in part, shapes the form that they take.[61] Furthermore, the fact that the words are mediated exclusively through dramatic characters means that the same words (signifiers) have different meanings and functions (signifieds) for the represented interlocutors and for the spectators. For the fictional characters, the words that are spoken are not taken as represented language but simply as a normal fact in their (represented)

60. Fischer-Lichte, *The Semiotics of theater*, p.137-39.

61. Roman Ingarden, *The Literary work of art: an investigation on the borderlines of ontology, logic, and theory of literature: with an appendix on the function of language in the theater*, translated by George G. Grabowicz (Evanston, IL 1973), p.392-93. First published as *Das literarische Kunstwerk mit einem Anhang von den Funktionen der Sprache im Theaterschauspiel* (Tübingen 1931).

life.[62] This dimension of the relationship of the *dramatis personae* to the words spoken is the same in the illusionistic and in most types of non-illusionistic theatrical codes, for even in plays which make use of verse and poetic language, the characters behave as if they are unaware that the language and delivery are not actually 'normal' in relation to the situations in which they find themselves.[63] For them, the special qualities of the language are overlooked and the words spoken by all the characters are treated as ordinary.

This is not, however, the case for the spectators. Since they are situated outside the world represented by the play, they do not participate in the conversation but merely observe it. As spectators, they are necessarily in what Roman Ingarden calls 'an aesthetic attitude', attuned to the apprehension of the work of art, but their relationship to the play language will differ according to whether the play they are watching is illusionistic or non-illusionistic. In the case of illusionistic drama, it appears to them as if the speech that is used addresses only the *dramatis personae* on the stage. Whilst it is true that the language has been created by the playwright with due regard for its necessary functions within a play, it nevertheless creates the impression that it is in no way directed at them, as spectators. In this kind of dramatic form, the speech does not betray the fact that it has been created 'for' an audience. This is not the case with theatre that is not illusionistic. In these forms, the special features of the dramatic speech (such as the use of verse and poetic language) are not there for the fictional characters, who affect not to notice them, but in order to enhance the pleasure of the spectators. These qualities exist to be perceived and appreciated by the audience as features of the artistic sign itself, or to perform whatever other tasks are ascribed to them within the given theatrical code. In the case of French neo-classical tragedy, for example, an important function of the language is to evoke pictures in the imagination of the audience, allowing them to recreate the world of the play in their mind, and this effect is brought about by the special, poetic qualities written into the speech of the fictional characters. Thus, it could be said that in non-illusionistic theatre, the linguistic signs do indeed 'address' the spectators as much as they address the represented persons. Ingarden suggests that this contrast between the two broad categories of play language is a fundamental difference between illusionistic and non-illusionistic theatre.

Eighteenth-century commentators approach these matters of theatrical code and types of dramatic language from the perspective of their own sign theory, which rests upon a primary distinction between natural and

---

62. Ingarden, *The Literary work of art*, p.394-95.

63. An exception in this category, in theory at least, would be the drama of Brecht in which the *Verfremdungseffekt* depends precisely upon the actor delivering the words as 're-presented' language.

artificial signs.[64] According to this analysis, all signs, both natural and artificial, communicate meaning by creating representations, essentially pictures, in the mind of the beholder or listener.[65] Natural signs are either those which constitute an aspect of a given phenomenon (thus smoke is a natural sign of fire) or those whose form as signs can be seen to resemble the thing signified. With natural signs, there is no hiatus between the signifier and the thing or idea it stands for. Artificial signs are those whose power to signify is established by convention and whose meaning cannot be deduced from the form of the sign itself. Images, and in particular painting, are therefore considered to be modes of communication that exploit natural signs, whereas language and the verbal arts rely on a system of artificial signs. This way of understanding the working of signs is very clearly expressed by the abbé Dubos in his *Réflexions critiques et historiques sur la poésie et sur la peinture*, which was first published in 1716. Citing the authority of Horace, Dubos argues that painting has a more powerful impact on people than poetry does because it uses natural signs which we take in through the physical eye, the most influential of the senses. He writes:

En second lieu, les signes que la peinture emploie pour nous parler ne sont pas des signes arbitraires et institués tels que sont les mots dont la poésie se sert. La peinture emploie des signes naturels dont l'énergie ne dépend pas de l'éducation. Ils tirent leur force du rapport que la Nature elle-même a pris soin de mettre entre les objets extérieurs et nos organes, afin de procurer notre conservation. Je parle peut-être mal quand je dis que la peinture emploie des signes, c'est la nature elle-même que la peinture met sous nos yeux. Si notre esprit n'y est pas trompé, nos sens du moins y sont abusés. La figure des objets, leur couleur, les reflets de la lumière, les ombres, enfin tout ce que l'œil peut apercevoir se trouve dans un tableau comme nous le voyons dans la nature, elle se présente dans un tableau sous la même forme où nous la voyons réellement.[66]

Poetry, on the other hand, takes longer to achieve its effects because the mind has to reconstitute its artificial signs as images:

Les vers les plus touchants ne sauraient nous émouvoir que par degrés et en faisant jouer plusieurs ressorts de notre machine les uns après les autres. Les mots doivent d'abord réveiller les idées dont ils ne sont que des signes arbitraires. Il faut ensuite que ces idées s'arrangent dans l'imagination, et qu'elles y forment ces tableaux qui nous touchent, et ces peintures qui nous intéressent.[67]

---

64. This distinction is formulated in the discussion of signs in the works of the Port Royal authors from the 1660s on. Nicholas Cronk, *The Classical sublime: French neoclassicism and the language of literature* (Charlottesville, VA 2002), p.3-6.

65. Wellbery, *Lessing's Laocoon*, p.9-12.

66. Abbé Jean-Baptiste Dubos, *Réflexions critiques et historiques sur la poésie et sur la peinture* (Paris 1993), p.133-34. This edition is based on Dubos's final edition of 1740 (republished posthumously by Pissot in 1755), but with modernised spelling.

67. Dubos, *Réflexions*, p.134.

Dubos does not distinguish, as Lessing later will, between the aesthetic and the non-aesthetic use of signs; he does not separate the art of painting from the use of images to communicate information, just as in the preceding quotation he does not differentiate between verse and words in general.[68] Similarly, he does not draw distinctions between the different arts that use language; Dubos discusses the ode in the same terms as he does tragedy and comedy. As a matter of fact, the poetic examples he most often gives in the *Réflexions* are drawn from French tragedies, and Dubos believes that tragic speech should, and does, function in the same way as any other kind of verse.[69]

This way of categorising signs into arbitrary and natural ones is able to accommodate another view of the linguistic signs as used in the context of dramatic representation. It is clear that many of the signs on which theatre draws (human figures, costumes, properties, painted sets) may be selected in such a way that they formally resemble the things they signify. In fact, theatre lends itself particularly well to the exploitation of natural artistic signs, even more so, perhaps, than the art that provides the model for natural signs, namely painting. Within the conceptual framework created by the classification of all signs into those that are natural and those that are artificial, it becomes apparent that language has a dual character and can, when used as a theatrical sign, also become natural. As language, it remains an artificial sign when considered as the medium of communication used by the characters of the play among themselves, but from the point of view of the spectators, the possibility exists for it to achieve the status of a natural sign, because language itself is being used to 'imitate' language, speech represents speech, talking persons represent talking persons. Theoretically then, there can be a type of dramatic language which formally resembles the thing it signifies, that is, a kind of dramatic speech that imitates ordinary, non-aesthetic ways of speaking and that creates, in effect, an illusion for the ear. In other words, the distinction made in eighteenth-century sign theory between natural and artificial signs made possible a conception of dramatic speech that resembles the one expounded by Ingarden. At the time when Lessing and Diderot began writing for the theatre, a form of dramatic speech designed to create an illusion for the ear did not exist within the contemporary tradition of literary drama. Tragedy was written in verse and made use of poetic language; comedy also sometimes exploited verse, but whether written in verse or prose, it relied on wit and other techniques for manipulating language to create humour. In both genres, words are being treated as arbitrary signs and attention is focused on language as a sign vehicle, displaying the resources of the sign itself. But various currents of aesthetic thought evolving from the late seventeenth century onwards

68. Dubos, *Réflexions*, p.135.
69. Dubos, *Réflexions*, p.95.

gradually gave rise to the idea that play language could be transformed into a natural sign, following the principles of the natural signs of painting, and thus contribute to a form of theatrical illusion comparable to the illusion created by visual art. This is the project to which the plays and dramatic theory of Diderot and Lessing made such a major contribution.

The new style exemplified in the plays of Diderot and, particularly, in those of Lessing has sometimes, as Van Stockum observed, been called 'realism', despite the difficulties, anachronistic and otherwise, associated with the use of this term. I have become convinced that this is much more our word than theirs and that what modern-day critics may feel inclined to describe as the 'realism' of writers such as Diderot and Lessing, they themselves conceptualised as the creation of aesthetic 'illusion', by which they mean, as Lessing tells us in the *Laokoon*, a pleasing deception that 'renders absent things as if present'.[70] As a way of testing this hypothesis, I have deliberately avoided use of the words 'realism', 'real' or 'reality' throughout the present study. If these words occur, it is only within direct quotations from other sources, not in the main body of the text. In fact, it proved surprisingly easy to leave these terms out, but readers will judge for themselves whether or not this strategy contributes to a better understanding of these writers' goals.

By and large, modern critics have taken Diderot's theatre as a starting point and have emphasised the ways in which his works initiate new trends, either from the perspective of genre, as with Félix Gaiffe's monumental study of the *drame*, or in relation to the increasing interest in the visual aspects of dramatic representation in the latter half of the century, as in the recently published study by Pierre Frantz.[71] This approach is, of course, easily justifiable, though it has sometimes served to conceal the extent to which Diderot's theory draws on the achievements of other dramatists and on other currents in aesthetics. Hans Robert Jauss, for example, opens an illuminating article on the *Entretiens sur 'Le Fils naturel'* with the completely inaccurate assertion that in the chapter about theatre in *Les Bijoux indiscrets*, Diderot introduces a brand new challenge to the principles of neo-classical theatre and in so doing lays the foundation for the development of a modern aesthetic theory.[72] In fact, the passage Jauss refers to is much less 'original' than he suggests, since its main ideas derive from earlier critiques of contemporary drama, in particular those associated with the names of Houdar de La Motte and Paul Landois. Alternatively, the background to Diderot's dramatic aesthetic is considered only in terms of very general literary and social developments. Gaiffe, in his study, discusses this background under

70. Göpfert, vi.9.

71. Félix Gaiffe, *Le Drame en France au XVIIIe siècle* (Paris 1910; 1971); Pierre Frantz, *L'Esthétique du tableau dans le théâtre du XVIIIe siècle* (Paris 1998).

72. Hans Robert Jauss, 'Diderots Paradox über das Schauspiel (*Entretiens sur le 'Fils naturel'*)', *Germanische-Romanische Monatsschrift* 11 (1961), p.380-413 (p.380).

headings such as the decadence of neo-classical tragedy and comedy, the influence of foreign literature and social change. Michel Lioure proceeds in similar fashion, emphasising literary factors, in his much briefer survey of the background to Diderot's innovations.[73] And despite Diderot's near silence on Nivelle de La Chaussée and the *comédie larmoyante* (a fact that is stressed by Derek Connon[74]), there are critics who simply assert that the *drame* is its offspring.[75] Even when commentators look into the matter of Diderot's sources in more detail, as Connon does, they have relatively little to say about the ways in which his concept of dramatic speech, of the spectator and of the stage *tableau* relate to earlier theatre or painting theory. This is the gap that the present work tries to fill in order to arrive at a reading of Diderot's theatrical writings that will better illuminate their significance for Lessing and for other writers of the age.

Diderot and Lessing were prolific writers and I have deliberately re-stricted my investigation to works directly relevant to the question at hand. As far as Diderot is concerned, I will draw mainly from the theatrical writings that we know Lessing read. These are the passage on theatre from *Les Bijoux indiscrets* (1748), the *Lettre sur les sourds et muets* (1751), *Le Fils naturel* and the *Entretiens* (1757), *Le Père de famille* (1758) and the *Discours de la poésie dramatique* (1758). In addition, I shall make occasional reference to articles from the *Encyclopédie* from the same period and to Diderot's 1758 letter to Mme Riccoboni, which help clarify points made in the other texts.

In the case of Lessing, the focus is on the principle plays and the drama theory from the pre- and post-Diderot periods. A comparison of his thinking and his dramatic practice before and after the Diderot trans-lation is necessary to show how his dramatic aesthetic evolved. The watershed date is 1759. Petersen and Wilfried Barner agree that the fifty-first *Literaturbrief* of August 1759 reflects Lessing's immediate response to Diderot's texts and that work on the translation must have started at about the same time. The quotation from the *Entretiens sur 'Le Fils naturel'* in the eighty-first *Literaturbrief* (dated 7 February 1760) is identical in wording with the published translation of later that year.[76] Lessing was

73. Michel Lioure, *Le Drame* (Paris 1963), p.12-15.

74. Derek Connon, *Innovation and renewal: a study of the theatrical works of Diderot*, *SVEC* 258 (1989), p.121-22. Connon thinks that Diderot may have failed to mention this genre because he saw it as a threat to his own reputation as an innovator. Perhaps more likely is that Diderot considered his dramatic aesthetic to be in essential ways different from the one that inspires La Chaussée's works, as maintained by Theodore E. D. Braun, 'From Marivaux to Diderot: awareness of the audience in the *comédie*, the *comédie larmoyante* and the *drame*', *Diderot studies* 20 (1981), p.17-29 (p.28).

75. Lioure, *Le Drame*, p.15.

76. Petersen, ix.14, and Gotthold Ephraim Lessing, *Werke und Briefe in zwölf Bänden*, ed. Wilfried Barner (Frankfurt am Main 1985-), v.547. Letter 103 also makes explicit reference to Diderot and will be mentioned. The *Literaturbriefe* continued to appear until 1765, although very few of them concern drama and Lessing's contributions became less and less frequent.

already familiar with Diderot's *Lettre sur les sourds et muets* which he had reviewed in June 1751 (in *Das Neueste aus dem Reich des Witzes*), identifying it as a work by the author of the *Lettre sur les aveugles* (1749), a publication he obviously also knew.[77] Lessing was not the first person to present Diderot's plays and theory to the German-speaking public. Reviews had already appeared in German magazines in 1759 and, unlike what happened in France, both plays received their first public performances (in Baden and Zurzach) in the late summer of that year.[78] But although other translations of the plays already existed, Lessing's versions of the *Entretiens* and the *Discours* were the first in German. As noted above, Lessing does not appear to have come across *Les Bijoux indiscrets* until some time after 1759.[79]

In the period immediately preceding 1759, Lessing's main preoccupation had been tragedy, and this is reflected in the letters on tragedy that he exchanged with Nicolai and Mendelssohn between 1756 and 1757.[80] This correspondence represents Lessing's most thorough attempt up until then to formulate a theory of tragedy and it covers a number of topics, including the contentious issue of illusion.[81] Two completed plays date from the same period, *Miss Sara Sampson* (1755) and the one-act tragedy, *Philotas*, written in 1758 and published anonymously in 1759. These works will be used to illustrate the main features of Lessing's dramatic theory and practice immediately before his study of Diderot. Lessing's earliest dramatic efforts, dating from the 1740s, were in the field of comedy. A respected body of critical commentary on the style of these plays, including the nature and role of language, already exists, and I shall invoke this work to highlight a certain consistency of technique between these early comedies and the tragedies of the following decade.

From the period following the Diderot translation, the major plays, *Minna von Barnhelm* (1767), *Emilia Galotti* (1772) and *Nathan der Weise* (1779), as well as two important theoretical and critical works, the *Laokoon*, published in 1766, and the *Hamburgische Dramaturgie* of 1767-1769, will be considered. Reference to the *Laokoon* may, at first glance, seem surprising, since it is not, ostensibly, a work about drama, but about the realms 'proper' to visual art (sculpture and painting) and to epic

77. Göpfert, i.115-23.

78. See Mortier, *Diderot en Allemagne*, p.51-57 and p.60-61; and Lessing, *Werke und Briefe in zwölf Bänden*, v.547.

79. See p.2, n.4 above.

80. These letters were first published in the 1794 edition of Lessing's *Sämtliche Schriften* (Göpfert, iv.831).

81. See Peter Michelsen, 'Die Erregung des Mitleids durch die Tragödie. Zu Lessings Ansichten über das Trauerspiel im Briefwechsel mit Mendelssohn und Nicolai', in *Der unruhige Bürger, Studien zu Lessing und zur Literatur des achtzehnten Jahrhunderts* (Würzburg 1990), p.107-36 (p.108). This is a revised version of an article that first appeared in the *Deutsche Vierteljahrschrift für Literaturwissenschaft und Geistesgeschichte* 40 (1966), p.548-66.

poetry. But it is Lessing's first work of theoretical aesthetics to appear following his study of Diderot's theatrical writings, and it sets out his theory of illusion and artistic signs, which are topics relevant to his mature plays. In addition, one of the unpublished fragments from the projected but never realised second and third volumes affords an interesting glimpse into the place that drama must logically occupy within Lessing's semiotic framework. This fragment is relevant to Diderot's theory, as are observations Lessing makes in the important letter to Nicolai of 26 May 1769. The *Hamburgische Dramaturgie*, an exercise in practical drama criticism, contains both explicit and implicit references to Diderot, most notably numbers eighty-four to ninety-five, which were prompted by a performance of Diderot's *Père de famille* in Lessing's translation. The latter include Lessing's German rendering of the passage from *Les Bijoux indiscrets* as well as a long discussion of the creation of dramatic characters. Other passages from the *Hamburgische Dramaturgie* that specifically mention Diderot or reflect Lessing's assimilation of French concepts will also be discussed. This selection of texts omits Lessing's many dramatic fragments. To include them would require a considerable amount of space and is not, I believe, necessary to the present purpose.[82] The works listed above were all published, and in the case of the plays performed, by 1780, the date of the second preface to *Das Theater des Herrn Diderot*, where Lessing acknowledges his creative debt to Diderot. They represent the public achievements underlying Lessing's reputation as a playwright and theatre critic and by which, he must have assumed, he would be judged by posterity. When he identified Diderot as a source of inspiration, he presumably expected his readers to interpret this acknowledgement in the light of his published works, and so this is largely what I have done. Since my intention is to explore the impact on Lessing's theatre of Diderot's theory of dramatic mimesis (his *Naturnachahmungslehre*), I shall also leave aside some topics that are often prominent in discussions of eighteenth-century domestic drama. Issues such as the social standing of the characters, the preferred types of plot, the didactic goals and the appeal to *sensibilité* will be raised where relevant, but I shall focus mainly on how language, supported by gesture, stage space and other visual effects, contributes to the creation of the kind of dramatic illusion that has come to be seen as characteristic of the new genres, that is, on plays as performing art, or as communication between stage and spectator. A number of commentators consider this to be Diderot's most valuable legacy to later generations of dramatists. The following chapters of this study will first examine the sources and the formulation of Diderot's conception of theatrical representation and then explore how his approach to dramatic form was assimilated by Lessing

---

82. A comprehensive discussion of the dramatic fragments of the 1750s can be found in Francis Lamport, *Lessing and the drama* (Oxford 1981), ch.1 and ch.4.

and helped shape the works through which he realised his potential as a dramatist of international importance. The stylistic developments embodied in the plays that Lessing completed after translating Diderot's dramatic writings can be seen to illustrate very well the profound effects that the widespread contemporary interest in illusion had on the dramatic writing of his time.

# I

## Theories of art and literature:
## the background to Diderot's innovations

# I. Theories of art and literature: the background to Diderot's innovations. Introduction

THEATRICAL codes as described in the previous chapter represent one kind of cultural sign system existing alongside many others, which all function in dynamic relationship with one another. As a result, the theatrical codes that shape the performance of plays at any given time are susceptible to influence from changes taking place in other areas of sign usage. Changes in codes which appear to be external to the theatre may also bring about changes in internal theatrical codes.[1] In France, the formation of the innovative theatrical code that is set out in the dramatic writings of Diderot was preceded by a significant struggle, both artistic and political, that took place in relation to painting. The debates concerning visual art modified contemporary conceptions of the painterly sign, and this, in turn, affected ways of looking at other artistic signs, including those deployed in dramatic representation. The present chapter will examine some of the developments that affected attitudes towards the painterly sign and consider how these changes were subsequently assimilated into dramatic theory by two of Diderot's immediate predecessors, Houdar de La Motte and Paul Landois.

---

1. Fischer-Lichte, *The Semiotics of theater*, p.5.

# 1. Roger de Piles and the painterly sign

FOR a period of approximately forty years, from the late seventeenth into the early eighteenth century, the Académie de peinture et de sculpture was the scene of a lively debate, reflected in a range of contemporary publications, about how to define painting. It was agreed that painting was to be understood as an art of imitation: the argument was about whether, in achieving this aim, it was *dessein* (design and drawing), or colour and chiaroscuro that was the most important aspect of the art. The dispute took the form of an attack on the official academic position, as represented by Le Brun and André Félibien, by the so-called *coloristes*, whose intellectual leader was Roger de Piles. It was, essentially, an argument about the nature of the painterly sign. The Academicians insisted on the importance of design over colour and light because colour and light are merely qualities of the material world, whereas design belongs to the intellectual and spiritual realm and is therefore superior, more worthy. For Le Brun, 'colour is not a quality of mind or reason, and is in fact unnecessary to reason's perception of the world. [...] Colour is degrading to the image because of its materiality, and painting ought to transcend its material base – its ignobly non-spiritual signifier.'[1] The emphasis on the importance of design and its intellectual character had been a fundamental aspect of the outlook of the Academy since its founding in 1648, and the significance attached to it formed the basis of the claim that painting was not a mere *métier*, a manual craft, but a liberal art on an equal footing with, for example, poetry.[2] To question the superiority of design appeared to many people to pose a threat not simply to a certain conception of painting but to its very status. On the other hand, the position of the *coloristes*, who defended the value of light and colour by arguing that this is how the physical world manifests itself to the human eye, conforms to the view of perception that would be outlined by John Locke in his *Essay concerning human understanding* of 1699. Like de Piles, Locke asserts that it is in the form of light and colour that the physical world is apprehended. In chapter ix of book II, in the section entitled 'Of perception', he writes:

When we set before our eyes a round globe of any uniform colour, v.g. gold, alabaster, or jet, it is certain that the idea thereby imprinted on our mind is of a

---

1. Norman Bryson, *Word and image: French painting of the ancien régime* (Cambridge 1981; 1983), p.60.
2. Bryson, *Word and image*, p.31-34; Nathalie Heinich, *Du peintre à l'artiste: artisans et académiciens à l'âge classique* (Paris 1993), p.7-37; Thomas Puttfarken, *Roger de Piles' theory of art* (New Haven, CT and London 1985), p.3.

flat circle, variously shadowed, with several degrees of light and brightness coming to our eyes. But we having, by use, been accustomed to perceive what kind of appearance convex bodies are wont to make in us; what alterations are made in the reflections of light by the difference of the sensible figures of bodies; – the judgement presently, by an habitual custom, alters the appearances into their causes. So that from that which is truly variety of shadow or colour, collecting the figure, it makes it pass for a mark of figure, and frames to itself the perception of a convex figure and an uniform colour; when the idea we receive from thence is only a plane variously coloured, as is evident in painting.[3]

In fact, as Jacqueline Lichtenstein notes, the conflict over the relative importance of design and colour can be see as a particular form of, or parallel to, the separation established by metaphysics between reason and the senses.[4] The long debate has been analysed in detail by Bernard Teyssèdre in his monumental study of 1957.[5] He dates the start of the dispute from 1668 with the publication of the then deceased Charles-Alphonse Du Fresnoy's *De arte graphica* by his friend and colleague Pierre Mignard. The same year de Piles published his translation of Du Fresnoy's poem into French, accompanied by extensive interpretative notes and commentary. In 1669 (*privilège* dating from December 1668), Molière published his poem *La Gloire du dôme du Val-de-Grâce*, which drew heavily, for its ideas, on Du Fresnoy and on de Piles.[6] It was written in response to Perrault's *La Peinture* (a poem glorifying Le Brun) in praise of the achievement of Molière's close friend and Le Brun's chief rival, Pierre Mignard, who had introduced the technique of the fresco to France.[7] After a series of *péripéties*, and the gradual infiltration of the official academic position by the ideas of the *coloristes* (all documented by Teyssèdre) the matter finally came to a close in 1699, when de Piles, by then a highly respected art critic, portraitist and man of the world, was himself named *conseiller honoraire* to the Academy. In this role, he delivered a number of lectures to the Academy and had the satisfaction of seeing the ideas he had been developing and promoting since 1668 absorbed into official doctrine.[8] The debate lived on in people's minds long after the dust had settled. Antoine Coypel, a painter of the next generation, remarked in a note to his *Epître à mon fils* (1708), 'Je me souviens encore des tems où les Ecoles de peinture retentissoient de ces fameuses disputes, dans lesquelles les uns cherchoient à détruire les charmes du coloris en faveur du dessein,

3. John Locke, *An Essay concerning human understanding*, ed. Alexander Campbell Fraser, 2 vols (New York n.d.; Oxford 1959), ii.186.

4. Jacqueline Lichtenstein, *La Couleur éloquente: rhétorique et peinture à l'âge classique* (Paris 1989), p.166.

5. Bernard Teyssèdre, *Roger de Piles et les débats sur le coloris au siècle de Louis XIV* (Paris 1957).

6. See Molière, *Œuvres complètes*, ed. Eugène Despois and Paul Mesnard, 11 vols (Paris 1886), ix.528, n.1.

7. Teyssèdre, *Roger de Piles et les débats sur le coloris*, p.92.

8. Teyssèdre, *Roger de Piles et les débats sur le coloris*, p.461.

et les autres passionnez pour le coloris, marquoient tant de mépris pour les solides beautez du dessein.'[9] Through the various works de Piles published between 1668 and 1708, the critique of the prevailing academic doctrine and the emerging theory of art were made known to a wide public, and his writings continued to exercise an influence on thought well into the eighteenth century.[10] Both Paul Landois, whose play *Silvie* will be examined in chapter 3 (p.62-76), and Diderot himself were familiar with de Piles's thought. Six of the articles which Landois contributed to the *Encyclopédie*, including the key entries 'Coloris' and 'Clair-obscur', quote de Piles or refer the reader to his work, and positions Landois adopts in other articles suggest that he was sympathetic to de Piles's views.[11] At the same time that Landois was receiving payment for his articles, Diderot was reading a number of works on art, including some by de Piles. The latter's translation of *De arte graphica* as well his *Cours de peinture* were among books which Diderot borrowed from the *bibliothèque du roi* in November 1747 and January 1748 respectively.[12] Numerous concepts and elements of vocabulary that Diderot later brings to his own writings on painting derive from the theory of de Piles.[13]

The art historian Svetlana Alpers argues that the overall importance of de Piles's contribution to art theory lies in the fact that his works articulate the developments that actually took place in seventeenth-century painting. They plot the shift from the Renaissance idea that art exploits representation in order to narrate, that is, that representation is employed in the service of a 'higher', essentially textual, aim, to the view that representation as such is a valid goal for painting. This trend is embodied in a number of important canvases executed by some of the leading artists of the period, including works by Caravaggio, Velazquez, Vermeer, and Rembrandt.[14] Other commentators on de Piles agree that his writings played an important role in freeing painting from the discursive emphasis imposed on it by Le Brun and the Academy.[15]

De Piles's thinking on artistic questions differs from the existing academic orthodoxy in that he consistently emphasises the importance of

9. Quoted in Teyssèdre, *Roger de Piles et les débats sur le coloris*, p.225, n.1.

10. Puttfarken, *Roger de Piles' theory of art*, p.125. Puttfarken points to the numerous editions and translation of de Piles's translation of Du Fresnoy, noting that it 'remained perhaps the most popular treatise on painting for most of the eighteenth century', p.39.

11. Romira Worvill, 'Recherches sur Paul Landois, collaborateur de l'*Encyclopédie*', *Recherches sur Diderot et sur l'Encyclopédie* 23 (October 1997), p.127- 40 (p.135).

12. Jacques Proust, 'L'initiation artistique de Diderot', *Gazette des beaux-arts* 55 (1960), p.225-32 (p.227 and p.230).

13. See for example Diderot's observations on the art of Chardin, DPV, xiii.379-81. See also Gita May, 'Diderot et Roger de Piles', *Publications of the Modern Languages Association* 85 (1970), p.444-55 (p.447 and p.455).

14. Svetlana Alpers, 'Describe or narrate? A problem in realistic representation', *New literary history*, 8:1 (1976), p.15-41 (p.16 and p.26-27).

15. Bryson, *Word and image*, p.62-63; Puttfarken, *Roger de Piles' theory of art*, p.80 and p.96; Heinich, *Du peintre à l'artiste*, p.155-58.

understanding painting as an art of visual imitation that is apprehended through the physical eye. There are two dimensions to his approach: on the one hand, he insists that a picture must be 'illusionistic', that is, it must evoke the look and feel of things in the world, but in addition it should be attractive as a particular kind of artefact, embodying an organisation that is inherently pleasing to the eye and easily assimilated.[16]

Although an unfashionable notion today, illusion is central to de Piles's understanding of the power that painting exercises on the viewer. He holds that it is through the illusion it creates, not by means of the story or situation to which the image refers, that painting imitates. He believes that the success of both painting and poetry depends ultimately upon the willingness of the viewer or the reader to be deceived and to surrender to illusion. Painting and poetry 'sont occupées du soin de nous imposer, & pourvu que nous voulions leur donner notre attention, elles nous transportent comme par un effet de magie d'un pais dans un autre'.[17] In the case of painting, this is achieved by its immediate and direct impact on the eye; its aim must be to capture and deceive the gaze of the spectator. In the opening section of the *Cours de peinture*, de Piles defines the essence of painting as 'l'imitation des objets visibles par le moyen de la forme & des couleurs'.[18] From this, he concludes that 'plus la Peinture imite fortement & fidèlement la Nature, plus elle nous conduit rapidement & directement vers sa fin, qui est de séduire nos yeux'. He insists repeatedly that the goal of painting 'est de surprendre les yeux et de les tromper, s'il est possible';[19] and he contrasts its effect on the eye with that on the mind, saying that the purpose of painting 'n'est pas tant de convaincre l'esprit que de tromper les yeux'.[20] No viewer, he asserts, can pass a good painting without being drawn to pause and study it. 'La véritable Peinture', he states 'est donc celle qui nous appelle (pour ainsi dire) en nous surprenant: & ce n'est que par la force de l'effet qu'elle produit, que nous ne pouvons nous empêcher d'en approcher, comme si elle avait quelque chose à nous dire.'[21]

The capacity of a picture to produce this effect on the beholder depends upon several factors, including, most importantly, a quality that he names

16. Puttfarken, *Roger de Piles' theory of art*, p.39.
17. Roger de Piles, *Cours de peinture par principes* (Paris 1708) p.428-29.
18. De Piles, *Cours de peinture*, p.3.
19. De Piles, *Cours de peinture*, p.17.
20. Roger de Piles, *Dialogue sur le coloris* (Paris 1673), p.69.
21. De Piles, *Cours de peinture*, p.4. Volker Schröder draws attention to the way de Piles consistently uses metaphors of language to describe the impact of painting. Schröder interprets this as a strategy to enhance the status of painting and assert its equality with (if not superiority to) poetry. '"Le Langage de la peinture est le langage des muets": remarques sur un motif de l'esthétique classique', in *Hommage à Elizabeth Sophie Chéron: texte et peinture à l'âge classique*, ed. René Démoris (Paris 1992), p.95-110 (p.108-10). For a detailed account of the rhetorical and argumentative tactics employed by de Piles in his campaign to change prevailing attitudes towards colour, see Lichtenstein, *La Couleur éloquente*, p.194-243.

'le vrai'. He argues that 'la veritable Peinture doit appeler son Spectateur par la force & par la grande verité de son imitation; & que le Spectateur surpris doit aller à elle, comme pour entrer en conversation avec les figures qu'elle represente. En effet, quand elle porte le caractere du vrai, elle semble ne nous avoir attirez que pour nous divertir, & pour nous instruire.'[22] 'Le vrai' is the foundation of painting, since 'tous ses objets peints parois-sent vrais, avant que de paroître d'une certaine façon; parce que le Vrai dans la Peinture est la baze de toutes les autres parties.'[23] The second chapter of the *Cours de peinture* is wholly devoted to an examination of 'le vrai' which de Piles divides into three categories: 'le vrai simple', 'le vrai idéal' and 'le vrai composé ou le vrai parfait'. Of these, the primary category is 'le vrai simple' which consists in a lifelike representation of the material world and constitutes the hallmark of all good paintings. De Piles defines it as:

une imitation simple & fidelle des mouvemens expressifs de la Nature, & des objets tels que le Peintre les a choisis pour modéle, & qu'ils se presentent d'abord à nos yeux, en sorte que les carnations paroissent de veritables chairs, & les draperies de veritables étoffes selon leur diversité, & que chaque objet en détail conserve le veritable caractere de sa nature.[24]

Although de Piles also discusses idealisation in painting, 'le vrai ideal', this is for him less important than 'le vrai simple', the true-to-life imita-tion or illusion, on which everything else depends. He thus reverses the order of precedence previously attached to simple and ideal truth.[25] Moreover, it is the capacity of painting to create such lifelike imitations that makes it superior to the other arts. 'Les autres arts', argues de Piles, 'ne font que réveiller l'idée des choses absentes, au lieu que la Peinture les supplée entièrement & les rend présentes par son essence qui ne consiste pas seulement à plaire aux yeux mais à les tromper.'[26] In this, the work of the painter can be said to resemble that of the creator himself. Painting, says de Piles:

imite Dieu dans sa Toutepuissance; c'est-à-dire dans la Création des choses visi-bles. Le Poëte peut bien en faire la description par la force de ses paroles, mais les paroles ne seront jamais prises pour la chose même, & n'imiteront point cette Toutepuissance, qui d'abord s'est manifestée par des Creatures visibles. Au lieu que la Peinture avec un peu de couleurs, et comme de rien, forme et represente si bien toutes les choses qui sont sur la Terre, sur les Eaux, et dans les Airs, que nous les croyons véritables.[27]

22. De Piles, *Cours de peinture*, p.6.
23. De Piles, *Cours de peinture*, p.9.
24. De Piles, *Cours de peinture*, p.31.
25. Puttfarken, *Roger de Piles' theory of art*, p.49.
26. De Piles, *Cours de peinture*, p.41.
27. De Piles, *Cours de peinture*, p.452-53. The references to 'un peu de couleurs, et comme de rien' are purely rhetorical: de Piles devotes a great deal of effort to demonstrating the complex and 'scientific' nature of the skills needed to master colouring and light and shade.

The contrast de Piles draws here between words, which can never be taken 'pour la chose même' and the appearance of the objects depicted in visual art, is the one that later commentators (such as Dubos) will express in terms of 'natural' and 'artificial' signs. Although de Piles does not apply this terminology, the underlying idea is present in his thought. In a later passage, where he cites Quintilian's commentary on the use of images in courts of law, he states that the reason for their effectiveness is 'que la parole n'est que le signe de la chose, & que la Peinture qui represente plus vivement la realité, ébranle & penetre le coeur beaucoup plus fortement que le discours'. [28]

In de Piles's theory, colouring and the distribution of light and shade are fundamental to the creation of this lifelike illusion because they are the means by which painting replicates how we see. It is in the form of colour and light that we perceive the visible world that painting imitates.

Le peintre qui est un parfait imitateur de la nature, pourvu de l'habitude d'un excellent dessein, comme nous le supposons, doit donc considérer la couleur comme son objet principal, puisqu'il ne regarde cette même nature que comme imitable, qu'elle ne lui est imitable, que parce qu'elle est visible, et qu'elle n'est visible que parce qu'elle est colorée. [29]

In the *Dialogue sur le coloris* (and in later writings), de Piles makes a number of important distinctions concerning colour which serve to reveal the underlying complexity of the painter's achievement in creating a lifelike representation of his subject with paint. He distinguishes between natural colour as a material quality of the objects we perceive around us; artificial colours, which are the colours the painter uses to reproduce an impression of the natural colours (these are subdivided into simple and local colours); and colouring (*le coloris*) which is the effective use of artificial colours by the painter to create a lifelike impression. He thus shifts colouring, or the 'intelligence des couleurs' (including chiaroscuro), from the rank of a secondary aspect of painting into one of its formal, and therefore noble components. [30] De Piles then goes on to demonstrate that colouring and light and shade are the principal characteristics that differentiate painting from any other artistic enterprise; they are the means of imitation unique to the painterly art, and it therefore follows that *le coloris* must be more important than *le dessein*. [31] In the *Cours de peinture*, de Piles asserts that 'on peut regarder le coloris comme la différence de la Peinture' and he argues that it is knowledge of *coloris*, and not intellectual mastery of subject matter, as Le Brun and Félibien had held, that distinguishes the painter from the craftsman and confers on painting the status of a liberal art. [32]

28. De Piles, *Cours de peinture*, p.470-71.
29. De Piles, *Cours de peinture*, p.311-12.
30. Teyssèdre, *Roger de Piles et les débats sur le coloris*, p.189.
31. Teyssèdre, *Roger de Piles et les débats sur le coloris*, p.192-93.
32. Puttfarken, *Roger de Piles' theory of art*, p.67-68.

Yet it is not truthful imitation alone that produces the seductive effect that interests de Piles; this is brought about by faithful imitation in combination with the way in which the picture is composed. The actual arrangement of the elements of the painting, in which colouring and light and shade play a major role, determines the overall visual effect and effectiveness of the work. De Piles refers to this diposition or order as the 'Œconomie du Tout-ensemble' and says that this quality 'donne de la force & de la grace aux choses qui sont inventées; elle tire les figures de la confusion & fait que ce que l'on représente est plus net, plus sensible & plus capable d'appeller, & d'arrêter son Spectateur.'[33] The 'Tout-ensemble' results from the harmonious interplay of all the different elements in the picture and is defined as 'une subordination générale des objets les uns aux autres, qui les fait concourir tous ensemble à n'en faire qu'un'.[34] De Piles compares this global effect brought about by mutually conspiring parts with other complex systems such as political entities 'où les grands ont besoin des petits, comme les petits ont besoin des grands', or with machines or living bodies. The 'Tout-ensemble' is 'comme une machine dont les roues se prêtent un mutuel secours, comme un corps dont les membres dépendent l'un de l'autre'.[35] A painting that embodies 'le vrai', and makes good use of the 'Œconomie du Tout-ensemble' communicates immediately and effectively with the viewer.

De Piles's understanding of the nature of the 'Tout-ensemble' underwent modification between his earliest and his later writings. At the time of the *Remarques*, he emphasises that the disposition of all the elements of a picture should serve to communicate the nature of the subject. 'Il y a une chose de très-grande consequence à observer dans l'Œconomie de tout l'ouvrage, c'est que d'abord l'on reconnoisse la qualité du Sujet, & que le Tableau du premier coup d'œil en inspire la Passion principale.'[36] This view became a generally accepted one, but de Piles himself later revised it, separating the overall effect of pictorial harmony from subject matter and defining it instead in terms of colour, lighting and oppositions, that is, those unique qualities of painting that serve to make a picture visually effective.[37] He bases this later concept of the 'Tout-ensemble' upon a theory of how the eye itself operates and how images can be constructed so as to capture and engage the eye by replicating structures that are easily accessible and pleasing to it.[38] These ideas are expounded around the concept of the 'unité d'objet' (explained by means of a diagram) and

33. De Piles, *Cours de peinture*, p.97.
34. De Piles, *Cours de peinture*, p.105.
35. De Piles, *Cours de peinture*, p.104-105 and p.113.
36. De Piles, *L'Art de peinture de Charles-Alphonse Du Fresnoy, traduit en français, avec des remarques nécessaires et très amples* (Paris 1668), p.135.
37. Puttfarken, *Roger de Piles' theory of art*, p.76 and p.78-79. See also his study *The Discovery of pictorial composition: theories of visual order in painting 1400-1800* (New Haven, CT, London 2000), p.269 and p.272-73.
38. Puttfarken, *Roger de Piles' theory of art*, p.81-83.

Titian's example of the distribution of light and shadow that occurs when light falls on a bunch of grapes (also illustrated). Thomas Puttfarken analyses this aspect of de Piles's theory in some detail, relating it both to modern views of vision and to the objections raised against the theory by contemporaries of the art theorist. He points out that de Piles's ideas led him to favour images based upon circular forms of composition and centred on a strongly illusionistic focus, exemplified in works by Rubens as well as some by Titian and Rembrandt.[39]

In terms of the impact de Piles's thinking had on other areas of aesthetics, the precise nature of his theory of vision is perhaps less important than its underlying principle, namely that the form an artwork takes should be shaped by reference to the manner in which the finished work will be perceived by the consumer. According to Puttfarken, de Piles's analysis of pictures in terms of a triangular relationship between artist, image and beholder, as well as his emphasis on the 'le vrai simple' (illusion) and on the capacity of disposition to communicate a visual idea, represent something new in art theory.[40] One consequence of his way of looking at disposition is the idea that every painter must work not simply from an intellectual concept of his subject, but also from a visual image of the whole work he wishes to produce. 'Il faut donc tellement prévoir les choses', he writes, 'que vostre Tableau soit peint dans vôtre teste avant que de l'estre sur la toile.'[41] For the notion of disposition as a 'careful almost rational ordering of subject-matter', de Piles substitutes the idea of 'an immediate, spontaneous vision'.[42]

The Cours de peinture includes an essay in defence of painting entitled 'Dissertation où l'on examine si la Poësie est preferable à la Peinture'. De Piles cites a number of classical sources to show that painting was highly regarded by many of the Ancients, including Aristotle and Horace. Du Fresnoy's De arte graphica was itself conceived as a parallel to Horace's Ars poetica, and in his own essay, de Piles exploits references to painting by these two great authorities on literature to enhance its reputation.[43] From Aristotle he quotes a passage from chapter four of the Poetics and another from the Politics to support the idea that painting is a socially useful imitative art with didactic value and wide appeal.[44] He also emphasises the high esteem that Horace had for painting and cites the famous lines

39. Puttfarken, Roger de Piles' theory of art, p.93 and p.96.

40. De Piles's notion of the 'Œconomie du Tout-ensemble', or simply the 'Tout-ensemble', found its way into literary and dramatic criticism. Fontenelle uses it, for example, in the preface to an edition of his plays published in 1757. Bernard Le Bovier de Fontenelle, Œuvres complètes, ed. G.-B. Depping, 3 vols (Paris 1813; Geneva 1968), iii.444-45.

41. De Piles, Remarques, p.133. Quoted in Puttfarken, Roger de Piles' theory of art, p.45, n.18.

42. Puttfarken, Roger de Piles' theory of art, p.45-46.

43. Teyssèdre, Roger de Piles et les débats sur le coloris, p.48; Puttfarken, The Discovery of pictorial composition, p.263; de Piles, Cours de peinture, p.425.

44. De Piles, Cours de peinture, p.425 and p.429.

on the power of what is seen over what is heard, as well as remarks on the capacity of both painting and poetry to transport us to other worlds.[45] The unstated intent of these numerous classical references is probably that of undermining Plato's condemnation of painting and painters in the *Republic*.[46] Indeed, I suspect that de Piles's constant emphasis on the positive aesthetic value of illusion succeeded, in the minds of many, in lifting the curse that Plato had laid upon it, a development greatly strengthened by the revaluation of sense experience in the philosophy of Locke.

A number of de Piles's ideas on painting have obvious parallels in the theory of the *drame*: the emphasis on communicating visually through arresting images as well as the importance attached to illusion and lifelike representation will both recur in the writings of Paul Landois and Diderot. Two works described in detail by de Piles at the end of his treatise are particularly suggestive in relation to theatrical representation. These are illusionistic wax sculptures (an *Adoration of the shepherds* and a *Descent from the cross*) by Giulio Gaetano Zumbo. De Piles first mentions Zumbo in the chapter on chiaroscuro, where he comments on the way that light and shade can be exploited to enhance the display of sculpture. He notes that these effects are heightened if the sculpture is also coloured, as in works by Zumbo. The two scenes he describes are three-dimensional works in coloured wax, displayed in wooden boxes with a modelled and painted background.[47] They involve numerous figures displaying a great variety of expression and involvement in the action. De Piles admires the diversity and the *vraisemblance* of these scenes, noting in particular the expressiveness and grouping of the figures, the minute observation of accurate detail, the lifelike textures and the 'wonderful harmony' of the whole.[48] He does not actually compare these works with stage representation, but the analogy readily comes to mind. The dramatic quality of Zumbo's creations is noted by a modern critic, who describes a series of works known as the Plague reliefs (not the ones referred to in the *Cours de peinture*) as 'a development into highly naturalistic, highly dramatic form

45. De Piles, *Cours de peinture*, p.426, p.429, p.450, p.455, and p.459.

46. *The Republic of Plato*, translated by Francis MacDonald Cornford (Oxford 1945), p.326 and p.328. Here, Socrates dismisses painters as illusionists, who merely hold a mirror up to nature and deal only in the appearances of appearances. For a succinct statement of Plato's position on representation and illusion, see Murray Krieger, 'Representation in words and in drama: the illusion of the natural sign', in *Aesthetic illusion: theoretical and historical approaches*, ed. Frederick Burwick and Walter Pape (Berlin and New York 1990), p.183-216.

47. At the time, these curiosities were in Paris, in the possession of the painter and engraver Elizabeth Chéron and her husband Jacques Le Hay. They were subsequently inherited by a M. Boivin. The comte de Caylus saw them in 1755 and refers to them in his 'Mémoire sur la peinture à l'encaustique'. See R. W. Lightbown, 'Gaetano Giulio Zumbo', *Burlington magazine* 106 (1964), p.486-96 and p.563-69 (p.564).

48. De Piles, *Cours de peinture*, p.478-79.

of well-established premises of imagery'.[49] Since the works described by de Piles were still in Paris in the 1750s, it is possible that Landois and Diderot may even have seen them. In any case, their illusionistic character, admired by de Piles as a successful realisation of the goal of deceiving the eye and capturing the viewer's attention, is a suggestive illustration of the possible effects of applying similar principles to the three-dimensional medium of the stage.

Prior to the development of the theory of the *drame*, however, the impact of the arguments about painting are evident in other, more general discussions of writing and literature which, in their turn, help foster the notion of theatre as a visual art. De Piles's conflict with the Academy seems to have had two particularly important consequences. Firstly, his emphasis on the perceptual impact of painting, that is, painting as a system of visual signs, had an effect on the contemporary re-examination of the linguistic sign system of its sister art, poetry. The debate concerning the use of prose in tragedy and the related dispute about the possibility of the prose poem are symptoms of this re-evaluation. Writers and commentators begin to question whether the formal constraints of metre and rhyme are essential to poetic expression or whether poetry consists in some other special features of language use, apart from these. Secondly, the attention de Piles focuses on painting's power to create illusion (its effect) and the technical means by which this is achieved (the distribution of colour, light and shade on a flat surface) highlights the particular qualities and power of the painterly sign. At the level of perception, it is not possible simultaneously to constitute a picture as an image of something and to view it as a surface pattern, that is, the actual distribution of paint on canvas. The spectator must either project the marks on canvas into three-dimensional space in order to form an image, or focus on the work of the brush and the patches of colour.[50] Thus, for the period of time that the viewer is absorbed in reconstituting the picture as a picture, the materiality of the sign, the paint, becomes, as it were, 'invisible' as a sign. The signifier disappears into the image, becoming what eighteenth-century thinkers call 'natural'. Like de Piles, Diderot uses the word 'magie' to describe the marvellous illusion that painting effects. 'Approchez-vous', he writes, 'tout se brouille, s'aplatit et disparaît. Eloignez-vous, tout se recrée et se reproduit.'[51] Following the debate about the relative importance of design and colour, this quality of the signifier, its invisibility or

49. Lightbown, 'Gaetano Giulio Zumbo', p.494. Lightbown's articles are an attempt to re-evaluate the work of Zumbo whose wax reliefs enjoyed a considerable reputation in the years following his death (1701) but later fell into disrepute on account of the supposedly sensational and macabre character of the Plague reliefs.

50. Ernst Gombrich, *Art and illusion: a study in the psychology of pictorial representation*, 2nd edn (New York and Princeton, NJ 1961), p.6 and p.199. See also Puttfarken, *The Discovery of pictorial composition*, p.89 and following.

51. 1763 *Salon*, DPV, xiii.380.

apparent assimilation into the thing signified, came to be seen as the condition to which all artistic signs, including the linguistic sign, should aspire. Evidence of the transposition of this view to writing can be found in Fénelon's *Dialogues sur l'éloquence*.

Although first published in 1718, after the author's death, they had been written much earlier, in the period 1677 to 1681, and most likely in 1679.[52] Fénelon's aim is to promote a type of pulpit oratory focused on the effective delivery of important truths rather than on the cultivation of pleasing style. He criticises orators who exploit dazzling displays of verbal virtuosity in order to elicit the admiration of the congregation for their own skills and urges instead a manner of composition and delivery that presents the listeners with a clear idea of the truths of faith, winning their commitment and their hearts. The *Dialogues sur l'éloquence* thus form part of the seventeenth-century reaction against the ornamental rhetoric of Ramus and Talaeus. Under the influence of the latter, effective communication had come to be perceived as language that shuns normal speech patterns; good style was equated with unusual style, the message subordinated to the manner in which it was expressed.[53] In attacking approaches that place 'words' above 'things', Fénelon is clearly engaged in the same project as Arnauld and Nicole in their *Logique, ou l'Art de penser* of 1662 (the Port Royal Logic), Bernard Lamy in his *De l'art de parler* (the so-called Port Royal Rhetoric), which was first published in 1675 and then frequently republished under a slightly different title, and Boileau in his widely acclaimed translation of Longinus, the *Traité du sublime* of 1674.[54] Fénelon, an Ancient, returns to classical sources (Plato, Demosthenes, Cicero, Longinus) to mount his attack against false eloquence (associated in the *Dialogues* with the name of Isocrates) and to draw up a guide not only to good preaching but to good writing in general.[55] In fact, he frequently illustrates his points with examples taken from the literature of Antiquity and he asserts that the difference between composing sermons and composing poetry is one of degree rather than kind.[56] It is from Plato and Longinus that Fénelon claims to draw his central argument in these *Dialogues*, the idea that truly effective rhetoric is hidden or 'invisible' rhetoric, rhetoric which leaves the listeners unaware of the mediating presence of the speaker and his words and brings them face to face with the truth (or message). This classical concept

52. François-Louis de Salignac, marquis de La Mothe-Fénelon, *Œuvres*, ed. Jacques Le Brun, 2 vols (Paris 1983), i.1233.

53. *Salignac de la Mothe Fénelon's 'Dialogues on eloquence': a translation with an introduction and notes*, ed. Wilbur Samuel Howell (Princeton, NJ 1951), p.37.

54. Fénelon, *Dialogues on eloquence*, ed. Howell, p.27, p.33 and p.37. Howell believes that if Fénelon's *Dialogues* had been published when they were written, they, rather than Lamy's work, might have been dubbed the Port Royal Rhetoric and with greater justification. On Fénelon and Boileau, see Cronk, *The Classical sublime*, p.130-31.

55. Fénelon, *Dialogues on eloquence*, ed. Howell, p.2.

56. Fénelon, *Œuvres*, i.35.

is reinforced through the discussion of examples from the writing of Homer and Virgil. Fénelon's particular interpretation and development of this guiding idea also bears the imprint of the contemporary debate about painting, which had entered a critical phase in the 1670s, the period when the dialogues were conceived and written.[57] Indeed, Fénelon appears to be recasting the classical idea of the invisible writer in the light of contemporary thinking about illusion and the painterly sign. This is apparent in various ways, including the prominence he gives to the terms *peinture* and *peindre*, together with the related expressions *voir* and *yeux*, which permeate the dialogues. The connection is clearly made in Ramsay's preface to the 1718 edition. Ramsay singles out for comment the three principles which Fénelon had identified as the essential parts of eloquence, *prouver*, *peindre* and *toucher*, and he explains the meaning of *peindre* by noting that the author 'veut que partout l'art se cache, ou du moins paraisse si naturel qu'il ne soit qu'une expression vive de la nature'.[58] *Peindre* is the term Fénelon substitutes for the more usual *plaire* among the aims of oratory, and when the concept is introduced in the second dialogue, interlocutor C is so puzzled by it that he has to ask A for a more detailed explanation. A continues: 'Peindre, c'est non-seulement décrire les choses, mais en représenter les circonstances d'une manière si vive et si sensible, que l'auditeur s'imagine presque les voir.'[59] The shift from *plaire* to *peindre* marks a fundamental divergence from the theory and practice of ornamental rhetoric and has quite particular consequences for style. To illustrate what he means by 'painting' with words, Fénelon's principal interlocutor, A, contrasts an account of the death of Dido as drafted by 'un froid historien' with Virgil's version. The main difference between them lies in the appeal that Virgil makes to the eye; the poet causes us to visualise the scene in our imagination, and the most important characteristic of his writing is that 'le poète disparaît; on ne voit plus que ce qu'il fait voir, on n'entend plus que ceux qu'il fait parler. Voilà la force de l'imitation et de la peinture.'[60] According to Fénelon then, painting is the art which sets the standard for effective imitation, and good writing is writing that comes as close as possible to that model. The disappearance of the hand behind the work, of the artifice in the art, is a constantly recurring theme in the dialogues, and Fénelon explicitly compares this quality of certain types of composition with the phenomenon noted above in relation to painting, namely that it cannot simultaneously be perceived as representation and as technique. Explaining what makes the works of Homer and Virgil so worthy of admiration, Fénelon writes:

57. De Piles's *Dialogue sur le coloris* appeared (anonymously) in 1673, the same year as the republication of his translation of Du Fresnoy's *De arte graphica*. His *Conversations sur la peinture* came out in 1679.

58. Fénelon, *Œuvres*, i.1239.

59. Fénelon, *Œuvres*, i.34.

60. Fénelon, *Œuvres*, i.35.

40

la nature se montre partout; partout l'art se cache soigneusement. Vous n'y trouvez pas un seul mot qui paraisse mis pour faire honneur au bel esprit du poète. Il met toute sa gloire à ne point paraître, pour vous occuper des choses qu'il peint, comme un peintre songe à vous mettre devant les yeux les forêts, les montagnes, les rivières, les lointains, les bâtiments, les hommes, leurs aventures, leurs actions, leurs passions différentes, *sans que vous puissiez remarquer les coups de pinceau*; l'art est grossier et méprisable dès qu'il paraît.[61]

This is not a simple comparison, a reiteration of the Horatian common-place; it is a conception that rests upon an analysis of the semiotic process. Fénelon's explicit reference to the 'coups de pinceau', the painterly sign, establishes a parallel between how painting was held to work (the use of transparent signs) and how good writing and speaking should work. Good writing, in Fénelon's view, strives for a verbal equivalent of the illusion created by painting. Moreover, it is these painterly qualities that con-stitute the essence of poetry, rather than the use of metre and rhyme. It is a common error to believe, he says, that one is a poet 'quand on a parlé ou écrit en mesurant ses paroles. Au contraire, bien des gens font des vers sans poésie, et beaucoup d'autres sont pleins de poésie sans faire de vers: laissons donc la versification. Pour tout le reste, la poésie n'est autre chose qu'une fiction vive qui peint la nature.'[62]

The distinctive character of Fénelon's account emerges more clearly when set against the comparisons made between writing and painting in one of his main sources, Boileau's translation of Longinus, which inter-locutor A recommends to his companions.[63] Altogether, there are four references to painting in the *Traité du sublime* and these seem principally to be intended as simple illustrations of the point at hand.[64] Fénelon is following the example of Longinus when he insists on the visual qualities of the writing of Homer and on its effectiveness, but for Longinus, the value of visual writing lies in its role as one of the sources of the powerful and arresting effect of the sublime, not in its potential for creating transparency.[65] When the sublime is achieved, the reader, distracted by this powerful effect, fails to notice the poetic figure(s) at work 'parce que l'Art ainsi renfermé au milieu de quelque chose de grand et d'éclatant [...] n'est plus suspect d'aucune tromperie'.[66] He considers these figures which pass unnoticed because overwhelmed by the sheer force of the sublime the best kind, and he goes on to explain the process by reference to the use of light and shade in painting. The sublime effect is like the most luminous part of a picture, which stands out ('semble sortir hors du tableau') and fully engages the attention of the viewer, with the result

61. Fénelon, *Œuvres*, i.37 (emphasis added).
62. Fénelon, *Œuvres*, i.35-36.
63. Fénelon, *Œuvres*, i.9-10.
64. Nicolas Boileau, *Œuvres complètes*, ed. Françoise Escal (Paris 1966), p.358, p.363, p.370, and p.381-82.
65. Boileau, *Œuvres complètes*, p.363.
66. Boileau, *Œuvres complètes*, p.370.

that the rest of the painting (or the figure) drops below their threshold of awareness. Fénelon transposes this straightforward illustration into the terminology of his own time, adapting it to fit the prevailing analysis of how art functions by invoking the 'invisible' brush strokes which are the technical means underlying the perceptual illusion achieved by painting. He also generalises the principle, applying it to all aspects of style and delivery, thus inviting a thorough re-examination of the practice of writing in the light of recent thinking about the effects created by visual art. Fénelon's approach to writing is illustrated in his highly popular prose epic, *Les Aventures de Télémaque* (1699), a work characterised by a compelling appeal to the sense of sight.[67] Both this literary example and the theory set out in the *Dialogues sur l'éloquence* were widely read both by his contemporaries and by writers of later generations, upon whom they must have left their mark.[68]

The impact of painterly values on literature is also visible in a shift of emphasis emerging in texts that take up the famous commonplace *ut pictura poesis*. For many years, the yoking together of poetry and painting as sister arts through the topos *ut pictura poesis* had stressed their similarities.[69] On the whole, though, this comparison had worked against a painterly understanding of visual art and imposed on art theory and criticism a decidedly literary character. Painting was evaluated not so much by reference to criteria proper to the nature of the medium but in terms of literary ones, particularly those applied to drama. Choice of subject matter, the representation of beautiful nature, the expression of the passions and respect for the unities of time, place and action were all invoked to assess the success of pictures.[70] This way of seeing, which placed content or subject matter at the centre of artistic expression and played down the significance of the technical (or manual) aspects of painting naturally accorded the place of honour to history painting, which drew its subjects from many of the same sources as tragedy and the epic, and placed still life painting (images of 'fruit and flowers'[71]) at the bottom.

---

67. Fénelon, *Les Aventures de Télémaque*, ed. Albert Cahen, 2 vols (Paris 1920), i.9; André Gabriel, 'Fénelon le peintre sourd', *Papers on French seventeenth-century literature* 13 (1980), p.117-34 (p.117-18).

68. Fénelon, *Dialogues on eloquence*, ed. Howell, p.46.

69. On the background to the changing fortunes of the *ut pictura poesis* topos see the following: Rensselaer W. Lee, '*Ut pictura poesis*: the humanistic theory of painting', *The Art bulletin* 22:4 (1940), p.196-269; Rémy Saisselin, '*Ut pictura poesis*: Dubos to Diderot', *Journal of aesthetics and art criticism* (1961), p.144-56; Dean Tolle Mace, 'Transformations in classical art theory: from "poetic composition" to "picturesque composition" ', *Word and image* 1 (1985), p.59-86; Henryk Markiewicz, '*Ut pictura poesis*: a history of the topos and the problem', *New literary history* 18:3 (1987), p.535-58; Simon Alderson, '*Ut pictura poesis* and its discontents in late seventeenth- and early eighteenth-century England and France', *Word and image* 11:3 (1995), p.256-63; Hans Christoph Buch, '*Ut Pictura Poesis': Die Beschreibungsliteratur und ihre Kritiker von Lessing bis Lukács* (Munich 1972).

70. See, for example, the discussion in Lee, '*Ut pictura poesis*'.

71. The term 'nature morte' entered French art vocabulary in 1756. Charles Sterling, *La Nature morte de l'antiquité à nos jours* (Paris 1952), p.xxxi.

The arguments of the *coloristes*, which foster a more sophisticated understanding of the visual and pictorial qualities unique to painting, draw
attention instead to the differences between the two art forms, and whilst
the painterly approach did not immediately dislodge the literary one,
it did succeed in broadening the categories that could be brought to
bear on the interpretation of pictures. In a number of eighteenth-century
texts, two rather different ways of assessing paintings can be seen to co-
exist. The abbé Dubos, for example, distinguishes between two types of
artistic composition, which he calls the 'poetic' and the 'picturesque'.
Dean Tolle Mace argues that these categories actually represent two distinct ways of seeing or habits of vision rather than two types of painting as
such. The first corresponds to the traditional, academic view and defines a painting that appears to obey the principles of unity governing
dramatic composition. The second definition, inspired by the criteria outlined by de Piles, rests upon an idea of the harmony which emerges
from the overall visual effect of a work, a harmony created through the
judicious use of colour and the skilful handling of light and shade.[72] The
new emphasis de Piles gave to the purely visual qualities and appeal of
pictures thus encouraged his contemporaries to begin looking at drama in
new ways, with the result that instead of imposing dramatic criteria on
painting, they eventually begin to apply the new values associated with
painting to drama, as Fénelon does with pulpit oratory and poetry.

One site where this revision of fundamental assumptions becomes visible
is in commentary about the unity of action. Adherents of the theory of
'poetic' composition may well compare a play to a painting, but in doing
so will say that a play is like a single painting, since both a painting and
a play should present only a single, unified action. This analogy is found
in neo-classical drama theory. The abbé d'Aubignac (in *La Pratique du
théâtre*) writes, for example:

Il est certain que le théâtre n'est rien qu'une image, et partant comme il est
impossible de faire une seule image accomplie de deux originaux différents, il est
impossible que deux actions (j'entends principales) soient représentés raisonna-
blement par une seule pièce de théâtre.[73]

D'Aubignac is not here talking about the impact on the eye, the image
as perceived, but about the organisation of subject matter, the image as
*dessein*. He is trying to describe how one tells a story in a play or a picture
in such a way that it will win the assent of the reasonable spectator. In the
following century, when writers compare the stage to painting, we increasingly find that the comparison is indeed intended as a visual one.
They compare a play not to a single painting but to a series of visual
images, which succeed each other like pictures in a gallery. Houdar de
La Motte will use this idea against Voltaire, who invokes the principle of

72. Mace, 'Transformations in classical art theory', p.60-61.
73. Quoted in Mace, 'Transformations in classical art theory', p.65.

pictorial unity as an argument for retaining the unity of action in dra-ma.[74] There are already traces of the change in the writings of de Piles who uses a theatrical metaphor to guide painters in the expression of the passions, observing that 'On doit considérer un tableau comme une scène où chaque figure joue son rôle.'[75]

Thus, the interest in form generated by the debates about painting stimulated reflection on the role of illusion and the means by which it can be achieved in the arts dependent upon language. This is particularly evident in Diderot's aesthetic of the *drame*, where the act of beholding and the concept of illusion associated with visual art are recruited to bring the experience of watching plays into line with that of viewing paintings. In the following section, however, I shall try to show how the kind of illusion embodied in figurative painting and the concept of the painterly sign as 'natural' first helped shape the controversial theory of tragic language that took form in the essays of Houdar de La Motte.

74. See chapter 2, p.58-59.
75. De Piles, *L'Abrégé de la vie des peintres avec un traité du peintre parfait* (Paris 1699), p.43. For polemical reasons, de Piles did not encourage the view that dramatic poetry had visual appeal. His aim was to enhance the status of painting by emphasising the idea that it was superior to poetry (including tragedy) on account of its appeal to the eye, the noblest sense. In accordance with existing tradition, he argues that the primary appeal of poetry is to the ear.

# 2. Houdar de La Motte and the 'invisible poet': the self-effacing linguistic sign

THE successful poet and playwright Antoine Houdar de La Motte, an author belonging to the generation before Voltaire, is responsible for introducing into French discussions of tragedy the concept of a self-effacing linguistic sign modelled on the painterly sign. He initiated a reaction against the form and function of dramatic language in neo-classical tragedy, the dominant dramatic genre of the time. Neo-classical tragedy is an example of a formal theatrical code. Its signs do not attempt to replicate the sign systems of the surrounding culture but constitute a unique theatrical code that depends for its success upon the audience's familiarity with the particular ways in which these signs are deployed. Since these theatrical signs are established by convention they are, in eighteenth-century terms, artificial or arbitrary. Before turning to La Motte's critique of this system, it might be useful to summarise some of its principal features as they existed in the early eighteenth century. The essential character of this code is described by the abbé Dubos in his *Réflexions critiques sur la poésie et la peinture*.[1]

Dubos begins by commenting on the conventions governing costume. Clothing for the male roles was based on Roman military dress, a costume Dubos characterises as 'noble par lui-même, et qui semble avoir quelque part à la gloire du peuple qui le portait'. Normal dress for actresses consists in 'ce que l'imagination peut inventer de plus riche et de plus majestueux'. Thus, costume is not determined by a will to respect the historical or social context of the represented fiction, but rather by the public character of theatrical performance and by the nature of the genre. As the noble genre, tragedy requires means of representation commensurate with its dignity; tragic actors dress in a manner that befits actors in a tragedy. The 1755 production of Voltaire's *L'Orphelin de la Chine*, with La Clairon in the lead role, is generally held to be one of the earliest attempts to introduce the use of authentic costumes into the performance of French tragedy.[2] The principles of costuming that Dubos describes typify, for him, the overall performance style of the neo-classical code, and were reinforced by the techniques of declamation and the kind of movement and attitude that were also used. Tragic actors, he tells us,

---

1. Dubos, *Réflexions*, Section 42, 'De notre manière de réciter la tragédie et la comédie', p.141-45.

2. Pierre Peyronnet, *La Mise en scène au XVIIIᵉ siècle* (Paris 1974), p.112-15; Frantz, *L'Esthétique du tableau*, p.95. Although Diderot praised La Clairon for the example she set, he thought that these costumes were still too costly and extravagant: DPV, x.406.

45

'parlent d'un ton de voix plus élevé, plus grave et plus soutenu que celui sur lequel on parle dans les conversations ordinaires'.[3] Their gestures must be 'plus mesurés et plus nobles', their movements 'plus graves' and their countenance 'plus sérieuse'. They should perform everything with 'un air de grandeur et de dignité' that matches the majesty and dignity of the poet's language. Modern research into the acting of the period emphasises its origins in formal rhetoric, as *actio* or bodily eloquence.[4] Close study of the detail of its conventions suggests that the actor 'did not pretend to *be* the character so much as to act out, to externalize the passions'.[5] Dubos does not mention set, but it is known that the backdrop and wings used at this period were multi-purpose and generic, not customised to suit individual plays as would be the case today. By the early eighteenth century, the Comédie-Française had come to rely on a total of five basic sets (a palace, a garden, a room in a middle-class home, a prison, and a public square), which served for many different plays.[6] The presence of spectators on the stage limited the amount of space that could be used for décor as well as the area available for acting.[7] The conventions applied to tragedy clearly do not have the creation of a unified visual illusion as their primary goal, and Dubos explicitly criticises the view, held by some, that illusion is the principle source of the pleasure to be derived from it. He insists that although we may be moved by what we experience in the theatre, 'rien n'y fait illusion à nos sens, car tout s'y montre comme imitation'.[8] The artifice is always apparent in the art. Of course, this, in essence, will be the burden of Diderot's critique of contemporary theatre, but in the dramatic aesthetic described by Dubos, the artistic signs associated with stage performance all serve to support and reinforce the component that is the dominant sign of neo-classical tragedy, its language.

From our modern point of view, language in neo-classical tragedy occupies a singular role for speech in a theatrical form. Dubos explains that tragedy makes its impact not by what is seen on the stage but by means of the images formed in the imagination of the audience by the poet's language. The 'poésie du style', which consists 'à prêter des sentiments

3. Dubos, *Réflexions*, p.142.

4. Angelica Goodden, *'Actio' and persuasion: dramatic performance in eighteenth-century France* (Oxford 1986), p.1.

5. Dene Barnett, 'The performance practice of acting: the eighteenth century', *Theatre research international*, new series 2:3 (1977), p. 157-86 (p.160).

6. Peyronnet, *La Mise en scène*, p.48.

7. Under the Regency the amount of on-stage seating at the Comédie-Française increased considerably, with the result that the acting area was reduced to a space fifteen feet wide at the front of the stage and eleven feet wide at the back, surrounded on at least three sides by spectators. Barbara G. Mittman, *Spectators on the Paris stage in the seventeenth and eighteenth centuries* (Ann Arbor, MI 1984), p.39-50.

8. Dubos, *Réflexions*, p.145. This section of the *Réflexions* (Section 43) is entitled 'Que le plaisir que nous avons au théâtre n'est point l'effet de l'illusion'.

intéressants à tout ce qu'on fait parler, comme à exprimer par des figures, et à représenter sous des images capables de nous émouvoir ce qui ne nous toucherait pas s'il était dit simplement en style prosaïque', constitutes so intense a pleasure for the audience that a play's other flaws will pass unnoticed, as long as each sentence brings with it fresh 'beauties of style'. The true measure of poetic genius is the ability to 'soutenir ses vers par des fictions continuelles et par des images renaissantes à chaque période'. Dubos invokes Horace's dictum *ut pictura poesis* not to suggest that the scenes of a tragedy present the audience with a series of actual visual images, like paintings with a verbal dimension, but to support his argument that tragic speech should constantly stimulate pictures in the mind of the spectators. It is these mental pictures that affect their emotions. Great writers such as Racine, he says, are those who succeed in converting commonplace ideas into striking forms of expression that activate our imagination.[9] Dubos's use of examples in this section shows that he makes no distinction between poetic language in general and the language of tragedy. Both function in essentially the same way, relying for their effect on literary qualities that 'address' the audience in the manner described earlier.[10] Not surprisingly, Dubos's account of the 'poésie du style' corresponds exactly with the role attributed to language in d'Aubignac's famous treatise of neo-classical theory, *La Pratique du théâtre*.[11] There are two areas in particular where d'Aubignac's comments on aspects of language vividly illustrate both its centrality to the traditional theatrical code and the gulf that will open between this code and that of the *drame*. These are his attitude towards the use of written stage directions and his account of the function of poetic figures. D'Aubignac begins his discussion of how the dramatic poet communicates details concerning time, setting, the identity of the characters and so on by invoking the classical distinction between the epic poet and the dramatic poet. In the epic, he writes, the delivery of this necessary intelligence is relatively straightforward since 'le Poète parle seul' and can simply tell the readers or listeners what they need to know. Not so in drama, where there are only the poet's fictional characters 'qui parlent, sans qu'il y prenne aucune part, et dans toute l'Action Théâtrale il ne paraît non plus que si les Acteurs étaient en vérité ceux qu'ils représentent'.[12] The conclusion that d'Aubignac derives from this principle is that 'toutes les pensées du Poète, soit pour les décorations du Théâtre, soit

---

9. Dubos, *Réflexions*, p.94-96.

10. See above, p.15-16.

11. D'Aubignac's treatise first appeared in 1657. It was republished in 1715, and for many eighteenth-century writers it came to represent the authoritative text of neo-classical drama theory. See Henry Carrington Lancaster, *French tragedy in the time of Louis XV and Voltaire: 1715-1774*, 2 vols (Baltimore, MD 1950), i.3.

12. Abbé d'Aubignac, *La Pratique du théâtre*, ed. Hélène Baby (Paris 2001), p.97. All future references will be to this edition.

pour les mouvements de ses Personnages, habillements et gestes nécessaires à l'intelligence du sujet, doivent être exprimées par les vers qu'il fait
réciter'.[13] He rejects stage directions as a violation of this basic principle,
since in such notes the poet is speaking in his own voice, not through
characters. In addition, by mixing prose with verse such directions con-
travene other fundamental rules of style. Since what distinguishes drama
from other literary kinds is its exclusive reliance on direct speech, the
dramatic poet must contrive to communicate everything relevant to the
representation of the action through the utterances of his characters. All
that is significant must happen as language, even if it is also present in
some other form. More than just the dominant sign ('car là *Parler*, c'est
*Agir*', to repeat the abbé's famous formula[14]), speech concedes none of the
significant representational functions to the other sign systems. Neo-
classical tragedy presupposes a replete text. When eighteenth-century
critics invoke the idea of the poet disappearing behind his characters
(often citing the same classical authors as d'Aubignac), they will mean
something very different, and their reliance upon stage directions allo-
cating signifying functions to other components such as setting and
gesture is one of the techniques used to achieve the effect of the disappearance of the hand behind the work.

D'Aubignac devotes considerable space to the discussion of figures,
which he considers even more important in drama than in poetry.[15] The
figures play a role in all the various categories of speech analysed by
the abbé ('narrations', 'délibérations', 'instructions' and 'discours pathétiques'), but they have two principal functions: to evoke the emotion felt
by the character, and to convey this emotion to the spectator. For this reason, they are particularly important in the 'discours pathétiques' where
they work in conjunction with disposition or structure. Striking poetic
figures convey an impression of the 'beau désordre' of nature, that is,
the unruly and disturbing nature of the passions, whilst disposition brings
this potential chaos under the degree of control necessary for artistic
representation. It is the successful combination of both elements that succeeds in communicating 'une image des mouvements d'un esprit troublé,
agité d'incertitude, et transporté de passion déréglée'.[16] In other words,
the range and intensity of the figures themselves evoke the intensity
of the emotion felt by the speaker. The heightened state of emotion is
conveyed by a heightened (in the literary sense) mode of expression.
Dramatic language is not the spontaneous expression of passion but an
artistic representation of it. A thorough training in rhetoric, which
provides a comprehensive analysis of all the figures and their effects in
different types of discourse was therefore considered a prerequisite for

13. D'Aubignac, *La Pratique du théâtre*, p.98.
14. D'Aubignac, *La Pratique du théâtre*, p.407.
15. D'Aubignac, *La Pratique du théâtre*, p.474.
16. D'Aubignac, *La Pratique du théâtre*, p.472.

any dramatist. Seventeenth-century treatises on drama generally stress the necessity for a dramatic poet to be well versed in the art of rhetoric, and they tend to relate particular recommendations they have for the composition of dramatic speech to the categories provided by traditional rhetorical theory.[17] D'Aubignac's rejection of stage directions and emphasis on the literary qualities of dramatic speech impose on the linguistic signs of the neo-classical code a role of considerable importance. In an interesting analysis of what d'Aubignac means when he speaks of theatrical illusion, Robert Morrissey demonstrates that ' "la realité" perçue par le spectateur est une réalité qui ne provient que des mots; c'est la parole qui fait voir'.[18] Hélène Baby concurs, describing the power that d'Aubignac attributes to dramatic speech as the 'capacité hallucinatoire du langage', which invests each line of verse with 'la force du spectacle'.[19] The 'visual' dimension of the tragic fiction exists primarily in the imagination of the spectator and language tends to substitute for the other sign systems.

In addition to the principles described above, tragic speech was also subject to the constraints imposed by versification. Despite the difficulties involved in trying to reconcile its use with the demand for *vraisemblance*, the rhymed alexandrine had become the norm for tragedy following the overwhelming success of *Le Cid* (1637). It is the simultaneous exploitation of metrical form and striking figures that places tragic speech in the same category of discourse as other kinds of poetry.[20] In fact, tragedy was considered its highest form and the genre in which it was necessary to prove oneself to earn the title of poet.[21] In the eighteenth century, Voltaire still defines good verse in the same terms as the preceding age, as language having 'tout le mérite d'une prose parfaite, en s'élevant au-dessus d'elle par le rhythme, la cadence, la mélodie, et par la sage hardiesse des figures'.[22] The difference between prose and poetry was held to be mainly a technical one: poetry was language submitted to a greater number of rules and therefore more challenging to the artist. It was known as 'le langage des dieux', an expression attributed to Plato, emphasising that poetry is a language quite distinct from normal modes of communication.[23] Since the skill of the poet lies in surmounting the

---

17. See for example H.-J. Pilet de La Mesnardière, *La Poëtique* (Paris 1640; Geneva 1972), p.326.

18. Robert Morrissey, '*La Pratique du théâtre* et le langage de l'illusion', *XVII<sup>e</sup> siècle* 146 (1985), p.17-27 (p.25).

19. *La Pratique du théâtre*, p.98, n.145.

20. A. Kibedi Varga, *Rhétorique et littérature: études de structures classiques* (Paris 1970), p.8-9.

21. Sylvain Menant, *La Chute d'Icare: la crise de la poésie française 1700-1750* (Geneva 1981), p.76.

22. Voltaire, 'Remarques sur Sertorius', *Commentaires sur Corneille*, ed. David Williams, in *The Complete works of Voltaire* (henceforward *OC*), (Geneva, Banbury, Oxford 1968-), vol.53-55 (Banbury 1974-1975), ii.833.

23. David Williams, 'Voltaire and the language of the gods', *SVEC* 62 (1968), p.57-81.

obstacles posed by bold language and versification, the primary pleasure that poetry affords the reader or listener is that of observing the *difficulté vaincue*, of appreciating how well the poet manages to express his ideas despite the constraints. Fontenelle notes that 'l'esprit est agréablement surpris que le poëte, gêné comme il était dans la manière de s'exprimer, ait pu s'exprimer bien', and he judges this effect all the more pleasing when 'la gêne de l'expression a été plus grande, et l'expression plus parfaite'.[24] The ability to express oneself well within the limits imposed by these various sets of rules made the poet 'un esprit supérieur', elevated above ordinary mortals confined to the use of the 'langage commun'.[25] In a letter of 1769, Voltaire compares skilled practitioners of poetry to priests in the service of sacred mysteries. They are 'le petit nombre des élus' and 'moins il y a d'initiés, plus les mistères sont sacrés'.[26] Defined primarily as poetry, the speech of tragedy is perceived as language characterised by highly distinctive features, speech designed to draw attention to itself as language and to elicit the admiration of the audience for the skills of the poet. Contemporary accounts of audience behaviour confirm that despite the rowdiness often associated with theatrical performances, spectators listened attentively to the language, acknowledging eloquent and striking lines with appreciative applause and mocking any that were awkward or susceptible of unintended *double entendre*.[27]

As a poetic sign, subject to these various rules and principles, the alexandrine of neo-classical tragedy has a distancing effect, and rests upon a 'séparation volontaire du signifiant et du signifié'.[28] The speech enhances the stature of the mythical and historical characters and contributes to the dignity and majesty of the form that commentators such as Dubos emphasise. The rigorous control of language is also an aspect of the moral purpose of the genre. Tragedy deals with unruly passions and the threat these pose, if unchecked, to both the social order and the integrity of the individual. But this subject matter is presented in the form of language carefully shaped by a human intellect and the orderliness the poet imposes on the material models the control members of society must enact upon their own passions. At the same time, the identification of tragic speech with poetry, a language apprehended by the listener as

24. Fontenelle, 'Sur la poésie en général', *Œuvres complètes*, iii.38-39.

25. Abbé d'Olivet, 'A M. le Président Bouhier, de l'Académie Française' in *Remarques de Grammaire sur Racine* (Paris 1738), p.151.

26. Voltaire, *Correspondence and related documents*, ed. Th. Besterman, in *OC* vol.85-135 (Geneva, Banbury, Oxford 1968-1977), Voltaire to Saint-Lambert, 7 March 1769 (D15504). The emphasis on poetry as a mystery, accessible only to the chosen few, is also present in Diderot's comparison of poetic expression with hieroglyphs in *La Lettre sur les sourds et muets* of 1751. See Kate E. Tunstall, 'Hieroglyph and device in Diderot's *Lettre sur les sourds et muets*', *Diderot studies* 28 (2000), p.161-72.

27. See, for example, Henri Lagrave, *Le Théâtre et le public à Paris de 1715 à 1750* (Paris 1972), p.424-29, p.431-32, p.440-42.

28. Roland Barthes, *Sur Racine* (Paris 1960; 1963), p.138, n.1.

speech issuing from a poet and demanding attention in its own right, gives rise to a tension, difficult to resolve, between the authorial voice and the voice of the *dramatis personae*. The 'presence' of the poet impinges on audience awareness in a manner that can appear problematic from a perspective of strict *vraisemblance*. Not surprisingly therefore, it was the linguistic sign of tragedy that was the first aspect of the neo-classical theatrical code to come under attack following the controversies surrounding painting, and Houdar de La Motte the courageous writer who led the charge. His highly controversial views on dramatic language (as well as on the prose poem) made him the object of numerous hostile attacks both during his lifetime and afterwards.[29] Nevertheless, his arguments for the use of non-literary prose speech in serious drama exerted a strong influence on dramatists of the next generation, and his achievement in putting dramatic theory on a path towards the effective integration of its visual signs is all the more remarkable in view of the fact that he was blind.[30] Two controversies in particular bring into sharp focus his new approach to tragic language: a debate with Boileau concerning figurative language, which took place between 1707 and 1711, and the intense discussion unleashed by the publication of his theatrical essays in 1730, in which he argues forcefully for prose tragedy. By attacking the two characteristics that served to define tragic language as poetry (its reliance on figures and its metrical form), La Motte opened the way for a new conception of dramatic speech.

The debate with Boileau was triggered by critical remarks that La Motte made of a line from Théramène's *récit* in Racine's *Phèdre* (1677). In the essay that introduces the 1707 edition of his odes, La Motte defines the ode in the traditional way, by reference to its metre and its use of figurative language. In passing, he draws a distinction between the composer of odes, who speaks as a professional poet ('Poëte de profession') and is therefore justified in using bold language, and tragic poets who must constantly strive to avoid excessive eloquence. Since dramatists 'ne font point parler des Poëtes, mais des hommes ordinaires', they should be careful to express only 'les sentimens qui conviennent à leurs acteurs' using only the type of words 'que la passion offre le plus naturellement'.[31] La Motte is taking the traditional distinction between poet and character

29. I shall confine my observations to La Motte's treatment of dramatic language. For his role in the debates about prose poetry see: Margaret Gilman, *The Idea of poetry in France, from Houdar de La Motte to Baudelaire* (Cambridge 1958); Jean Ranscelot, 'Les manifestations du déclin poétique au début du XVIII<sup>e</sup> siècle', *Revue d'histoire littéraire* 33 (1926), p.497-520; Vista Clayton, *The Prose poem in French literature* (New York 1936); P. W. K. Stone, *The Art of poetry: 1750-1820* (London, New York 1967); and Menant, *La Chute d'Icare*.

30. 'Portrait de M. de la Motte par feue Madame la Marquise de Lambert', in Antoine Houdar de La Motte, *Œuvres*, 9 vols and supplement (Paris 1753-1754), i.iii-v. She contrasts his physical blindness with the luminosity of his intellect.

31. La Motte, *Œuvres*, i.26.

literally and applying the criterion of *vraisemblance* to evaluate language as
an expression of character and of passion. As an example of a speech in
which the poet's voice drowns out that of the character, La Motte cites
Théramène's *récit*, in particular one of the lines describing the arrival of
the monster: 'Le flot qui l'apporta, recule épouvanté'. Although acceptable in an ode, this striking personification is out of place in a tragedy,
where it violates either *vraisemblance* or *bienséance*. The spectator, claims
La Motte, 'est choqué de voir un homme accablé de douleur, si recherché
dans ses termes, & si attentif à sa description'.[32] As Racine's friend and 'le
législateur de Parnasse', Boileau responded in his eleventh 'Réflexion sur
Longin', included in the 1710 edition of his translation of the *Traité sur
le sublime*. Boileau advances three arguments to justify Racine's choice of
expression; all of them, in various ways, reassert the fundamental idea
that tragic speech is poetic language and may therefore incorporate bold
figures. His first point is that as poetry, Théramène's line 'porte son
excuse avec soi' and is therefore beyond the reach of the criticism La
Motte makes. Secondly, he justifies Théramène's heightened expression in
terms familiar from d'Aubignac, by reference to the intensity of the
emotion involved. It is through the use of such figures that Théramène's
passion is represented and communicated to the spectators. According to
Boileau, a dramatic character in the grip of powerful emotion must be
allowed the same freedom of expression as a poet in the throes of inspiration ('un Poëte en fureur').[33] Finally, he appeals to the assertion made
by Longinus that the approval of a large number of different people of
various ages, backgrounds and temperaments demonstrates that something is great. Boileau reminds La Motte that this particular line is almost
always applauded vigorously whenever *Phèdre* is performed. This may
well be one of the reasons that La Motte fixed on this example, since the
audience response clearly proves his point. If the spectators applaud, then
they are responding to the language as 'poetry' and showing their
appreciation of Racine's skill; they are not absorbed in the illusion of
character and situation, which is exactly what La Motte had claimed.
Boileau died in 1711, but La Motte nevertheless replied to his comments
in an open letter published in the fourth edition of his odes. In opposition
to Boileau's reassertion of the neo-classical position, La Motte emphasises
two points that are fundamental to a new conception of dramatic speech.
He says that when introducing speaking characters the writer must use
ordinary language, enhanced only by the grace and elegance commensurate with the social rank of the speaker. In other words, if tragic
characters speak nobly it is because they are noble, not because they are
characters in a tragedy. He goes on to deny the validity of the equival-
ence neo-classical commentators establish between poetic expression and

32. La Motte, *Œuvres*, i.27.
33. Boileau, 'Réflexion XI', *Œuvres complètes*, p.559-62 (p.561).

heightened emotional states. According to La Motte, the bold language known as 'le langage des dieux' is never a true expression of the passions because it is 'le fruit de la méditation & de la recherche, & l'impétuosité des passions n'en laisse ni le goût ni le loisir'.[34] For La Motte, *vraisemblance* means that tragic speech should reflect both the social background of the characters and the spontaneity of the expression of powerful emotion.

The confrontation between Boileau and La Motte is a watershed, and others soon took up La Motte's argument that the use of figurative language represents an unacceptable intrusion of the poet's voice. In 1714, Fénelon raised similar points in his *Lettre sur les occupations de l'Académie*. Like La Motte, Fénelon sets himself against Boileau. He criticises the latter's approval of some instances of Corneille's use of figurative language and repeats La Motte's arguments about elegant expression in relation to social rank and the spontaneity of passionate utterances.[35] He has harsh words for Théramène's *récit*, condemning 'la description la plus pompeuse et la plus fleurie de la figure du dragon' in the mouth of Hippolyte's tutor, and he contrasts this speech with examples of more natural and convincing expressions of emotion found in the plays of Sophocles, in particular the anguish of Oedipus and the pain of Hercules and Philoctetes. Fénelon's letter no doubt gave these notions wider currency in France and elsewhere. This section of it, as well as the part on comedy, was later reproduced in German translation in Gottsched's *Deutsche Schaubühne*, and both Diderot and Lessing refer to the language of Philoctetes as a model.[36]

La Motte returned to the issue of dramatic speech in the context of a more wide-ranging examination of dramatic aesthetics in 1730. During the 1720s he had written four successful verse tragedies.[37] In 1730 these were republished in a two-volume edition, accompanied by four essays on drama in which La Motte makes a number of controversial suggestions for improving French tragedy. He not only recommends abolishing the unities of time, place and action in favour of a single 'unité d'intérêt', but also calls for tragedies in prose.[38] The 1730 edition of his plays includes a

---

34. La Motte, *Œuvres*, v.92.

35. Fénelon, *Œuvres*, ii.1171-72.

36. J. C. Gottsched, *Die deutsche Schaubühne nach den Regeln und Exempeln der Alten*, 2nd edn, 2 vols (Leipzig 1746-1750), i.9-41. References to the dispute between La Motte and Boileau resurface in the 1730s (in the *Journal des savants*, for example) at the time of the debate about verse and prose. Saint-Marc, the editor of the 1775 edition of Boileau's works, includes information about their dispute in his footnotes.

37. *Les Machabées* (1721), *Romulus* (1722), *Inès de Castro* (1723), and *Œdipe* (1726). His masterpiece was considered to be *Inès de Castro*, one of the most popular tragedies of the eighteenth century. For details of performances and La Motte's royalties, see Marie-France Hilgar, 'Théorie et pratique de la tragédie dans l'œuvre de Houdar de la Motte', *Littératures classiques* 16 (1992), p.259-67 (p.262-63 and n.3).

38. Paul Dupont, La Motte's biographer, emphasises what a bold and progressive conception his views represented for the time. See *Un poète-philosophe au commencement du dix-huitième siècle: Houdar de La Motte* (Paris 1898), p.280-81. J. G. Robertson suggests that some

prose version of his own *Œdipe*, a transposition into prose of the first scene from Racine's *Mithridate* with a brief introduction, and two odes on the relative merits of prose and verse. The inclusion of all this material gives some indication of how important he thought this issue was.[39] The need to efface the sense of an authorial presence, invoked in the debate with Boileau, plays a key role in La Motte's commentaries on tragedy, not only in relation to language but in connection with all aspects of the tragic form. La Motte condemns the supremacy of language in contemporary tragedies, which for the most part 'ne sont que des dialogues & des récits', and he urges the replacement of speech by action and visual effects, 'ces actions frappantes qui demandent de l'appareil & du spectacle'.[40] Action and spectacle, he says, are the essence of tragedy, 'une beauté qui semble être de son essence'. La Motte supports both points – the effacement of the poet and the importance of visual effects – by reference to the authority of Horace. The demand for more spectacle, such as that he tries to use in his own *Romulus*, is justified by quoting Horace's maxim that 'les esprits sont plus vivement frappés par les yeux que par les oreilles'.[41] La Motte offers the opinion that French playwrights have got it the wrong way round.

His source for the concept of the 'invisible poet' is mentioned in the introduction to his prose version of the first scene of *Mithridate*. La Motte explains that he has chosen a scene from Racine because he thinks that of all the tragic poets, Racine is the one whose language is least burdened by 'poetic' qualities. Transposed into prose, Racine's dialogue will readily demonstrate how superfluous metrical form is. But La Motte does allow himself to cite another instance of one of Racine's lapses: he quotes four lines spoken by Œnone in the opening scene of *Phèdre*, remarking that 'on ne reconnoît pas à ce discours la nourrice de Phœdre, mais l'Auteur qui se met à sa place'.[42] This passage fails the litmus test established by Horace,

of La Motte's ideas derive from Pier Jacopo Martelli, via Luigi Riccoboni: 'Sources italiennes des paradoxes dramatiques de La Motte', *Revue de littérature comparée* 3 (1923), p.369-75.

39. Here, I shall consider only La Motte's theory, not his tragedies. The theory was written after the plays and not with the purpose of justifying his own practice, although it includes commentary on his own works. La Motte's aim was to use his experience of writing for the theatre to propose new directions for French tragedy, distilled into his outline for a play about Coriolanus. For an account of his plays, see Lancaster, *French tragedy*, i.71-94, and Hilgar, 'Théorie et pratique de la tragédie', p.262-67, although Hilgar's judgements imply that she thinks La Motte's theory preceded the plays (p.265).

40. La Motte, *Œuvres*, iv.183.

41. La Motte, *Œuvres*, iv.185. 'But things entrusted to the ear / Impress our minds less vividly than what is exposed / To our trustworthy eyes so that a viewer informs himself / Of precisely what happened', Horace, *The Art of poetry* in *The Satires and epistles of Horace*, translated by Smith Palmer Bovie (Chicago, IL 1996; 1959), p.271-91 (p.278).

42. 'Les ombres par trois fois ont obscurci les cieux / Depuis que le sommeil n'est entré dans vos yeux; / Et le jour a trois fois chassé la nuit obscure, / Depuis que votre corps languit sans nourriture' (that is, 'You haven't eaten or slept for three days'). See La Motte, *Œuvres*, iv.414.

according to whom (in La Motte's words), 'l'éloge du Poëte épique est que, si l'on rompt la mesure de ses Vers, on retrouve toûjours les membres épars d'un Poëte, l'éloge de l'Auteur Dramatique, c'est qu'en rompant de même les mesures, le Poëte disparoisse & ne laisse voir que le Person-nage'.[43] The passage comes from the fourth satire of the first book of Horace's satires. Uncomfortable with the hostile attitude some people have towards poets, Horace argues that his satires cannot be classified as poetry at all. He says that his writing is more like the language of the New Comedy, which is simply the speech of ordinary people transposed into verse, and he contrasts this type of language with some lines typical of the lofty style of the epic, pointing out that one cannot rewrite as prose:

> After foul discordant Fate
> Broke down War's brazen pillars and her gate [...]

'For in these lines you'll find, though dismembered, the limbs of a poet.'[44] The underlying thought obviously impressed itself on La Motte and may even have guided his own writing. His concern here, though, is to invoke the authority of Horace against the practice of neo-classicism in relation to both language and the role of visual effects. In substituting the authority of Horace for that of Boileau, in the service of a theatrical form that would be less verbal and more visual, La Motte is anticipating a strategy that Diderot will later employ.[45]

In the essay accompanying his tragedy *Œdipe*, La Motte gives his reasons for experimenting with prose dialogue in tragedy. He appeals to the principle of *vraisemblance*, 'qui est absolument violée par la versifica-tion' and implies that introducing ordinary language will have a positive effect on the representation of both character and action: 'par le langage ordinaire, les Personnages & les sentimens n'en paroîtroient-ils pas plus réels; & par cela même, l'action n'en deviendroit-elle pas plus vraye?'[46] He argues that metrical form contributes nothing essential to the language of drama and that if it is dropped, nothing will be lost except 'cet agencement étudié qui vous distrait de l'Acteur, pour admirer le Poëte'.[47] To an individual with common sense ('tout homme de bon sens'), who happened never to have encountered poetic form, verse dia-logue would appear to be nothing but 'un abus de la parole'. What the dramatic poet must do is identify with his *dramatis personae* and remain 'fi-dèle aux caractères & aux passions qu'il représente; & sur-tout imiter de près le discours naturel de gens importans qui, sans préparation, se parlent

43. La Motte, *Œuvres*, iv.414-15.
44. Horace, *The Satires and epistles*, p.53-54.
45. Russell Goulbourne, 'Diderot et Horace, ou le paradoxe du théâtre moderne', in *Etudes sur 'Le Fils naturel' et les 'Entretiens sur le Fils naturel' de Diderot*, ed. Nicholas Cronk (Oxford 2000), p.112-22 (p.122).
46. La Motte, *Œuvres*, iv.392-93.
47. La Motte, *Œuvres*, iv.394.

selon leurs intérêts & selon leur passion présente'.[48] La Motte is calling for dialogue that imitates the way that people naturally speak in a given set of circumstances, speech that does not attract attention in its own right, as artistic language.

The idea of the intrusive poet recurs in connection with a number of La Motte's other recommendations for better dramatic writing. He con-demns *sententiae*, the maxims that were thought to enhance the moral value of tragedy, as a mere 'ornement ambitieux, qui ne sert qu'à rendre le dialogue moins naturel & moins vrai'.[49] Characters in the grip of a powerful emotion cannot possibly 'arranger des réflexions générales, au lieu de sentir vivement ce qui les touche en particulier'. Expressions of this type in Corneille's plays have always stood out as 'des morceaux dis-tingués, où brilloit plus qu'ailleurs le génie du Poëte, quoiqu'aux dépens du naturel et des convenances'.[50] The poet must resist the temptation to turn his characters into 'raisonneurs'; they should express only 'des sen-timens ou des pensées personnelles que le Poëte doit laisser généraliser aux Spectateurs'. In this same section, La Motte criticises the tendency to create long, carefully composed speeches declaimed without interruption. This violates the *vraisemblance* of normal human interaction. Dramatic dialogue should be lively, with frequent interruptions. Characters should respond appropriately, as soon as something is said that would naturally provoke a reaction, and when not speaking themselves, they should respond to what they hear with gestures and facial expressions.[51] These exchanges should not give the impression of being composed by a poet, but imitate the give and take of conversation. La Motte dislikes mono-logues, although he acknowledges that these may occasionally be neces-sary to aid the comprehension of the spectators. As they are traditionally employed in tragedy, he considers them a violation of the principle of the imitation of nature since there is no model in nature for such coher-ent passages of reflection, addressed by a speaker to him or herself. 'Où trouveroit-on dans la nature des hommes raisonnables qui pensas-sent ainsi tout haut! [...] Où prendre encore un coup les originaux de semblables discoureurs?'[52] He suspects that the reason monologues are tolerated at all is that although the character is supposed to be alone, we are conscious of the presence of the audience. 'Nous voyons des auditeurs; & dès-là, le parleur ne nous paroît pas ridicule; ce n'est pas à eux qu'il s'adresse, mais c'est pour eux qu'il s'explique.' This makes us forget that the actor 'devrait se taire'. If a monologue must be introduced, it should

48. La Motte, *Œuvres*, iv.415.
49. La Motte, *Œuvres*, iv.300.
50. La Motte, *Œuvres*, iv.302.
51. La Motte, *Œuvres*, iv.299. La Motte considers the habits of actors, accustomed to the declamatory style, to be one of the main obstacles to the introduction of a more natural form of tragic speech (iv.391).
52. La Motte, *Œuvres*, iv.280-81.

never take the form of a *tirade* or a *récit* (much less of *stances* 'où le Personnage devient tout-à-coup un Poëte de profession'): it should consist
solely in 'quelques mouvemens entrecoupés, quelques résolutions brus-
ques' which transform it into something 'plus naturelle et plus rai-
sonnable'.[53] Accounts of off-stage events and the use of confidants are
both techniques that encourage unnecessary verbalisation at the expense
of action. They create opportunities for poetic rather than dramatic
modes of representation and should be avoided as much as possible.[54] The
remedies La Motte suggests are the relaxing of the unity of place, so that
the dramatist can show events instead of having them narrated, and
involving the secondary characters in the action, so that they do more
then merely listen. In these passages, La Motte makes various appeals to
*vraisemblance* and to 'l'imitation de la nature' to justify his criticisms of the
conventional emphasis on language and the *dédoublement* of voices he finds
so disquieting.

His comments on the artificiality of conventional scenes of exposition
link the concept of the invisible poet explicitly with that of illusion. The
weakness of traditional opening scenes, in La Motte's view, is that they are
really no more than prologues, setting out basic facts concerning the events
about to unfold.[55] What the spectator sees is not the imitation of an action
but a poet laying the groundwork. As a result, these scenes are cold, boring
and all very much alike. The solution, says La Motte, is for the writer to get
out of the way. Since tragedy is supposed to take the form of action,

il faut que le Poëte se cache dès le commencement, de maniere qu'on ne s'ap-
perçoive pas qu'il prend ses avantages, & que c'est lui qui s'arrange, plutôt que
les Acteurs n'agissent [...] C'est par cette méthode que le Spectateur est d'abord
dans *l'illusion*; il n'apperçoit pas le Poëte sous les personnages, parce que l'art des
préparatifs disparoît & qu'il se tourne en mouvemens & en passion.[56]

For La Motte, 'illusion' is an effect that comes into being when the spectator no longer attends to the artifice in the art but becomes absorbed in
the fiction that it embodies. The invisibility of the poet in the play is like
the invisibility of the painter in the picture.

Comments that La Motte makes in his *Discours sur Homère* suggest that
he was familiar with the theory of de Piles and the *coloristes* and that he
held painting to be the most imitative of the arts. Intelligent composition
and skilful design, he notes, would not be enough to make a good picture
'si le coloris n'achevoit de donner aux objets toute leur ressemblance'.[57]
He also alludes to the traditional parallel drawn between poetry and painting in order to point out that there are significant differences between

53. La Motte, *Œuvres*, iv.283.
54. La Motte, *Œuvres*, iv.278 and iv.185.
55. La Motte, *Œuvres*, iv.154.
56. La Motte, *Œuvres*, iv.153 and iv.156, emphasis added.
57. La Motte, *Œuvres*, ii.83.

them. 'Quoique l'imitation & le choix soient nécessaires au Poëte comme au Peintre, le mérite du choix caractérise davantage le Poëte, & le mérite de l'imitation caractérise davantage le Peintre.'[58] In terms of its capacity to create an imitation of nature, La Motte, like de Piles, considers painting to be superior even to the art of sculpture.[59] It is not surprising therefore, that La Motte's attack on the dominance of the linguistic sign in tragedy should be accompanied by a corresponding interest in visual effects, for which he uses the terms 'spectacle' and 'tableau'. He cites the altar scene from his play *Romulus* as an example of the replacement of narration by action and says that he knows of only two other 'grands tableaux' of this type in French tragedy, the wedding ceremony in Corneille's *Rodogune* and the crowning of Joas in Racine's *Athalie*. His brief descriptions of these scenes show that he visualises them as pictures set before him, which achieve their effect through the distribution of the figures and the use of meaningful objects. The 'coupe suspecte [...] passant d'une main à l'autre' in *Rodogune*, or the crown, the sword and the book, with the priest kneeling at the feet of the young prince, in *Athalie*, 'frappent bien autrement que les plus beaux Vers'. Only before scenes of this kind can it truly be said that the spectator 'assiste à des événements & non pas simplement à des discours, comme dans la plûpart des Pieces'.[60] La Motte maintains, as Diderot later will, that drama must offer the spectators physical images which are taken in through the physical eye. This, for him, is the basis for comparisons between the theatre and painting. When Voltaire attacks La Motte's questioning of the unities and invokes the traditional comparison made between drama and painting in order to defend the unity of action, La Motte rejects it as invalid. Voltaire argues (in the preface to the 1730 edition of *Œdipe*) that a poet should not include more than one action in a play any more than a painter should attempt to depict two events on the same canvas.[61] La Motte agrees that a painting should not show two events, since a picture can only properly represent a single moment. He goes on to say, however, that this does not apply to tragedy, which represents 'une action successive & qui en renferme plusieurs autres'. Consequently, 'il y auroit vingt tableaux à faire des différens moments & des différentes situations d'une Tragédie'.[62] This will be Lessing's argument about the differences between painting and the epic in the *Laokoon*. In a sense La Motte and Voltaire are talking at cross-purposes. At the same time, their disagreement shows that La Motte has come to think of a play as a series of physical images that communicate with the spectator

58. La Motte, *Œuvres*, ii.53.

59. La Motte, *Œuvres*, iv.444.

60. La Motte, *Œuvres*, iv.187-88.

61. Voltaire, *Œdipe. Avec une préface dans laquelle on combat les sentimens de M. de la Motte sur la poësie* (Paris 1730), p.vi.

62. La Motte, *Œuvres*, iv.431-32.

both visually and aurally. He is focusing on the impact it has on spectators as viewers, who watch the drama unfold on the stage before them. This is the significance that the comparison between painting and drama will have for later eighteenth-century dramatists, rather than the one Voltaire invokes. This reorientation in perspective is captured in a passage from a section in La Motte's third *Discours*, entitled 'De la conduite d'une tragédie'.[63] La Motte announces it as the essential rule of dramatic composition, the one governing everything else. The trick, he says, is to control every single element in such a way that they all contribute to the verisimilitude of the whole, 'de maniere enfin que le Spectateur voïe toûjours une action, & ne sente jamais un Ouvrage: car dès que l'Auteur prend ses avantages aux dépens de la moindre vraisemblance, il les peut perdre par cela même. L'illusion cesse. On ne voit plus que le Poëte au lieu des Personnages.'[64] The goal of drama is the creation of the illusion of an event taking place in present time; the means are those which successfully conceal the poet's art. The point is so important that La Motte feels it needs further elaboration, and he goes on to explain the different ways in which the writer and the spectator relate to the play. The writer works according to a preconceived plan, but the spectators respond to what they simultaneously see and hear before them:

Le Poëte travaille dans un certain ordre; & le Spectateur sent dans un autre. Le Poëte se propose d'abord quelques beautés principales sur lesquelles il fonde son succès. C'est de là qu'il part; & il imagine ensuite ce qui doit être dit ou fait pour parvenir à son but. Le Spectateur au contraire part de ce qu'il voit et de ce qu'il entend d'abord; & il passe de là aux progrès & au dénoûment de l'action [...] En un mot, tout est art du côté de celui qui arrange une action Théatrale; mais rien ne doit le paraître à celui qui la voit.[65]

This paragraph brings together two sets of aesthetic values and seems to encapsulate the paradigm shift that is taking place in conceptions of the art of dramatic composition. The poet that La Motte here evokes is like the neo-classical writer, schooled in rhetoric and poetics and thinking in terms of beautiful effects that will earn him the admiration of the audience. The spectator is a member of the audience to come, ready to surrender to the physical illusion that dramatic representation offers to the senses of sight and hearing. La Motte's description of the theatre spectator as one who simultaneously hears and sees will recur in discussions of dramatic form throughout the century, most strikingly perhaps in Diderot's theatre writings. La Motte's point is that dramatic poets must learn to write from the perspective of the spectator; he has repositioned the writer in front of the stage, like the painter before his canvas.

63. Diderot takes up a number of the same points in the section of his *Discours* entitled 'Du plan de la tragédie et du plan de la comédie', DPV, x.353-67.
64. La Motte, *Œuvres*, iv.284-85.
65. La Motte, *Œuvres*, iv.285.

Despite the attention they attracted, La Motte's theories did not lead to the creation of many prose tragedies. Apart from his own *Œdipe*, which was not performed, only four prose tragedies from the period are known.[66] The most important are *Silvie*, the first French *tragédie bourgeoise* (1741), which will be discussed in the next section, and Sedaine's *Maillard, ou Paris sauvé*, of 1771, a play on the theme of the 1358 revolt of the people of Paris against Jean II. The play was performed in a private theatre in 1782 and published in 1788, but was never accepted at the Comédie-Française, a fact which Sedaine attributed (wrongly perhaps) to the influence of Voltaire.[67] In his preface to the published edition, Sedaine makes clear that he sees his play as a fulfilment of the theories of La Motte.[68] Although the subject is historical, the representational style of the play situates it in the illusionistic tradition of the *drame*, a genre in which Sedaine had already distinguished himself.[69] Indeed, the *drame* seems to be where La Motte's influence was felt most, particularly in relation to the nature and function of dramatic speech. Contemporary evidence of the gradual infiltration of his ideas is supplied by the critic Trublet, who states in a 1759 edition of some republished essays that 'le prétendu paradoxe de M. de la Motte sur les Tragédies en prose, n'en est presque plus un', and he offers a mock apology for devoting space to 'une vérité aujourd'hui assez généralement reconnue'. Nevertheless, he provides his own brief analysis of the role of language in tragedy, summarising all the main points made by La Motte. Trublet invokes the concept of the invisible poet and asserts that the pleasure proper to tragedy consists in the illusion it creates. He insists that this effect can only come about if all the elements of the work contribute harmoniously to this aim, appealing simultaneously to the emotions and the senses, and he sees the use of prose and natural language as essential ingredients of it. He rejects the opposing argument, according to which the use of verse helps create illusion by enhancing the dignity of tragic characters, with the statement 'ce sont les auteurs des tragédies qui vous en paraissent plus grands, plus importants; c'est eux seuls que vous allez chercher au théâtre, et que vous y voyez'.[70] The appreciation of the artist's skill, which listening to verse

---

66. The two factors limiting the implementation of La Motte's theories were the lack of a successful model and the influence of Voltaire: Lancaster, *French tragedy*, p.4.

67. Günther Ladislas, *L'Œuvre dramatique de Sedaine* (Paris 1908), p.279-82. Ladislas considers the political content of the play a more likely explanation for the decision taken by the Comédie-Française.

68. Michel-Jean Sedaine, *Maillard, ou Paris sauvé: tragédie en cinq actes en prose* (Paris 1788), p.xi.

69. The other prose tragedies that are known were never performed. They are Fontenelle's *Idalie*, written in 1719 and published in 1757, and Charles-Jean-François Hénault's *François II*, published in 1770 in his *Pièces de théâtre en prose*.

70. N. C. J. Trublet, 'Réflexions sur la prose et les vers françois, par raport à la tragédie', in *Essais sur divers sujets de littérature et de morale*, 4 vols (Paris 1760; Geneva 1968), iv.390-404 (p.399-400).

entails, is a delight for the mind rather than the heart, a pleasure 'de l'homme de lettres plutôt que de l'homme'.

Trublet's statements seem to be confirmed by various writers associated with the *drame*, who often reproduce La Motte's arguments, both with and without acknowledgement. The concept of the invisible poet reappears with astonishing frequency in their writings, especially in relation to language. Diderot already uses it in his earliest published commentary on the theatre, the critique of tragedy in *Les Bijoux indiscrets*.[71] Beaumarchais, in his essay on the *genre sérieux*, rejects La Motte's suggestion that prose be adopted for heroic tragedy, but he insists that prose is essential to the creation of illusion in the middle genre, and he goes on to praise Sedaine's achievement in *Le Philosophe sans le savoir*, in terms of the absent poet.[72] In the 1760s and 1770s, the invisible poet figures in the pages of the *Correspondance littéraire* where Grimm (who continues to call for French tragedies in prose) defines the nature not just of a single genre but of dramatic art in general in terms of the disappearance of the poet.[73] Mercier openly acknowledges his debt to La Motte in his *Nouvel Essai sur l'art dramatique* (1773), where he defends the use of prose with the familiar argument that verse is appropriate in the epic, where it is the poet 'qui embouche la trompette' but not in the *drame*, in which it is 'le personnage seul qui doit paroître, & non l'auteur'.[74] So although La Motte's ideas may not have inspired a truly successful prose tragedy, they appear to have helped launch a genre. His application of the classical topos of the invisible poet goes far beyond its role in the thinking of neo-classical theorists such as d'Aubignac. For them, it is a way of describing a literary device, the use of direct speech. La Motte exploits it to communicate his vision of a new theatrical code, in which the illusion that drama strives to create conforms to the standard established by the art of painting.

---

71. DPV, iii.164.

72. Pierre-Augustin Caron de Beaumarchais, *Œuvres*, ed. Pierre Larthomas (Paris 1988), p.133.

73. See, for example, his comments on Jean-François de La Harpe's *Mélanie, ou la Religieuse*, in Friedrich Melchior, baron de Grimm, Denis Diderot, Guillaume-Thomas Raynal, Jacques-Henri Meister, *et al.*, *Correspondance littéraire, philosophique et critique*, ed. M. Tourneux, 16 vols (Paris 1877-1882), viii.461.

74. Louis-Sébastien Mercier, *Du théâtre, ou Nouvel Essai sur l'art dramatique* (Amsterdam 1773), p.296.

# 3. Paul Landois and the 'hidden spectator': the use of natural theatrical signs in *Silvie*

In August 1741, a little more than a decade after the publication of La Motte's essays on tragedy, the first French *tragédie bourgeoise*, a work composed in prose, was given two performances at the Comédie-Française.[1] The following year it was published by Prault *fils*.[2] The unusually named *Silvie*, with its equally provocative subtitle (*Tragédie, en prose, en un acte*), is both a development of the theory outlined by La Motte and an anticipation of Diderot's dramatic aesthetic. The play deals with the time-honoured theme of jealousy, but the story comes from a widely read work of prose fiction written by Robert Challe, the collection of stories entitled *Les Illustres Françaises*, which was first published in 1713. The use of fictitious rather than historical or legendary characters in a play styling itself a tragedy is, in itself, a significant innovation. The particular form the prose dialogue takes, the stage setting and directions and the visual conception that shapes the play are also unique for the time. Details of Paul Landois's life remain much of a mystery, but we do know that when he turned his hand to writing in the 1740s (he wrote articles on art for the *Encyclopédie* as well as *Silvie*) he had already trained as a painter in his father's studio.[3] He was therefore uniquely positioned to grasp how painterly values might effectively be applied to dramatic composition.

Diderot considered *Silvie* an important play. Moi draws attention to it in the *Entretiens*, where it enjoys the distinction of being one of the rare contemporary works to merit a mention.[4] Dorval describes it as a work original enough to inspire 'un homme de génie', but thinks it will take something more to convert the nation as a whole to domestic tragedy in prose. Some of the reasons for the play's significance are implied by the position it occupies in Diderot's text, where the references to it form the

---

1. It is referred to as a 'Tragédie Bourgeoise' in the prologue to the play, and is also listed as such in the *Registres* of the Comédie-Française. Paul Landois, *Silvie*, ed. Henry Carrington Lancaster, *The First French 'tragédie bourgeoise': 'Silvie', attributed to Paul Landois*, The Johns Hopkins studies in romance literatures and languages 48 (Baltimore, MD 1954), p.12 and p.xiii. All future references to *Silvie* will be to this edition.
2. At the time of the performances and publication, the author remained anonymous. The abbé de La Porte identified the play as the work of Paul Landois, author of articles on painting in the *Encyclopédie*, in 1769, in the 'Auteurs vivants' section of *La France littéraire*. This is the earliest known association of his name with the play. Worvill, 'Recherches sur Paul Landois', p.130.
3. His father was Michel Landois, a master painter of the Académie de Saint-Luc (Worvill, 'Recherches sur Paul Landois', p.131-32).
4. Connon, *Innovation and renewal*, p.125.

transition between the discussion of stage *tableaux* and that concerning the use of prose, the two issues central to La Motte's dramatic aesthetic.[5] Persuaded of the historical importance of Landois's neglected work, Henry Carrington Lancaster brought out a modern edition in 1954, which he hoped would have the effect of stimulating further critical interest.[6] In that spirit, I shall here try to show how it brings together in dramatic form the thinking concerning illusion and natural theatrical signs that had come to the fore in the debates about painting and about the use of prose in tragedy.

The play itself is preceded by a witty and entertaining prologue in three scenes, designed to prepare the audience for the novel style of the play. The prologue opens as the Commandeur arrives at the Théâtre français in search of his friend, the author of the one-act tragedy in prose that is about to be performed. It is thus set in the 'here and now' of the audience. The Commandeur informs the Auteur that he has just come from the café where a number of minor literati ('petits faiseurs de Vers') are busy demonstrating 'dogmatiquement' that a tragedy not composed in verse can only be 'pitoyable, & digne du sifflet'.[7] The Commandeur and the Auteur briefly discuss the Auteur's decision to have the play performed (premature and hazardous in the opinion of the Commandeur, who fears the public humiliation to which they are now both exposed) and they are then joined by three other spectators, the Marquise, the Chevalier and M. Grosset who have come to watch the controversial performance. As they approach, the Commandeur urges his friend to keep his identity secret, and this mystification, along with the irreverent and satirical commentary on traditional tragedy, engenders a good deal of the ensuing humour. The Marquise, the Chevalier and M. Grosset are simultaneously intrigued and sceptical about the new play. Their attitude is probably not unlike that of the members of the audience watching the prologue, and in fact, the Commandeur later refers to these three characters as 'un échantillon du Public'.[8] The Auteur, whose true identity remains unknown to the new arrivals, goads them into expressing their theatrical

5. DPV, x.115. Diderot later planned to include *Silvie* in a volume containing three other domestic tragedies in prose (Lillo's *The London Merchant*, Moore's *The Gamester* and Lessing's *Miss Sara Sampson*). This project never came to fruition, but a 1762 draft of the preface remains, in which Diderot admiringly and quite incorrectly describes *Silvie* as 'la première tragédie en prose qui ait paru sur quelque théâtre que ce soit'. He goes on to attribute the development of domestic tragedy in England and Germany to this model. We do not know what lead him to make such extravagant claims (which he must have known were wrong) but it is obvious that he considered the 1741 play a significant milestone. DPV, x.549.

6. Landois, *Silvie*, p.xx.

7. Landois, *Silvie*, p.5-6. The café is presumably the Procope, situated opposite the Comédie-Française on the rue des Fossés Saint-Germain.

8. Landois, *Silvie*, p.12. Lancaster shows that the prologue to *Silvie* is inspired by the one that introduces Dumas d'Aigueberre's *Trois Spectacles* of 1729 (Introduction, p.xiv-xv and Appendix I).

prejudices without constraint, whilst the Commandeur does his best to defend the innovative principles on which the one-act tragedy is based. The prologue thus dramatises the themes of illusion and identification (which also figure in the dialogue) by collapsing the gap between the stage scene and the world of the audience. The latter are confronted with an image of themselves, spectators who have come to watch a provocative new play, and of the preconceptions and assumptions that they bring to bear on that experience.

Both the figurative language and the verse of neo-classical tragedy are implicitly criticised. The Commandeur defends the Auteur's decision to avoid the use of 'poetic' speech, by mocking the inflated terms and classical allusions associated with tragic language. He notes that the Auteur, 'ami de la nature', has deliberately avoided 'le pompeux galimathias tragique' in this work, and that 'les choses y sont nommées par leur nom'. Morning is not 'le blond Phœbus qui va sur son char lumineux fournir sa brillante carrière'; it is 'tout uniment le matin'.[9] The characters, caught in the grip of strong passions, 's'expriment conformément à leur situation, ne se mêlent que de ce qui les touche'.[10] Fénelon had criticised French writers who considered it demeaning to call things by their names,[11] and there are also distinct echoes of La Motte in the Commandeur's observation about the expression of emotion.

The main theme of the prologue discussion, however, is the use of prose and the Marquise, the Chevalier and M. Grosset each represent a different opinion. Whilst the Marquise is prepared to consider the play on its own merits ('Si elle est bonne en Prose, peut-on faire un crime à l'Auteur de ne l'avoir point faite en vers?'), the Chevalier insists that by definition, a tragedy in prose cannot possibly succeed ('Si elle est bonne, décide la question. Mais Madame me permettra de lui dire, que c'est supposer l'impossible').[12] M. Grosset, a buffoon, visibly modelled after Molière's M. Jourdain, extols the merits of the kind of tragedy he is used to in terms of the characteristic features of its dialogue, features he fears may be lacking in *Silvie*. These include the majestic cadences of tragic verse, as well as 'ces maximes, ces rêves, ces beaux traits de morale, ces portraits' and especially 'leur Acteur au récit, qui vient apprendre quel est celui duquel les affaires ont mal tourné': all the elements, in short, which La Motte had criticised as announcing the presence of the poet. The Commandeur insists that there will always be some spectators who appreciate representation of 'le vrai', and he justifies the suppression of verse as La Motte does, by an appeal to illusion. Although there are many occasions, he says, when he tolerates, admires or approves of the use of verse, 'ce ne sera jamais dans la représentation d'une Scene de la vie

9. Landois, *Silvie*, p.8.
10. Landois, *Silvie*, p.9.
11. Fénelon, *Œuvres*, i.56.
12. Landois, *Silvie*, p.6-7.

64

humaine, qu'on ne met sous les yeux que pour faire illusion, & où elle ne subsiste qu'à proportion que les choses sont exactement dans le vrai-semblable. Et quelque chose y est-il moins que de faire parler les gens en Vers?'[13]

There is no reference to La Motte's invisible poet, but the statement just quoted, which introduces the word 'illusion' for the first time, leads directly into the earliest version of the hidden spectator story, a topos that Diderot will subsequently take up and exploit in *Les Bijoux indiscrets* and the framework to *Le Fils naturel*. In the 1741 prologue, the idea of the hidden spectator plays the same role as that of the disappearance of the poet for La Motte; it is a way of conceptualising what is meant by 'il-lusion', but whereas La Motte approaches the issue from the perspective of the relationship between the play and the writer, the author of the prologue to *Silvie* focuses on the relationship between the play and the spectator. Indeed, how to be an enlightened spectator is a major theme of this prologue, where typical spectator attitudes are perceived to be one of the greatest obstacles to change.

The Commandeur asks the Chevalier what he would do if, concealed near the royal chambers, he happened to see and overhear some courtiers discussing a plot to kill the prince, and then saw them poised to carry it out. The Chevalier replies that he would immediately break down the door, sword in hand, and attack the traitors. The Commandeur then invites him to compare the scene he has just imagined with the impression that would be made on him if, knowing nothing about either theatre or the performance conventions of tragedy, he were to witness the same situation being enacted on the stage. The Chevalier is at a loss for an answer, but the Commandeur sketches in his likely reaction:

Ton courage & ton zéle ont dicté ta réponse dans le premier cas. Dans le second, sans crainte de passer pour sujet témeraire, ce même zéle te feroit faire des vœux au Ciel pour qu'il fit recouvrer la raison à ton Prince; car tu dirois; 'Si ce n'est point une Mascarade, dans laquelle il s'est engagé, il est fou; & sa Cour est folle.'[14]

The individual of common sense, ignorant of the conventions of tragedy but otherwise familiar with the ways of society, would never take a theatrical performance to be 'a scene from human life'. This story directs attention to the process that occurs at the moment of performance. It highlights the nature of the interaction between stage play and spectator and of the means of imitation that drama in performance exploits. This is to consider thea-trical representation as semiosis, the deployment of a system of theatrical signs. The Commandeur's example makes the point that the words and gestures of contemporary tragedy constitute a system of theatrical signs so far removed from normal human experience as to be incomprehensible to

13. Landois, *Silvie*, p.10.
14. Landois, *Silvie*, p.11.

the uninitiated. In order to respond to the play, the audience must know and understand these particular conventions. By contrast, the style of representation embodied in *Silvie*, which avoids the heightened declamation of tragedy and makes use of ordinary language and everyday objects, exemplifies a code that would readily be intelligible to the kind of naïve spectator that the Commandeur describes. These are theatrical signs that resemble the things they signify; they are therefore natural theatrical signs that share the self-effacing character of the signs of painting.

Where the image of the hidden spectator came from, and whether or not it is a conscious reformulation of the trope of the naïve spectator used in d'Aubignac's *Pratique du théâtre*, I have not been able to establish. It is, however, interesting to compare this eighteenth-century use of it with its role in d'Aubignac's treatise. In his chapter on *vraisemblance*, d'Aubignac introduces a hypothesis: 'supposons qu'un homme de bon sens n'ait jamais vu le Théâtre, et qu'il n'en ait même jamais ouï parler'.[15] Such a man, says d'Aubignac, will not be able to tell whether the actors are 'des Rois et des Princes véritables' or merely 'des fantômes vivants'. But even when he has learned that all is merely 'une feinte, et un déguisement', he will still not be capable of evaluating the play or knowing whether or not it is *vraisemblable*. This is only possible after seeing many plays and having had adequate time to reflect on them. 'Pour juger parfaitement du Poème Dramatique, il faut que cette raison naturelle soit parfaitement instruite en ce genre d'image dont les hommes ont voulu se servir pour représenter quelque action.' D'Aubignac's conception emphasises the conventional, contractual nature of artistic representation. In the prologue to *Silvie*, the topos is intended to show that under the existing theatrical *régime* any confusion of actors with kings is impossible. It also implies that a play should be immediately intelligible to a spectator of common sense, in the same way that good painting was held to employ a universal 'language', accessible to all.[16] Both tropes used by eighteenth-century dramatists (the invisible poet and the hidden spectator) emphasise concealment, either of the poet or the spectator, because the idea of concealment allows them to evoke a dramatic style based on showing rather than telling, a style in which both text and actors perform as if no audience were present. As time progresses, this effect will be fostered by the gradual introduction of lighting techniques that permit the physical concealment of the auditorium from the stage, and of the spectators from one another, by restricting light to the acting area.[17]

15. D'Aubignac, *La Pratique du theatre*, p.127.

16. 'En effet, si les Poëtes ont le choix des Langues, dès qu'ils se sont déterminés à quelqu'une de ces Langues, il n'y a qu'une Nation qui les puisse entendre: et les Peintres ont un langage, lequel (s'il m'est permis de le dire) à l'imitation de celui que Dieu donna aux Apôtres, se fait entendre de tous les Peuples de la Terre.' De Piles, *Cours de peinture*, p.449.

17. Fischer-Lichte, *The Semiotics of theater*, p.100.

Whilst opinions will differ on whether, or to what extent, *Silvie* can be considered a successful play (eighteenth-century views certainly diverge on this), it does fulfil the expressed intent of the Auteur in the prologue to provide the model of a new genre.[18] The work embodies an original approach to the two main aspects of representation considered here, the integration of visual effects and a corresponding transformation of dramatic speech in the service of illusion.

Dorval highlights the importance of the visual conception of the play when he describes the opening scene as a 'tableau charmant'.[19] The opening stage directions supply the basic elements of the set:

Le Théatre represente l'interieur d'une chambre où l'on ne voit que les murs; une table sur laquelle est une lumiere, un pot à l'eau et un pain: un habit d'homme & une mauvaise robbe de femme.

Des FRANCS, en habit de campagne, se promenant comme un homme furieux, UN LAQUAIS, portant un miroir.[20]

There is also a chair, not mentioned in these opening directions, and the mirror, which the servant is removing as the play opens, is restored to its place in the first exchange of dialogue. Des Francs, changing his mind about this item, instructs the servant to leave it with the words 'Je veux que lui présentant sans cesse son image, la perfide ait horreur de son crime.' The text does not say where the servant is to place this mirror, but the logical choice, in view of the prevailing stage conditions and the reference to the bare walls, would be the table. The visual impact created by the table evokes the art of still life: bread, water pitcher, light, a reflecting surface (here, the mirror) and fabric somewhere nearby – these are basic elements of still life painting as it was practised by Dutch artists and increasingly by French ones. The total décor has both denotative and connotative value. It represents the place where the action of the play takes place (the room in which Silvie is confined) and, as Moi points out in the *Entretiens*, it reveals something of Des Francs's state of mind: 'voilà le séjour et la nourriture qu'un mari jaloux destine, pour le reste de ses

18. Landois, *Silvie*, p.13. There is little evidence of contemporary response to the play (perhaps not surprising since it was performed in August). A female friend of Mme de Graffigny, the abbé Leblanc and Palissot (who was too young to have seen the play performed in Paris) all express negative opinions; Devaux, the marquis d'Argenson, Diderot, and Mouhy positive ones.

19. DPV, x.115.

20. Landois, *Silvie*, p.15. This differs from the description in Challe's story. Des Francs reports that the room 'avait pour tout meuble un méchant lit de camp, et une paillasse sans linceuls ni couvertures, une selle de bois de trois pieds comme elles sont en province, sans tapisserie, sans foyer, ni cheminée, ni fenêtre, ne recevant le jour que par un œil-de-bœuf, que j'avais fait laisser en haut, et qui était condamné par une grille de fer'. The bread and water are only mentioned later, although Des Francs does allude here to the 'paquet de hardes qui pouvaient servir à la dernière des paysannes', which will serve as her dress. Robert Challe, *Les Illustres Françaises* (1713), ed. Frédéric Deloffre and Jacques Cormier, new edition (Geneva 1991), p.414. Future references are to this edition, unless otherwise stated.

jours, à une femme innocente dont il a soupçonné la vertu'.[21] The bread
and water represent food and drink, but also suggest that the place is a
type of prison. The mirror is the classic symbol of female vanity and also
of illusions in the sense of errors. The 'mauvaise robbe de chambre' hints
at Des Francs's anticipated unmasking of Silvie. Together, the two gar-
ments visible on stage at the beginning (the 'robbe de chambre' and the
male 'habit') are a visual allusion to the theme of adultery. The light
offers a gleam of hope and suggests the possibility of innocence. The décor
is thus simultaneously imitative and symbolic, and the objects within it
communicate meaning visually, as in a picture. The audience grasps
things that are unmentioned in the dialogue. As an opening scene it is
very original, bringing together La Motte's suggestions for creating lively,
action-based exposition (it begins *in medias res*) and de Piles's analysis of
the impact made by good painting, which captures the attention of
passing viewers and draws them into its world.[22]

The dialogue and stage directions also include references to other visual
theatrical signs exploited in the play, such as costume, properties and
lighting. These too are chosen to foster the illusion of an event drawn from
life. The stage directions contain six references to costume (worn or used
as properties), and the dialogue contains nine. Although these references
are sketchy, there are enough of them to show that the dramatist was
trying to impose on the cast the consistent use of the costumes required
by the fictional context. Des Francs is dressed 'en habit de campagne'.
Silvie's costume is not described in the stage directions, apart from the
reference to the 'mauvaise robbe de chambre' meant for her, but when she
enters she has just been woken and is weak and still drugged. In scene v
she has to fall to the ground in a faint. It seems likely that informal dress
of some kind was what Landois intended for her, and there is a precedent
for this in Challe's novel. In a passage to which the dialogue of scene vii of
the play specifically refers, Silvie is described as wearing 'un déshabillé de
satin blanc'.[23] Des Francs's statements in the play (which take up the
novel's account of her efforts to seduce him by wearing a garment she
knew he found attractive) are consistent with her being similarly attired
in the play, although it would have been very unusual for the heroine of a
tragedy to appear on stage *en négligé*. The dialogue and stage directions
also make reference to various pieces of jewellery, needed for some stage
business in scene v, and the hunting knife and box of poison Des Francs
produces in scene vii. The allusions to clothing and accessories would
make it difficult for the actors to ignore the wishes of the dramatist who
seems to have a clear vision of the play's intended visual effects, although
the Auteur in the prologue says that he fears that the exploitation of

21. DPV, x.115.
22. De Piles, *Cours de peinture*, p.4.
23. Landois, *Silvie*, p.26, and Challe, *Les Illustres Françaises*, p.419.

costumes and furniture in a tragedy may give rise to inappropriate mirth among the spectators.[24] Items such as these, however, all represent elements to which a painter would give careful consideration in creating a picture. Landois's entries in the *Encyclopédie* show that artists disposed of a specialised vocabulary for this kind of detail, and he defines some of these terms under the headings 'Accessoires', 'Accompagnements' and 'Ajustements'.

Particularly intriguing in Landois's play are the references in both the stage directions and the dialogue to lighting. In addition to the mention of the lamp on the table in the opening description of the set, both Silvie and Des Ronais comment on the surrounding darkness of the room, so he seems to have imagined the scene in terms of the distribution of light and shade that might be used in a painting. Whether or not Landois could possibly have expected the Comédie-Française actors to try and implement such ideas is difficult to say, but this period saw significant changes in the use of lighting in Paris theatres.[25] The seventeenth- and early-eighteenth-century practice of using lighting to illuminate the entire theatre and add lustre to the event as a whole was gradually giving way to a tendency to concentrate more light on the stage and less on the auditorium. At the Comédie-Française, the lighting arrangements changed sometime between 1719 and 1757, although the exact date remains uncertain. Before the middle of the century, there had been some limited experimentation with lighting as a theatrical sign, for example to create 'night' scenes. This was technically feasible since it only involved extinguishing a sufficient number of candles. In the absence of any documentation about the Paris performances of *Silvie*, it is impossible to know whether Landois's conception of the distribution of light and dark in his play had any practical consequences. But his attempt to introduce painterly principles of lighting to the visualisation of stage scenes anticipates, by quite a few years, the proposals made by Algarotti and Noverre whom Gösta Bergman cites as the earliest proponents of such ideas.[26] In his *Essai sur l'opéra* (Italian edition 1755; French edition 1773), Algarotti recommends the paintings of Rembrandt, Giorgione and Titian as suitable models to follow for stage lighting and Noverre, in his *Lettres sur la danse* (1760), suggests that people responsible for theatre lighting consult with painters to learn their art. But regardless of whether or not Landois's ideas for lighting were realisable in the theatre of the day, their presence in his text shows that in his mind, Landois had conceived the setting in relation to the way light and shade are exploited in pictures to enhance illusion and focus the spectator's gaze. His approach to play

24. Landois, *Silvie*, p.9.
25. Gösta Bergman, *Lighting in the theatre* (Stockholm, Totowa, NJ 1977), p.144-95. Developments in theatre lighting were advanced as a result of efforts to improve Paris street lighting (p.144-45).
26. Bergman, *Lighting in the theatre*, p.178-80.

writing is a painterly one and the details given in the text, although less extensive than Diderot's stage directions, show that he was writing from the perspective of a visual conception of the whole, as de Piles recommends for painting.

In view of the fact that Landois was an artist as well as a writer, one cannot help wondering whether he might even have had specific paintings in mind as he composed *Silvie*. There are several examples from later in the century (that is, following the publication of Diderot's theatre writings) of plays that exploit scenes deliberately modelled on well-known paintings, the best known being act II, scene iv of *Le Mariage de Figaro* (1784), where Beaumarchais instructs that the Comtesse, Suzanne and Chérubin should arrange themselves like the figures in Van Loo's painting entitled *La Conversation espagnole*.[27] Diderot's memory of Landois's play suggests that in this case too, existing works of art may have inspired the visual conceptualisation of the play. The account given in the *Entretiens* is not simply a description of the opening set, as Diderot's text seems to imply; it in fact reconstitutes a later scene that includes a female figure at the table, a weeping Mlle Gaussin in the role of Silvie. The *tableau* that Dorval evokes (bare walls, table and light, informally dressed female figure) suggests the basic elements and general concept of a series of paintings by Georges de La Tour on the theme of the repentant Magdalen. These pictures, which are examples of La Tour's *Nuits*, depict Mary Magdalen, simply dressed, seated at a table on which stand a candle, a book and, in several versions, a mirror. Other accessories include a skull and, in some treatments, a rope scourge and a jar of ointment. The number of these works that survive today implies that the Magdalen paintings were the most popular of La Tour's nocturnes.[28] There are five autograph versions still in existence as well as three variations known from contemporary copies. Although explicit references to La Tour and his works are rare in the eighteenth century, art historians today believe that his pictures must have been known to people involved in the art world of the time.[29] Despite variations of detail, La Tour's images all exploit the basic elements identified above as well as the same distribution of lighting as that evoked in Landois's play through the references to the lamp and the surrounding obscurity. That the painter Landois might turn to familiar Magdalen iconography to enrich the visual impact of his play is not surprising in view of the literary allusions that link Silvie with Mary Magdalen in the source text. In Challe's novel, Des Francs explicitly compares Silvie to Magdalen, and Henri Coulet has demonstrated that one scene in particular (preserved in the play version

27. Angelica Goodden, '"Une peinture parlante": the *tableau* and the *drame*', *French studies* 38 (1984), p.397-413 (p.404).

28. Philip Conisbee, *Georges de La Tour and his world* (New Haven, CT 1996), p.102.

29. Pierre Rosenberg, Jacques Thuillier and Pierre Landry, *Georges de La Tour, Paris, Orangerie des Tuileries, mai-septembre* (Paris 1972), p.91.

and also exploited in works by Prévost and Diderot) is modelled on a biblical story about her.[30] Diderot's description of Landois's setting, in the second *Entretien*, highlights all the elements that suggest this iconography and it seems entirely plausible that the painter would conceptualise his play in terms of imagery that is thematically consistent with the biblical allusions used by the novelist.[31] But whether or not Landois's play is, in fact, another example of a deliberate allusion to known works of art, it is clear that he has approached the creation of his text with a painterly eye and from the same angle that he would approach a painting, enlisting visual theatrical signs in a way that is new in serious drama in France.

His use of prose speech is equally original, and the dialogue of *Silvie* can be seen to embody many of La Motte's suggestions. The replete text typical of neo-classical tragedy gives way to dialogue that is not simply a prose transcription of speeches intended for verse format, but a new type of dramatic language, capable of evoking the spontaneity of conversation. Many of the lines are short, and sentences are frequently left incomplete or change direction in mid-course. Characters interrupt each other and one-word answers to questions are not infrequent. Suspension points are used to indicate dramatic pauses, not only in monologues, such as the one in the opening scene, but also in exchanges between two characters. In Des Ronais's second speech in scene ii, there are several lengthy pauses as he waits, in vain, for a response from Des Francs. In pace and rhythm, this dialogue imitates everyday patterns of communication.

Landois's choice of Challe's novel as a model proves more effective than La Motte's idea for rewriting Racinian verse. Modern critics single out the language of *Les Illustres Françaises* as one of its most original characteristics. Frédéric Deloffre describes Challe's style as 'un véritable style de conversation' that is unique for a novel of the period, and Lawrence Forno also considers it a successful depiction of 'the speech patterns of middle-class Parisians in the late seventeenth century'.[32] Landois's play seems to capture the tone of the novel, including some of its idiosyncrasies. In both works, Des Francs's speech is characterised by the presence of expressions that evoke the linguistic conventions of tragedy. In the play, he refers to Silvie as 'la perfide', to Gallouin as 'le traître', to himself as 'lâche' and describes his emotional state as 'ma rage' or 'ma fureur'. He speaks of 'funestes effets', of 'cet instant fatal' and he threatens to 'souiller

30. Henri Coulet, 'Le thème de la Madeleine repentie chez Robert Challe, Prévost et Diderot', *Saggi e ricerche di letturatura francese* 14 (1975), p.287-304.

31. For a more detailed consideration of this question, see Romira Worvill, 'Le rôle de la peinture dans l'adaptation théâtrale d'une nouvelle de Robert Challe par Paul Landois', in *Challe et/en son temps: actes du colloque de l'Université d'Ottawa, 24-26 septembre 1998*, ed. Marie-Laure Girou Swiderski and Pierre Berthiaume (Paris 2002), p.99-112.

32. Robert Challe, *Les Illustres Françaises* (1713), ed. Frédéric Deloffre, 2 vols (Paris 1959), i.xlvii, and Lawrence J. Forno, 'Robert Challe and the eighteenth century', *SVEC* 79 (1971), p.163-75 (p.169).

ma main de ton sang perfide'.[33] Silvie only addresses Des Francs once as
'cruel' and twice as 'barbare', but otherwise avoids figures of this kind,
and Des Ronais uses none. Michèle Weil suggests that the function of
these remnants of 'noble' language in both Challe's novel and in the
various dramatisations based on it, including *Silvie*, is to 'ennoble' the
non-aristocratic characters by endowing them with heightened *sensibilité*.[34] This perceptive observation does not, however, seem entirely to
explain the function of such expressions in Landois's play, where they are
concentrated in the speech of Des Francs and appear rather to serve the
goal of characterisation, by marking him as the passionate individual, in
contrast with the more phlegmatic Des Ronais. In Landois's treatment,
this kind of language seems to represent a personal rhetoric, rather than
a rhetoric of the emotions in general. Moreover, the speech in this
first French *tragédie bourgeoise* is considerably less 'poetic' than that of its
English counterpart, Lillo's *The London merchant*, with its discernible
echoes of Shakespearean blank verse and the rhyming lines that conclude
each act.[35] To an unprejudiced or well-disposed spectator of the eighteenth century (such as Diderot), Landois's text must have seemed to
achieve the invisibility of the poet that La Motte calls for.

There are no confidants in the play, but there are three monologues
(if Des Francs's remarks to himself in scene i are counted) and two *récits*
(Des Francs relates the events of the previous evening to Des Ronais in
scene ii, and this is balanced by Des Ronais's account, in the final scene,
of Gallouin's confession and death). All of these speeches are relatively
short and functional. The monologues serve the purpose of revealing character and allowing time to pass, whilst Des Francs's account in scene ii
is broken up by Des Ronais's questions and interjections, which help
disguise its narrative form. The goal of the concluding *récit* is to convey
information in a plausible manner, and there is no attempt to exploit it
for literary or rhetorical effect. The brevity of the one-act form and
respect for the unities prevented Landois from eliminating *récit* altogether.
Des Francs's exposition of the situation could only be avoided by showing
his return and discovery of the 'guilty' couple, which would not have been
possible on account of decorum as well as the unity of place, and the same
constraints explain the need for Des Ronais's *récit* at the end, although the
German translation of the play dispenses with it by bringing the wounded

33. In the novel, Des Francs uses expressions such as 'perfidie', 'rage', 'fureur', 'cruauté',
'gloire', 'amour offensé', 'coups mortels', 'outragé', and swears, to an absent Silvie, that he
will return to Paris 'pour laver dans ton sang ton infidélité et mon infamie'. The relevant
sections of the novel are reproduced in Appendix II in Lancaster's edition, p.36-48.

34. Michèle Weil, 'Du roman bourgeois au drame bourgeois', *Cahiers d'histoire des littératures romanes* 4 (1977), p.433-63 (p.450-51). The other works she examines are *La Veuve*
(composed in 1756, published in 1764) and *Dupuis et Desronais* (1763) by Collé.

35. F. M. Wilkshire, 'Lillo and Moore in France: English influences on the dramatic
theory of Diderot', *Man and nature/l'homme et la nature* 5 (1986), p.201-13 (p.208-209).

Gallouin (Adrast) on stage to confess, apologise and expire.[36] But although La Motte's call for the substitution of action for speech is not fully resolved in *Silvie*, Landois's text does imply a desire to limit and contain the narrative and descriptive tendencies of traditional tragic dialogue.

The language is reinforced by a style of gesture and movement that invests the speech with visual qualities consistent with the goal of illusion. Stage action is indicated in enough detail to show that the dialogue was composed with the intention of allowing gesture and movement to play a significant and, at times, autonomous role in the communication of meaning. At the beginning of scene v, for example, when Silvie first sees Des Francs, who has returned home unbeknownst to her, gestures are used to reveal the very different states of mind of the two characters. Some of the action is dictated in the traditional manner, by the dialogue, for example Silvie's question 'Mais qu'avez-vous?' or her later exclamation 'Quels regards vous jettez sur moi.'[37] At other times, movement is prescribed through stage directions: 'elle veut l'embrasser, et il la repousse', 'elle veut lui prendre la main, il la repousse'.[38] Gesture and movement bring out the inward emotions of the two characters, as well as transitions from one emotion to another: Silvie's initial pleasure at unexpectedly finding her husband at home, quickly followed by bewilderment and anxiety in the face of his unexpected coldness towards her; Des Francs's inner turmoil as he struggles to master the feelings stirred by what he believes is her betrayal and to retain an outward air of composure. His words consistently understate what he thinks and feels, and throughout this brief section gesture supplies the subtext. Here, the playwright has recourse to less language, not more, and it is gestures that do the job of figures in neo-classical discourse. They do not simply reinforce the spoken lines but express things left unsaid. The form that this body language takes appears to reflect the cultural code with which the spectators would be familiar from ordinary social life.

The gestures prescribed in *Silvie* fall into two broad categories: those that are required by the plot, and those that function simply to express emotional tension. The first category includes examples such as Des Francs showing Silvie the 'mauvaise robbe de chambre', confronting her with Galouin's 'habit' or offering her the choice between the poison and the hunting knife. These actions call for a greater degree of interaction

---

36. *Serena, ein Bürgliches Trauerspiel in Prose von einem Aufzuge. Nebst einem Vorspiel. Aus dem Französischen übersetzt* (Frankfurt, Leipzig 1764), p.61 and p.63. The unidentified translator was Gottlieb Konrad Pfeffel. *Serena* was subsequently reprinted in his *Theatralische Belustigungen. Nach französischen Mustern* (1765), and again in 1776 in the first volume of *Neue Schauspiele, aufgeführt [...] zu München* (Karl S. Guthke, *Das deutsche bürgerliche Trauerspiel*, Stuttgart 1972, p.25-26). A Danish version, *Serena, et skuespil*, appeared in 1779, translated by Peder Topp Wandall.

37. Landois, *Silvie*, p.20 and p.21.

38. Landois, *Silvie*, p.20 and p.21.

between people and objects, of the use of props, than in conventional tragedy. The second category, gestures serving to express emotional tension, consists of four principal actions: agitated walking ('se promener'), falling at the feet of another character ('se jeter aux pieds de'), sitting and standing that have no purpose other than as the physical expression of emotion (for example, 'se laisser aller dans un fauteuil'), and physical collapse. In *Silvie*, agitated walking is indicated twice in the directions, 'se jeter aux pieds de' three times, use of the 'fauteuil' three times and total collapse once. Particularly innovative is the use of the chair as a means to increase the opportunities for the actors to express feeling through natural-looking gesture and movement. This is its sole function.[39] It is never mentioned in the dialogue and only appears in the stage directions when a character drops into it under the strain of emotion. In all three cases, the act of sitting is associated with a reference to death, literal or figurative. In scene ii, Des Francs sits after delivering the line 'Non, ma mort vous l'apprendra' (the pronoun 'it' refers to the troubling suspicion that he cannot put into words). He gets to his feet again three speeches later when he seems to have decided what his course of action with Des Ronais will be.[40] In scene vii, Silvie 'se laisse aller dans le fauteuil' after the line 'Rappellez vos sens... quelqu'illusion... je me meurs' after Des Francs claims to have surprised her in bed with Gallouin (an accusation she cannot understand).[41] Nine speeches later Des Francs sits briefly after announcing that his anger towards Silvie has become contempt and that he is ready to exact vengeance. He sits following the line 'C'en est fait' and rises again, seconds later, after pronouncing the second part of the sentence, '& me voilà tranquille.'[42] In this last case the movement again serves to contradict what the character actually says. Perhaps Landois felt that references to death were necessary to justify these frequent acts of sitting, which run counter to the traditional idea of the dignity of tragedy and of tragic characters. Whilst physical movement certainly had a place in the neo-classical tradition, actions such as sitting, rising and kneeling were used relatively sparingly and are often shaped by questions of social etiquette as well as theatrical effect.[43] Moreover, such bodily action remained the servant of speech, preparing for it or

39. Later in the century, stage accessories will acquire symbolic significance, for example the barrow in Mercier's *La Brouette du vinaigrier* or the *fauteuil de malade* in Beaumarchais's *Le Mariage de Figaro* (see Georges Bérubé, 'A la recherche du malade dans *Le Mariage de Figaro*: quel(s) sens faut-il donner à l'objet-fauteuil?', *Man and nature/l'homme et la nature* 5, 1986, p.15-28).

40. Landois, *Silvie*, p.17.

41. Landois, *Silvie*, p.26.

42. Landois, *Silvie*, p.27.

43. David Maskell, *Racine: a theatrical reading* (Oxford 1991), p.61-83; Michaela Sambanis, 'Mettre en scène Racine: à propos des didascalies', *Zeitschrift für Französische Sprache und Literatur* 113:1 (2003), p.27-38.

supporting and enhancing it.[44] Most of the gestures specified in Landois's drama bear the stamp of the ordinary, and serve to create the illusion of characters totally absorbed in the events represented in the play. As gestures and movements modelled on those of the surrounding culture, they constitute natural theatrical signs, dedicated to conveying an impression of spontaneous behaviour. Words and actions are thus fused into a single impression in the way that Diderot will later recommend.

It is interesting to note that Landois's experimentation with this type of ordinary action in tragedy precedes the development of a widespread interest in natural acting sparked by the publication of works such as Rémond de Sainte-Albine's *Le Comédien* (1747) and François Riccoboni's *L'Art du théâtre* (1750). The best example of a 'natural' style in the theatre of the time was that of the Italians. In a letter of 1739, the président de Brosses describes their manner as a harmonious interaction of word, tone and gesture:

Le geste et l'inflexion de la voix se marient toujours avec le propos de théâtre, les acteurs vont et viennent, dialoguent et agissent comme chez eux. Cette action est tout autrement naturelle, a un tout autre air de vérité que de voir comme aux Français, quatre ou cinq acteurs rangés à la file sur une ligne, comme un bas-relief, au devant du théâtre, débitant leur dialogue chacun à leur tour.[45]

Diderot, too, likes the improvisational style of the Italian actors who, he says, perform with greater freedom than the French and 'font moins de cas du spectateur', although he considers the total effect marred by other features of this theatrical code, such as 'les insipides discours et l'intrigue absurde'.[46] He implies, though, that this style could be successfully adapted to plays in written form. In the same section of the *Discours*, Diderot invokes the effectiveness of the harmonious interplay of speech with descriptions of movement and gesture in the novel and he also draws a parallel between the principles of good acting and rules of pictorial representation.[47] The last two, in particular, seem like obvious sources for Landois's exploitation of such techniques. The four emotive gestures mentioned in his play (agitated pacing, unmotivated sitting, kneeling, and fainting) are all used in the same manner in contemporary prose fiction such as Challe's novel and Prévost's *Manon Lescaut* (1730).

Thus, in Landois's *Silvie*, unlike a play such as La Chaussée's *Mélanide* of the same year, all the theatrical signs of the contemporary code for serious drama have been simultaneously modified. Language, gesture, movement, costume and décor all conspire to create the illusion of an event drawn from contemporary life, in the manner suggested by the hidden

44. Bryson, *Word and image*, p.78.
45. Quoted in Xavier de Courville, *Un Apôtre de l'art du théâtre au XVIII^e siècle: Luigi Riccoboni dit Lélio*, 3 vols (Paris 1943) iii.231.
46. DPV, x.408.
47. DPV, x.411 and x.416.

spectator topos presented in the prologue. An eighteenth-century 'hidden spectator' seeing a performance of *Silvie* would take it to be the representation of 'a scene from human life' and Dorval's comment on the power of the opening scene ('un tableau charmant') suggests that Landois had succeeded in achieving the kind of arresting effect that in de Piles's theory characterises good painting. Landois has crafted his play not from the perspective of the trained poet composing a literary work, but from that of a visual artist, positioned before the scene he paints. *Silvie* is constructed according to principles that Diderot will later set out as the theoretical foundation of a new dramaturgy: one that takes the topos of the hidden spectator as its guiding idea.

# II

## Synthesis and innovation in Diderot's dramatic writings

# 4. The 'invisible poet' and the 'hidden spectator' in Diderot's dramatic theory and plays: the new theatrical code

THE importance of the role of the beholder in Diderot's thought and writing has been recognised ever since the publication of Michael Fried's widely read study of the aesthetic values that reverberate through Diderot's art criticism and the body of paintings which, in various ways, exemplify them.[1] Fried explores Diderot's insistence on the paradox that in order to succeed in capturing the attention of the viewer and holding him or her in thrall before the image, a painting must convey the impression that it was not created for a beholder. Despite the fact that the existence of pictures presupposes viewers, the image must appear to be 'unconscious of' the presence of the spectator before it, for it is this effect which grips the beholder and draws him or her into its represented world.[2] For Fried, the particular significance of Diderot's art criticism lies in the fact that it articulates clearly the issues with which French artists of the time were actually engaged, as they worked to resurrect and renew a tradition of absorptive painting that had largely disappeared during the dominance of the rococo.[3] Fried emphasises the fact that the criteria Diderot brings to bear on the paintings discussed in his *Salons* are the same as those that he applies to dramatic representation in his theatre writings of the late 1750s. Fried cites a number of passages from the *Entretiens* and the *Discours* to show how frequently the recommendation that both the dramatist and the actor forget or ignore the presence of the spectator recurs, although he makes no mention of the hidden spectator figure (Moi) from the framework to *Le Fils naturel et les Entretiens* or of the example of the hidden spectator that Mirzoza uses in *Les Bijoux indiscrets*. For Fried, Diderot's conception of the relationship between the audience and performance is epitomised in the stage *tableau*, which, he writes, 'helped to persuade the beholder that the actors themselves were unconscious of his presence'.[4]

Since the appearance of Fried's study, other critics have addressed the act of beholding as it appears in Diderot's writings, either to enlarge upon

---

1. Michael Fried, *Absorption and theatricality: painting and beholder in the age of Diderot* (Berkeley and Los Angeles, CA, London 1980).
2. Fried, *Absorption and theatricality*, p.103. He refers to this conception of the relationship between painting and beholder as the 'supreme fiction'.
3. Fried, *Absorption and theatricality*, p.3-4, p.43-45, p.76.
4. Fried, *Absorption and theatricality*, p.96.

or qualify his findings. Some take issue with his use of words such as 'negate', 'neutralise' and 'exclude', since these terms open up the problem of how an artwork that 'denies' or 'ignores' the presence of the spectator succeeds in eliciting a response.[5] Others question the extent to which the parallel that Fried sets up between painting and drama can be maintained, and they emphasise the importance of recognising the specificity of Diderot's theatre aesthetic, which relies on the sympathetic identification between the audience and the *dramatis personae* for its moral effect.[6] There is agreement, though, that 'beholding' is central to Diderot's thought and aesthetics and that the position of the spectator represents 'une des postures de base' in his work as a whole.[7] Philip Stewart does give brief consideration to the framework to *Le Fils naturel*, asserting that Moi, whom he describes as a 'voyeur', 'typifie toute l'esthétique théâtrale de Diderot'. But he does not explore this in detail, and simply notes a number of aesthetic ambiguities he finds implied by the use of this figure before going on to examine other examples of beholding in Diderot's writing.[8] Only Jauss, in an article published many years before Fried's study, seems to have considered the hidden spectator of *Les Bijoux indiscrets* an important element in Diderot's drama theory. He begins his discussion of Diderot's *comédie sérieuse* and its related paradoxes (principally as explored in the *Entretiens*) with a careful analysis of Mirzoza's comments on tragedy and illusion.[9] For Jauss, the example of the hidden spectator is a strikingly simple and succinct formulation of the new principle of imitation that Diderot establishes in opposition to the neo-classical one. Jauss regards it as Diderot's first attempt to evoke a way of representing human events on the stage in such a manner as to make them appear not only probable according to the rules of art but true according to the laws of nature.[10] Apparently unaware of the earlier use of the same image in the prologue to *Silvie*, or of any connections with the dramatic theory of La Motte, Jauss mistakenly identifies the passage from *Les Bijoux indiscrets* as the site where a new paradigm for conceptualising theatrical representation was first articulated. Moreover he does not explore the relationship of Diderot's spectator figure to an evolving semiotic analysis

5. Suzanne Pucci, 'The art, nature and fiction of Diderot's beholder', *Stanford French review* 8 (1984), p.273-94 (p.277). Pucci examines the relationship between the beholder and his/her object in Diderot's discussions of painting, of nature and of the novel.

6. Alain Ménil, ' "Ut pictura poesis erit"? Théâtre et antithéâtralité dans la théorie du drame', in *Etudes sur 'Le Fils naturel' et les 'Entretiens sur le Fils naturel' de Diderot*, ed. Nicholas Cronk (Oxford 2000), p.89-111 (p.91-92).

7. Philip Stewart, 'Diderot absconditus', in *L'Encyclopédie, Diderot, l'esthétique: mélanges en hommage à Jacques Chouillet, 1915-1990*, ed. S. Auroux, D. Bourel, and C. Porset (Paris 1991), p.149-57 (p.152).

8. Stewart, 'Diderot absconditus', p.150-51.

9. Jauss, 'Diderots Paradox über das Schauspiel', p.381.

10. Jauss, 'Diderots Paradox über das Schauspiel', p.383.

of dramatic representation or to the kind of illusion associated with painting. Thus, whilst various studies take up aspects of the role of the spectator in Diderot's aesthetic thinking, none examines in detail the function and effects of the topos of the hidden spectator as a unifying element in Diderot's theatrical writings. This is what I propose to under-take here, in an effort to show that Diderot uses this topos, and its com-panion, the invisible poet, in the same way as his predecessors La Motte and Landois, to articulate concepts of dramatic illusion and dramatic speech that are modelled on art theory. Michael Fried's book draws attention to the continuity that exists between criteria that Diderot elab-orates in his drama theory and the art criticism of the *Salons* and related essays and fragments. The present study tries to show that the aesthetic values set out in the drama theory themselves derive from the contemporary discourse concerning the nature of the painterly sign and painterly illusion. The kind of illusion that Diderot recommends for dramatic representation is modelled on the effect created by figurative painting, as he understood it, and constitutes the means through which the theatre spectator becomes emotionally engaged in the fiction and thus susceptible to the moral influence of drama.

The invisible poet and the hidden spectator both figure in the con-versation about theatre that takes place between Mirzoza, Sélim and Ricaric in *Les Bijoux indiscrets* (1748). Mirzoza considers contemporary plays inferior to those of the Ancients for reasons of both their content and their performance style. She finds fault with the unfolding of the action, the dialogue and the dénouements (all elements embodied in the writer's text) as well as with the techniques of declamation and the movements and gestures through which the story is brought to expression on the stage. In both areas, it is the all-too-apparent artifice of form that she condemns, evident as much in the highly improbable plots as in the stylised manner in which the actors walk and move. When Sélim counters that the artificiality of the plots is at least mitigated by the 'illusion' (his word) created through the use of dialogue (by which he means the use of direct speech, as opposed to narrative form), she at once rejects this claim, invoking the familiar topos of the invisible poet to condemn the 'em-phase', 'esprit' and 'papillotage' of the language, which is utterly remote from nature. 'C'est en vain,' she continues, 'que l'auteur cherche à se déro-ber; mes yeux percent, et je l'aperçois sans cesse derrière ses person-nages.'[11] As an example, she cites the characters of Corneille who, she claims, are little more than mouthpieces for the author. The visual emphasis of her references to the presence of the poet is particularly striking. Although she is talking about an aural impression, the impact that the spoken language has is expressed by reference to the sense of sight; her eyes penetrate beyond the *dramatis personae* and allow her to 'see'

11. DPV, iii.164.

the poet hiding behind them, a tangible presence on the stage.[12] The paradox expressed here – that hearing a certain type of speech causes the listener to 'see' a writer on the stage – identifies Diderot as a successor to La Motte and neatly illustrates the increasing encroachment into dramatic theory of criteria derived from visual art. The poet must disappear so that language will cease to impinge on spectator awareness and achieve the 'transparency' of the painterly sign.

An alternative approach to the creation of dramatic speech is expressed in Mirzoza's concluding remarks on dialogue, where she articulates a principle that will be reiterated by Dorval in the second *Entretien* and subsequently cited by Lessing in the eighty-first *Literaturbrief*. The formula she proposes – 'Messieurs, au lieu de donner à tout propos de l'esprit à vos personnages, placez-les dans des conjonctures qui leur en donnent'[13] – inverts the neo-classical approach by emphasising that the linguistic virtuosity of the writer must be subordinated to the demands of character and situation. The poet's task is not to transpose thoughts, passions and traits of character into artful and striking verbal form ('esprit'), but to find words that foster the illusion of a spontaneous reaction. Drama requires a kind of language that suggests immediacy, not reflection. It must appear to be the language of the moment and not strive to impress as language. Diderot's use of the word 'esprit' in this context situates his analysis in the tradition of Fénelon's critique of verbal inventiveness for its own sake;[14] and in the *Entretiens*, when Diderot suggests alternative models for dramatic speech, he invokes one of the examples cited by Fénelon, the suffering Philoctetes.[15] This attitude towards superfluous wit has its parallel in art theory, where overt cleverness is also held to be an obstacle to the creation of illusion. In an essay that Diderot knew, Shaftesbury states that the 'completely imitative and illusive' art of painting, whose goal is to deceive and command our sense of sight, 'must of necessity abandon whatever is over-learned, humorous, or witty; to maintain herself in what is natural, credible, and winning of our assent'.[16] In both art and drama, successful illusion rests upon the invisibility of the artist in the work.

---

12. Mercier will put the matter in the same vivid terms: 'Le Poète veut toujours être apperçu & se mêler parmi ses personnages; il ne sçait pas combien il gagneroit à disparoître tout-à-fait; plus on l'oubliera, plus il devra être satisfait', *De la littérature et des littératures suivi d'un nouvel examen de la tragédie française* (Yverdon 1778; Geneva 1970), p.113.

13. DPV, iii.164; DPV, x.100; Göpfert, v.262.

14. For an explanation of the literary connotations of the word 'esprit', the *Encyclopédie* simply refers readers to Voltaire's articles on 'Elégance' and 'Eloquence', which take a traditional rhetorical approach to the literary use of language.

15. Fénelon, *Œuvres*, ii.1172.

16. Anthony Ashley Cooper, Earl of Shaftesbury, 'A notion of the *historical draught* or *tablature* of the judgment of Hercules', *Second characters, or the Language of forms*, ed. Benjamin Rand (1713; New York 1969), p.55. Diderot knew the works of Shaftesbury, including this essay. He published his free translation of Shaftesbury's *Inquiry concerning virtue and merit* in 1745.

Mirzoza goes on to relate a modified version of the hidden spectator story first found in the prologue to *Silvie* to highlight the weaknesses of customary performance styles. She argues that a naïve spectator, endowed with common sense and some basic knowledge of the world, who was introduced into a 'loge grillée' overlooking a stage and told that the performance he was witnessing was a scene from life, would not for a moment be taken in. Everything he perceived would betray the artifice: 'la démarche empesée des acteurs, [...] la bizarrerie de leurs vêtements, [...] l'extravagance de leurs gestes, [...] l'emphase d'un langage singulier, rimé, cadencé, et [...] mille autre [*sic*] dissonances'.[17] Considered as sense data, the theatrical performance does not conform to the spectator's experience of life and human interaction. Diderot is here using the spectator trope in the same way it is used in the prologue to *Silvie*, to focus attention on drama as a performing art, rather than on the play as text. From the perspective of the hidden spectator, a play represents a system of theatrical signs constituting a code, and the story is designed to suggest that the code of neo-classical tragedy would be unintelligible to a spectator of common sense 'qui n'ait jamais entendu parler de spectacles'.[18]

Diderot elaborates on the idea of a theatrical code in the second *Entretien*, where Dorval compares French tragedy with the theatre of the Ancients from which it was claimed to derive (the drama of Antiquity is also Mirzoza's model for good practice). Dorval explains that the dramatic system of the Ancients was shaped by conditions of representation that required a measure of exaggeration.[19] The huge theatres and large numbers of spectators account for the masks and the buskins, the unusual style of speech, the pronounced movements and the use of verse. Every performance code has its own unity, shaping all the parts, whether this be the system of high tragedy or the style adopted by the colourful charlatan, be-feathered and be-ringed, of the place Dauphine.[20] Change one of the elements and the others will change with it: 'tout ce que l'action dramatique a d'énorme, se produit et disparaît en même temps'. The French neo-classical manner, which appropriates from the Ancients the heightening effects of verse, whilst neglecting their simplicity of plot and dialogue and the use of *tableaux*, has built on the wrong parts of the system.

When Mirzoza defines the kind of illusion for which drama should strive, she does so in the same terms as Roger de Piles. A play, she says, is the imitation of an action so exact 'que le spectateur, trompé sans interruption, s'imagine assister à l'action même'. In de Piles's theory, 'tromper' is the verb which expresses the impact that painting has on the physical eye, although he also holds that the viewer is simultaneously aware that

17. DPV, iii.165.
18. DPV, iii.165.
19. DPV, x.117.
20. DPV, x.119.

the painting is an artefact. Mirzoza agrees that when we watch a play we know that it is a form of art and therefore an imitation, but she likewise stresses that this is not a reason to reject illusion and prefer artifice. She argues that drama should imitate in the most natural manner possible, asserting that 'il n'y a que le vrai qui plaise et qui touche'. The word 'vrai' means for her what it does in de Piles's theory and the prologue to *Silvie*: the accurate reproduction of the texture of things in the world, that is, illusion. Lessing will later define illusion in the *Laokoon* as 'the rendering present of things absent' and Lord Kames, in his *Elements of criticism* (1762), will call it 'ideal presence', an effect he finds exemplified in the achievements of drama and painting.[21] In all these instances, painting provides the basic model for the effect called 'illusion', and 'illusion' is understood as the effect that painting has. The theatrical ideal articulated by Diderot in *Les Bijoux* is the same as that described by La Motte in his theory and put into practice by Landois in his play. All three hold that whilst the form taken by a dramatic work must always posit its reception by spectators, the play should not in any explicit way betray the author's consciousness of creating 'for' them. The appearance of the topoi of the invisible poet and hidden spectator in Diderot's novel of 1748 is an indication of how attuned he was to contemporary trends in art and drama theory. Although in the *Entretiens* and the *Discours* he will elaborate much more fully on the ideas expressed so succinctly here, his vision of theatrical representation will not basically alter. This passage, as Lessing points out in the *Hamburgische Dramaturgie*, articulates its essentials.[22]

The topos of the hidden spectator is subsequently enlisted as the key structural device for *Le Fils naturel* and the *Entretiens*, although it is applied here in a constructive rather than a critical way. It serves to demonstrate the strengths of Dorval's approach to representation rather than to expose the weaknesses of an outworn code. This viewer is a witness to the re-enactment of an event drawn from the lives of the play's protagonists, which they perform themselves in a private setting. The hidden spectator relates his experience in the first person, in the prologue and epilogue to the text of the performance, and this is followed by the three conversations between Moi (the spectator) and Dorval (the dramatist), where the experience is analysed in relation to principles of dramatic form. The prologue and epilogue thus reformulate Mirzoza's example of a hidden spectator as a fictional situation that allows a redefinition of the two mutually determining poles of the theatrical experience, the play and the spectator.

The circumstances leading to the creation of the play confer on it a commemorative function that is a reminder of the connections between

---

21. Eric Rothstein, ' "Ideal presence" and the "non finito" in eighteenth-century aesthetics', *Eighteenth-century studies* 9 (1976), p.307-32 (p.309).
22. Göpfert, iv.262.

theatre and meaningful social ritual.[23] The performance witnessed by Moi takes place on a Sunday, a reflection of the ideal role Dorval imagines for theatrical representation in the utopian community of the island of Lampedouse.[24] In the *Discours*, Diderot describes his complete text as 'une espèce de roman', accompanied by 'l'histoire véritable de la pièce', and he insists upon the importance of the premise that the subject of the play was an experience drawn from life.[25] Both the 'play' and the narrative framework are presented as rooted in fact; we are lead to believe that the dramatised events actually happened to Dorval a year prior to the salon performance and that the narrated encounter with Dorval actually happened to Moi–Diderot whilst he was on holiday in the country in the summer of 1756. Both components, the dramatic and the narrative, therefore have 'a model in nature' towards which Diderot's text gestures.

Moi is a more developed personality than either Mirzoza's foreign visitor or the Chevalier from the prologue of 1741. As an individual of common sense, curious and interested, familiar with the theatre and yet not without prejudices that Dorval has to try and overcome, Moi is a figure with whom the readers of *Le Fils naturel* can more readily identify and he exemplifies the kind of educability found in numerous other figures from Enlightenment fiction. As with the prologue to *Silvie*, the fictional framework of *Le Fils naturel* invites the eighteenth-century spectator to set aside habitual assumptions and reconsider both dramatic form and the watching of plays from a fresh perspective.

At the end of the prologue, Moi describes how he gained access to a hiding place in the salon from where 'je vis et j'entendis ce qu'on va lire'.[26] Here, as elsewhere in the *Entretiens*, the emphasis is placed on both sensory dimensions, seeing and hearing. Despite the awkwardness of always using 'voir' and 'entendre' together, Diderot is careful to invoke both verbs when referring to the experience of watching plays, and the consistency with which he follows this practice in all his writings on theatre from this period (the *Entretiens*, the *Discours*, the letter to Mme Riccoboni) shows how important he felt it was to impress upon readers the idea that both senses are simultaneously involved in the response to drama. This is how Diderot differentiates between the illusion created by a painting and that created by a play: painting creates an illusion for the eye but drama must create an illusion for eye and ear. In the epilogue, Moi describes his immediate reaction to the experience of watching the salon performance. It was so lifelike ('vraie') that 'oubliant en plusieurs endroits que j'étais spectateur, et spectateur ignoré, j'avais été sur le point

23. Béatrice Didier, 'Images du sacré chez Diderot', *Travaux de littérature* 6 (1993), p.193-209 (p.202).
24. DPV, x.105.
25. DPV, x.364.
26. DPV, x.17.

de sortir de ma place, et d'ajouter un personnage réel à la scène'.[27] The
power of the theatrical illusion so engages his attention that he is ready to
emerge from his hiding place to take part, just as the Diderot of the *Salons*
will be drawn into conversation with the young girl weeping over her
dead bird in a painting by Greuze, or write as if he has physically stepped
into Vernet's inviting landscapes.[28] Such responses are a reflection of de
Piles's criterion for good painting, which draws the viewer into its world.

   An event related in the epilogue makes explicit the nature and the force
of theatrical illusion, although the term 'illusion' is not used. Since
Lysimond is dead, his role is taken over by a friend of similar appearance
and voice (he has the same age, build and hair colour), who appears
dressed in the deceased man's prison clothes. The friend is thus an actor,
equipped with the basic resources exploited by any thespian: appearance,
gesture, voice and setting. Confronted with this 'copy' of Lysimond, who
both looks and speaks like the original, the other performers find themselves in the situation of spectators. The impersonation, which renders the
absent man as if present ('remettant sous les yeux de toute la famille, un
homme qu'elle venait de perdre'), is for them an illusion, the appearance
of the former Lysimond. They do not take this figure to be Lysimond,
because they know it is not him. Their response is not a response to a
living Lysimond, but to an artistic illusion of Lysimond, and seeing this
illusion, they break down and weep, causing the play to end. Even Moi,
unacquainted with the deceased man and familiar in advance with
Dorval's story and its outcome, is moved to tears by what he has witnessed. Reflecting on this experience, he wonders why, if this was just 'une
comédie comme une autre', the participants had been unable to perform
the final scene. 'Quelle était la cause de la douleur profonde dont ils
avaient été pénétrés à la vue du vieillard qui faisait Lysimond?'[29] The
answer lies in the illusionary effect. Aesthetic illusions possess the power to
shake people to their foundations and connect them with their spontaneous, 'natural' self, manifested in tears. This is an autonomous effect
belonging to artistic illusions; it is different from the effect that would be
caused by the original phenomenon, and Diderot (unlike Plato) places a
positive value on it. His insistence, here and elsewhere, that the goal of
serious drama is to arouse emotion in the spectator, is one of the essential differences between his aesthetic and the seventeenth-century one
which was based on distance, not identification.[30] The creation of emotional identification between the spectator and the characters is crucial to

27. DPV, x.84.

28. DPV, xiv.179-82, and DPV, xvi.174-224.

29. DPV, x.84.

30. Jauss, 'Diderots Paradox über das Schauspiel', p.388-89 and p.392-93. See also
Alain Ménil, *Diderot et le drame: théâtre et politique* (Paris 1995), p.64. Ménil compares and
contrasts Diderot's theory of identification with the neo-classical view of how tragedy
affects the spectator.

Diderot, since it is the cornerstone of his argument that drama is moral. According to his theory, sympathetic identification is fostered by a number of different techniques, including the representation of *conditions* and the speech of the characters. The evocation of *conditions* obliges the members of the audience to recognise their own situation in that of the *dramatis personae* and to apply the lessons of the play to themselves. In the language used by the characters, the dramatist must aim to capture a quintessentially human response, 'ce que tout le monde dirait en pareil cas; ce que personne n'entenda, sans le reconnaître aussitôt en soi'.[31] These qualities, which the dramatist writes into the play, are conducive to the creation of illusion, but they are also greatly enhanced by a style of representation that takes painterly illusion as its model. The reaction of Moi and the others to the impersonation of Lysimond anticipates Dorval's explanation of the interest domestic tragedy would hold for contemporary audiences, in which both subject matter and the means of imitation contribute to the effect: 'C'est le tableau des malheurs qui nous environnent. Quoi! Vous ne concevez pas l'effet que produiraient sur vous une scène réelle, des habits vrais, des discours proportionnés aux actions, des actions simples, des dangers dont il est impossible que vous n'ayez tremblé pour vos parents, vos amis, pour vous-même?'[32]

The reaction of Lysimond's family to the appearance of the actor playing him also confirms something that Lysimond himself had said earlier to Dorval, namely that theatrical performance is much more powerful than visual representation alone. In the prologue, Dorval quotes remarks his father had made contrasting the re-enactment he has in mind with the value of family portraits. Lysimond considers portraits limited, since they capture only 'un moment de notre visage', whereas the kind of work he wants Dorval to compose would conserve 'nos propres idées, nos vrais sentiments, les discours que nous avons tenus'. These observations rest upon a distinction of the kind that Lessing will later make between poetry and painting in the *Laokoon*. As a purely spatial art, portraiture is confined to the representation of a single moment and therefore disposes of a much narrower range of material than a form that includes language and unfolds over time. The illusion of Lysimond that is brought about through performance elicits in the viewer an emotional response that is far more intense than that generated by a portrait.[33]

Diderot's account of the response precipitated by the impersonation of Lysimond would have been of particular interest to Lessing, since it amounts to a refutation of an argument he makes in a letter to Nicolai and Mendelssohn about the effects of viewing a statue. The context is their discussion of the nature and effects of tragedy. In the late 1750s,

31. DPV, x.100.
32. DPV, x.140.
33. DPV, x.16. The abbé Dubos speculates on why paintings rarely cause spectators to shed tears, whereas tragedies often do, even mediocre ones: *Réflexions*, p.136.

87

before reading Diderot's dramatic theory, Lessing rejects Mendelssohn's belief that illusion contributes to aesthetic response and insists that illusion is irrelevant to the emotional effects brought about in the spectators of tragedy. To prove his point, he argues that a man who suddenly became aware that a physical form he had earlier taken to be a living woman, gesturing mysteriously to him, was in fact a statue, would merely feel cheated and disappointed. This is not an aesthetic response, and Lessing dismisses this man's 'illusion' as a simple 'mistake' that is irrelevant to the workings of art.[34] In contrast to this, Diderot's account of the reincarnation of Lysimond demonstrates that aesthetic illusion is not founded upon a confusion of the art object with something else, but produces its own, unique effect. Dorval and the others are not deceived or mistaken, but they are moved. Lessing has much to say in the *Briefwechsel* about sympathetic identification, but he attributes this effect to qualities of subject matter (character and story); Diderot stresses that it is also a function of the theatrical means of imitation or signs.[35]

The parallel between the relationship spectators have to theatrical representation and the situation of human beings vis-à-vis nature is subtly reinforced by references to the natural environment where the *Entretiens* take place. At the end of the epilogue, Moi laments the inadequacy with which his words convey the impression made on him by the combination of Dorval's presence and 'le spectacle de la nature'.[36] The first conversation concludes with Dorval's description of the spectacle of the setting sun, evoked by means of an appeal to the two senses of seeing and hearing. '*Voyez* comme les ombres particulières s'affaiblissent [...] *Voilà* toute la région [...] On n'*entend* plus [...] *Le bruit* des eaux courantes.'[37] Dorval also explains what these various sense impressions signify: good weather the next day, the end of this day's work. The forms, colours and sounds are all natural signs from which the observer constructs meaning, like the spectator of a play constructing meaning from theatrical signs. The second conversation opens with an account of Dorval's rapt contemplation of the 'spectacle de la nature' and his thoughts on nature as

---

34. This example is discussed further on p.153-54.

35. The emotional reaction of Lysimond's family embodies exactly the elements that Lessing defines, in the *Briefwechsel*, as the causes of tearful response: 'alle Betrübnis, welche von Tränen begleitet wird, ist eine Betrübnis über ein verlornes Gut; kein anderer Schmerz, keine andre unangenehme Empfindung wird von Tränen begleitet. Nun findet sich bei dem verlornen Gute nicht allein die Idee des Verlusts, sondern auch die Idee des Guts, und beide, diese angenehme mit jener unangenehmen, sind unzertrennlich verknüpft' ('any sadness that is accompanied by tears is sadness for the loss of something good; no other form of sorrow, no other negative feeling is accompanied by tears. Now, this good which is lost contains not only the idea of loss but also the idea of good, and the two aspects, the pleasant and the unpleasant, are inseparably linked') (13 November 1756) Göpfert, iv.166.

36. DPV, x.84.

37. DPV, x.97-98, emphasis added.

the true source of all inspiration.[38] Thus, a connection is made between our mode of being in the world, as observers of the spectacle of nature, and our role as spectators in relation to dramatic representation. The laws of perception determine both the style of drama and the subject matter appropriate for such representation. Dorval emphasises the difference between the task of the epic or the novel, which is to 'peindre à mon imagination', and the goal of drama, which is to 'mettre en action sous mes yeux'.[39] It is on these grounds that he rejects both 'le genre burlesque' and 'le genre merveilleux', stating that these forms can have no poetics since they are not based on a 'modèle subsistant dans la nature'.[40] The standard for evaluating the illusion of drama is the same as it is for painting, that is, the impression made on us by nature; and in both media, the art must reflect the workings of the natural world.

The topos of the invisible poet, introduced by La Motte to suggest the idea of a play that successfully effaces the traces of its own production in the manner of painting, is soon taken over in Diderot's theory by a more direct comparison. His concept of the stage *tableau* embodies the same ideal of the transparency of all the theatrical signs, including linguistic ones. What Diderot says about the visual and auditory artistic signs at work in stage *tableaux* shows that he consistently gives priority to theatrical signs that formally resemble the things they signify, that is, to theatrical signs that eighteenth-century semioticians call 'natural'. Theatrical signs that are visual include setting, props, costume (and everything else relating to the actor's appearance), gesture, movement and lighting. Diderot addresses almost all of these, either in his theory, or in his plays, or both. Auditory theatrical signs are language, non-verbal utterances, music and sounds (knocking, thunder, gunshots, etc.). I shall leave aside music, since Lessing does not indicate or prescribe the use of musical accompaniment in his mature plays, and sounds, which Diderot does not mention or specifically exploit, in order to focus here on his treatment of dramatic speech. Diderot does not use the vocabulary of signs to discuss these matters, but his theory is a semiotic one nonetheless.[41]

Diderot defines a stage *tableau* as an arrangement of characters on the stage 'si naturelle et si vraie' that it would be equally pleasing if transferred to canvas by a painter; elsewhere he refers to a scene with action

---

38. DPV, x.99.

39. DPV, x.147. In the *Discours*, where Diderot returns to this idea, he claims that the novelist, who only has to persuade the imagination by his use of words, can always find a solution to problems posed by subject matter; not so the dramatist. DPV, x.357-58.

40. DPV, x.146.

41. Dennis Fletcher, '"Ut pictura spectaculum": Diderot and the semiotics of the stage', *Romance studies* 4 (1984), p.79-96 (p.82). In the *Paradoxe sur le comédien*, Diderot does use the word 'signes' to denote the linguistic and gestural resources that actors exploit to create the illusion of a living character. See DPV, xx.55 and xx.104.

and no speech as a 'décoration animée'.[42] In the context of painting, Diderot means by '*tableau*' not any kind of picture but a coherent and integrated image, as defined in his article entitled 'Composition' in the *Encyclopédie*. There, he characterises a well-composed picture as 'un tout renfermé sous un seul point de vue, où les parties concourent à un même but, & forment par leur correspondance mutuelle un ensemble aussi réel, que celui des membres dans un corps animal'.[43] This definition, which is the one Shaftesbury gives in his essay on *tablature*, derives from de Piles's notion of the 'Œconomie du Tout-ensemble'.[44] A scenic *tableau*, therefore, is not super-added spectacle but a coherent whole, generating meaning from the interaction of all its parts whilst creating the lifelike illusion considered the hallmark of good painting.[45] The examples of stage *tableaux* that Diderot identifies, both from his own plays and from Landois's *Silvie*, conform to these criteria, as do the various suggestions for potential *tableau* scenes mentioned in the theory. Achieving this effect requires a complete reorganisation of both the visual and auditory sign systems of contemporary tragedy so that plays can offer spectators images more powerful even than those of painting. Diderot laments the failure to recognise that the means of imitation proper to drama, 'où les hommes mêmes agissent', are ideally suited to the creation of such powerful illusionistic images.[46]

Diderot exploits the *tableau* concept to expose and attack the two major factors limiting the expressive potential of traditional drama: the influence of *bienséance* (which imposed restrictions on costume and gesture, as well as on subject matter and speech) and the material conditions of stage representation (which made it impossible for dramatists and actors to exploit the three-dimensional space of the Comédie-Française stage to create images with depth). Diderot draws attention to the inconsistency of excluding from stage representation scenes that are found moving when treated in painting, giving as one example some visual details suggesting the nativity, a venerated and popular image in painting, that no poet would dare present on the French stage for fear of ridicule.[47] Moi is

42. DPV, x.92 and x.112.

43. DPV, vi.475. Diderot's definition of pictorial unity, and other passages from his article on composition, are drawn from Shaftesbury's essay on tablature. (See Shaftesbury, 'A notion of the *historical draught* or *tablature* of the judgment of Hercules', p.32, for his definition of *tableau*.) The original version of this essay was published in French in the Amsterdam edition of the *Journal des savants* in November 1712 (see Fried, *Absorption and theatricality*, p.209, n.56).

44. Puttfarken, *The Discovery of pictorial composition*, p.279-82.

45. Fried argues that the concept of pictorial unity which Diderot sets out in the *Essais sur la peinture* (1766), the *Pensées détachées sur la peinture* (1776-1777) and in a 1760 review of Watelet's didactic poem entitled *L'Art de peindre* goes further than that of his contemporaries in that Diderot insists that this unity must reflect the causality inherent in nature (Fried, *Absorption and theatricality*, p.85-87).

46. DPV, x.93.

47. DPV, x.403.

appalled by the scenes Dorval sketches out to demonstrate the potential of dual sets and alternating spoken and silent scenes, which would include (in a tragedy) 'un lit de repos, une mère, un père endormi; un crucifix; un cadavre'.[48] Beds, sleeping figures, crucifixes, and dead bodies could all appear in painting. In the *Discours*, Diderot compares his suggested scenario for a play on the death of Socrates (not possible on the French stage) with the striking effect achieved by Poussin's *Testament d'Eudamidas*, the painting that was for him emblematic of the emotional force communicated by a simply conceived scene, drawn from ordinary human experience and rendered with naturalness and truth to life.[49] Diderot's position appears simple: anything spectators are prepared to 'look at' on canvas, they should be prepared to view in the theatre. In fact his argument goes further than this; the ultimate standard, for both arts, is nature, and he considers suspect the taste of any nation 'lorsqu'il admettra dans la nature des choses dont il interdira l'imitation à ses artistes, ou lorsqu'il admirera dans l'art des effets qu'il dédaignerait dans la nature'.[50] The only constraint that Diderot admits for theatrical images is a purely practical one: whether or not they can sustain illusion in performance. In this connection, he contrasts the impact of the *tableau* from La Noue's *Mahomet II*, in which Mahomet, a dagger raised above Irène's breast, tries to decide whether to act, with the illusion-disrupting effect of more complex actions 'qui me rappelleront que je suis dans un parterre; que tous ces personnages sont des comédiens; et que ce n'est pas un fait qui se passe'.[51] Much of the visual action that occurs in Diderot's plays, such as the taking of tea in *Le Fils naturel* (which shocks Moi), or the display of differently textured fabrics which forms the background to the scene depicting *condition* in *Le Père de famille* (II.i), are simple in this sense, and are also familiar themes from visual art. Action that cannot be represented effectively on stage may be suitable material for a *récit*, where the poet can use words to evoke the scene in the imagination of the spectators. But even narrated events are subject to constraints; they must be possible in nature. Dorval insists that 'il ne faut ni réciter ni montrer au spectateur un fait sans vraisemblance'.[52] Thus, it is not decorum that should determine what can be depicted in the form of a stage *tableau*, but the laws of nature and the potential of such action for illusionistic representation.

It is also the quality of the illusion afforded by painting that shapes Diderot's suggestions concerning visual signs in the theatre. These theatrical signs must have the 'invisibility' or 'transparency' of the painterly

---

48. DPV, x.114.
49. DPV, x.416.
50. DPV, x.404.
51. DPV, x.141. The similarity between this image and the concluding *tableau* in Lessing's *Emilia Galotti* was noted above, p.11.
52. DPV, x.141. Théramène's *récit* would fail this test too.

sign. Thus, plays should unfold in a décor that is constructed and painted to look like the fictional setting of the action ('transporter au théâtre le salon de Clairville, comme il est'[53]), whilst at the same time never attracting attention as art; the theatre painter 'est borné aux circonstances qui servent à l'illusion'.[54] Similarly with costumes; these should be appropriate to the circumstances of the action and express character and *condition*, yet remain simple (Diderot illustrates this by reference to some of the costumes he envisages for *Le Père de famille*). He recommends that comedy should be performed 'en déshabillé', the actors being 'ni plus apprêté[s] ni plus négligé[s] que chez soi', and this is reflected in his own plays, which, like Landois's *Silvie*, defy the prevailing *bienséances* by prescribing 'casual' dress (by eighteenth-century standards) for some of the characters.[55] All members of the cast should adopt the same principles, in order to create a harmonious overall impression.[56] Ostentation, which is motivated by a desire to impress the spectator, violates the principle of the invisibility of artistic signs and should be avoided. 'Le spectateur', says Diderot, 'n'est rien pour vous', and he urges actors to visit art exhibitions for inspiration on this point.[57]

In painting theory, 'costume' or 'le costumé', a term adopted into French from Italian art vocabulary, applied to more than clothing. Jaucourt, in his article 'Costumé' in the *Encyclopédie*, defines it as 'l'observation exacte de ce qui est, suivant le tems, le génie, les moeurs, les lois, le goût, les richesses, le caractère et les habitudes d'un pays où l'on place la scène d'un tableau'. It also concerns 'les bienséances, le caractère et les convenances propres à chaque âge, à chaque condition'.[58] In other words, it is about accuracy of context and was therefore also evidence of a painter's learning. Frantz identifies it with what the nineteenth century would call 'local colour' and emphasises its relevance to historical subjects.[59] Diderot uses the term in this sense in his sketch for a play on the death of Socrates ('Il faut ici s'assujettir au costumé').[60] Observation of 'le costumé' is fundamental to the illusion of painting since it guarantees that the scene depicted on the canvas will be free from inconsistencies such as the inclusion of animal or plant life alien to the supposed location,

53. DPV, x.110.
54. DPV, x.405.
55. Similarly Lessing, in *Miss Sara Sampson*, specifies that Sir William and Waitwell make their first entrance dressed in travelling clothes: Göpfert, ii.11.
56. DPV, x.406-408.
57. These principles were applied by Alain Bézu in his 1993 production of *Le Fils naturel*.
58. Denis Diderot, Jean D'Alembert *et al.*, *L'Encyclopédie, ou Dictionnaire raisonné des sciences, des arts et des métiers par une société de gens de lettres*, 17 vols (Paris 1751-1765) iv.298-99.
59. Frantz, *L'Esthétique du tableau*, p.87 and p.91.
60. DPV, x.340.

or the representation of people from other countries as if they were compatriots of the painter (Dürer's main failing, according to Jaucourt). A number of Diderot's proposed innovations can be seen as applications of the principle of 'le costumé' to enhance the illusion afforded by drama, where it would shape not only visual effects, as in painting, but also become integrated into plot and dialogue. The representation of contemporary manners, the depiction of *conditions* and *relations*, and the requirement that the moral values expressed in a play be consistent with 'l'esprit du siècle' are aspects of 'le costumé', manifested in drama through things seen and things heard, which strengthen the illusion through the accumulation of natural theatrical signs.[61]

Diderot does not discuss lighting as such, and the possibilities for exploiting lighting effects were limited, as noted above (p.69), but the opening scenes of *Le Père de famille* include the stage business of calling for new candles to replace the dying ones, a piece of action that uses visual means to indicate the length of time the family has been waiting and the advanced hour. Regardless of how early productions treated this scene in terms of theatre lighting, it is a good example of Diderot anticipating a time in the future when this piece of business could be reinforced by bringing up the on-stage lighting (a natural theatrical sign).

Visual theatrical signs of major importance to Diderot are those of gesture and movement, but I shall consider these in conjunction with dramatic speech.[62] His concept of the stage *tableau*, with its reliance on visual theatrical signs that are natural, has implications for dramatic speech, since it follows that words too will have to embody the qualities of natural artistic signs. Here, Diderot's theory and practice of dramatic speech represents a development of the innovations pioneered by La Motte and Landois. In Diderot's theory, dramatic speech comprises three elements: the words that are spoken, the gestures and movements that accompany them and what one might call the vocal quality that informs certain kinds of oral expression ('cri', 'accent' and 'ton'). For each of these dimensions of expression, Diderot's suggestions are shaped by the goal of achieving a form of dramatic speech in which the conventional or artificial theatrical signs of traditional tragic language (its verse, stylised gestures and formal declamation) are converted to natural ones.

In a late-nineteenth-century study of La Chaussée, Gustave Lanson asserted that 'L'emploi de la prose est peut-être ce qu'il y a de plus original, de plus logique, de plus judicieux et de plus grave dans les doctrines et les essais dramatiques de Diderot.'[63] Surprisingly, though, the

---

61. DPV, x.88, x.144 and x.123.
62. 'A tout moment, le geste ne répond-il pas au discours?' DPV, x.101.
63. Gustave Lanson, *Nivelle de La Chaussée et la comédie larmoyante* (Paris 1887), p.270.

significance of this choice has received little attention, despite the fact that Dorval seems to see the development of prose dialogue as a key to bringing about greater naturalness on the stage. Alluding obliquely to arguments used in the context of the French *querelle des vers*, he asserts that prose tragedy will exist in France as soon as a poet 'nous fera pleurer avec de la prose'. He goes on to point out that in art, as in nature, 'tout est enchaîné'. Consequently, 'si l'on se rapproche d'un côté de ce qui est vrai, on s'en rapprochera de beaucoup d'autres'.[64] This passage echoes La Motte's arguments in his *Réponse à M. de Voltaire*, in particular the way in which Dorval justifies innovation by a simple appeal to spectator response (considered a stronger and more reliable indicator than received opinion), as well as the notion that if one of the components of a play is modified, the others will follow.[65] Dorval sees the introduction of prose as the best hope for undoing the damage caused by the influence of *bienséance*: 'c'est alors que nous verrons sur la scène des situations naturelles qu'une décence ennemie du génie et des grands effets a proscrites'. The arguments all hark back to La Motte but the French example Diderot invokes to point the way forward is Landois's *Silvie*.

In view of the significant break with tradition that the use of prose in a 'serious' play represents, Diderot's commentary on this point seems remarkably low-key. This is true, too, in the *Discours*, where Diderot again appears oddly hesitant about the role of prose, stating that he feels prose to be the most appropriate medium for domestic tragedy 'sans trop savoir pourquoi'.[66] He goes on to offer some tentative suggestions in the form of a series of rhetorical questions that leave the matter unresolved. The following two paragraphs then slyly summarise arguments used in the context of the earlier prose–verse debate to arrive at a definition of poetry independent of the use of verse and rhyme. Diderot concludes that 'une tragédie en prose est tout autant un poème qu'une tragédie en vers'.[67] No more than this is stated explicitly, and so the attention Diderot overtly gives to the role of prose in his theory of the *drame* appears inversely proportional to its actual significance.

An explanation for the subterfuge is hinted at in the *Paradoxe sur le Comédien*. There, the two interlocutors condemn the French alexandrine as 'trop nombreux et trop noble' for theatrical dialogue, whilst they see the

---

64. DPV, x.116.

65. La Motte, *Œuvres*, iv.441-42. La Motte writes 'Pourquoi des vers dans nos tragédies? pourquoi ce reste de musique dans la représentation des choses ordinaires? Puisque vous faites agir des hommes, faites-les parler comme des hommes. Vous vous êtes rapprochés de la nature: encore un pas et vous l'atteindrez. Faites parler vos acteurs en prose, et vous aurez une imitation parfaite, et dans sa plus grande naïveté.'

66. DPV, x.358.

67. DPV, x.359. Russell Goulbourne also sees in this passage a reference to La Motte. 'The eighteenth-century "querelle des vers" and Jean Du Castre d'Auvigny's *La Tragédie en prose*', *SVEC* 2000:05, p.371-410 (p.386).

ten-syllable line as 'trop futile et trop léger'.[68] They do not specify any another option, although the attentive reader is left thinking it must be prose, especially since the two speeches that the first speaker offers as examples of simple and effective dramatic speech are both given in prose translation. He describes French tragic authors as 'ampoulés', and claims that the simplicity of tone the stage requires could never be achieved within the framework of 'nos tendres jérémiades' or 'nos fanfaronades à la Corneille'. He goes on to add that he would never dare voice such a critique of French tragic language to anyone other than his interlocutor, for fear of being 'lapidé dans les rues, si l'on me savait coupable de ce blasphème'.[69] This had been La Motte's fate, metaphorically speaking, and Diderot's noticeable reticence, in all his dramatic writings, when commenting on the function and the implications of the use of prose is probably a consequence of the virulence of the reaction unleashed against La Motte. Comments Grimm makes in his *Correspondance littéraire* suggest as much. In the September 1767 issue, he notes that following Diderot's example, Beaumarchais, too, recommends the use of prose for the *drame sérieux*.[70] But he goes on to predict that sooner or later, this trend will provoke another 'querelle littéraire', since M. de Saint-Lambert 'ne peut pardonner à M. Diderot d'avoir donné la préférence à la prose sur les vers pour les ouvrages dramatiques'.[71] Grimm seems to think it quite likely that Saint-Lambert will take issue with Diderot on this in a public forum. Diderot's choice of prose clearly appeared more radical to his contemporaries than it does to us, and from this point of view, his plays can be seen to constitute a further episode in the continuing saga of the role of prose on the French stage.[72] The lines from Horace, which are placed at the beginning of *Le Fils naturel* and state that a play with a few sound ideas and good character portrayal is worth more than 'verse which lacks substance but is filled with well-sounding trifles', take up the distinction between form and content that was fundamental to the debate about French verse. Diderot's substitution of prose discourse for the alexandrine

68. DPV, xx.107. This goes further than the opinion voiced in his *Encyclopédie* article 'Alexandrin', where he writes, 'Le nombre & la gravité forment le caractère de ce vers; c'est pourquoi je le trouve trop éloigné du ton de la conversation ordinaire pour être employé dans la comédie' (DPV, v.319).

69. DPV, xx.109.

70. In his *Essai sur le genre sérieux*, Beaumarchais concludes his exposition of the merits of prose (a section which makes reference to both La Motte and Diderot) with the words 'c'est ce qui ramène tout naturellement à préférer la prose, et c'est ce qu'a sous-entendu M. Diderot'. See *Œuvres*, p.132.

71. Grimm *et al.*, *Correspondance littéraire*, vii.415.

72. In the February 1770 issue, for example, Grimm asserts that 'toutes nos plus belles pièces sont de la poésie épique'. He criticises Voltaire's verse in *Mahomet* as inappropriate to the subject matter (a regrettable blemish in 'le plus bel ouvrage du Théâtre-Français'), and calls for French tragedies in prose, referring to his own views as a theory 'qu'il serait aisé d'approfondir davantage et d'exposer dans tout son jour, si l'on était curieux de se faire lapider en face de la Comédie-Française'. Grimm *et al.*, *Correspondance littéraire*, viii.460-62.

is not an innocent choice, and the connection with La Motte is made explicit by Naigeon, in his rather hostile commentary on Diderot's *drame*. Naigeon does not hesitate to blame La Motte for Diderot's decision to use prose, and he adds that La Motte's convictions about the possibility of creating prose tragedies 'a dû nécessairement donner la première idée de la tragédie domestique et bourgeoise'.[73]

The choice of prose for the new genres naturally leads to the question of what kind of prose. Diderot's criticism of 'wit', first mentioned in *Les Bijoux*, is accompanied by open disdain for the effects of rhetoric. Dorval explains to Moi how he went about trying to compose dialogue for act III, scene v, in which Clairville reacts to Rosalie's rejection of him (the 'scène de désespoir'). Recalling only the strong impression left by the event, and unable to remember what was actually said, Dorval turns for inspiration to scenes from other plays and creates a most eloquent despairing lover. When Clairville reads the resulting text, he rejects it as worthless: 'il n'y a pas un seul mot de vérité dans toute cette rhétorique'.[74] He rewrites the scene himself, insisting that 'il ne s'agit que de se remettre dans la situation, et que de s'écouter'. For Clairville, observation of one's own feelings and the promptings of the imagination are more reliable than tradition and literary example. The result is dialogue that successfully captures 'le ton de la nature', and it is this practical experiment in generating dramatic text that provides the jumping-off point for the discussion about the expression of the passions, declamation and mime in the second conversation. This is the only occurrence of the word 'rhétorique' in Diderot's dramatic theory of this period, a significant departure from the practice in neo-classical treatises; and whilst Diderot's like-minded predecessors allude to rhetoric in order to criticise its effects, he barely even mentions it. His approach implies that one can write drama perfectly well without any knowledge of formal rhetoric, and even that it might be to one's advantage to be ignorant of it.

Consistent with his rejection of speech organised according to the rules of versification and rhetoric, Diderot exploits in his plays the effects of broken or incomplete phrases, disconnected utterances, unanswered questions, exclamations, repetitions, pauses in the dialogue and so on, which replicate the pace, rhythm and form of spontaneous and uncensored discourse. Landois's *Silvie* is an early model of this approach and

73. Jacques-André Naigeon, *Mémoires historiques et philosophiques sur la vie et les ouvrages de Denis Diderot* (Paris 1821; Geneva 1970), p.177. There are a number of other passages and concepts in Diderot's theatre writings that seem to reflect ideas found in La Motte. One example is the idea that the greatest obstacle to the development of theatrical form is the weight of custom, maintained by prejudice. See La Motte, *Œuvres*, iv.390-91 and iv.439-43, and DPV, x.331. The wording of the subtitle of *Le Fils naturel* (*Les Epreuves de la vertu*) echoes La Motte's suggestions for enriching a simple action by inventing circumstances 'qui mettent le même caractère et la même vertu à diverses épreuves', La Motte, *Œuvres*, iv.30. La Motte's formula is not inappropriate for Diderot's play.

74. DPV, x.97.

La Motte, too, recommends introducing variety of pace, although it is doubtful that he had in mind the form this takes in Diderot's dramas.[75] The effect to aim for, as well as the means to achieve it, is explained by the anecdote that Dorval relates to illustrate the merits of the speech composed by Clairville. Dorval tells how a local peasant woman sent her husband to visit his relatives in a nearby hamlet. There he was killed by one of his brothers-in-law, and when Dorval visited the house the next day, he found the peasant woman kneeling at the feet of her husband's dead body, weeping and lamenting. Dorval's account again stresses the combined effect of visual and aural cues upon himself, as a spectator ('J'y vis un tableau, et j'y entendis un discours').[76] The words that Dorval heard the woman utter ('Hélas, quand je t'envoyai ici, je ne pensais pas que ces pieds te menaient à la mort') are cited as an illustration of acceptable wit. For Dorval, they represent a direct expression of 'l'âme du moment' and could as easily have sprung from the lips of a woman of rank as from those of a peasant because they are dictated solely by circumstance and emotion. Although they embody a conceit, the words do not have an overtly literary character, nor are they a product of background or education. They leave the impression that anyone else might have said the very same thing. Clairville's text for act III, scene v does not contain any examples of wit, but Dorval approves of the way it gives direct expression to feeling, representing nothing other than 'ce que la passion inspire, quand elle est extrême'.[77] Clairville's speech consists of fifteen brief sentences or fragments (two of them questions) and an exclamation, amounting to a total of a mere five lines of text. In a neoclassical verse play, a speech expressing despair would take the form of a lengthy, verbal analysis of this emotional state, exploiting a range of rhetorical figures (*tirade*). In Diderot's play, emotional intensity is evoked by means of the agitated movement and gestures that accompany oral expression or fill the pauses in between. The gestures described are not conventional, but imitate the gestures Clairville spontaneously used when he lived this experience. They are therefore natural theatrical signs of the natural signs of Clairville's emotion. He paces to and fro, leans on the back of a chair for support, buries his face in his hands, drops into a chair, stands up, paces some more, and so on. In the anecdote of the peasant woman, Dorval describes the attitude she spontaneously fell into when confronted with her husband's corpse. She is kneeling on the ground, clasping her husband's feet, which protrude from the bed, and weeping. The description focuses on details that bring to mind iconography associated with Mary Magdalen: the kneeling woman, her unruly *coiffure* (she is 'échevelée') and the tears she sheds over the feet of her husband are all

75. For a detailed description of Diderot's style, see Connon, *Innovation and renewal*, p.52-74.
76. DPV, x.100.
77. DPV, x.101.

elements from the image of the Magdalen bathing the feet of Jesus with her tears and wiping them dry with her hair.[78] Both scenes (Clairville's despair and the woman's grief) illustrate the reciprocal influence of speech and action, and the words themselves only communicate their meaning when they are associated with the action and embedded in their specific context. Dorval stresses the integration of verbal and gestural elements in human expression. 'Pourquoi avons-nous séparé ce que la nature a joint? A tout moment, le geste ne répond-il pas au discours?', he asks, criticising contemporary drama for its excessive verbalising at the expense of the visual resources of gesture and movement. The dramatic set pieces known as *tirades*, he insists, are the very opposite of 'ces vraies voix de la passion', because they are far too articulate to seem natural and they violate illusion. Dorval again invokes the topos of the too-visible poet to condemn such speeches. As long as they last, it is as if both the writer and actor have come down from the stage to mingle with the spectators. 'Ils descendent tous les deux du théâtre. Je les vois dans le parterre.'[79] The dramatic speech created for Clairville possesses the same qualities as the spontaneous expression of the peasant woman; natural gestures and attitudes supply the intensity and nuance that in the neo-classical style is imparted to speech through the resources of poetic language. The task Diderot ascribes to *actio* is that of the rhetorical figures in high tragedy, and his account of the expressive force of the visual signs of gesture and movement, corresponds, in his aesthetic, to d'Aubignac's explanation of the way in which the range and variety of rhetorical figures serve to evoke the 'beau désordre' created by the passions (discussed above, p.48).

In his theoretical writings, Diderot recommends two sources for developing an appropriate gestural system for the stage, a study of 'la peinture des mouvements' found in novels such as those of Samuel Richardson, and the principles of composition in painting.[80] A survey of the gestures and actions prescribed in Diderot's stage directions quickly reveals that he himself made considerable use of Landois's model. The four principal movements prescribed to express emotion in *Silvie* (agitated walking, unmotivated sitting and standing, throwing oneself at the feet of another, and fainting) all occur with significant frequency in Diderot's stage directions. 'Se promener' is mentioned thirteen times in *Le Fils naturel* and fourteen times in *Le Père de famille*. The use of a chair as a

---

78. There are other allusions to Magdalen imagery in Diderot's work. See Coulet, 'Le thème de la Madeleine repentie'. No one has identified a visual source for act III, scene v, although Jacques Chouillet has suggested that a moment from another scene with Dorval and Clairville (II.iv), where the two men embrace, may be an echo of Domenico Ghirlandajo's *L'Ultima cena*. See 'Le rôle de la peinture dans les clichés stylistiques et dramatiques de Diderot', *Europe* 661 (1984), p.150-58 (p.153-54). In the 1765 *Salon*, Diderot describes a painting of the Magdalen by Lagrenée, which he purchased for 300 livres (DPV, xiv.91).

79. DPV, x.103.

80. DPV, x.411 and x.416.

means for the actor to express intensity of emotion ('se jeter dans', 'se renverser dans', 's'appuyer contre', and so on) occurs nine times in *Le Fils naturel* and ten times in *Le Père de famille*. Two of these examples appear to be straightforward imitations of similar moments in *Silvie*.[81] The direction 'se jeter aux pieds' or 'aux genoux' of another *dramatis persona* occurs four times in *Le Fils naturel* and ten times in *Le Père de famille*; and total collapse occurs once, in *Le Père de famille*, although at one point in *Le Fils naturel*, Dorval 'tombe presque sans sentiment dans un fauteuil'. Two of the directions in *Silvie* make use of a comparison introduced by the word 'comme', 'comme un homme furieux', 'comme un homme troublé'. The same formula occurs five times in *Le Fils naturel* and four times in *Le Père de famille*. Although Diderot's plays reveal a more extensive gestural repertoire than *Silvie*, he seems to have adopted Landois's basic stock of gestures expressing emotion, as well as the technique of using elements of the set, especially chairs, to broaden the range of physical expression. The identity of Diderot's source did not escape some of his contemporaries. Palissot, for example, describes *Silvie* as the work that first set the example of 'ces minutieuses innovations [details concerning gestures and *tableaux*], qui ont été depuis si ridiculement imitées, et vantées si fastueusement par M. Diderot'.[82] The objections raised against Diderot's treatment of gesture by actors such as Riccoboni and Grandval are an indication of how novel his conception was at the time.[83]

Diderot also recycles, in *Le Père de famille*, the *tableau* of the weeping woman with table and lamp from Landois's play (the 'tableau charmant' described in the second *Entretien*). Because of the constraints imposed by the unity of place, he cannot show this scene on stage but he incorporates it verbally into Saint-Albin's account, in act I, scene vii, of his meeting with Sophie in her lodgings the previous evening.[84] Sophie is seated, weeping, at her table, her neglected sewing on the floor at her feet. 'Elle avait les coudes appuyés sur sa table, et la tête penchée sur sa main. Son ouvrage était tombé à ses pieds. [...] Des larmes s'échappaient d'entre ses doigts, et coulaient le long de ses bras.' Saint-Albin relates their conversation and concludes: 'A ces mots ses pleurs redoublent, et elle retombe

81. Landois, *Silvie*, p.25-26, and DPV, x.45 (*Le Fils naturel*, III.iv), and DPV, x.262 (*Le Père de famille*, III.vi).

82. Charles Palissot, *Œuvres de M. Palissot*, 6 vols (Paris 1788), iii.238. There are also some interesting thematic connections between *Le Fils naturel* and the *Lettre à Landois* of 1756. The recycling of phrases from the letter in the play suggests links, in Diderot's mind at least, between Landois and the fictional Dorval, whose choices in the play (the sacrificing of the self to virtue) embody the type of decision that Diderot, in the letter, tells Landois he needs to learn to make.

83. Angelica Goodden, '*Le Fils naturel*: langage du corps et discours sur le corps', in *Etudes sur 'Le Fils naturel' et les 'Entretiens sur le Fils naturel' de Diderot*, ed. Nicholas Cronk (Oxford 2000), p.53-64 (p.57).

84. In his letter to Mme Riccoboni, Diderot mentions several possible scenes set in the *grenier* where Sophie and Mme Hébert live, that he would have liked to include, but for the unity of place. DPV, x.446-47.

sur sa table comme je l'avais trouvée. La lueur pâle et sombre d'une petite lampe éclairait cette scène de douleur qui a duré toute la nuit.'[85] Diderot here reworks the basic elements supplied by Landois into a *tableau de genre*, illustrating *condition* through the references to the needlework and décor. This image has affinities with the stage *tableau* of Rosalie weeping at her loom in act II, scene i of *Le Fils naturel*, which Dorval cites as an example of *tableau* in the *Entretiens*. Such images suggest the work of Chardin and others whose paintings depict domestic interiors with figures engaged in the humble tasks of everyday life.

But if on the one hand Diderot visibly draws inspiration from examples set by Landois, he also carries these suggestions further, broadening the range of gestures and increasing the opportunities stage furniture offers for varying movement and attitudes. His characters inhabit the physical space of the salon with an ease and a spontaneity not possible in the prison-like setting of Silvie's room. They take things up, set them down, lean against the backs of chairs and sofas, on tables and against walls; they engage in everyday activities, such as drinking tea, playing board games, taking breakfast, weaving, sewing, writing and inspecting fabric for possible purchase. Activities such as these greatly increase the visual interest of gesture and movement and provide characters with natural things to do as they talk, although they do not necessarily talk about these things, as a system like that of d'Aubignac would require. Diderot's stage directions suggest, too, that he was trying to exploit the use of recurring or typical gestures as a means of enriching character portrayal. Dorval's folded arms and 'air sombre' are mentioned more than once. These techniques are an essential part of the creation of life-like illusion and the possibilities opened up by these various kinds of stage business, including their use to depict *condition*, were not lost on Lessing.

Dorval's discussion of expression includes reference to the vocal quality of speech; he praises the 'ton de la nature' that Clairville achieves in his scene and he urges actors to seek the 'vraies voix de la passion'. Traditional tragic declamation involved a special use of the voice, over and above the attention to diction and projection necessary for an actor's words to be heard. The broad vocal range and the modulations of the voice exploited for verse declamation imparted to it something akin to the complexity of a musical performance and widened the gap between tragic

---

85. DPV, x.206-207. In a note to an earlier passage from Saint-Albin's account, Jacques Chouillet draws attention to the similarity between the setting of Landois's play and Sophie's simple room and furniture, 'Une table de bois, deux chaises de paille, un grabat; voilà ses meubles', DPV, x.205, n.14. In the *Paradoxe*, Diderot alludes to a painting by Lagrenée entitled *La Philosophie* which exploits elements very similar to those in his verbal description of Sophie. Lagrenée had exhibited this picture and its companion piece, *La Poésie*, in the Salon of 1767. Diderot purchased the pair (DPV, xvi.142-43, and DPV, xx.84).

speech and non-theatrical discourse. Diderot's attention to the expressive effects of 'cri', 'accent' and 'ton' in both his theory and his stage directions is an implicit rejection of this artificial system in favour of a use of the voice that creates the impression of being spontaneous and natural. The exploitation of these vocal theatrical signs ('la voix', 'le ton') plays a significant role, along with gesture and action, in building the illusion of a living character, and are all the responsibility of the actor, 'qui donne au discours tout ce qu'il a d'énergie'.[86]

By 'cri' Diderot means the pre-rational, uncensored sounds 'torn' out of the body under the impact of intense or violent emotion.[87] 'Cri' only occurs once as a stage direction in his plays, in act III, scene iii of *Le Fils naturel*. The servants (less constrained by etiquette than the other characters), and the passionate Clairville all utter 'un cri de douleur' when André quotes Lysimond's account of how other prisoners had taken advantage of his age to steal his food and straw bedding.[88]

'Accent' and 'ton', as Diderot uses them, have both a singular and a collective application. Dorval states that every emotion has its own 'accent' but, unlike theorists such as Grimarest, who try to characterise the intonation typical of various emotions, Dorval adds that these accents are 'si fugitif[s] et si délicat[s]' that it is impossible to describe them or submit them to notation.[89] It is part of the genius of the actor to intuit and express them.[90] In addition, there is an 'unité d'accent' governing the overall vocal register of a play in a manner that distinguishes not just one genre from another but also each individual work. Learning how to find and blend into this 'unité d'accent' is, says Dorval, the work of an actor's lifetime. The general direction of these thoughts is clear: Diderot is recommending a use of the voice that is based not on considerations of genre or formal descriptions of how each passion manifests itself, but on the direct observation of human behaviour and on intuition. Two of the stage directions in *Le Fils naturel* suggest the 'accent' appropriate to a particular piece of speech: Constance adopts 'l'accent de la tendresse' when she evokes her first meeting with Dorval, and Clairville, rejected by Rosalie and unable to speak, falls back on 'l'accent inarticulé du désespoir'.[91]

The most frequently used of all these terms is 'ton'. It is discussed in the *Entretiens*, merits an independent section in the *Discours* and figures in a total of nineteen stage directions (a fact that probably did not escape the

86. DPV, x.102.

87. Dennis Fletcher, 'Primitivisme et peinture dans les théories dramatiques de Diderot', *Actes du colloque international Diderot* (Paris 1985), p.457-67 (p.463).

88. DPV, x.50. The stage directions do not make it entirely clear whether Clairville utters a cry like those of the servants or expresses his emotion in some other way.

89. Peter France and Margaret McGowan, 'Autour du *Traité du récitatif* de Grimarest', *Dix-septième siècle* 132 (1981), p.303-17, p.306.

90. DPV, x.104.

91. DPV, x.24 and x.46.

attention of Lessing as he was translating these texts). 'Tone' is very difficult to define. Generally speaking, the word is used to identify a particular degree of sound (or colour) within a range and it is often invoked to make quite fine distinctions. As Diderot uses the term in his theory, it seems to mean a combination of what is said and how it is said; the choice of words and the register. It can also refer to a quality of a play considered as a whole. Dorval states that tone, along with passion, characters and interest, is a more important factor than subject matter in determining whether a play is comic, serious or tragic.[92] More frequently though, tone is discussed as a function of character where it is subject to many variables and sometimes seems to be synonymous with 'accent'. According to Diderot, every character has his or her own tone, which shapes speech in relation to the passions or interests of the moment.[93] A fictional character must be allowed to say whatever is appropriate to the circumstances, regardless of *bienséance*. 'Il n'y a rien de sacré pour le poète, pas même la vertu, qu'il couvrira de ridicule, si la personne et le moment l'exigent.' Diderot goes on to emphasise the radical separation between the things the *dramatis personae* say and the personal beliefs of the writer; their tone (or voice) is not his. Tone differentiates; it is an expression of character and individuality. The remarks with which Moi concludes the *Entretiens* show that Diderot believed he had succeeded in giving each of his characters a unique tone. He tells the reader that despite the wide-ranging nature of the dinner table conversation, he had no difficulty in recognising the temperament with which Dorval had endowed each of his characters. '[Dorval] avait le ton de la mélancolie; Constance, le ton de la raison; Rosalie, celui de l'ingénuité; Clairville, celui de la passion; moi, celui de la bonhomie.'[94] Moi objects to Constance's tone in act IV, scene iii, because it does not conform to his expectations of either women or the theatre ('ce ton est bien extraordinaire au théâtre'); Dorval defends it by appealing to the particular qualities of her character. In the play, it was this accent and tone that seduced him into changing course: 'O raison! qui peut te résister quand tu prends l'accent enchanteur et la voix de la femme?'[95] The term 'tone' thus seems to evoke the highly individual quality of human speech as manifested in both choice of words and oral expression, a rhetoric that is entirely personal. Modern critics have drawn attention to the fact that the characters in Lessing's mature plays often allude to the tone of each others' speech (noticeably so in both *Minna von Barnhelm* and *Emilia Galotti*), and some have identified the exploitation of tone as one of the most successful aspects of his later dialogue.[96]

92. DPV, x.134.
93. DPV, x.392.
94. DPV, x.162.
95. DPV, x.69.
96. See Metzger, *Lessing and the language of comedy*, p.215, and Schröder, *Sprache und Drama*, p.212.

Diderot's choice of prose, his rejection of rhetoric and wit, his use of dislocated and interrupted speech, his emphasis on the importance of gesture and movement to reinforce or substitute for words, and his interest in the nuance imparted to language by natural inflections of the voice cohere into a formula for a type of stage speech that formally resembles the thing it signifies. This is play language transformed into natural theatrical signs, which do not draw attention to themselves as signs (the language of a poet) but create, for the audience, the illusion of speech belonging to the fictional characters. This conception of dramatic language is modelled on the sign system of painting, and the theatrical signs for speech are created from the perspective of a viewer positioned before the work, who is interpreting the aural cues of language in the context of related visual stimuli. It is language that is 'seen' as much as it is heard. As Diderot notes in the *Discours*, 'ce ne sont pas des mots que je veux remporter du théâtre, mais des impressions'.[97] These various innovative features that characterise Diderot's dramatic texts can be observed particularly clearly in his treatment of letters and in his scenes of exposition. I shall briefly consider some examples of these in order to illustrate the ways in which his practice differs from that of other dramatists of the time and to show what contemporaries such as Lessing found so suggestive in his approach.

Several of the most popular plays from the period prior to the publication of Diderot's theatre writings exploit letters. Voltaire's *Zaïre* (1732; IV.v), La Chaussée's *Mélanide* (1741; IV.iii) and Mme de Graffigny's *Cénie* (1750; III.iii and IV.iii) all make use of letters, and there is also one in Landois's *Silvie* (1741; I.viii). Regardless of genre and linguistic form, however, there are obvious similarities in the way in which letters are handled in all these works. In *Zaïre* and in *Mélanide*, the text of the letters is built into the verse structure of the speech of the characters who read them. All the letters are of more or less the same length (approximately six lines of verse or the equivalent in prose) and the text containing the relevant material is read aloud, in full. In *Mélanide*, *Cénie* and *Silvie*, the letters are used to provide information, either about something that takes place in another location (*Mélanide*, *Silvie*) or about events from the past (*Cénie*). In *Silvie* and *Cénie*, the letters are deathbed confessions, and therefore serve as a proxy for a character who cannot be present to speak on his or her own behalf. Voltaire gives the letter that figures in *Zaïre* a more dramatic function and uses it more effectively. It is sent by Nérestan to the heroine, but it falls into the hands of Orosmane, who reads it. Orosmane projects onto the letter his own emotions and preoccupations, and this leads to new complications not intended by the sender. In addition, the letter provides an opportunity to supply further evidence of

97. DPV, x.339.

Orosmane's jealousy, and it creates dramatic irony by placing the spectators in the position of knowing more than the characters.

Whilst Diderot's use of letters in *Le Fils naturel* (II.vi, II.vii, II.viii and II.ix) has some similarities with these earlier examples, it is the differences in his approach that are the most striking. Like Voltaire, Diderot exploits the letter's potential for dramatic effect when the one written by Dorval falls into the 'wrong' hands and is misinterpreted, thus causing further repercussions in the plot. Formally, though, his treatment is quite original. In *Le Fils naturel*, the final four scenes of the second act exploit the delivery and reading of one letter, and the writing and misreading of a second. Rosalie's letter to Dorval is, first of all, the object of a comic device. Charles has to search his pockets at length to find it and the delay builds tension and provides Dorval with the opportunity for silent action. Left alone, Dorval peruses the letter, but he reads aloud only fragments and these fragments, which nevertheless convey the drift of the whole, are interrupted by his reactions to what he reads. His decision to pen a response, and the drafting of the reply, are enacted silently, as mime, which Diderot outlines in stage directions indicating that the gestures and movements should reveal that Dorval finds the task difficult. This action is interrupted when Charles enters to summon immediate help. Constance then arrives and finds Dorval's letter. She, too, scans the whole, but reads aloud only four key phrases, which sum up the main idea. The remainder of the speech is made up of her response to the misunderstood text. The strategy Diderot exploits is that of reducing the text of the letters to the minimum number of phrases necessary to convey the essential idea, whilst exploiting the letter's materiality to motivate natural-looking gesture and movement; not so much the content of the letter as the letter as object. This is a fundamental transformation of earlier treatments and although nothing is said about it in his theory, it appears as though Diderot is consciously providing an example of the potential visual interest to be derived from the everyday activity of writing and receiving letters. The depiction of figures reading and writing, whether in relation to letters or other kinds of text, is a common theme in the painting of the period, particularly in works belonging to the absorptive tradition described by Fried.[98] Diderot's use of the letter as a stage property demonstrates how it can be exploited theatrically, and not just as a plot element, or as a solution to problems posed by the unity of place or by the need to communicate information to the audience.

---

98. Fried, *Absorption and theatricality*, p.7-70 and p.111-15. Two portraits of Diderot from the late 1760s exploit this very theme. Louis-Michel van Loo, nephew of Carle van Loo, depicts him in the act of writing and Jean-Honoré Fragonard shows him reading. Both activities can be seen as functions of his *condition*, although Diderot did not like the Van Loo treatment and criticises it in his 1767 *Salon*.

The way Diderot handles the opening scenes of his plays also departs from existing tradition and demonstrates a similar reorganisation of the verbal and visual elements. Neo-classical doctrine included rules for dramatic exposition. The dialogue of the expository scenes was expected to supply the audience with a certain amount of basic intelligence concerning the time and place of the action, the principal characters and any other background information considered relevant to the events about to unfold. These principles are concisely formulated by Boileau in his *Art poétique*, in a passage which Voltaire invokes to expose the weaknesses, as he sees them, of La Motte's tentative efforts to provide a livelier opening scene in *Inès de Castro*.[99] The opening scene of Landois's *Silvie* violates Boileau's principles even more thoroughly, leaving unstated almost all the details traditionally considered essential in favour of supplying a different kind of information visually. The milieu is communicated through setting, costume and the role of the servant. Des Francs's state of mind is revealed in his disconnected speech and restless, angry pacing. The spectator does not receive factual information from the things the characters say, but is expected to piece together the necessary essentials from the diverse visual and aural clues.

The first two scenes of *Le Fils naturel* work in a similar fashion. When the play opens, Dorval is alone on stage; he is then joined by his servant, and a dialogue between them ensues in scene ii. The monologue of scene i conveys Dorval's emotional stress and distraction, apparently brought on by an amorous entanglement. The final sentences imply forbidden love and a sense of guilt, although nothing is stated clearly. Gesture plays a major role in communicating the inner conflicts. Décor, which is described in more detail in Diderot's play, and costume (like Des Francs, Dorval is dressed 'en habit de campagne', rather than the conventional 'habits de ville'[100]) help communicate an impression of the social setting. The most striking difference between the two scenes is the massive reduction in the amount of language in Diderot's play, and the greater reliance on visual effects. Dorval's monologue consists in only eleven brief sentences and these transmit very little in the way of hard information, other than that it is early in the morning and that he cannot sleep. Language has receded in importance in relation to the visual impression, although the lines do still supply some facts. In *Le Père de famille*, this is no longer the case. In the first scene of this play, language conveys none of the information that neo-classical theorists such as Boileau would expect. The play opens with a group of characters assembled in a setting that Diderot's stage directions describe in some detail. Attitudes, movements and even facial expressions are prescribed for some characters and there

99. Boileau, *L'Art poétique*, in *Œuvres complètes*, p.155-85 (p.169-70); Voltaire, 'Vers et poésie', *Dictionnaire philosophique*, in *Œuvres complètes*, ed. Louis Moland, 52 vols (Paris 1877-1885) xx.565.

100. Dubos, *Réflexions*, p.141.

are several points of visual interest to engage the spectators' attention. The dialogue itself is confined to a polite question, the summoning of a servant to replace the candles and remarks concerning the game in progress between Cécile and her uncle. Here, speech has completely given up specific reference to the story or situation, that is to things outside the scene itself, and has been completely assimilated into the visual image. This language does not appear to 'address' the audience, either in terms of its content or its form. Considered from the perspective of the spectator, the words uttered in the opening scenes composed by Landois and Diderot achieve the status of natural theatrical signs; to use Lessing's phrase, they have become 'natural signs of arbitrary things'.[101]

Diderot's treatment of letters and of opening scenes typifies the form and function attributed to dramatic speech in his theory. The realisation that the audience does not need to hear the complete text of a letter, or to be told a lot of background detail in an opening scene, suggests the artistic principle known as *non finito*. From the writings of Roger de Piles onwards, it became a commonplace in art criticism to observe that sketches could have an appeal as great or greater than that of a finished drawing because they call upon the intervention of the viewer's imagination to complete them.[102] Painters, too, exploited the fact that not all parts of a canvas need to be 'finished' in the same amount of detail, since the imagination of the viewer has a natural capacity to complete parts of the image from a few visual cues. The possibilities for imaginative expansion afforded by both unfinished and finished works became an increasingly important concept in all branches of aesthetics in the period.[103] Diderot was familiar with this principle, and in his letter to Mme Riccoboni he applies it to the actors' gestures, citing the example typically associated with the effect, a painting by Timanthes of the sacrifice of Iphigenia, in which Agamemnon's face was shown covered by a mantle, thus obliging the viewer to imagine his grief.[104] In this passage, Diderot is talking about the effects of ensemble acting, and notes that 'celui dont je n'aperçois que certains mouvements qui mettent en jeu mon imagination, m'attache, me frappe et me désole plus peut-être qu'un autre dont je vois toute l'action'.[105] He makes a similar remark in response to Riccoboni's comments about the difficulty of seeing actors' facial expressions if they move more than three feet from the lights at front-stage. Diderot waves aside her objections with the remark, 'Mettez

---

101. Compare the letter to Nicolai of 26 May 1769, discussed below (p.164-65): Göpfert, vi.896-98.

102. Rothstein, ' "Ideal presence" and the "non finito" ', p.326. This idea goes back to classical writers (p.308).

103. Rothstein, ' "Ideal presence" and the "non finito" ', p.330.

104. Rothstein, ' "Ideal presence" and the "non finito" ', p.327-28.

105. DPV, x.440.

mon imagination en train, et je verrai au plus loin, et je devinerai ce que je ne verrai pas.'[106] His treatment of language reflects the same idea; the audience does not need complete text, especially when the mind is stimulated by the visual impact of the scene as a whole. The principle of *non finito*, applied to dramatic speech, is the opposite of the neo-classical assumption that everything that occurs in a play must be fully realised in language.

In assessing whether or not Diderot was successful in his enterprise, it is easy to find fault with his dialogue. It has become a tradition in Diderot criticism, reaching back to the earliest reactions to his plays, to claim that there is a hiatus between his theory and his practice, and to criticise his characters for being too verbose and grandiloquent. I think it important to notice that, alongside the long speeches (which tend, after all, to be concentrated in scenes of argument and persuasion), there are many occasions when exchanges are shorter, more rapid and enriched by visual interest. These passages do suggest practical alternatives to the speech-bound tradition of neo-classical tragedy, as the works of later dramatists inspired by Diderot, such as Sedaine, Mercier and Lessing, show.[107] Moreover, if one compares the length of speeches in Diderot's two plays with La Motte's experiments (his transposition into prose of the first scene of *Mithridate* and the prose version of his own *Œdipe*), it is clear that Diderot's efforts, like those of Landois, represent significant progress towards a new style. Certain types of speech typical of the neo-classical tradition are either absent or seriously modified in Diderot's plays. The principal *récit* from *Le Fils naturel* (III.vii) is broken up into short sections, interspersed with visual and spoken reactions on the part of the other characters present;[108] and although his plays contain monologues, Diderot avoids the lengthy analyses of emotional states that characterise French tragedy.[109] In addition, the humour (there is some in these plays!) does not rely on audience-directed wit and word play, but arises from the interplay of character and situation, for example in the scene where Charles searches his pockets for the elusive letter, or when Justine questions Rosalie about her feelings (II.i) or when the *père de famille* slowly removes the hat from the *inconnu* passing through his salon, only to discover his missing son (I.vii). These and other devices allow Diderot to

---

106. DPV, x.442.

107. Recognising the positive effect Diderot's example had on later dramatists, Connon dubs Diderot's efforts to transform dramatic speech a 'heroic failure'. See Connon, *Innovation and renewal*, p.74.

108. DPV, x.47-52.

109. Goodden notes that speech in *Le Fils naturel* is still permeated with figures typical of neo-classical diction (apostrophe, metonymy, antithesis, periphrasis), although she also points out how difficult it must have been for innovators such as Diderot to liberate themselves from 'le fardeau de la grande tradition dramatique du siècle précédent'. Goodden, '*Le Fils naturel*', p.58-59.

avoid the techniques that in both the tragic and comic tradition privilege verbal expression in ways that direct attention to language as such. In an article written in 1973, Richard Whitmore puts the emphasis on the progress that can be seen in the handling of dialogue between *Le Fils naturel* and *Le Père de famille*, and he argues that in the second play, the dramatic speech goes a long way towards fulfilling Diderot's stated aims by successfully capturing the individuality of each character.[110] The stage success of *Le Père de famille*, in France and elsewhere, suggests that Diderot must have got something right.[111]

The influence his ideas exercised on other writers may be due to the fact that in addition to the examples in his plays, his theory offers concrete advice to potential writers on how to go about writing plays in this style. Here, too, the distance separating Diderot from the neo-classical tradition is considerable. In contrast with the analytical approach, shaped by formal rhetoric, described in many seventeenth-century dramatic treatises, Diderot recommends the cultivation of imagination and the complete mental visualisation of each scene before and while writing. In the *Discours*, he reminds readers that the word 'imagination' means, precisely, the faculty of recalling images. All reasoning and intellectual activity can ultimately, Diderot claims, be pursued back from abstract words and concepts to 'quelque représentation sensible' ('sinnliche Vorstellung' in Lessing's text). The capacity to access these original images and express them in their fullness is the distinguishing characteristic of both the painter and the poet.[112]

The specific suggestions Diderot makes for writing more effective drama all rely on the exploitation of the imagination's picturing capacity. He draws attention, for example, to the value of creating visual images of all the characters, and of attaching to each figure an appropriate physiognomy. 'Tout peintre, tout poète dramatique sera physionomiste.'[113] The dramatist should visualise each scene by evoking the 'masque' and 'démarche' of the characters involved and imagining their movements and gestures. 'C'est ce simulacre qui inspire le premier mot; et le premier mot donne le reste.' The importance of visualising gesture and movement, and their interaction with the spoken word, is mentioned several times in both the *Entretiens* and the *Discours*, and Diderot gives a concrete example of this procedure in the section on 'entractes', where he makes the more unusual suggestion that the dramatist sketch out for himself and for the

---

110. Richard Prescott Whitmore, 'Two essays on *Le Père de famille*', *SVEC* 116 (1973), p.137-209 (p.144-45).
111. Anne-Marie Chouillet, 'Dossier du *Fils naturel* et du *Père de famille*', *SVEC* 208 (1982), p.73-166 (p.77). Her study lists eighteen editions of *Le Père de famille* between 1757 and 1770 and demonstrates that it was one of the most frequently performed plays of the eighteenth century.
112. DPV, x.359-60.
113. DPV, x.389.

actors all the important off-stage encounters that the action presupposes. This tactic will ensure that the playwright has a thorough grasp of the subject and this, passed on to the actors, will help them sustain their roles. He describes in detail an 'off-stage' scene associated with *Le Père de famille*, and his sample text is an interesting model of what he means by creating the simulacrum of a character and by blending visual and aural elements into a total impression. 'Il me semble que je le [le Commandeur] *vois* arriver d'une démarche composée, avec un visage hypocrite et radouci, et que je lui *entends* dire d'un ton insinuant et patelin: LE COMMANDEUR – Germeuil, je te cherchais.'[114] This account embodies the viewing point of the dramatist and shows that to write plays, Diderot situates himself before the scene, at the front of the house, where the spectators are. He writes entirely from their perspective. This emerges with even greater clarity from his letter to Mme Riccoboni, where he describes his 'façon de composer' and the way he exploits the spatial configuration of his own study to define an area within which the action of the developing play can be envisaged.[115] The window wall, he states, 'est le parterre, où je suis'. Opposite, in the area of the bookshelves, is the stage. He visualises each scene being played out there, in front of him, and adds that whenever a character enters, 'je le suis de l'œil, je l'entends et j'écris'. As he writes plays, Diderot casts himself in the role of the hidden spectator who records and transcribes the events as they unfold before him, but leaves no trace of his presence in the finished work.[116]

Diderot's observations on the importance of theatre space are closely related to his own choice of theatrical studio. He points out that dramatists compose plays in the context of the conditions of representation prevailing in their cultural milieu. These conditions shape the creative possibilities they can entertain. 'Faute de scène, on n'imaginera rien', notes Dorval, invoking the recently constructed theatre in Lyon as a stage space capable of inspiring a multitude of new works and possibly new genres.[117] The dramatist must visualise his drama in two senses: as the illusion of a scene from life and as a performance taking place in a given physical space, since the available stage space determines the particular form that the dramatisation of the action can take. Large stages allow the possibility of simultaneous scenes; an acting space eleven feet wide at the back, fifteen feet wide at the front and surrounded by spectators does

114. DPV, x.386, emphasis added.
115. DPV, x.440. Lessing did not have access to this document, but the passage provides a revealing articulation of the conception of play writing that informs Diderot's theory and plays.
116. This description of how Diderot writes plays has interesting affinities with a scene from Richardson's novel, *The History of Sir Charles Grandison*, which will be discussed in chapter 5 (p.150-51).
117. DPV, x.110-11.

not.[118] This reciprocal relationship between stage space and the writer's task is stated more forcefully in the letter to Mme Riccoboni, where Diderot stresses the need to change stage conditions in order to permit freer acting styles (and therefore plays that support them).[119]

Diderot's suggestions for creating dialogue are also based on use of the imagination. Speech should be modelled on the discourse the dramatist hears around him; the art of dialogue is cultivated by holding conversations with oneself. This two-fold approach is summarised in the formula: 'Ecouter les hommes, et s'entretenir souvent avec soi; voilà les moyens de se former au dialogue.'[120] This is very different from the importance attached to rhetorical training in dramatic treatises of the preceding age.[121]

The attitude underlying the rhetorical slant of neo-classical drama is that in art forms centred on language, the 'message' passes from author to consumer in a manner that is felt to be linear or face-to-face. Words used aesthetically issue from a poet; they embody a voice and are 'addressed to' someone. Diderot's theatre theory transforms this relationship. The creation of illusion requires that the dramatist compose the play from a perspective that is more or less identical with that of the viewer for whom it is intended, that is, the writer should position him or herself 'in front' of the play, where the spectators are, and write from this vantage point. This is the arrangement that obtains in painting, where the position the viewer adopts to contemplate the work is close to that taken by the artist as he or she created it. The topos of the hidden spectator thus serves not only as an image for the beholder of a play but also as an image for a new kind of writer. Diderot's recasting of dramatic form and dramatic writing in the light of painting theory succeeds in inverting all the main features of the neo-classical model: the visible artist becomes invisible; artificial signs give way to natural ones; textual fullness is replaced by suggestive *non finito*; the poet adopts the viewpoint of the painter; a rhetoric of language surrenders to the language of form. This amounts to a new theatrical code, and the authority who lends his name to these transformations is not Boileau but Horace.[122] In fact, theatrical representation, as it emerges from Diderot's theory, can be construed as a combination of the painterly categories of *dessein* and *coloris*. At the level of story and characters, drama requires careful planning, structuring and design, qualities of which Diderot frequently stresses the importance. At the level of performance,

---

118. The dimensions of the acting area at the Comédie-Française. See above, p.46, n.7.

119. DPV, x.437-38 and x.446.

120. DPV, x.346.

121. Rhetorical principles were, of course, originally derived from effective speech practices, but they evolved over time into a body of prescriptive doctrine.

122. Goulbourne, 'Diderot et Horace', p.121-22.

the work will only bring about illusion if speech, gesture, costume and setting confer upon the action the texture of life, the *coloris*, which seduces and deceives the senses of the spectator. Diderot does not make this comparison, but Lessing does, in the eighty-first *Literaturbrief*, considered by critics to be one of the earliest expressions of his reaction to the discovery of Diderot's theatre writings.[123] The sections which follow will show how coming to terms with Diderot's painterly approach to theatrical form caused Lessing to change the way he went about writing plays.

123. Göpfert, v.265. Diderot is quoted in this letter, but in relation to another point.

# III

## Lessing's assimilation of the new theatrical code

# III. Lessing's assimilation of the new theatrical code. Introduction

LESSING'S dramatic output falls naturally into three periods: the early comedies of the Leipzig years, the tragedies and the tragic experiments of the 1750s, and the post-*Laokoon* plays of his maturity. At each phase, Lessing's treatment of dramatic speech was shaped by the global theory of language and literature that he held at the time. Thus, Paul Böckmann (whose views are discussed below) has argued that the early comedies need to be understood in relation to the concept of wit that informed literary thinking in the early eighteenth century.[1] I shall suggest that dramatic speech in the two tragedies completed in the 1750s owes a great deal to the idea of poetry that evolved in Germany out of the semiotic approach to aesthetics initiated by Baumgarten, and that the language of the mature plays reflects Lessing's assimilation of the new concepts of dramatic speech and dramatic writing formulated by Diderot. Although, in the first two phases, Lessing was writing in different genres, his treatment of dramatic language rests, in both cases, on a concept of language as a system of arbitrary signs that speak directly to the audience. Considered from this perspective, dramatic speech in the early works can be seen to share a common orientation, although given a particular form by genre, as Hans Rempel argues.[2] But by the time Lessing composed his mature plays, he thought – and wrote – differently. Whilst stage speech remains a system of arbitrary signs for the fictional characters communicating with each other, it represents for the audience (and for the dramatist creating it) the 'natural signs of arbitrary things'.[3] This transition, from the concept of dramatic language as a system of arbitrary signs in the service of a specific effect (humour, sensibility, the activation of intuitive cognition) to that of dramatic language as a system of natural theatrical signs in an art form dedicated to the creation of illusion, accounts, I believe, for the change that affects Lessing's dramatic technique in the mature plays. The young Lessing writes as a poet still imbued with the neo-classical attitude towards language; the mature Lessing creates plays from a visual perspective analogous to that of the painter positioned before his subject.

1. Paul Böckmann, *Formgeschichte der deutschen Dichtung*, 2 vols (Hamburg 1949).
2. Hans Rempel, *Tragödie und Komödie im dramatischen Schaffen Lessings* (Berlin 1935; Darmstadt 1967).
3. Göpfert, vi.897-98.

# 5. Lessing's treatment of dramatic language in the early comedies and in *Miss Sara Sampson* and *Philotas*

IN the early comedies, Lessing exploits the ambiguities and the multiple facets of words as tokens of meaning to generate humour. Böckmann shows how the principle of wit, in the eighteenth-century sense, shapes both the language and the plots or situations typical of Lessing's early dramas. Wit was held, by the thinkers of the early Enlightenment, to constitute the defining characteristic of the successful poet.[1] It is the product of a felicitous combination of *Scharfsinn* ('acumen') and *Phantasie* ('imagination') and consists in the capacity to perceive similarities between dissimilar things and to express these in a striking and effective manner. Pope said it best:

> True wit is Nature to advantage dress'd,
> What oft was thought, but ne'er so well express'd.[2]

Poetry gives expression to the similarities detected by wit, both at the level of the words in which thought is expressed and in the content of the thought itself. According to Böckmann, 'Die Dichtung ist hier nur soweit Sprachkunst, als sie witziges Spiel mit der Sprache sein kann [...] Und entsprechend ist der Gehalt der Dichtung auf die witzigen Gedanken und Maximen angewiesen; auf das scharfsinnige Wahrnehmen von Ähnlichkeiten zwischen auseinanderliegenden Gedankenreihen.'[3] The principle of imitation in literature is, in fact, subordinated to the ideal of witty expression; imitation presupposes imitation enhanced by wit, which perceptively brings to light unexpected similarities and relationships between things. Wit, therefore, is not only a quality of thoughts and words, but is also invoked as a principle that shapes literary structure, as, for example, in the critical writings of Gottsched.[4]

This reliance on wit rests on the belief that language is a system of arbitrary signs standing for thoughts and concepts. Imagination is the capacity to produce new images out of memory and observation and to bring things together in a manner that is both perceptive and ingenious.[5]

---

1. Böckmann, *Formgeschichte der deutschen Dichtung*, i.506.
2. Alexander Pope, *Essay on criticism*, lines 297-298, in *The Poems of Alexander Pope*, ed. John Butt (London 1965), p.153.
3. Böckmann, *Formgeschichte der deutschen Dichtung*, i.507. 'What makes poetry an art of language is precisely its capacity to play with language [...] and correspondingly, poetic content consists in witty ideas and maxims; in the penetrating discernment of similarities between very disparate sets of thoughts.'
4. Böckmann, *Formgeschichte der deutschen Dichtung*, i.517.
5. Böckmann, *Formgeschichte der deutschen Dichtung*, i.504.

Böckmann shows that Lessing's early comedies from the period 1747-1750, which were written in prose, reflect these presuppositions, both in their language and their dramatic form. He goes on to argue that in *Minna von Barnhelm*, Lessing questions the principle of wit and succeeds in adapting conventional comic language to the expression of true feeling. He thus transcends the limits of wit and founds a new form of dramatic language. The evolution of Lessing's drama, as Böckmann sees it (and here, his argument about the comedies parallels Staiger's analysis of Lessing's tragic speech[6]), perfectly illustrates the transformation in the German conception of poetry between the time of Gottsched and the *Sturm und Drang*. 'Und zugleich wird man die Problemstellung wie die Form auch seiner späteren Dramen am besten verstehen können, wenn man sich klar macht, wie in ihnen der Witz wirksam bleibt, und wie zugleich eine neue Grundlage in ihnen gewonnen wird, die echte Symbolgestaltung.'[7] Wit is not abandoned in *Minna von Barnhelm*, but is integrated in an entirely different way. Böckmann contrasts statements Lessing made about wit in the 1740s with the very different opinions expressed later on, in the *Hamburgische Dramaturgie*. He invokes in particular number 30, where Lessing asserts the superiority of genius over wit and has clearly rejected the latter as a primary aesthetic value.[8] In fact, the contrast between wit and genius had already come up much earlier, in number 103 of the *Literaturbriefe* (1759), where it underlies the distinction made there between versifiers and true poets. Lessing quotes explanations given by Joseph Warton and Diderot to illustrate the differences between a mere wordsmith (someone who knows the rules of poetry and applies them effectively) and what Warton calls a writer of 'a lively plastic imagination'. Diderot contrasts them as 'un Hercule' (the poet) and 'un Apollon' (the versifier), and the passage Lessing refers to here comes from Diderot's discussion of poetry, prose and the imagination in the *Discours de la poésie dramatique*.[9]

Lessing believed that comedy must have a moral purpose, and the topics he treats (the effects of ill-digested book learning, the un-free nature of free-thinking, anti-Semitism, misogyny) make clear his intent to provoke intelligent thought on a range of contemporary follies. He achieves this aim not by striving to create a lifelike illusion, but by entertaining his audience with the laughter occasioned by various kinds of witty and clever insight. He quite consciously and deliberately exploits the artifice of the comic form inherited from the European (and particularly the French)

---

6. See below, p.179-80.

7. Böckmann, *Formgeschichte der deutschen Dichtung*, i.530. 'Both the way in which conflicts are framed and the dramatic form of his later plays can best be understood when it is recognised that although wit is still at work in them, a new principle, that of true symbolic form, here comes into being.'

8. Böckmann, *Formgeschichte der deutschen Dichtung*, i.531-32.

9. Göpfert, v.273; DPV, x.359.

tradition. This is apparent in various ways. References within the works themselves often remind the audience that they are watching a play. In *Der Misogyn* (1748), which revolves around Hilaria's disguise, the lovers themselves exploit theatre to overcome Wumshäter's prejudice against women. Valer and Hilaria develop at some length a comparison between their plotting and the writing of comedy and Valer questions whether they will ever be able successfully to unravel the plot they have created. Hilaria (as Lelio) reassures him that 'wenn er [der Knoten] nicht wieder aufzuwickeln ist, so machen wir es, wie die schlechten Komödienschreiber, und zerreißen ihn'. To which Valer responds, 'Und werden ausgezischt, wie die schlechten Komödienschreiber.'[10] Moreover, the play concludes with a remark directed to the spectators by Lisette, who says, 'Lachen Sie doch, meine Herren, diese Komödie schließt sich wie ein Hochzeitkarmen!'[11] In *Die Juden* (1749), Christoph explains that the bag on which he invites Lisette to sit contains his master's travelling library. It consists 'aus Lustspielen, die zum Weinen, und aus Trauerspielen, die zum Lachen bewegen; aus zärtlichen Heldengedichten; aus tiefsinnigen Trinkliedern, und was dergleichen neue Siebensachen mehr sind'.[12] In *Die alte Jungfer* (1749), Herr Kräusel asks 'Sie haben doch wohl die erbauliche Komödie gelesen, die ich wider Edelmannen gemacht habe? O! das ist ein Stück, als schwerlich jemals auf das Theater wird gekommen sein.'[13] All such comments are winks at the audience, reminders that they are participating in a form of entertainment in which ordinary modes of human interaction are suspended in the interests of humour and art. The frequent asides (seven in *Der junge Gelehrte*, 1748; fourteen in *Die Juden*; six in *Der Misogyn*; twelve in *Der Freigeist*, 1749; fourteen in *Der Schatz*, 1750) are part of the same aesthetic. They constantly testify to the presence and involvement of the audience.[14] In his study of Lessing's use of imagery, Helmut Göbel notes various occasions on which language itself becomes self-reflexive, for example in *Der junge Gelehrte*, when Anton, whose imagination is normally rich in colourful images, has to declare himself unable to find an appropriate one.[15] Göbel sees these various authorial allusions as the means by which Lessing consciously fosters awareness of the creative process that gives rise to the form itself ('die Bewußtheit der

10. Göpfert, i.435. 'If this tangle cannot be unravelled, then we'll do what bad playwrights do and cut through it.' 'And get ourselves hissed off, just like the bad playwrights.'
11. Göpfert, i.472. 'Laugh, gentlemen, laugh; this comedy is ending like a wedding-song.'
12. Göpfert, i.394. 'In comedies that make you cry and tragedies that make you laugh; in tender epics; in profound drinking songs and in all manner of other novelties'.
13. Göpfert, i.762. 'You have surely read the edifying comedy that I wrote attacking the nobility? Now that is a play the likes of which has never been performed before.' This is reminiscent of Molière's reference to his own plays in *Le Malade imaginaire*.
14. See for example, the six asides which follow one after another in scene vi of *Die Juden*.
15. Göpfert, i.299-300; Helmut Göbel, *Bild und Sprache bei Lessing* (Munich 1971), p.71.

Gestaltung in der Gestaltung').[16] Artifice is not concealed; it is openly acknowledged.

The cursory treatment of setting in the majority of these comedies belongs to the same tradition and is quite unlike Lessing's approach in the later plays. He simply does not tell us where *Der Misogyn*, *Die Juden* or *Damon* (1747) are supposed to take place, presumably because he expected any company performing them to rely on their standard comic décor. In the case of *Der Freigeist* and *Die alte Jungfer*, the stage directions simply call for a room ('ein Saal') and *Der Schatz*, Lessing's adaptation of Plautus's play, is set in the street as classical convention required. Only in Lessing's first comedy, *Der junge Gelehrte*, which unfolds in Damis's study, equipped with a desk and books, does he relate setting to theme. Here, interestingly enough, there is an intimation of a practice Lessing would later develop to great effect. The stage directions for the opening scene, which read, '*Damis (am Tisch unter Büchern). Anton*' ('*Damis, at a table, surrounded by books. Anton*'), suggest that Lessing thought of the table and books primarily as props, that is as extensions of Damis's costume and character (like Solbist's large wig and package of legal documents in *Der Misogyn*). At the same time, stage space also has a more significant, expressive role. The fact that all the action takes place in Damis's study and that the other characters have to come to this location to interact with him, introduces a humorous paradox. The study emphasises the isolation from life that immersion in books has imposed on Damis, but the constant invasion of this space by others gives rise to comic conflict as Damis seeks in vain to create around him the quiet he thinks he needs for his intellectual endeavours. In fact, this choice of setting occasions a number of difficulties when it comes to motivating the presence of the other characters there, but this does not have great importance in a work that is a comedy.

In all of these early works, Lessing makes extensive use of exaggeration, of improbable situations, of disguises capable of deceiving only in a comedy, of farce and of humorous stage business, which are all the stock-in-trade of this tradition. The majority of the characters, as their names suggest (Lelio, Damis, Oront, Lisette, etc.), are the types of the comic tradition, drawn with broad strokes that serve the purposes of humour. Wit, in the early Enlightenment sense, characterises the ploys (*Einfälle*) that they exploit to achieve their ends and around which the plots revolve: the false letter in *Der junge Gelehrte*, Hilaria's disguise in *Der Misogyn*, Theophan's efforts to overcome Adrast's prejudice against clerics in *Der Freigeist* and so on. Wit is apparent too, in the underlying idea that drives some of the plays. In *Der Freigeist*, for example, the unfolding of the plot leads to a more balanced reconstitution of the proposed marital alliances. Lisidor neatly summarises the final situation: 'Der Fromme sollte die Fromme,

---

16. Göbel, *Bild und Sprache*, p.73.

und der Lustige die Lustige haben'; instead 'der Fromme will die Lustige, und der Lustige die Fromme', a linking of opposites that points in the direction of the need to harmonise *Witz* and *Herz*.[17] In *Die Juden*, Lessing exploits a plot that throws into relief the positive moral qualities of the principal character and thus exposes the irrational and destructive nature of anti-Semitism. Lessing would have expected audiences to recognise the play's obvious affiliations with the parable of the Good Samaritan, one of the essential lessons of Christianity. Although these early plays include some topical references, for example, the Berlin Academy's essay prize in *Der junge Gelehrte*, the purpose of these is not to foster illusion, but to draw the audience into a theatrical conspiracy and amuse them with references to their own world, outside the theatre.

Böckmann is not the only critic to highlight the clear conception that underlies these dramas and the clever manipulation of situation to make an intellectual point. What Böckmann attributes to the influence of wit in its broadest sense, Peter Pütz explores as a manifestation of the comic principle of reversal (*Umkehrung*), a device he considers particularly appropriate to the goals of Enlightenment.[18] He sees this principle at work at all levels of the plays: in the relationship between their titles or themes and the expectations the audience bring to the theatre; in the treatment of the underlying ideas; in the shaping of individual scenes and in the dialogue itself. There is a constant movement between the initial status quo and its transformation into something else, often its opposite. Thus Pütz, like Böckmann and Göbel from their respective points of view, emphasises the central role that the intervention of self-conscious artistry exercises in these works. Lessing is not here striving to create the illusion of a lifelike event; he is aiming to create effective comedies within a tradition that fully recognises the essential artifice of the comic form, and it is from within this perspective that their language must be considered.

For the most part, the interaction of situation and character is exploited in a manner calculated to give rise to humorous and witty exchanges, not in order to dissect and analyse emotions and motives. Wordplay is a dominant feature. A linguistic device of which Lessing makes frequent use in all his plays is anadiplosis, the repetition by one character of words drawn from the last lines of his interlocutor's previous speech.[19] In the comedies, this technique is one of the basic mechanisms in the service of comic effect. Expressions and phrases used by one speaker are taken up and echoed by another, but in the process are wrongly interpreted (consciously or unconsciously), reinterpreted or simply repeated in a new context or with different implications. In his study, Böckmann analyses

17. Göpfert, i.554; Böckmann, *Formgeschichte der deutschen Dichtung*, i.537. 'The serious man was supposed to get the serious woman, and the merry man, the merry woman [...] the serious man wants the merry woman, the merry man the serious one.'

18. Peter Pütz, *Die Leistung der Form: Lessings Dramen* (Frankfurt am Main 1986), p.67-99.

19. Metzger, *Lessing and the language of comedy*, p.35.

several examples from *Der Freigeist*, and all the plays are rich in similar passages.[20] Lessing exploits many other verbal devices typical of comic dialogue. Repetition for humorous effect, for example, figures in act II, scene xi of *Der junge Gelehrte*, where Damis dismisses all the failings Lisette claims to find in Juliane with the word 'Kleinigkeit' ('a trifle'), which Anton counters with 'Lügen!' ('Lies!');[21] or in act II, scene vii of *Der Misogyn*, where Lisette forces Wumshäter to utter the words 'my daughter' against his will.[22] Another form of repetition is the catch-phrase, such as Chrysander's 'Wie wir Lateiner zu reden pflegen',[23] that certain characters trot out on cue. Lessing also likes to make use of words or groups of words that appear humorous, simply as words, in the context in which they occur. The names of the Greek poetesses that Damis reels off to his father and Chrysander's ignorant distortion of these in act I, scene ii of *Der junge Gelehrte* is one example.[24] In similar fashion, Wumshäter and Solbist from *Der Misogyn* list off, with comic exaggeration, the names of all the world's evil women from Eve down to Wumshäter's three wives.[25] In this same section Lessing exploits one of Molière's favourite techniques, the satire of rhetoric and professional jargon, as Solbist launches into, and then forgets, the speech he has prepared on this topic for the court. Literary pretensions are the object of humour in *Der junge Gelehrte* and *Die alte Jungfer*. Even the language of love is not immune from comic treatment, as we see in act II, scene ii of *Der Misogyn* where Laura tries to draw Hilaria, disguised as Lelio, into an exchange of *galanteries*. This scene is a good example of a dramatic strategy Lessing uses often (both here and in his later plays): that of casting speech in an ironic perspective by allowing the audience to know more than some of the *dramatis personae*. The effects generated from the layers of meaning that remain hidden from the speaker can be both humorous and thought-provoking. The concealed identities in both *Der Misogyn* and *Die Juden* lead to scenes of this type. Once the audience knows that Lelio is Hilaria and that the Traveller is a Jew, the words they utter, and those spoken to them by the characters ignorant of their true identity, do not merely produce comic effects but also invite reflection on the contradictory relationship between beliefs, action and character.

To a large degree, then, language has what one might consider an autonomous role in these comedies. Lessing constantly plays with speech, using it not primarily as a vehicle of expression for feelings and actions but for its own sake, and to produce comic effects from within itself. Rempel emphasises these playful and independent qualities of Lessing's comic

20. Böckmann, *Formgeschichte der deutschen Dichtung*, i.534-35 and i.538-39.
21. Göpfert, i.329.
22. Göpfert, i.458.
23. 'As we Latin scholars like to say.'
24. Göpfert, i.290.
25. Göpfert, i.452-53.

dialogue, which is subordinated to logic rather than character.[26] Similarly, Böckmann points to the fact that in numerous passages, speech develops directly out of the meanings and ambiguities of the words themselves, creating the impression that language is playing hide-and-seek with itself.[27] This approach to dramatic speech and the reliance on wit as a driving force in much of the dialogue derives from Lessing's highly developed awareness of words as things in themselves. He treats them as autonomous entities, calculated to elicit specific responses in the audience to whom they are addressed as much as they are to the stage interlocutors.

For this reason, Metzger's suggestion that Lessing 'set out to create in *Der junge Gelehrte* a linguistic world closely resembling in its vocabulary and tone the actual conversation of middle-class Leipzigers as they might speak at home' is perhaps to misplace the emphasis.[28] It seems more likely that Lessing, who in a letter dated 28 April 1749 told his father that his ambition was to become a German Molière, actually set out to be funny, and that the authenticity Metzger finds in the dialogue is a side-effect rather than a goal. The studies of Rempel and Böckmann, which stress the influence of contemporary conceptions of wit, offer, perhaps, a more accurate assessment of Lessing's achievement than an interpretation which approaches the dialogue of the early comedies as steps on the way towards the language of *Minna von Barnhelm*. This observation is not, however, intended to diminish the value of Metzger's study, which provides an illuminating account of the various linguistic techniques that Lessing uses and the specific devices that imbue the dramatic speech of the comedies with its great liveliness. In addition to anadiplosis and interruption, Metzger identifies a number of features including contraction, elision, ellipsis, interjections, oaths, and exclamations, as well as choice of vocabulary, which all contribute to the creation of the generally colloquial tone he considers appropriate to the Leipzig society for whom Lessing wrote.[29] Within this framework, Metzger distinguishes in several of the plays two perceptible tonal levels, that of the comic characters, including the servants, and that of the non-comic, or less comic, middle-class figures. The speech of the former seems to capture more successfully the rhythms and patterns of everyday usage, although without degenerating into dialect or slang. Göbel's study of the use of imagery in the comedies confirms this finding. He notes that the language of the servants, rooted in the experiences of day-to-day life, is 'viel bildhaftere und teilweise auch anschaulichere Sprache als die der Kaufleute oder des jungen

---

26. Rempel, *Tragödie und Komödie*, p.13-14.
27. Böckmann, *Formgeschichte der deutschen Dichtung*, i.543.
28. Metzger, *Lessing and the language of comedy*, p.30-31.
29. Metzger, *Lessing and the language of comedy*, p.43 and p.54; Böckmann, *Formgeschichte der deutschen Dichtung*, i.533.

Gelehrten'.[30] The language of the other characters displays much less variety and liveliness and has a tendency towards more elevated speech. The distinction between the two styles is partly a reflection of different social standing, and partly the result of character typology, for Lessing's early comedies continue to rely on the traditional types of the comic tradition (the old men, the young lovers, the saucy servants) and to embody, in the principal character, a folly to be satirised. All these figures express themselves in a manner consistent with the type, not as unique individuals with a personal rhetoric. In fact, Lessing often exploits the apparently ordinary form of their language to expose the absurdity of what is actually being said. In act I, scene iii of *Der Misogyn*, for example, Wumshäter is spurred on by the sly promptings of Lelio to formulate his views in a way that shows exactly how nonsensical they are. The opinions he holds are pushed to the limits of the ridiculous and go far beyond what the audience might expect a misogynist to express. The contrast between the absurdity of his beliefs, and the matter-of-fact, everyday tone in which he utters them, serves to show how laughable they are. Lessing is deliberately exploiting the gap between the signifier and the signified.

Of course, dramatic speech in these works does not always serve comic aims, and the plays influenced by the sentimental comedy of the period, such as *Der Freigeist*, often contain passages of quite serious dialogue. The opening scene of *Der Freigeist*, in which Adrast and Theophan hold a detailed discussion of the nature of friendship in relation to their divergent world views, is a non-humorous confrontation of ideas, which requires attentive listening on the part of the audience. The same is true of the conversation between Adrast and Juliane in act IV, scene iii. But in the major scene between Adrast and Theophan, in which Adrast finally recognises that he has misjudged the young cleric (V.iii), Lessing exploits the reversal in a comic manner, using displays of anger and surprise, reinforced by sections of short, rapid exchanges and asides, to defuse emotion. Both Metzger and Göbel agree, though, that the non-comic roles and scenes are the ones in which the language is the least lively and well differentiated. When Lessing is not being witty, his language is not as dramatically effective.

In short, language in the early comedies, lively and persuasive as it may be in many of its particulars, is still shaped by an overall aesthetics of effect rather than representation. Many of its features are such that considered purely from the point of view of form, it can be seen to resemble everyday, colloquial speech; nevertheless, its content and the way in which Lessing exploits qualities of language *qua* language for comic effect make it unlike ordinary speech. It is not ordinary language dedicated to the creation of illusion, but ordinary language in the service of comedy,

---

30. Göbel, *Bild und Sprache*, p.69. 'More picturesque and vivid language than that of the merchants or the young scholar'.

and this makes it very different from the dramatic speech that characterises Lessing's mature drama. Although not poetic language, it is nevertheless audience-directed in the sense discussed in the Introduction.[31] The same orientation, as I shall now try to show, is evident in the two tragedies Lessing produced in the 1750s. Although written in prose, they too exploit a form of language that is self-consciously literary.

*Miss Sara Sampson* (1755) and *Philotas* (1759) are the only finished works to emerge from a period of experimentation during which Lessing tried to massage diverse story materials into plays that would both achieve the tragic effects defined by Aristotle and suit the modern age.[32] Individually, the fragments embody the various attempts that Lessing made to adapt the tragic form to contemporary taste, but the general tendency of them is to suggest that he was striving to create tragedy that would remain close enough to traditional norms to enhance German cultural prestige. *Miss Sara Sampson* therefore emerges as a surprising and innovative work. It was the first successful middle-class tragedy in German, and a play quite unlike Lessing's other experiments of the period.[33] It is set in contemporary England, the characters are fictitious, not historical, and the emphasis is on 'private virtues'. In addition to the unusual subject matter, Lessing's choice of prose and his intent that the work be performed in accordance with the new, natural acting style show that he was moving towards the kind of theatrical code that Diderot would articulate two years later. But Lessing's conception of dramatic language, and its relationship to acting, is, at this time, very different from Diderot's, and although he chooses prose as the linguistic medium, he still approaches play language as if it were a form of poetry rather than an autonomous theatrical sign.

Lessing has left no record of the reasons he opted for prose in *Miss Sara*. The two tragic fragments pre-dating his domestic tragedy (*Giangir, oder der verschmähte Thron* and *Samuel Henzi*) are written in verse (unrhymed and rhymed alexandrines, respectively). Twentieth-century critics attribute Lessing's choice of prose to various factors: continuing awareness of seventeenth-century examples of prose tragedy,[34] the influence of English models and the success of the first performances of English middle-class tragedies in Germany (1754),[35] the influence of some types of sentimental comedy, and the contemporary novel. But Daunicht, whose study of the

31. See above, p.15-16.
32. Francis Lamport, 'Lessing and the "Bürgerliches Trauerspiel"', in *The Discontinuous tradition: studies in German literature in honour of Ludwig Stahl*, ed. P. F. Ganz (Oxford 1970), p.14-28 (p.18-19 and p.21-22).
33. Daunicht, *Die Entstehung des bürgerlichen Trauerspiels*, p.276-79.
34. Paul P. Kies, 'The sources and basic model of Lessing's *Miss Sara Sampson*', *Modern philology* 24 (1926), p.65-90 (p.90).
35. Curtis C. D. Vail, *Lessing's relation to the English language and literature* (New York 1936) p.134; Robert R. Heitner, *German tragedy in the age of Enlightenment: a study in the development of original tragedies, 1724-1768* (Berkeley and Los Angeles, CA 1963), p.170 and p.308.

question is the most thorough, situates Lessing's views in the context of the German debate concerning the use of verse or prose in drama that took place in the 1740s.[36] Both Daunicht and Claus Schuppenhauer (in a study of 1970) connect German interest in this topic with the French debate, with which German-speaking writers and critics were familiar. Gottsched's ambiguous position on the appropriate linguistic form for tragedy appears to be a reflection of the difficulty he had in deciding between the merits of existing practice (widespread use of the alexandrine), the progressive French position (prose) and English example (blank verse).[37] In the *Deutsche Schaubühne*, he had published, in German translation, Fénelon's short essays on tragedy and comedy from the *Lettre sur les occupations de l'Académie*; later, he also makes explicit, and in fact positive, reference to La Motte.[38] Numerous German essays and articles, both for and against the use of prose in comedy, as well as in tragedy, appeared.[39] Lessing was aware of these controversies, and his cousin Mylius was the author of a piece entitled *Von den Reimen und dem Sylbenmaasse in Schauspielen*, in which he defends the idea of prose tragedy in the name of probability and truth to life.[40] The debate never achieved resolution in the realm of theory, but increasingly, the younger dramatists came to favour the use of prose, even in tragedy, as conducive to a more natural style.[41] Daunicht describes Lessing's position as open-minded and flexible, one that would allow the writer discretion in the choice of form. To illustrate this, he reproduces the few short passages from the early 1750s where Lessing's views are expressed. In fact, as far as poetry is concerned, Lessing appears still to accept neo-classical definitions. In the April 1751 issue of *Das Neueste aus dem Reiche des Witzes*, for example, he defends rhyme in poetry by reference to the concept of the *difficulté vaincue*. Criticising the opponents of rhyme, Lessing writes, 'Rechnen sie das Vergnügen, welches aus der Betrachtung der glücklich überstiegnen Schwierigkeit

36. Daunicht, *Die Entstehung des bürgerlichen Trauerspiels*, p.201-206.

37. Daunicht, *Die Entstehung des bürgerlichen Trauerspiels*, p.144. In his critical writings, Gottsched often seems to favour blank verse as used by English dramatists as the most appropriate form for German tragedies. On the other hand, his model play, *Der sterbende Cato*, is written in rhymed alexandrines, and all the tragedies in the *Deutsche Schaubühne* are in rhymed verse. Daunicht claims that in the end, Gottsched was unable to shake free from the power of theatrical tradition, despite his insistence on the importance of *vraisemblance* (p.111). See also Claus Schuppenhauer, *Der Kampf um den Reim in der deutschen Literatur des 18. Jahrhunderts* (Bonn 1970), p.261-66 and p.279-80.

38. Gottsched, *Neuer Büchersaal der schönen Wissenschaften und freyen Künste*, 10 vols (Leipzig 1745-54), iv.370. Quoted in Daunicht, *Die Entstehung des bürgerlichen Trauerspiels*, p.206.

39. Daunicht discusses a range of works on this theme from the decade 1741-1751, including essays by Gottlob Benjamin Straube, Johann Elias Schlegel, Adam Daniel Richter, and Lessing's cousin, Christlob Mylius. See Daunicht, *Die Entstehung des bürgerlichen Trauerspiels*, p.144-55.

40. Daunicht, *Die Entstehung des bürgerlichen Trauerspiels*, p.154.

41. Daunicht, *Die Entstehung des bürgerlichen Trauerspiels*, p.206.

entsteht, für nichts?'[42] The reader's recognition of the artist's technical achievement is an important principle for Lessing. Nevertheless, he concludes this item with the statement, 'Daß aber ein Heldendichter und ein Dramatischer Poet die Reime wegläßt, ist sehr billig; denn da verursacht der Übelklang eines fast immer gleichen Abschnitts einen größern Verdruß, als das Vergnügen sein kann, welches jene schön überwundenen Hindernisse erwecken.'[43] The qualification in relation to the epic and drama concerns the use of rhyme (not metre), and Lessing decides the issue by weighing relative pleasure quotients, not by appealing to *vraisemblance* or illusion, as La Motte and Mylius do.[44] His position implies a dislike of the French alexandrine and a preference for the blank verse of English drama, rather than an interest in a fundamentally new conception of dramatic speech.[45]

Flexible, then, on the issue of metrical form, Lessing was also familiar with the new ways of defining poetry to emerge from contemporary German aesthetic and semiotic theory.[46] Drawing on Wolff's map of the human mind, Baumgarten, Mendelssohn and others were formulating a view of poetry that was based on the distinctions made between symbolic and intuitive cognition and between arbitrary and natural signs. This theory produced a conception of poetry that has some similarities with the one that Fénelon articulates in the *Dialogues sur l'éloquence*, although developed from the perspective of language and cognition theory, not in response to thinking about the effects of visual art.

According to German theory, works of art do not appeal to 'symbolic' cognition ('symbolische Erkenntnis'), the realm of discursive knowledge, but communicate directly with 'intuitive' cognition ('anschauende Erkenntnis'), which is related to the lower faculties of sense and imagination.

---

42. Göpfert, iii.96. Quoted by Daunicht, *Die Entstehung des bürgerlichen Trauerspiels*, p.202. 'Do they think that the pleasure arising from the contemplation of a difficulty felicitously overcome counts for nothing?'

43. 'It is entirely reasonable for the epic poet and the dramatist to avoid the use of rhyme; in those genres, the unpleasant effect arising from the recurrence of the same sounds causes an annoyance which is greater than the pleasure that can be derived from the perception of the difficulty which is overcome.'

44. Lessing makes reference to La Motte's 'unité de l'intérêt' in the *Kritik über die Gefangnen des Plautus* from the *Beiträge zur Historie und Aufnahme des Theaters* (1750), Göpfert, iii.498.

45. Lessing subsequently repeated some of these statements in other pieces of writing (Daunicht, *Die Entstehung des bürgerlichen Trauerspiels*, p.201-202). In the year preceding the composition of *Miss Sara Sampson*, Lessing alludes positively to a one-act tragedy in prose, *Emirene*, published in the *Hamburgische Beyträge* (1753). However, his remarks do not really illuminate his position on dramatic speech, since he merely uses the opportunity to encourage German companies to experiment with tragedies other than those based on the traditional formula of five acts and verse. See Gotthold Ephraim Lessing, *Sämtliche Schriften*, ed. Karl Lachmann, 3rd edn revised by Franz Muncker, 23 vols (Stuttgart, Berlin and Leipzig 1886-1924), v.381. Future references to this edition will use the abbreviation LM.

46. I am indebted to Wellbery's lucid study (*Lessing's Laocoon*) for my grasp of these issues.

Only objects presented to the soul in intuition are capable of moving the recipient and producing an aesthetic effect, which David Wellbery defines as 'an energetic, self-sustaining attentiveness in which emotional response and sensate representation are enriched and ramified'.[47] The act of intuitively apprehending the art object, through which the recipients feel themselves feeling, connects them with the workings of their own soul and allows them to experience a transpersonal, universal dimension of themselves, something which was thought to have a socialising influence.[48] Art is able to exert these effects on intuitive cognition when it represents its objects through the kind of signs that allow us to attend more fully to the idea of the signified object than to the presence of the sign itself.[49] In France, as we have seen, it was on these grounds that aesthetic thinkers adopted the painterly sign as the model for linguistic signs, and compared aesthetic uses of language with the effects of visual art. In German theory the attitude is different. Although language is considered a system of arbitrary signs, with the primary task of conveying a clear and distinct idea of things to symbolic cognition, it was also regarded as ideal for communicating objects to intuitive cognition. This is because words bear no physical resemblance to the thing they signify, and language therefore 'cleaves to the movement of the imagination while leaving its materiality behind'.[50] According to German thinkers, language which is used aesthetically allows the recipient to attend fully to the object of representation, because it is unencumbered by the distracting presence of a material, signifying medium. In order to achieve this effect, however, language in its aesthetic role must transform itself in such a way as to convert the symbolic cognition usually associated with language use into the kind of intuitive cognition that can move the soul. Poetry (aesthetic language) can achieve this goal in two main ways. Firstly, it can avoid such obviously artful devices as wit, puns, rhetorical figures, and rhyme that divert attention away from the signified object towards the presence of the sign itself. Secondly, poetic language can privilege types of word and expression that are particularly conducive to an intuitive actualisation of the represented object. One notable feature of this theory of poetic language, which derives ultimately from the fact that linguistic signs function, essentially, as 'names' for the things they represent, is that it gives great prominence to individual words and tends to emphasise effective words or lexical tropes at the expense of syntactical figures.[51] Examples of the kinds of words believed to enhance the sensate quality of aesthetic language are emphatic terms, proper names, painterly epithets, and metaphors. What they all have in common is that in different ways

47. Wellbery, *Lessing's Laocoon*, p.62.
48. Wellbery, *Lessing's Laocoon*, p.65.
49. Mendelssohn, quoted in Wellbery, *Lessing's Laocoon*, p.61-62.
50. Wellbery, *Lessing's Laocoon*, p.68.
51. Wellbery, *Lessing's Laocoon*, p.75.

they convey the mind beyond the stage of symbolic cognition and call up clusters of representations in intuitive cognition which provide a quasi-perceptual mental experience of the object or quality to which they refer.[52] They let us 'see' or 'feel' the thing represented. The reason why words of this type were thought to stimulate such forceful and dynamic representations is that they replicate the natural signifying procedures – mimesis, naming, metaphor, expressive speech – believed to be at the origins of language and culture. They were considered vestiges of the processes whereby language first came into being. Lessing's reliance on this grasp of the form and function of aesthetic language is evident in two ways in *Miss Sara Sampson*. It emerges in certain features of the text itself and it also underlies Lessing's theory of how dramatic speech shapes the expressions and gestures of the actor.

I shall consider the text itself first, where it is clear that a number of the linguistic features privileged in *Miss Sara Sampson* are precisely those which contemporary semiotic theory held to be the acme of poetic expression. Two prominent examples are name–adjective combinations and imagery. Proper names were considered a class of words that enhance sensateness as their use causes the recipient to actualise the named individual in a way that is imaginatively rich.[53] Similarly, the well-chosen epithet serves to characterise an object by its salient feature and thus helps the recipient to proceed to a fuller intuition of it. Traces of this thinking are apparent in one of the most noticeable (to the modern ear) features of Lessing's dialogue in *Miss Sara Sampson*, the frequency with which the characters are referred to in the dialogue, by their name, or by a word designating their state in life or their relationship to others (father, daughter, *Buhlerin* ['courtesan' or 'whore']), accompanied by an adjective. Marwood is on different occasions 'die böse Marwood', 'eine buhlerische Marwood', 'die gefährliche Marwood', 'die barbarische Marwood'; Sir William is 'der zärtliche Vater', 'der unglückliche Vater', 'der wimmernde Vater' and, according to Marwood, 'ein zu guter alter Narr'. Sara is 'das beste, schönste, unschuldigste Kind', 'die teuerste Miss', 'die vernünftige Sara', 'die zärtliche Tochter', 'eine reuende gehorsame Tochter', 'die einzige, geliebteste Tochter', and so on. The climax of this naming process is the curse Mellefont pronounces on Marwood, after learning of her flight: 'Verzehrend Feuer donnre der Himmel auf sie herab, und unter ihr breche die Erde ein, der weiblichen Ungeheuer größtes zu verschlingen!'[54] To a modern consciousness, the adjectives seem oddly superfluous in view of the fact that, in performance, the characters are constantly present before the spectators. The use of such language cannot be accidental, however; nor is it a reflection of ordinary ways of speaking.

52. Wellbery, *Lessing's Laocoon*, p.76.
53. Wellbery, *Lessing's Laocoon*, p.75.
54. Göpfert, ii.90. 'May the heavens send down fire upon her to consume her, and may the earth open beneath her and swallow her up, this most monstrous of female monsters!'

Lessing appears to be consciously manipulating the language according to poetic principles believed to activate the intuitive cognition of the spectators or the reader, whom he also has in mind. The linguistic device is used to elicit a specific response in them.

Sustained and recurring imagery and metaphor also play an important role in the play. Göbel's detailed study examines various recurring image clusters, for example the metaphors of light associated with Sara.[55] Waitwell first uses light imagery in the opening scene where he says, 'Aus jeder kindischen Miene strahlte die Morgenröte eines Verstandes, einer Leutseligkeit'.[56] Sara falls back on the contrast of light and darkness when she reflects, though with a sense of foreboding, on the happiness that her father's forgiveness may or may not bring: 'Vielleicht erscheinet mir dieser Strahl von Glückseligkeit nur darum von ferne, und scheinet mir nur darum so schmeichelhaft näher zu kommen, damit er auf einmal in die dickste Finsternis zerfließe, und mich auf einmal in einer Nacht lasse, deren Schrecklichkeit mir durch dieses kurze Erleuchtung erst recht fühlbar geworden.'[57] When Sir William appears at his poisoned daughter's bedside, she compares him to a heavenly apparition,[58] and he then uses similar imagery (in contrast to the fire and earthquake Mellefont calls down upon Marwood) in speaking of her: 'Nicht mehr meine irdische Tochter, schon halb ein Engel, was vermag der Segen eines wimmernden Vaters auf einen Geist, auf welchen alle Segen des Himmels herabströmen? Laß mir einen Strahl des Lichtes, welches dich über alles Menschliche so weit erhebt.'[59] When Lessing reviewed the play eleven years later (in number 13 of the *Hamburgische Dramaturgie*) he reiterated this imagery in his commentary, describing the final gesture of Sophie Friederike Hensel in the role of the dying Sara (a spasm of the fingers such as dying people sometimes exhibit) as 'das letzte Aufflattern eines verlöschenden Lichts; der jüngste Strahl einer untergehenden Sonne'.[60] The use of this sustained imagery structuring Sara's brief life is a self-conscious stylistic element in the conception of the play and forms a contrast with corresponding evocations of darkness and foreboding.[61] Together these recurring antitheses serve to present Sara as a character caught in a battle

---

55. Göbel, *Bild und Sprache*, p.79-87.

56. Göpfert, ii.11-12. 'From every childish feature there shone the rosy light of dawning reason and good nature'.

57. Göpfert, ii.62. 'Perhaps this ray of happiness is only appearing to me from afar and lulling me into the belief that it is drawing nearer because it is going to disappear suddenly into deepest darkness and plunge me back into a night whose terror I shall truly feel only because of this short period of light.'

58. Göpfert, ii.95.

59. Göpfert, ii.98. 'No longer my earthly daughter, but already half an angel, what can the blessing of a wimpering father do for a spirit upon whom heaven is pouring out all its blessings? Leave me a ray of that light which is raising you so high above all that is human.'

60. Göpfert, iv.294. 'The final flicker of a dying light; the last beam of a setting sun'.

61. Göbel, *Bild und Sprache*, p.87.

between good and evil and thus lead the spectator towards an intuitive actualisation of the crisis the play presents.[62] Metaphors of imprisonment occur in connection with Mellefont and the influence of Marwood, and Göbel also examines the frequency of fire, sea, and heart metaphors as they relate to the passions and feeling, as well as the prolific tear imagery. This extensive web of metaphor is consistent with the importance attached to it in contemporary semiotic accounts of poetic language that accord metaphor a central position. It is not considered an ornamental device, as in rhetorical teaching, but held to be the product of a natural cognitive operation, which therefore allows poetry to present its objects vividly to intuition.[63] Göbel concludes that embedded in prose, the metaphors and similes carry a more intense charge 'weil sie herausragen aus der sonst vorwiegend begrifflichen Rede'.[64] For Göbel, the poetry is clearly 'visible'!

From the foregoing it is clear that Lessing is structuring the language in order to achieve specific effects on the spectators. The poetic features just identified are designed to appeal directly to their intuitive cognition and to enable them to actualise the content of the speeches and the situation. A similar orientation is apparent in Lessing's conception of the relationship between the dramatist's text and the role of the actor. His view, at this time, is rather different from the one Diderot articulates in his dramatic theory. Whereas Diderot sees the actor as an autonomous artist, who breathes life into the writer's text and deserves a degree of creative freedom in the delivery of lines,[65] Lessing uses dramatic speech to control the actors' interpretation. In fact, he situates both actor and spectator in a similar relationship to the writer's text.

Lessing's early interest in acting is well known, and he published extracts he had translated from works on acting by François Riccoboni and Rémond de Sainte-Albine in the *Beiträge* (1750) and the *Theatralische Bibliothek* (1754).[66] At the end of the piece from Sainte-Albine, he announces that he hopes shortly to publish his own text on acting; however this never appeared and all that remains of it is the title with an outline and some notes.[67] In this fragment, Lessing divides stage gestures into two broad categories: controlled gestures and spontaneous gestures. The controlled gestures are those that can be learned and reproduced at

---

62. Göbel, *Bild und Sprache*, p.80. This theme is evoked in Waitwell's very first speech when he says of Mellefont, 'Böse Leute suchen immer das Dunkle, weil sie böse Leute sind' ('Wicked people always seek out the dark because they are wicked people'), Göpfert, ii.11.

63. Wellbery, *Lessing's Laocoon*, p.77-78.

64. Göbel, *Bild und Sprache*, p.93. 'Because they stand out from the otherwise predominantly abstract speech'.

65. DPV, x.102. Diderot writes, 'il y a des endroits qu'il faudrait presque abandonner à l'acteur. C'est à lui à disposer de la scène écrite.'

66. Göpfert, iii.751 and iv.816.

67. *Der Schauspieler: Ein Werk worinne die Grundsätze der ganzen körperlichen Beredsamkeit entwickelt werden*, Göpfert, iv.721-33 and iv.912.

will, whereas the spontaneous gestures presuppose 'eine gewisse Beschaf-
fenheit der Seele' ('a certain disposition of the soul') that causes the
speaker to produce them without understanding how.[68] One of the
striking features of the dialogue of *Miss Sara Sampson* is the presence of
numerous references to movement, facial expressions and gestures, including the shedding of tears.[69] These lines amount to stage directions
through which the characters prescribe controlled gestures for themselves
or others. Theodore Ziolkowski believes that it was only by writing action
into the text in this way that Lessing thought he could impose on the
actors the new, mimetic acting style he envisaged for the play, and he
points out that in the later plays, lines of this kind are largely replaced by
stage directions, as we now know them.[70] The references to gesture have
an oddly descriptive effect in the dialogue, and the spectators often find
themselves listening to characters giving a blow-by-blow account of the
movements and gestures being performed before them.[71]

Ziolkowski focuses his attention on Lessing's treatments of the controlled gestures. In a letter to Mendelssohn of 1757, Lessing explains his
technique for evoking the spontaneous gestures that he saw as the hallmark of the skilled actor. Taking as an example, the speech in which
Marwood threatens to murder Arabella (II.vii) he gives a clear account of
how the dramatist can use language to shape the actor's expression.[72]
Lessing says that if all he had required was that the actress allow her voice
to rise to the highest pitch of intensity, then he would have ended the
speech with the words 'verstellen, verzerren und verschwinden'. But since
he also wanted the words to be enhanced by eloquent facial expressions of
rage of a kind the actor cannot reproduce at will, he added more text in
an effort 'ihre Einbildungskraft durch mehr sinnliche Bilder zu erhitzen,
als freylich zu dem bloßen Ausdrucke meiner Gedanken nicht nötig
wären'.[73] The sensate images influence the actor's imagination and give
rise to the physiognomic responses that are the 'natural signs' of the emotion. The lines following the words 'verstellen, verzerren und verschwinden' read 'Ich will mit begieriger Hand Glied von Glied, Ader von Ader,
Nerve von Nerve lösen, und das kleinste derselben auch da noch nicht
aufhören zu schneiden und zu brennen, wenn es schon nichts mehr sein

68. Göpfert, iv.733.
69. Ziolkowski, 'Language and mimetic action', p.270-73. Ziolkowski argues that Lessing's intention in *Der Schauspieler* was to achieve a fusion of the theories of Rémond de
Sainte-Albine, who argued that actors act best by identifying with the emotions to be
portrayed, and François Riccoboni who maintained that the actor must remain detached
in order to have full control of his movements and expressions (p.265-67).
70. Ziolkowski, 'Language and mimetic action', p.270-73.
71. Ziolkowski, 'Language and mimetic action', p.270. See, for example, Sara's
description of Marwood's features in her penultimate speech in act IV, scene viii.
72. LM, xvii.120-22.
73. LM, xvii.121-22. 'In order to stimulate her imagination through more sensate
images than were strictly necessary for the simple expression of my thoughts.'

wird, als ein empfindungsloses Aas. Ich – ich werde wenigstens dabei empfinden, wie süß die Rache sei!'[74] The image this evokes both for the actor saying it and the spectator hearing it is certainly calculated to create an effect. The references to limbs, veins and nerves itemise the successive stages of dismemberment and build towards the climactic 'empfindungsloses Aas'; the verbs 'schneiden' and 'brennen' are strategically placed in mid-sentence and acquire additional force from pronunciation; and the adjective 'begierig' applied to the hand performing these terrifying gestures succinctly invests the deed with a horrific sadism. The predominance of nouns and verbs intensifies the impression of an act in progress. This concrete evocation of an act of cruel and brutal destruction reverses the commonplace of woman as a giver of life and turns Marwood into the anti-mother and literary descendant of Medea, the prototype of the role.[75] But although these sensate images would probably elicit striking physiognomic expression on the face of the actor, they push psychological plausibility and verbal *vraisemblance* beyond their limits, and their use confers on the dialogue the same premeditated and artistic quality as the figures to which Fénelon and La Motte object.

The passages of this type are not all this extreme. The second example Lessing cites is Mellefont's reaction to Sara's announcement of the arrival of her father's letter (III.v). Lessing concedes that the natural moment for Mellefont to seize the letter would have been following the first sentence of his fourth speech, 'Geschwind reißen Sie mich aus meiner Ungewißheit.'[76] But, argues Lessing, the additional lines, which postpone this moment until part-way through Sara's response, afford the actor a much better opportunity to express this impatience through subtle and eloquent acting. The rhetorical questions and the regretful reflection on the past which make up the remaining ten lines of Mellefont's speech allow time for the necessary images to arise in the mind of the actor. These images then translate into the involuntary facial expressions that communicate the fictional Mellefont's anxious anticipation to the spectator.[77] Such techniques, whether in the form of descriptions of controlled gestures or the use of sensate images designed to stimulate spontaneous ones, all freight the dialogue with extra language that in fact makes it difficult for the mimetic acting style to achieve its full effect.[78]

Whilst Lessing's text shows evidence of his interest in contemporary theories of poetry, it can also be seen to be still anchored in rhetorical theory. This is evident in the function of language itself and in the

74. Göpfert, ii.41. 'My eager hand will separate limb from limb, vein from vein, nerve from nerve and will not cease to cut and to burn even the smallest of them until nothing is left but a senseless carcass. I – I, at least will feel the sweetness of revenge.'
75. Lamport, 'Lessing and the "Bürgerliches Trauerspiel" ', p.15-16.
76. 'Quick, put me out of my uncertainty.'
77. LM, xvii.122.
78. In modern performances of the play, Lessing's text is cut and modified.

structure of the dialogue. Rempel has pointed out an interesting parallel in the way in which language is treated in both the early comedies and Lessing's first middle-class tragedy. He argues that in both forms, language can be seen to be shaped by the purpose of the genre itself and the effects that each seeks to bring about. Just as the language of the comedies exploits various kinds of wit to provoke the comic effect of laughter, so, in *Miss Sara Sampson*, the detailed articulation of the emotional suffering of the sympathetic characters seems intended simply to stimulate emotions of sadness in the audience and to make them weep.[79] In both cases, language is being consciously manipulated to bring about a certain reaction in the audience rather than create the illusion of the ordinary discourse of the characters. Rempel's analysis of the speech in *Miss Sara* has recently been reinforced by Stefan Trappen, who relates the prevalence of tears and references to weeping in that play to principles deriving from rhetorical theory about how sympathy may be evoked in the listener. He agrees that Lessing's text is deliberately designed to cause this response in the audience when the play is performed.[80]

Further evidence that, at this time, Lessing still conceptualised both language and acting within a rhetorical framework can be found in *Der Schauspieler*, the above-mentioned fragment on acting in which Lessing had planned to provide an account of all the principles of 'bodily eloquence'.[81] Lessing begins his introduction by defining eloquence in general as 'die Kunst einem andern seine Gedanken so mitzuteilen, daß sie einen verlangten Eindruck auf ihn machen'.[82] The art of organising thought to achieve the desired effect he calls 'Geistige Beredsamkeit' ('spiritual eloquence'); the art of communicating these organised thoughts in such a manner as to enhance that impression ('diese so geordneten Gedanken dem andern so mitzuteilen, dass jener Eindruck befördert wird') is 'körperliche Beredsamkeit' ('bodily eloquence'). In other words, although interested in mimetic acting, Lessing's conception of its function is still a traditional one. In drama, both the words and the gestures that support and reinforce them, are conceived in terms of a linear or face-to-face relationship with the audience upon whom they exert an immediate effect. This is the orientation of neo-classical tragedy.

Structurally too, *Miss Sara* has much in common with the traditional forms shaped by rhetorical methods. Jakob Mauvillon, a contemporary of Lessing, draws attention to the similarities in a review of *Emilia Galotti*

79. Rempel, *Tragödie und Komödie*, p.39-40. This was also an element in the wager between Lessing and Mendelssohn, which, according to legend, led to the composition of *Miss Sara* (Daunicht, *Die Entstehung des bürgerlichen Trauerspiels*, p.278).

80. Stefan Trappen, 'Von der persuasiven Rhetorik zur Ausdruckssprache: Beobachtungen zum Wandel der Formensprache in Lessings Trauerspielen', *Cahiers suisses de littérature comparée* 30 (1999), p.67-87 (p.74-75).

81. Göpfert, iv.732.

82. 'The art of communicating one's thoughts in such a way that they make the desired impression on the listener.'

that appeared in 1772. Looking back at Lessing's achievement in *Miss Sara*, Mauvillon concludes that despite the brilliant death scene ('ein wahres Meisterstück'), the dialogue as a whole contains too much declamation and too many long speeches, all of which make it quite unnatural. This, he says, 'ist die Manier der Franzosen, das ist gewiß; und es ist ebenso gewiß, daß sie von der Natur, die allein wahrhaftig gefallen kann, ganz weit entfernt ist'.[83] The judgement seems fairly accurate, for despite the use of prose and the obvious attempts to inject into the dialogue a sense of the give and take of ordinary discourse, the text is still organised in a recognisably traditional way.

There is extensive use of speeches embodying the kind of amplification that is typical of the neo-classical tradition. In such speeches, the essential point is made in a couple of sentences at the beginning, and the remaining lines elaborate on this idea in stylistically ingenious and affecting ways. A good example is Sir William's fourth speech in act I, scene i.[84] The ten-and-a-half-line speech opens with a command to Waitwell ('O schweig!') and a rhetorical question that explains it ('Zerfleischt nicht das Gegenwärtige mein Herz schon genug?').[85] This first rhetorical question is then repeated in another form. Following that, a new element is added: 'Ändre deine Sprache, wenn du mir einen Dienst tun willst',[86] and this thought is then developed through the remaining seven lines of the speech in a string of imperatives, showing Waitwell what he could have said, instead of what he did say. If Sir William were speaking to Waitwell alone, his speech would consist solely in sentences one, two and four, which occupy three lines of the entire speech. The remaining seven and a half lines simply elaborate on these basic elements in such a way as to allow various items of expository information to be communicated to the audience. Or consider Mellefont's thirteen-line speech to Sara on the nature of virtue.[87] The main point is contained within the two questions that open the speech and the penultimate sentence: 'Wie? muß der, welcher tugendhaft sein soll, keinen Fehler begangen haben? [...] Nein, Miß, Sie sind noch die tugendhafte Sara, die Sie vor meiner unglücklichen Bekanntschaft waren.'[88] The nine intervening lines develop the theme that one sin does not a sinner make. This is Lessing, speaking through Mellefont and talking past Sara to the audience, inviting them to reflect on how to define a virtuous person.

---

83. Jakob Mauvillon, *Rezension über 'Emilia Galotti'* (1772), Göpfert, ii.694. 'This is the French style, that is certain; equally certain is that such a style is far removed from nature, which alone can truly please.'

84. Göpfert, ii.11-12.

85. 'Be silent!' 'Is not the present situation enough to rend my heart in two?'

86. 'If you wish to be kind, speak of something else!'

87. Göpfert, ii.21.

88. 'What? Must the person who strives after virtue be someone who has never made a mistake? [...] No, Miss, you are still the same virtuous Sara you were before you were unlucky enough to meet me.'

This technique is pushed to the limit in act III, scene iii, in which Waitwell first brings Sir William's letter to Sara. Almost all Sara's speeches consist in lengthy amplifications of an idea or response expressed in the initial sentences, a phenomenon that provoked Gerhard Fricke to compare the dialogue in this scene to arias from an opera. He aptly characterises Sara's outpourings on the theme of guilt and forgiveness as 'lyrical'.[89] In their studies of Lessing's dramatic speech, both Staiger and Schröder maintain that these lengthy emotional speeches reflect the influence of traditional rhetorical doctrine, which fostered the idea that each quality and passion can be given discrete verbal form.[90] They might also be seen as illustrations of its teaching methods, which were largely based on amplification exercises.[91]

Lessing also relies quite heavily on narration in this play. *Miss Sara* obeys the unity of time and, like traditional tragedy, focuses on the moment of crisis (the arrival of Sir William and then Marwood at the inn where Sara and Mellefont are staying) and the ensuing catastrophe. As a result, there are numerous passages of narration that relate earlier events or recount scenes that happen off-stage. There are twenty-four such passages in the entire play, ranging from short sections of about four lines in length (for example, Norton's brief account of Marwood's departure from the inn[92]), to the major narration in act IV, scene viii – Marwood's telling of her own story – which occupies seventy-six lines in all, interrupted from time to time by Sara's interjections.[93] This passage is quite openly presented as a piece of narration, for Marwood, under the sobriquet of Lady Solmes, asks Sara 'Soll ich Ihnen die Geschichte der Marwood in wenig [!] Worten erzählen?'[94] Altogether these passages of narration represent between 10 and 11 per cent of the whole play. Although on the low side, this does fall within the normal range for a neoclassical work in the French tradition.[95] Typically, the majority of the

89. Gerhard Fricke, 'Bemerkungen zu Lessings *Freigeist* und *Miss Sara Sampson*', in *Festschrift für Josef Quint*, ed. Hugo Moser (Bonn 1964), p.83-120 (p.109-10). In an insightful and authoritative article, Heinrich Bornkamm argues that guilt and forgiveness are the main themes of Lessing's play and that his attitude to these conforms to the Lutheran one. 'Die innere Handlung in Lessings *Miss Sara Sampson*', *Euphorion* 51 (1957), p.385-96.

90. Staiger, 'Rasende Weiber', p.27-31; Schröder, *Sprache und Drama*, p.163-64.

91. Peter France, *Rhetoric and truth in France: Descartes to Diderot* (Oxford 1972), p.17-22.

92. Göpfert, ii.90.

93. Göpfert, ii.77-80.

94. 'Should I tell you Marwood's story in a few [!] brief words?'

95. Nina Ekstein, *Dramatic narrative: Racine's 'récits'* (New York, Bern, Frankfurt 1986), p.3-4. Ekstein invokes narratology theory to establish a minimal definition of narrative and then applies this to Racine's plays. Her study shows that 'the average percentage of the number of lines of *récit* in relation to the total number of lines in each play is 16.2%, varying from a low of 9.68% (*Alexandre*) to a high of 19.4% (*Bajazet*)'. Since Lessing's play is in prose, it is not so easy to arrive at as exact a calculation. Using Göpfert's edition, I simply counted the number of lines of prose for each narrative passage, calculated how many pages of text this represents and converted the result to a proportion of the whole.

narrative passages are found in the exposition or in the dénouement. In the case of *Miss Sara*, this is true for the exposition (eighty-two lines of narration in act I) but not for the dénouement. Act V has only forty lines of narration, less than the amounts in acts I, II and IV. The lesser amount in the final act is explained by the fact that the catastrophe (Sara's death) happens on stage, in view of the audience. What is related, through short pieces of narration supplied by Betty, Norton, Mellefont, and Marwood herself (in the form of the note which Mellefont reads aloud) is its cause, Marwood's poisoning of Sara and her subsequent flight to the coast with Arabella.

The longest piece of narration, Marwood's story (or history) occurs not in the dénouement, but in a scene of major importance, act IV, scene viii, where Marwood, whom Sara takes to be Lady Solmes, gives an account of her life and character intended to persuade Sara to abandon her claims to Mellefont. It is therefore a key element in the conflict of the play, the struggle between Marwood and Sara for possession of Mellefont. Since the audience has already heard other versions of this story from Mellefont and Norton (in I.iii and I.iv), and witnessed Marwood's unscrupulous attempts to win back Mellefont, they are in a good position to recognise the distortions of fact that she exploits in order to achieve her goal. The narration reinforces our impression of Marwood's duplicitous and calculating nature but also contributes to the action through the effect on Sara, the stage listener, by precipitating her collapse and the subsequent poisoning.

The second-longest piece of narration occurs in the exposition; it is Sara's account of her dream in act I, scene vii (twenty-six lines), a *récit* prepared by Betty's report of Sara's disturbed night in act I, scene iv (eleven lines). Sara's dream is the most obvious case of a lengthy narration intended primarily for the audience. It foreshadows the outcome of the play and Lessing uses it as a device to create a sense of fear and tragic inevitability.[96] Within this narration, he exploits numerous stylistic effects appropriate to prose (choice and placing of adjectives, word order, questions, exclamations, quotation of direct speech, building towards a climax, and so on) to enhance the interest for the listening audience.

There is some indication that Lessing is trying to motivate these narrative passages by making them part of the portrayal of character. Of the twenty-four narrative passages, Marwood narrates ten and is the main subject of four others. The extent of her participation as both narrating

I deliberately erred on the side of a conservative estimate. In an appendix to her main study, Ekstein provides statistics concerning the *récits* that figure in plays by Corneille and Molière.

96. In his essay 'Von den lateinischen Trauerspielen welche unter dem Namen des Seneca bekannt sind' of 1754, Lessing suggests that since contemporary sensibilities no longer tolerate the intervention of gods, dramatists treating the Hercules story could replace Juno's chorus-like role with a priest's dream. Göpfert, iv.88.

voice and as agent in the narratives of others is an indication of her active and manipulative role. Marwood uses language, including narrative, as a means of controlling those around her. None of the other characters can be compared with her in terms of their use of narration. Betty has two passages relating off-stage events and Waitwell has only one, evoking the young Sara. Mellefont has three narrations and Sir William and Norton each have two. All three of these characters deliver one short passage in the dénouement, relating an off-stage event. In addition, Norton and Sir William have one longer and more personal passage earlier in the play and Mellefont two of this kind. Norton and Mellefont both contribute accounts of Mellefont's past life and character; Sir William relates his role and, as he sees it, his responsibility in the elopement of Sara and Mellefont. These personal narratives give the audience some information about the past and also provide each character with an opportunity to express his sense of guilt in relation to the present. This distribution of narrative passages reflects the power structure in the play. The most active and self-determining character is the one who does most of the narrating. But however it is motivated, talking about the past takes up much more space in this play than it will in Lessing's mature works, which successfully shift the emphasis to action happening in the present.

*Miss Sara* also contains a number of passages that evoke possible future developments or hypothetical states of affairs, for example Sara's reaction to Mellefont's revelation that he plans to marry her in France, where she imagines her departure from England as a criminal and expresses her fear of exposing herself, as such, to the risks of a sea voyage (I.vii); or again her reflections on whether or not her father's life will be shortened as a result of her actions, the possible role her mother, had she lived, might have played in changing the course of events, and the life she and Mellefont will share with Sir William (IV.ii). Similarly Marwood predicts the (limited, she thinks) duration of Mellefont's passion for Sara (II.iii), describes how she will continue to pursue Mellefont (II.iii) and evokes in horrific terms the vengeful murder of Arabella (II.vii). These sections, which are all developed at some length (they range from ten lines to more than twenty), resemble narrative, in that they evoke situations or actions beyond the immediate stage world. But their virtual character (they deal only with possibilities, not facts or things presented as facts) puts them in a category apart. They serve above all to reveal character by allowing the audience into the inner mental world of the *dramatis personae*. The expression of their hopes and anxieties intensifies the audience's feelings of fear, horror or loss through comparison of this universe of the mind with the events that actually occur. In terms of Lessing's aims, they all afford ample opportunity for the actors to display their skills.

The play also includes numerous asides. Traditionally, asides were more typical of comedy than of tragedy, because of their overtly 'theatrical' nature and also because they are inconsistent with the dignity of tragic characters. In *Miss Sara*, sixteen lines in all are preceded by the direction 'bei Seite', eleven of them spoken by Marwood, four by Mellefont and one by Waitwell. This distribution makes clear that Lessing uses them primarily as a means of underscoring the duplicity of certain *dramatis personae*, especially Marwood. Since she adopts the role of actress within the action of the play, the use of asides may have seemed to Lessing an appropriate technique for expressing character; nevertheless, they draw attention to the artifice of the representation.

Thus, despite Lessing's use of prose, the dialogue in *Miss Sara* rests upon a conception of the dramatic text as artistry, exploiting language that addresses the audience. Whilst the factors shaping the form of Lessing's dramatic speech are varied and complex, the fact remains that language is still the primordial sign, dedicated to giving the inner world of the characters verbal form and often duplicating the natural signs of facial expression and physical gesture. All that happens still happens as language, and that language is still literary and 'poetic', even though it is cast in prose.

The treatment of dramatic speech in *Philotas*, in terms of both structure and expression, is very much like that in *Miss Sara Sampson*, although without some of its more flagrant weaknesses. There are very few stage directions in the dialogue, in comparison with *Miss Sara Sampson*, which is probably an indication that Lessing expected the play to be read rather than performed.[97] As in *Miss Sara*, narrative and quasi-lyrical or self-revelatory passages dominate the dialogue, especially in the speeches of Philotas. There are two main narratives, both of which relate exchanges that would have been dramatically interesting, had Lessing chosen to make them scenes in the play. Philotas's long narrative in scene ii describes his efforts to persuade his unwilling father to let him go into battle, his restless anticipation of the event and his subsequent capture. His account even includes quotations of direct speech, which prompts the thought that Victor Hugo was to articulate seventy years later in the preface to *Cromwell*, 'mais conduisez-nous donc là-bas! On s'y doit bien amuser, cela doit être beau à voir!'[98] Showing this particular scene could

97. Written in 1758 and published anonymously in 1759, *Philotas* was not performed until 1774, Göpfert, ii.697.

98. Victor Hugo, 'Préface de Cromwell', *Théâtre complet*, ed. Roland Purnal, J.-J. Thierry and Josette Mélèze, 2 vols (Paris 1963), i.428. Many critics interpret Lessing's enigmatic play as a satirical attack on French neo-classical tragedy. Seen in this light, his decision to respect the unities of time and place, which are among the major conventions of that style, makes sense. See Helmut Schneider, 'Aufklärung der Tragödie: Lessings *Philotas*', in *Horizonte: Festschrift für Herbert Lehnert zum 65. Geburtstag*, ed. Hannelore Mundt, Egon Schwarz and William J. Lillyman (Tübingen 1990), p.10-39 (p.31); Robert E. Norton, '"Ein bitteres Gelächter": tragic and comic elements in Lessing's *Philotas*', *Deutsche Vierteljahrsschrift für Literaturwissenschaft und Geistesgeschichte* 66:3 (1992), p.450-65 (p.462-63). Julia Gädeke Schmidt argues that *Philotas* is a parody of Racine's *Alexandre le Grand*, which Gottsched had cited as a model: *Lessings Philotas: Ästhetisches Experiment mit satirischer Wirkungsabsicht* (New York, Bern, Frankfurt, Paris 1988), p.90 and following. Gisbert Ter-Nedden

only have been accomplished by violating the unity of place, to which the play, as it exists, conforms. But Strato's narrative at the beginning of scene viii, in which he relates what happened when he went to retrieve Philotas's sword from his captor and which is made up largely of the soldier's own words, could have been shown on the stage by summoning the soldier to the tent where Philotas is being held. Lessing prefers to render it as narrative, perhaps because it might have been pushing the limits of *vraisemblance* to contrive to present this character too as a father, as all the others are.[99] Both *récits* are effective as narrative in that they evoke a vivid impression of the scene, and both concern Philotas either directly or indirectly. As stage dialogue, though, they are weak and their length suggests epic rather than dramatic form.

The significance of the dramatic situation is again reinforced through the use of imagery. The main metaphors discussed by Göbel are those relating to fire, which characterise the volatile emotions of the main figure, and the plant metaphors, which throw into relief the adolescence of the protagonist and emphasise the transition between the promise of youth and the fulfilment of adulthood.[100] There are also metaphors drawing on the imagery of *Herz* and *Tränen* and a number of similes such as that of the balance used by Aridäus.[101] These figures are a vivid way of summing up the existing situation in a form adapted to assimilation by intuitive cognition. Göbel notes similarities in the way in which imagery is exploited in both *Miss Sara* and *Philotas* and observes that although, in both plays, it helps to communicate inner action and emotions effectively, its use also interrupts the forward movement of the drama and introduces moments of reflection that are a feature of epic style.[102] Göbel concludes that even though Lessing avoids such devices as the epic simile, his writing still owes much to the model of epic poetry.[103]

The use of language in *Philotas* does not therefore represent any significant advance over Lessing's earlier techniques. Whilst the emphasis on monologue could be seen to fulfil an artistic function in a work whose protagonist is characterised by his inability to listen to and absorb the reasoning of others, Lessing's extensive reliance on this technique makes the play as a whole less like drama. This is particularly striking in the opening scene, a monologue, which leaves the expository function to a single speaker. There are no explicit stage directions prescribing action for Philotas as he speaks, although the words he utters draw attention to his

maintains that Lessing's model was Sophocles's *Ajax*: *Lessings Trauerspiele: der Ursprung des modernen Dramas aus dem Geist der Kritik* (Stuttgart 1986), p.114-63.

99. Schneider points out that all the dialogue scenes take place between Philotas and a 'father' substitute: 'Aufklärung der Tragödie', p.19.

100. Göbel, *Bild und Sprache*, p.101-103.

101. Göpfert, ii.108.

102. Göbel, *Bild und Sprache*, p.112-16.

103. Göbel, *Bild und Sprache*, p.113.

wound and to the tent in which he finds himself, things the audience or reader needs to notice. Although the pace and tone are varied by the use of numerous exclamations, a couple of rhetorical questions and some pauses, the information that is included for the sake of the audience does tend to stand out. Peter Burgard, who notes that Philotas literally speaks to himself in this speech ('Schmeichle dir nur, Philotas!'), sees it as presenting an important theme of the play by depicting a personality divided against itself.[104] In performance, however, an audience would probably feel as if Philotas were speaking directly to them, like a narrator, telling them his story and justifying himself to them.

Overall, Lessing's practice in both plays suggests that he views dramatic dialogue not from the perspective of tragedy considered as performing art, but from that of tragedy as a genre of literature. Because there is a genre named tragedy, there is also a 'tragische Sprache' (a 'tragic language'), a particular way of writing that is appropriate to the form, more or less regardless of who the characters are.[105] Whilst it is true that Lessing wanted to reform what he saw as the excesses of the French tragic manner, he does not yet have a coherent view of an alternative theatrical code with a different role for dramatic speech. He affirms the centrality of language in the 1757 letter to Mendelssohn, where he remarks that even if Mendelssohn could prove to him, with mathematical certainty, that the passages he had criticised in *Miss Sara* were out of place, he still would not expunge them, 'wenigstens so lange nicht, als noch immer mehr Leute Trauerspiele lesen, als vorstellen sehen'.[106]

At the same time, Lessing does write into these two tragedies scenes that seem to me to conform to Diderot's idea of a stage *tableau*. The scene that occupies what is technically the centre of *Miss Sara* is act III, scene iv.[107] Sara is alone on stage. The stage directions indicate that she sits down at a table to write. Her intention is to pen a reply to her father's letter of forgiveness (received in the previous scene), and as she tries to find the best words to express her feelings, she meditates, writes, crosses out her words, thinks again and muses aloud about the act of writing itself and the problem of how to give her thoughts and feelings appropriate verbal form:

Ja, die Feder hab' ich in der Hand. – Weiß ich aber auch schon, was ich schreiben soll? Was ich denke; was ich empfinde. – Und was denkt man denn,

104. Peter Burgard, 'Lessing's tragic topography: the rejection of society and its spatial metaphor in *Philotas*', *Deutsche Vierteljahrsschrift für Literaturwissenschaft und Geistesgeschichte* 61:3 (1987), p.441-56 (p.445). 'Go on, Philotas; flatter yourself!'

105. Lamport notes that in *Miss Sara Sampson*, 'Language is not used as a means of differentiating between the characters: they all speak in the same manner, masters and servants, parents and children', *Lessing and the drama*, p.86.

106. LM, xvii.117. 'At least, not as long as there are more people who read tragedies than see them performed'.

107. It is the fourth scene of seven in act III. It is preceded by a total of twenty scenes and followed by a total of twenty-three.

wenn sich in einem Augenblicke tausend Gedanken durchkreuzen? Und was empfindet man denn, wenn das Herz, vor lauter Empfinden, in einer tiefen Betäubung liegt? – Ich muß doch schreiben – Ich führe ja die Feder nicht das erste Mal.[108]

Sara's situation, expressed visually through the act of writing, can be taken as an image for what eighteenth-century semiotics posits as the primary cultural gesture, that of conferring signs on human thought and experience. Sara and the other morally good characters all wrestle with the problem of giving adequate semiotic expression to their experience and of finding the right signs to name their thoughts and responses so as to communicate them to others.[109] It is their failure to do this in time that precipitates the tragedy. They are thwarted by a character who knows how to manipulate the gap between signifier and signified, and is ready to exploit the arbitrary nature of verbal signs to gain power over others. Marwood's 'history' or 'story' is largely a lie, and indeed, Sara finally dismisses it as 'einen blendenden Roman' ('a dazzling novel').[110] The play thus addresses the issue of the dual nature of the linguistic sign, seen by eighteenth-century thinkers as both an instrument permitting the progress of knowledge and reason, and also as a source of error, when human beings allow themselves to be distracted by words in themselves, and fail to attend to the ideas they signify.[111] In *Miss Sara*, the victory goes to the forces of ideology and the figure Fritz Brüggemann characterises as 'der typische politische Mensch der vorbürgerlichen Zeit'.[112] The letter-writing scene thus articulates, in word and image, a central theme of the play and it would, I think, be accurate to call it a *tableau*. It is interesting to note that although Sara's speech is long (too long), it is among the

108. Göpfert, ii.55. 'So, I have the pen in my hand. – But do I know yet what I should write? What I think; what I feel? – And what can one think when one is besieged, in a single moment, by a thousand different thoughts? And what can one feel, when one's heart turns numb, under the sheer weight of sensation itself? – But I must write. – It's not as though I've never picked up a pen before.'

109. Waitwell is often at a loss to translate his feelings into language: 'Wo soll ich die Worten finden, die ich schon so lange suche?' ('Where am I to find the words I have been looking for in vain?') (Göpfert, ii.94).

110. Göpfert, ii.82.

111. Wellbery, *Lessing's Laocoon*, p.36-38. Schröder characterises these two relationships with language this way: 'Wahrheit ist nachahmende, Lüge nachgeahmte Sprache. [...] beide stehen die Worte als willkürliche Zeichen zu Gebote' (*Sprache und Drama*, p.163-65). ('Truth is speech which imitates; lies are speech that is imitated. [...] both exploit words as arbitrary signs.') However, I question Schröder's assertion that the morally good characters are blind to the problematic nature of linguistic signs, and that this is what causes their downfall (p.166).

112. Fritz Brüggemann, 'Lessings Bürgerdramen und der Subjektivismus als Problem', in *Gotthold Ephraim Lessing*, ed. G. and S. Bauer (Darmstadt 1968), p.83-126 (p.84). This article was first published in the *Jahrbuch des freien deutschen Hochstifts* (1926), p.69-110. 'The typical political individual of the pre-bourgeois age'.

most natural in the play for tone; this might be because Lessing identified with it, or because he visualised it.[113]

*Philotas* concludes with a powerful *tableau* for which the audience has been prepared by the protagonist himself, who announces it two scenes earlier: 'es muß ein trefflicher, ein großer Anblick sein: ein Jüngling gestreckt auf den Boden, das Schwerd in der Brust!'[114] This great and wonderful spectacle (Lessing intends the adjectives ironically) is then realised in scene viii, where, as a result of his rejection of genuine dialogue and an extraordinary effort of the imagination, Philotas succeeds in turning himself into the subject of this picture and an image of the heroic tragedy that Lessing rejects. 'Ein wunderbarer Jüngling', comments Strato; 'Beweine ihn nur!', adds Aridäus, and in a final question that could be addressed to the audience, he asks 'Glaubt ihr Menschen, daß man es nicht satt wird?', the 'es' meaning the inhuman role he is forced to play as statesman in international power politics or, perhaps also, the French neo-classical tragic model that dominated the German stage.[115] Philotas dies because he refuses to engage in dialogue with others, choosing instead to express himself through the sword, the tool of those who privilege might over negotiation, personal glory above peace. The sword must rule, says Philotas, because in deciding the fates of men, it expresses the will of the gods:

Die Götter aber, du weißt es, König, sprechen ihr Urteil durch das Schwerd des Tapfersten! Laß uns den blutigen Spruch aushören! Warum wollen wir uns klein-mütig von diesem höchsten Gerichte wieder zu den niedrigern wenden? Sind uns-ere Fäuste schon so müde, daß die geschmeidige Zunge sie ablösen müsse?[116]

Seduced by an image, Philotas loses touch with others and with the world around him; his self-inflicted death is also a form of self-gratification.

The concluding *tableau* from *Philotas*, centred on a death-dealing sword, and the letter scene from *Miss Sara*, in which the main character wields a pen, therefore offer a pair of contrasting and yet complementary images that link the two works, and express Lessing's belief in the importance of

---

113. In the essay *Über eine zeitige Aufgabe*, Lessing remarks about himself, 'Nur Schade, daß ich nicht nachdenken kann, ohne mit der Feder in der Hand!' ('What a pity that I cannot think things over without a pen in my hand!') (Göpfert, viii.549). For a different perspective on the role of letters in this play, see Steven R. Cerf, '*Miss Sara Sampson* and *Clarissa*: the use of epistolary devices in Lessing's drama', in *Theatrum mundi: essays on German drama and German literature*, ed. Edward R. Haymes (Munich 1980), p.22-30.

114. Göpfert, ii.118-19. 'It must be a splendid, a mighty spectacle: a young man stretched out on the ground with a sword through his breast!'

115. 'A wondrous young man.' 'Just weep for him.' 'Do you people think that one doesn't get tired of it?' Schneider argues that the phrase 'ihr Menschen' shows that the last line includes the audience.

116. Göpfert, ii.120. 'The gods, as you know, O King, pronounce their judgement through the sword of the most fearless! Let us hear the bloody ruling! Why turn timidly from this, the highest tribune to a lesser one? Are our fists already so tired that they must be relieved by the honeyed tongue?'

language as an instrument of culture. The pen and the sword symbolise the age and evoke the opposition between the traditional feudal regime that, in the last analysis, was still prepared to defend its privileges by the sword, and the Enlightenment writers, who strove to bring about a new order through the judicious use of their pens. Sara's question – 'Weiß ich aber auch schon, was ich schreiben soll?'[117] – also seems to sum up quite well the feeling behind Lessing's experiments in tragedy from this decade. One answer appears to have come from the theatre writings of Diderot, a writer to whose ideas Lessing's existing interest in the use of prose, natural acting and stage pictures, must have made him singularly receptive.

117. 'But do I know yet what I should write?'

# 6. Illusion, signs and speech in Lessing's dramatic theory and criticism from the *Briefwechsel* to the *Hamburgische Dramaturgie*

SHORTLY before Diderot began to draft *Le Fils naturel*, Lessing became engaged in a correspondence on the subject of tragedy with his friends Friedrich Nicolai and Moses Mendelssohn. The exchange of letters unfolded between July 1756 and May 1757, and its importance both for the insights it provides into Lessing's developing theory of sympathy (*Mitleid*) and for the unique glimpse it affords of a turning point in the history of German aesthetics is well recognised. But it would also to be true to say that criticism has not yet reached a consensus on the matter of its interpretation.[1] The difficulties stem in part from the fact that the three participants approach the issues from different angles and with different aims.[2] Furthermore, the positions they elaborate are all to a certain extent transitional, combining both progressive and traditional elements. Here, this correspondence will be considered from the perspective of two specific questions: what do these letters reveal about Lessing's conceptualisation of the way in which drama exerts an effect upon its audience, and what is the relative importance, for all three correspondents, of two of the defining elements in Diderot's approach to theatre, illusion and the idea of the playwright as spectator?

The debate was triggered by Nicolai's summary of his essay, entitled *Abhandlung vom Trauerspiele*, which he sets out in his letter to Lessing of 31 August 1756.[3] Nicolai's conception of tragedy is progressive in as far as it builds on the new approaches to art fostered by Dubos's emphasis on the role of emotion. Nicolai rejects the Aristotelian view of catharsis and argues that the purpose of tragedy is to stimulate passions in the spectator, not to purge them or to fulfil a moral goal.[4] This aspect of Nicolai's theory has implications primarily for what one might call story material; it affects how the playwright handles plot and character. What is clear

---

1. Michelsen, 'Die Erregung des Mitleids', p.108; Jost Schillemeit, 'Lessings und Mendelssohns Differenz. Zum Briefwechsel über das Trauerspiel', in *Digressionen: Wege zur Aufklärung: Festgabe für Peter Michelsen*, ed. Gotthardt Frühsorge, Klaus Manger and Friedrich Strack (Heidelberg 1984), p.79-92 (p.79). See also Lessing *et al.*, *Briefwechsel über das Trauerspiel*, ed. Schulte-Sasse.

2. Schillemeit, 'Lessings und Mendelssohns Differenz', p.84-85.

3. Nicolai's essay was published in the *Bibliothek der schönen Wissenschaften und der freyen Künste* in 1757. The correspondence was first published in the 1794 edition of Lessing's *Sämtliche Schriften* (Göpfert, iv.831).

4. Michelsen, 'Die Erregung des Mitleids', p.110-11.

from Nicolai's letter, though, is that in terms of tragedy viewed as a system of theatrical signs, he envisages no real change. He notes, for example, that although it is not necessary that the unities of time and place be strictly observed, it is best to leave both time and place somewhat vague ('Zeit und Ort nicht allzu genau zu bestimmen').[5] In other words, the evocation of milieu, an element that would be greatly enhanced at the level of performance through the visual sign systems of costume and décor, is underplayed. As far as linguistic expression goes, Nicolai is again traditional; he says that his theory presupposes a poet who thinks nobly ('edel denke') and that the writer must also express himself in a manner that is noble, sensate and beautiful ('edel, sinnlich und schön').[6] Language, in Nicolai's theory, is still conceived as the voice of the poet and style is determined by genre: it is the language of tragedy. Thus, although progressive in terms of the role it ascribes to feelings and to moral intent, Nicolai's theory does not appear to represent any advance in terms of the semiotics of performance.

Mendelssohn's views are very different from Nicolai's in this respect. In his letter of November 1756, in connection with remarks on the emotion of terror, he states that he considers it essential to understand the conflict between, specifically, 'theatrical illusion' and symbolic cognition. In this, and in his subsequent comments on illusion, it becomes increasingly clear that what Mendelssohn means by the term 'illusion' is the combined, simultaneous impact on the spectator as a viewer of the visual and auditory elements of the play in performance. In fact, Mendelssohn's understanding of theatrical illusion in these letters corresponds to the one developing in France.

In the November letter, Mendelssohn offers two examples to illustrate his contention that feelings of terror can be pleasurable for the spectator, even when no feeling of sympathy is present. These are the painted representation of a snake and the appearance of a ghost on stage, the latter being a reference to an example Lessing had used earlier.[7] Mendelssohn takes as his starting point examples that depend on the sense of sight and whose power to affect the audience will be greater the closer the phenomena come to approximating the viewer's own experience or (in the case of the ghost) their beliefs about human experience. Further clarification relating to the snake example is provided in the notes entitled *Von der Illusion*. In these notes, Mendelssohn dismisses the (supposedly) Aristotelian explanation of the pleasure caused by the image of a snake. According to this theory, the feeling of pleasure arises from the realisation that the snake is not alive and therefore has no power to harm. Mendelssohn disagrees; he believes that the pleasure arises from the intui-

---

5. Göpfert, iv.157.
6. Göpfert, iv.158.
7. Göpfert, iv.162.

tive realisation that the painted image of the snake successfully captures the original on which it was modelled (that 'das Urbild getroffen sei').[8] For Mendelssohn, whose approach to these questions is driven by his over-riding interest in the sources of aesthetic pleasure (as opposed to Lessing's teleological and ethical approach to tragedy), the pleasure derived from art rests on the virtually simultaneous perception that the art object successfully evokes its model but that it is not the 'Urbild selbst'.[9] He describes this effect as one of deception ('Betrug'), stating that 'Wenn eine Nachahmung so viel ähnliches mit dem Urbilde hat, daß sich unsere Sinne wenigstens einen Augenblick bereden können, das Urbild selbst zu sehen, so nenne ich diesen Betrug eine ästhetische Illusion.'[10] As we have seen, this is the definition of illusion disseminated in the writings of Roger de Piles to explain the power of painting. Mendelssohn is aligning what he means by theatrical illusion with the illusion created by art; he is thinking of tragedy as visual representation, as well as in literary terms, as plot and character. Lessing however, considers illusion irrelevant to their discussion. He concludes his long letter of 18 December 1756 with the assertion, supported by a reference to Aristotle's *Poetics*, that the doctrine of illusion does not concern the dramatic poet and that the representation of a play is not the task of literature but of a different art.[11] He argues that successful tragedy must be able to achieve its full effect on the reader, without actors and stage representation, and that to do this, tragedy has no more need of illusion than any other story ('jede andere Geschichte'). Lessing's observations suggest two things. First, the word 'illusion', used in a theatrical context, still has for Lessing the sense that it did in the previous century, when it served to describe the 'spectacular' effects associated with opera and stage machinery; it does not mean a total effect that includes *vraisemblance* and arises from the combined effect of subject matter and theatrical performance.[12] Secondly, Lessing does not view tragedy as being primarily an art intended for stage representation and he does not believe that its form is determined, in any essential way, by that consideration. The fact that tragedy may be performed is not funda-mental to the manner in which the writer conceives the work. For Lessing, the dramatist's concerns should be focused on the emotional and moral goal of tragedy, the creation of sympathy. His aim is to achieve a satisfying level of *vraisemblance*, the likely probability inhering in

8. Göpfert, iv.836. The example of the image of a snake is a reference to an argument used by Batteux in *Les Beaux-Arts réduits à un même principe* (1746) which Mendelssohn rejects: Schillemeit, 'Lessings und Mendelssohns Differenz', p.90, n.21.

9. Göpfert, iv.835. Schillemeit, 'Lessings und Mendelssohns Differenz', p.87 and p.89.

10. Göpfert, iv.835. 'When an imitation so closely resembles its original that our senses are momentarily persuaded that they see the original itself, I call this deception an aes-thetic illusion.'

11. Göpfert, iv.195.

12. Hobson, *The Object of art*, p.32-36.

characters and events and fully controlled by the writer: that is, tragedy as a form of literature, like 'jede andere *Geschichte*' (emphasis added).

This basic orientation towards tragedy as literature is equally evident in the arguments he presents about admiration. Lessing differentiates between tragedy and the epic in terms of the principal emotion that each seeks to arouse (sympathy in the case of tragedy, admiration in the case of the epic) and the corresponding type of hero that each genre typically treats.[13] He maintains that it is crucial not to confuse different kinds of poem but to maintain the appropriate boundaries between genres. In his letter of January 1757, Mendelssohn takes issue quite specifically with Lessing's point about different kinds of poem and he rejects Lessing's way of defining forms. He appeals to the progress made over the previous century in terms of the understanding of natural phenomena, and he points out that nature does not create watertight boundaries between them. Art, he argues, should follow nature in this matter. To the traditional classifications in terms of genres (based, he says, simply upon custom, the habits of language and the authority of the Ancients) Mendelssohn opposes the claims of reason. Reason tells us that in the selection of an appropriate subject for tragedy, the deciding factor should be that the action in question '*nur durch die lebendige Vorstellung eines größern Grades der Nachahmung fähig ist*' (Mendelssohn's emphasis).[14] It is enough, believes Mendelssohn, for the subject to be suitable material for 'live representation'. He then refers Lessing to the notes he has included on aesthetic illusion and adds that the only criterion for admitting a given passion into tragedy is that the imitated passion convincingly resembles the original ('die nachgeahmte Leidenschaft überzeugen kann, daß die Nachahmung dem Urbilde ähnlich sei').[15] This seems to me to be one of the key passages from these letters. Mendelssohn here quite consciously attacks the traditional manner of classifying tragedy within the existing system of literary genres and proposes instead a definition based on the fact that tragedy is, in some way that is essential to it, a performing art, a 'lebendige Vorstellung'. He wants to define tragedy not in terms of the kind of story that it is, but in terms of the kind of imitation that it is, and this includes stage representation. He clearly sees that he and Lessing are using the word 'illusion' in different ways and he concludes his letter by drawing attention to this misunderstanding. Moreover, in trying to pinpoint where they differ, he alludes to the opera, the theatrical genre previously

13. Göpfert, iv.186.
14. Göpfert, iv.196. 'Is capable of a higher level of imitation only through live representation'.
15. In his essay entitled *Von der Illusion*, Mendelssohn returns to Lessing's point that tragedy can achieve its full effect when read and states that only those readers able to assess whether the written text is so constituted that the play would be capable of this higher level of imitation in live representation can dispense with the performance experience. Göpfert, iv.836.

thought of as specialising in illusions. Mendelssohn stresses that by the term 'illusion' he does not mean the use of the sumptuous sets typical of the opera, which, he agrees, do not belong in tragedy; and he adds that if the use of the word 'illusion' to identify the effect that he, Mendelssohn, is talking about is inappropriate in terms of normal usage, Lessing should simply give the effect a different name.[16] Thus, for Mendelssohn, the term 'theatrical illusion' means the total effect that would be created by the play as performed, with all its sign systems working together. Mendelssohn does not use the language of semiotics in these letters, but his comment that stage scenery should never draw attention to its own beauty and never disrupt illusion through glaring contradictions shows that he is thinking in terms of the harmonious interplay of all the elements involved.[17]

Further evidence of the progressive nature of Mendelssohn's view emerges from one of the literary examples he gives. Throughout the letters, there are numerous references, both explicit and implicit, to other works.[18] Many of these allusions are to plays (ancient, classical and modern), but there are two interesting exceptions in Mendelssohn's long letter of early December, where he makes reference to episodes from novels by Richardson, one in *Clarissa* (1747-1748) and one in *The History of Sir Charles Grandison* (1753-1754). Richardson's novels, which offer numerous examples of scenes in which natural-sounding speech is allied to descriptions of gesture and movement in such a way as to create an illusion for the eye of the mind, inspired other thinkers on drama, including Diderot. In Mendelssohn's brief evocations of both these scenes he puts the emphasis on the total effect created, including the visual

16. Göpfert, iv.200.

17. Hasselbeck points out that Mendelssohn introduces the idea of signs into his discussion of these issues in a work written shortly after the exchange of letters, his *Betrachtungen über die Quellen und die Verbindungen der schönen Künste und Wissenschaften* (1757). Here he recommends to poets the choice of 'Ausdrücke, die das Bezeichnete deutlicher empfinden lassen, als das Zeichen. Hierdurch wird der Vortrag lebendig und anschauend, und die bezeichnete Gegenstände unsern Sinnen gleichsam unmittelbar vorgestellt' ('expressions which allow the signified to be felt more strongly than the signs. In this way, the representation becomes lively and vivid and at the same time, the signified objects are presented directly to our senses'). In the expanded version of the *Betrachtungen* published in 1761, Mendelssohn writes that 'die untern Seelenkräfte werden getäuscht, indem sie öfters der Zeichen vergessen, und der Sache selbst ansichtig zu werden glauben' ('the lower faculties are deceived, in that they often forget the presence of the signs and believe they are looking at the thing itself'). Quoted in Hasselbeck, *Illusion und Fiktion*, p.102.

18. The letters on tragedy were not written with publication in mind, and the correspondents often make elliptical reference to views they have expressed elsewhere, to shared reading material and so on. Both Michelsen and Schillemeit have demonstrated the importance of pursuing these intertextual allusions in order to arrive at an accurate analysis of the exchange. Their work has revealed the role played by Dubos's *Réflexions* in Nicolai's theory of tragedy, as well as the importance of other works by Mendelssohn (notably his *Briefe über die Empfindungen*, 1755, and his *Sendschreiben*, 1756, on Rousseau's critique of culture) as sources of Lessing's definition of sympathy. Michelsen, 'Die Erregung des Mitleids', p.118-19; Schillemeit, 'Lessings und Mendelssohns Differenz', p.81.

dimension. The moments to which he alludes are presented as things seen. The scene from *Sir Charles Grandison* is particularly illuminating, however, and is introduced specifically in connection with the question of imitation. Mendelssohn takes up Lessing's assertion that the poet must make the hero feel his misfortune if the audience is to be moved. Mendelssohn agrees with the main point, but insists that Lessing is wrong to believe that this can be accomplished merely through the narration of the pressing circumstances, such as Lessing gives in the story of the beggar, which he uses to demonstrate what he means. According to Mendelssohn, narration is not sensate enough and the dramatist should always try to convince the audience of the imminent danger threatening the hero and those around him by appealing to their senses in a different way. To illustrate this argument, he refers to the scene from *Grandison* where the hero calls at the home of Hargrave, who has challenged him to a duel.[19] Mendelssohn's description of the moment he has in mind focuses not on what is said, but on Grandison's demeanour, and the contrast between his deportment and the situation in which he finds himself: 'Wie erstaunet man aber, als Grandison selbst mit seiner gewöhnlichen Munterkeit erscheint, und den größten Verdruß, der ihm hatte begegnen können, mit mehr als gleichgültigen Augen ansiehet!'[20] From Mendelssohn's use of the words 'erscheint' and 'Munterkeit' it is clear that he is referring to a passage from a document entitled '*The PAPER*', included in a letter from Harriet Byron to Lucy Selby.[21] This document, which was penned by Henry Cotes, a young man described in the novel as 'honest, discreet, and one of the swiftest short-hand writers of the age', is a verbatim transcription of the conversation that transpires between Hargrave, his associates and Sir Charles.[22] Hargrave's friend, Bagenhall, has arranged for Cotes to be hidden in a large closet from where he can hear and record what is going on. It turns out that Cotes can also see what is taking place. When Sir Charles is summoned into the room, Cotes notes: 'And then [as I saw through a knot-hole, that I just then, hunting for a crack in the wainscot-partition, discovered] Sir Charles entered; and I saw, that he looked very sedate and chearful; and he had his sword by his side, though in a morning-dress.'[23] Almost the entire conversation that follows is reported in the form of direct speech, set out as in a play, beside the

19. Samuel Richardson, *The History of Sir Charles Grandison*, ed. Jocelyn Harris, 3 vols (London, New York, Toronto 1972), i.248. This scene is the culmination of an episode that begins on p.116 with Hargrave's abduction of Harriet Byron from a costume ball.

20. Göpfert, iv.184. 'How amazed the reader is when Grandison himself appears in his usual cheerful mood and so calmly faces up to what could have been the worst moment of his life.'

21. Richardson, *Grandison*, i.247-68.

22. Richardson, *Grandison*, i.267. The readers and the characters (except for Grandison, though the readers do not know this) all expect the scene to end in a duel. Bagenhall arranges for the secret transcription of the conversation as a legal precaution.

23. Richardson, *Grandison*, i.248.

names of the characters. From time to time, the note-taker also records visual impressions, the movements and gestures of the participants, and there is one section that is entirely made up of commentary on movement and attitude, with no speech at all. Sir Charles has agreed to accompany Hargrave into the garden alone. They leave the room and Cotes is let out of his closet. Then, along with Bagenhall, Jordan and Merceda, he watches through the window the scene that unfolds between the other two men in the garden below. They are too far away for their words to be heard, so Cotes simply describes in detail their movements and gestures as Sir Charles persuades Hargrave to lower his sword and return to the house. This is the most intense moment of the entire episode and it is conveyed solely through the visual description of the action as seen from the perspective of the observers at the window. This particular part of the scene is an example of teichoscopy, the reporting of an event taking place 'out of sight' of the reader or spectator by a character whose vantage point allows him or her to observe it.[24] As Sir Charles and Hargrave return to the room, Cotes goes back into his closet and continues to record the conversation. This situation, Cotes recording what he sees and hears, the words and the actions of the characters exactly as they happen, is yet another instance of the topos of the hidden spectator. Particularly suggestive is the emphasis it throws on the idea of recording something that is happening in present time.

Mendelssohn's allusion to this passage in the context of a discussion of imitation shows that the scene must have impressed itself on his mind. It obviously coincides with the view of illusion he presents in the letters to Lessing, and can be seen to exemplify the position of the playwright as he now thinks of it. Cotes, the unseen non-participant, transcribing what is (within the framework of Richardson's novel) an actual event, is a metaphor for the playwright creating an 'imitation' of nature. Cotes is another figure like the hidden spectators evoked by French dramatists, though in their version the spectator is merely a viewer, not a writer as well. Mendelssohn's theatrical aesthetic, like theirs, posits the presence of both the recipient and the writer as non-participating viewers. Although Mendelssohn merely alludes to this passage from Richardson, without discussing it in any detail, his obvious knowledge of it and its relevance to his concept of illusion highlights the similarities between his conception of theatrical representation and the one that informs the dramatic theory that Diderot will publish two months later, in February 1757.

---

24. Gero von Wilpert, *Sachwörterbuch der Literatur*, 4th edn (Stuttgart 1964), p.704-705. The technique of teichoscopy derives from Homer. The model is the scene from book III of the *Iliad*, where Helen describes the heroes of the Greek army from the walls of Troy. Aeschylus exploits teichoscopy in the opening scene of *Agamemnon*, where the watchman on the roof of Atreus's palace sees the beacon announcing the fall of Troy. It is also used in Shakespeare's *Julius Caesar* (V.iii).

Mendelssohn refers to this scene from *Grandison* as an example of a method of representation that offers an alternative to two features of dramatic writing mentioned by Lessing, and which in fact characterise his own practice in *Miss Sara Sampson*. In the letter of 18 November 1756, Lessing takes up the issue of how to achieve the right balance between moral courage and suffering so as to ensure that the audience or reader will feel sympathy for the hero rather than admiration. Lessing holds that although the hero should demonstrate enough moral strength for the audience not to have contempt for him, the dramatist should nevertheless allow him to feel his misfortune ('er muß es ihn recht fühlen lassen'), in order to gain our sympathy.[25] The idea of 'feeling one's misfortune' is a good description of what often happens in *Miss Sara* in the passages Fricke identified as 'lyrical' and that Rempel and Trappen see as designed to provoke tears.[26] What Lessing seems to mean by allowing the characters to feel their pain is elaborating on it in linguistic form as in the neo-classical tradition. In his next letter, sent to Nicolai on the following day, Lessing breaks sympathy down into three components or degrees: 'Rührung' (emotion), 'Tränen' (tears) and 'Beklemmung' (anguish).[27] To show what these terms signify for him, and how these different degrees of sympathetic emotion can be evoked in an audience, he uses the example of the beggar, mentioned above, who relates how and why he has fallen on hard times. As the story unfolds, Lessing varies or adds to the surrounding detail to show how these different ingredients affect the emotional response of the listener. What is particularly interesting about this example is that although Lessing is ostensibly talking about how plays work, what he actually explains is how narration works, and in fact Lessing twice uses the word 'Erzählung' to refer to the beggar's speech. The various emotional effects Lessing is interested in creating will be brought about, he tells Nicolai, by the manner and the order in which the beggar tells his story. In other words, the beggar's success or failure in causing a certain affective response in his listener will depend upon how good a narrator he is and how skilled a rhetorician. Why does Lessing consider this example of narration an appropriate model of how drama communicates? It is because the beggar is speaking in his own voice to a listener; the scene Lessing evokes is therefore in the form of dialogue ('dialogisch'). But it is not 'dramatic' in Mendelssohn's sense, because narration is not sensate enough ('sinnlich genug'). Lessing thinks of tragedy as a whole composed in dialogue ('ein dialogisches Ganze'),[28] which has its origins in the epic; for Mendelssohn it is live representation ('lebendige Vorstellung').

There is a visual component in Lessing's example; however, this is strictly subordinated to linguistic effects. The interlocutor's emotion ('Rührung',

25. Göpfert, iv.174.
26. Fricke, 'Bemerkungen', p.109-10; Rempel, *Tragödie und Komödie*, p.39-40.
27. Göpfert, iv.177.
28. Göpfert, iv.175.

the first level) is triggered by the spectacle of the beggar ('der Anblick'), but this visual impression only produces an obscure idea ('dunkler Begriff') in him. It is not until he acquires a clear conception of the beggar's perfections and his misfortunes, as a result of hearing his story, that the other two levels of sympathy can be attained. Lessing's example thus orders visual and verbal components of the experience according to a chronological and qualitative hierarchy in which the visual element is the least significant. This is in vivid contrast to Mendelssohn's evocation of Grandison's appearance at Hargrave's, which he introduces as a counter-example to Lessing's beggar. Lessing's beggar and Cotes in his closet (present in Mendelssohn's mind, though not in his text) are images for two different types of theatrical communication. The beggar who relies on narration and rhetoric to win his listener is a model of the neo-classical writer. Cotes in his closet is an apt figure for contemporary and future dramatists who will write as witnesses to an unfolding event, fusing aural and visual effects into a coherent single impression.

The gap between Lessing and Mendelssohn is further illustrated by two other concrete examples Lessing develops to reiterate his opposition to Mendelssohn's concept of illusion and the pleasure we derive from it. These are the female statue and the sympathetic string (2 February 1757). The female statue is the counter-example Lessing introduces to refute Mendelssohn's argument about the painted snake. He tries to invalidate Mendelssohn's account of why negative emotions are experienced as pleasurable when occasioned by art by simply reversing the argument and considering the case of a work that triggers a positive response. A viewer would not experience pleasure but disappointment, he claims, upon discovering that a statue he had taken to be a living woman gesturing mysteriously to him was 'merely' a statue.[29] But this refutation of Mendelssohn's argument is not sound. It does not at all follow from Mendelssohn's explanation of why unpleasant emotions are pleasurable when mediated by art that positive feelings might equally well be transformed into negative ones. Lessing's opinion is based upon an assumption that Mendelssohn does not make, namely that an artwork, in as far as it is an imitation, is necessarily 'inferior' to the thing that it imitates. He takes it as axiomatic that the *Urbild* is 'better' than the imitation, and so for Lessing the statue is deceptive in a negative way and simply proves that we cannot trust our visual impressions. It is clear from this that Lessing is being influenced by the Platonic view of art and illusion; indeed, his unwavering insistence that tragedy must exert a positive moral effect on its audience appears to be motivated by the need to have an answer for Plato, who would otherwise, says Lessing, be justified in having poets banned from his Republic.[30] Mendelssohn, however, is using

29. Göpfert, iv.203.
30. Göpfert, iv.189.

the term 'imitation' in an Aristotelian way. For him, to say that a work of art is a 'Nachahmung' is simply an attempt to name the relationship that obtains between the work and the human experience to which it refers. It does not serve to rank the two experiences, but rather to allow for a detailed description of the characteristics of the work in question. Mendelssohn thinks of stage representation in terms of its perceptual as well its emotional impact; imitation and illusion together account for this. This amounts to a semiotic theory of tragedy like the one that Diderot expounds. As we saw in Part II above (p.86-87), Diderot's discussion of the effect brought about by the illusion of the deceased Lysimond effectively counters the view of the response to art that is implied by Lessing's female statue.

Lessing's theory of how drama communicates with the audience is explained by the analogy of the sympathetic string. This metaphor supports the position already conveyed through the example of the beggar and his narration. Lessing points out that when two strings are tuned to the same pitch and one of them is struck, the other resonates in sympathy with it. The characters of a play in the grip of emotion are like the string that is touched to make it sound; the readers or spectators vibrate in response, but for them, the feeling is pleasant rather than stressful because they are not directly affected ('touched') by the original cause of the emotion, which is without consequences in their own life.[31] Lessing is not suggesting that it actually is by means of vibrations that tragedy exercises its effect, but simply that the process can be compared to this. What is significant about this analogy, when set against Mendelssohn's concept of illusion, is that it leaves out all reference to the visual effect that drama has. Lessing seems to think of tragedy as a form that exerts its effect through sound; the string analogy is aural and in that sense, it reflects the traditional association of poetry (including tragedy) with the ear, in contrast with its sister art, painting, which makes its appeal to the sense of sight. Moreover, throughout these letters, Lessing uses the word 'Zuhörer' far more frequently than 'Zuschauer' to denote the reader or audience of tragedy. The sympathetic string analogy confirms that for Lessing, as in the neo-classical tradition, words are the dominant theatrical sign; they are what really count.

Jost Schillemeit concludes his illuminating study of the *Briefwechsel*, which focuses on various aspects of Mendelssohn's position, with the

---

31. Göpfert, iv.203-204. The popularity of the metaphor of the vibrating string (which Diderot also uses) may have been enhanced by contemporary interest in a related mathematical problem. The 'wave equation' was the subject of a number of important mathematical papers published in the period 1747-1753 by D'Alembert, Euler and Bernoulli. This work in mathematics marks the beginning of the theory of partial differential equations, and the debate over vibrating strings led to a new understanding of the notion of a function. Victor J. Katz, *A History of mathematics: an introduction* (New York 1993), p.522-25.

observation that the disagreement between Lessing and Mendelssohn on the matter of illusion is historically the most important and, indeed, the decisive divergence of opinion in their debate.[32] I agree with him on this point, although not with his final assessment of the respective positions of the participants. Schillemeit argues that Lessing's analysis of sympathy presupposes a spectator fully in the grip of illusion ('den vollkommen illusionierten Zuschauer') and he refers to Lessing's account of the relationship between the emotions represented by the *dramatis personae* and those experienced by the audience as 'Lessing's concept of total illusion' ('Lessings Begriff der vollkommenen Illusion'). He characterises Mendelssohn's view of art as ' "durchschaute" Nachahmung' (' "perceptible" imitation') and sees this as harking back to an older tradition, which places the emphasis on art as art, and stresses the gap between it and life. I think that this should be put the other way round. It seems misleading to me to use the word 'illusion' in connection with Lessing's essentially non-visual theory, especially in view of his own adamant rejection of this term throughout the letters. Moreover, Lessing's plays from this period were not written with the intent of creating this kind of aesthetic illusion. It might be more accurate to describe Lessing's position as a theory of identification: the listeners (*Zuhörer*) identify with characters they believe to be like themselves and whom they consider deserving of their sympathy. This occurs, Lessing maintains, when the writer correctly gauges the levels of misfortune and perfection in story and character. He does not address the issue of the artistic means by which this story and these characters are mediated to the audience, other than to suggest that it happens in some way akin to the transmission of vibrations. This is the role played by theatrical illusion in Mendelssohn's theory, where it constitutes the interface between play and audience. His understanding of it is the newly developing one, which means deriving the dramatic text from a mental or visual representation. He already approaches theatre as a form of aesthetic semiosis, whilst Lessing still conceives of drama as a virtuoso performance, anchored in rhetoric.

It is unfortunate, I think, that Mendelssohn merely alluded to the Cotes episode instead of expounding it more fully. Had he done so, Lessing would no doubt have understood Mendelssohn's position straightaway instead of having to wait until he came upon it in the framework to Diderot's *Fils naturel* two years later. As it is, the concept of illusion that Mendelssohn puts forward in the *Briefwechsel* is the one that Lessing will only later adopt as his own, when he sees its relevance to his theory of sympathy. Despite his interest in contemporary acting styles, he will only begin to consider illusion seriously when he finds it allied to a commitment as strong as his own to a vision of a morally and socially responsible

---

32. Schillemeit, 'Lessings und Mendelssohns Differenz', p.92.

theatre that achieves its impact through the combined effect of illusion and sympathetic identification.

In the period following his translation of Diderot's writings, Lessing changed his position on all the essential points that make up the viewer-focused dramatic aesthetic. His concept of illusion, his understanding of the means of imitation in different literary and artistic kinds, and his approach to the creation of dramatic language all alter. Some of theses changes are apparent in the three *Literaturbriefe* (51, 81 and 103), which reflect Lessing's immediate response to Diderot's theatrical writings. The relevant passages principally concern poetic and dramatic language. Moreover, the visual perspective, which is so conspicuously absent in Lessing's contributions to the *Briefwechsel*, here starts to emerge as he re-evaluates a complex of ideas that were fundamental to contemporary views of writing: illusion, elevated language, the role of wit in dramatic speech and the definition of a poet.

Letter 51, dated August 1759, includes Lessing's account of a recently published essay by Klopstock on poetic language. Towards the end of this piece, which summarises Klopstock's analysis of the chief differences between prose and poetry, Lessing introduces a comparison of his own between the language of poetry and that of drama. Surprisingly, in view of the attitudes expressed in the *Briefwechsel*, he here draws a distinction between these two forms of aesthetic writing by means of an appeal to illusion and an oblique reference to the notion of the invisible poet. Whilst he agrees with Klopstock that in poetry the writer should choose the noblest and most forceful expressions ('die edelsten und nachdrücklichsten Wörter'), this is precisely the kind of language that does not belong in drama, where the poet does not speak for himself ('nicht in seiner eignen Person spricht').[33] In drama, the use of elevated language betrays prior reflection ('die vorhergegangene Überlegung'), transforms the stage characters into orators ('Declamatores') and destroys illusion. This is precisely the position set out by Diderot in the wake of the French debates about tragic language, and Lessing's reproduction of the argument here shows that his attitude towards illusion has changed significantly since the *Briefwechsel*. He now subscribes to the view that the creation of illusion is one of the goals of drama and that illusion is a factor shaping dramatic speech.

Letter 81 (7 February 1760), in which Lessing makes explicit reference to Diderot and quotes extracts from his *Entretiens*, illustrates in several important ways the reorientation taking place in Lessing's thinking. He first introduces a reference to Diderot in support of the idea that Germany needs more and better theatres if play writing is to flourish, and he quotes Diderot's remarks about the place theatre occupied in ancient Greek society as compared with its role in contemporary France, where

33. Göpfert, v.183 and v.184.

its potential for positive social impact is seriously underrated and under-exploited. All the more reason, notes Lessing, to deplore the situation in Germany where theatre does not even command the level of public interest and support that it does in Diderot's France.[34] He then goes on to mention Christian Weisse's first tragedy, *Eduard der Dritte*, and this leads him into a series of remarks on wit and the nature of dramatic language. Digressing from the subject of Weisse's play, Lessing sets out the context for a clever and striking remark attributed to the father of Edward III, the historical Edward II. Edward II, who had been forced to abdicate in favour of his son, was moved from one uncomfortable prison to the next. He bore his adversities with fortitude until one day, he found himself out in the open, with only a bowl of cold muddy water his guards had drawn from a nearby ditch to wash his beard. At this, he began to lament his fate. Among the reproachful comments addressed to his indifferent guards, was the remark that he was not going to give them the satisfaction of de-priving him of warm water to wash his beard. As he said this, two streams of warm tears began to flow down his face. The scene Lessing evokes for his readers is noteworthy not only because it encapsulates Edward's dignity and pain in a moment of humiliation and suffering, but also for the way in which it combines both language and action. Edward's refer-ence to hot water alludes simultaneously to the undignified treatment he receives at the hands of his guards and the tears flowing down his cheeks. Lessing says that if these words were given to a character in a play, critics would almost certainly challenge them as too 'witty' for a suffering person and therefore unnatural in a serious dramatic work. As noted in the previous chapter in connection with Lessing's early comedies, the word *witzig* refers both to self-conscious wordplay that displays an author's skill with language, and to other forms of clever juxtaposition.[35] Here, Lessing alludes to what the historical Edward said as a way of showing that pain can and does give rise to remarks that can be seen as witty in this sense. He adds that such language is acceptable in a play when, as in his example, what the character says is not wit for its own sake, but wit that is inspired by the circumstances ('was ihm die Umstände in den Mund legen'). Any witty expressions that arise naturally out of the situations created by the playwright will not only be above criticism but will also exercise a powerful emotional effect ('er kann gewiß sein, daß alle der Witz, den ihnen diese Situation gibt, nicht nur untadelhaft, sondern höchst pathetisch sein wird'). These words paraphrase a state-ment Diderot makes in the *Entretiens*.[36] The thought seems almost trivially self-evident to a present-day reader and it would be easy to overlook its

34. Göpfert, v.260-61. Lessing repeats these ideas in the *Ankündigung* of the *Hamburgische Dramaturgie*, Göpfert, iv.232.

35. See above, p.117.

36. 'La première [idée], c'est qu'il ne faut point donner d'esprit à ses personnages, mais savoir les placer dans des circonstances qui leur en donnent', DPV, x.100.

significance for Lessing. It is important for a number of reasons. First, it means that dramatic speech does not have to be determined principally by genre but is justified by its power to persuade the audience that it is natural, that is, that it is successful as illusion (although Lessing does not use the word here). If the surrounding context warrants it, wit can have a place in tragedy (as, indeed, it will in Lessing's *Emilia Galotti*). Lessing then quotes in full Diderot's anecdote of the peasant woman, weeping as she clutches the feet of her murdered husband, to show that people from any class are capable of these forceful and penetrating utterances in extreme situations. A peasant woman can be as witty as a king, which means (second point) that dramatic speech is not primarily dependent on character typology. Witty remarks do not need to be reserved for those figures whose character or role it is to be 'witty'. All human beings are capable of this type of wit, because in the grip of the passions, all people are the same ('die Leidenschaften machen alle Menschen wieder gleich').

These two examples of speech show that Lessing has fundamentally revised his view of how dramatic language represents emotion. The words of Edward and of the peasant woman are a vivid expression of their emotional pain and suffering, but these short, pithy utterances are the very antithesis of the lengthy speeches that Lessing puts into the mouths of his characters in *Miss Sara* and *Philotas*. The examples quoted in Letter 81 only make sense as the articulation of suffering when taken in their total visual context, that is, as a verbal element integrated into action and setting. Taken alone, the words do not communicate their full import. They have meaning and force only for spectators who see the action before them or for readers who put themselves into the spectator role and visualise it in their imagination. Lessing is obliged to supply a lengthy, narrative and descriptive context to make his Edward II example comprehensible, and Diderot has to do the same to explain the effect of the peasant woman's speech. Dorval presents this anecdote as an example of a *tableau* and his account includes spectators who respond to the woman's language and action with tears.[37] Their presence structures the scene in a manner analogous to theatrical representation, with a central action and non-participating viewers who react sympathetically to the woman 'feeling her pain' as intensely, but a great deal more concisely, than the characters in, for example, Lessing's early tragedies.

Lessing is here embracing a view of dramatic speech as language that expresses emotional response directly, as it is happening; not language as the product of a reflective, artistic reorganisation. The principal formal constraint he recognises now is that speech should serve to foster the illusion of an action happening before us, as if for the first time. He has obviously reassessed the relative value of the visual and aural components of dramatic representation, and is now willing to accord a larger role to

37. DPV, x.100; Göpfert, v.262.

what is visual. The connection between this change of attitude and the French debates concerning painting is made clear several paragraphs later by the comparison he goes on to draw between dramatic language and painting. Lessing states that 'Charaktere und Situationen sind die Contours des Gemäldes; die Sprache ist die Colorite; und man bleibt ohne diese nur immer die Hälfte von einem Maler, die Hälfte von einem Dichter.'[38] The contours of character and situation were all that Lessing was interested in discussing in the *Briefwechsel*, not the impact on the senses of the means of imitation. Now he includes both. He praises the opening lines of Weisse's play as equal to the writing of Schlegel, but he goes on to complain that in the rest of the work, the verse is very uneven and fails to meet the same standard throughout. This weakness in the area of speech undermines the portrayal of both character and situation and diminishes the overall effectiveness of the play. In de Piles's theory, as we saw, colouring is the means by which illusion is brought about in painting.[39] Lessing's observation on language and colouring thus implies that he now considers it essential for dramatic speech to be consistent with illusion, even when the play, as here, is in verse. Because Weisse fails to sustain the tone struck at the beginning of the play, the uneven quality of the speech intrudes on the spectators' consciousness and disrupts the illusion. Lessing's equation of dramatic speech with colouring not only reflects the theory of dramatic speech outlined in Diderot's theory but relates it to its source.

The final explicit reference to Diderot in the *Literaturbriefe* is in number 103, mentioned above (p.118), where Lessing discusses the distinction made by English and French critics between the *versificateur* and the poetic genius.[40] Warton is somewhat scathing about the mere 'man of rhymes', but Diderot insists, and Lessing with him in this letter, that the *versificateur* is also a person of rare talent.[41] The difference between the two lies in the breadth and power of their imagination. The contrast between skill with words and strength of imagination is an aspect of the reassessment of the verbal and the visual taking place in Lessing's view of creativity. He is thus simultaneously reorienting both his conception of poetry and his

---

38. Göpfert, v.265. 'Characters and situations are the contours of the painting; language is the colouring; without the latter, one is only half a painter, half a dramatist.'

39. See above, p.34. This view is promoted in works which Lessing is known to have read later, in connection with his *Laokoon*, for example de Piles's translation of Du Fresnoy and Jonathan Richardson's *Essay on the theory of painting* of 1725 (which Lessing actually read in French translation).

40. Göpfert, v.273. Lessing describes Diderot as 'der neueste, und unter den neuen unstreitig der beste französische Kunstrichter' ('the newest, and among the new, unquestionably the best French critic').

41. DPV, x.359. This is the section entitled 'Du plan de la tragédie et du plan de la comédie', in which Diderot discusses illusion, the relationship between history and tragedy and between history and comedy, prose tragedy and dramatic speech, and the functioning of the imagination.

definition of the poet. Lessing returns to the distinction between versifier and poet ('the true *Maker* or *Creator*', as Warton calls him) several times in the *Hamburgische Dramaturgie*, though he is rarely again as generous in his assessment of the versifier as he is here.[42]

Brief though these passages relating to Diderot are, they do, I believe, lie at the heart of his influence on Lessing. The explicit reference and implicit appeals to the idea of illusion, the reassessment of the expressive force of dramatic speech, the positive spin put upon the visual dimension of poetry, the equation of dramatic speech with colouring and the emphasis on the role of the imagination in creative writing all show that Lessing has begun to think about drama from the perspective of both spectator and writer as viewers. The two main works of theory and criticism that Lessing subsequently published (the *Laokoon* and the *Hamburgische Dramaturgie*) confirm and enrich in various ways the reorientation apparent in the *Literaturbriefe*. Without going into great detail, I shall briefly indicate some salient points from each of these two works to illustrate this development.

Lessing began work on what was to become the *Laokoon* in the early 1760s.[43] The text published in 1766 deals with painting and poetry (in fact the epic, or narrative form). According to the title page, this was to be the first part of a larger work that would discuss all the arts. This project was never brought to completion, however, and so we do not have a formal semiotic analysis of drama written by Lessing. Nevertheless, the *Laokoon* is of major importance in charting the development of Lessing's aesthetic thought in ways that are relevant to style in his mature plays. It opens with the assertion that the common goal of both poetry and painting is to create illusion, for which Lessing uses the word 'Täuschung' ('deception'). Illusion is defined as the effect by means of which poetry and painting 'stellen uns abwesende Dinge als gegenwärtig, den Schein als Wirklichkeit vor'.[44] He then proceeds to explore the ways in which poetry and painting can best bring about illusion, given the nature of the means of imitation over which each disposes. Lessing differentiates between poetry and painting in terms of their use of signs and the definitions at which he arrives are well known. Painting uses the visible signs of figures and colours in space. These visible signs are considered natural, and the effects of painting are achieved through the appeal to the imagination via the eye. Poetry uses articulated sounds in time. These are arbitrary signs, and the effects appropriate to poetry are achieved

42. It comes up in *HD* 32 where he attacks Corneille (Göpfert, iv.376), in *HD* 42 where it is invoked to criticise Maffei (Göpfert, iv.425), and in *HD* 81 against Gottsched (Göpfert, iv.606). In *HD* 34, Lessing contrasts genius in general with knowledge of rules and mere bookish learning (Göpfert, iv.388).

43. Göpfert, vi.865 and vi.987. The *Laokoon* is believed to be based on material Lessing had originally intended to publish under the title *Hermäa*, mentioned in his correspondence in 1762 and 1763.

44. Göpfert, vi.9. 'Present absent things to us as if they were present, appearances as if they were life itself'.

through the appeal to the imagination through the ear. The various rules that Lessing prescribes for each art are the direct consequence of the means on which it relies. These determine the type of material suitable for treatment in each art form. In order for each art to realise its highest aesthetic form as an art of imitation that appeals to intuitive cognition, there must be an appropriate relationship ('ein bequemes Verhältnis') between signifier and signified.[45] Painting, which deploys colours and shapes in space, is ideally suited to represent beautiful objects; poetry, which relies on articulated, consecutive sounds should represent actions. Lessing is not saying that this is what they always, in fact, do, but that this what they ought to do in order to realise their highest form as arts.[46]

The fact that the signs of painting are considered 'natural' and those of poetry 'arbitrary' has significant implications for the value Lessing himself places on each of the two media. In France the belief that the signs used by painting were 'natural' had conferred on them a kind of superiority and contributed to the positive re-evaluation of painting that occurred in the period. This is not the case in Lessing's theory. For him, the use of arbitrary signs represents a more advanced stage of semiosis, and therefore of imaginative freedom, than painting and sculpture have or can achieve.[47] Poetry thus enjoys certain advantages in comparison with the visual arts. It has access to a much larger range of potential material, and its appeal to the imagination is freer, because it is unencumbered by the materiality that characterises the signs of the latter. These qualities make poetry the superior art in Lessing's view.[48] Nevertheless, it is important to recognise that Lessing's concept of the aesthetic functioning of the sign itself is derived from the nature of the painterly sign.[49] On this issue, Lessing's views accord with French theory. This point emerges from his analysis of the nature of signs in chapter 17, where he responds to comments that Mendelssohn had made on his second draft. Mendelssohn had objected to Lessing's exclusion of the depiction of bodies from poetry on the grounds that since poetry uses arbitrary signs, it can represent anything you want

---

45. Göpfert, vi.102-103.

46. This point is clearly stated in one of the fragments, where Lessing writes: 'Ausdrückliche Schilderungen von Körpern sind daher der Poesie versagt. Und warum sie es tut so tut sie es nicht als nachahmende Kunst, sondern als Mittel der Erklärung. So wie die Malerei nicht nachahmende Kunst, sondern ein bloßes Mittel der Erklärung ist, wann sie verschiedene Zeiten auf einem Raume vorstellet.' ('Detailed descriptions of bodies are therefore to be excluded from poetry. And if they are included, then poetry is acting not as an art of imitation but as a means of explanation. Just as painting is working not as an art of imitation but merely as a means of explanation when it depicts different moments of time in the same space.') Göpfert, vi.602.

47. Wellbery, *Lessing's Laocoon*, p.128-30.

48. Critics have interpreted this preference in various ways, but their speculations remain inconclusive. See Ernst Gombrich, 'Lessing (lecture on a master mind)', *Proceedings of the British Academy* 43 (1957), p.133-56 (p.144); Buch, '*Ut Pictura Poesis*', p.63.

49. Wellbery stresses this point: '*In the Laocoon poetry is still viewed in terms of the paradigm of painting*.' (Wellbery's emphasis). *Lessing's Laocoon*, p.182-83 and p.227.

it to. That is the value of arbitrary signs.[50] Lessing deals with this objection by drawing a distinction between the aesthetic and the non-aesthetic use of arbitrary signs. Although the signs of poetry are arbitrary, their application and effect are determined by the goal of poetic writing, which is to create the illusion of the signified in the imagination of the listener. This is very different from the function of arbitrary signs in ordinary discourse, where words convey merely a discursive knowledge of the object to symbolic cognition and can thus readily provide an account of bodies. The poet, however, does not appeal to symbolic but to intuitive cognition:

> Der Poet will nicht bloß verständlich werden, seine Vorstellungen sollen nicht bloß klar und deutlich sein; hiermit begnügt sich der Prosaist. Sondern er will die Ideen, die er in uns erweckte, so lebhaft machen, daß wir in der Geschwindigkeit die wahren sinnlichen Eindrücke ihrer Gegenstände zu empfinden glauben, und in diesem Augenblicke der Täuschung, uns der Mittel, die er dazu anwendet, seiner Worte bewußt zu sein aufhören.[51]

The aesthetic use of signs in poetry imposes the condition that the signs achieve transparency. The listener must have no consciousness of the words as signs; he or she should be able to attend only to the actions rendered present to the imagination through the medium of the words. The efficacy of poetic signs is thus directly related to their invisibility as signs. As with the French writers discussed in Parts I and II, Lessing's ideal of transparency for language in poetry is modelled on the transparency of the natural signs of painting. He makes this clear in his explanation of what he means by a poetic, or verbal, picture:

> Ein poetisches Gemälde ist nicht notwendig das, was in ein materielles Gemälde zu verwandeln ist; sondern jeder Zug, jede Verbindung mehrerer Züge, durch die uns der Dichter seinen Gegenstand so sinnlich macht, daß wir uns dieses Gegenstandes deutlicher bewußt werden, als seiner Worte, heißt malerisch, heißt ein Gemälde, weil es uns dem Grade der Illusion näher bringt, dessen das materielle Gemälde besonders fähig ist, der sich von dem materiellen Gemälde am ersten und leichtesten abstrahieren lassen.[52]

---

50. Göpfert, vi.565n.

51. Göpfert, vi.110. 'The poet does not seek merely to be understood, his representations do not simply have to be clear and distinct; this is enough to satisfy only the writer of prose. The poet wants to make the ideas he stimulates in us so lively that in the heat of the moment, we believe that we are receiving the authentic sense impressions of the objects themselves, and that in this moment of deception, we cease to be conscious of the words which are his means.'

52. Göpfert, vi.100. 'A poetic picture is not necessarily one that can be transformed into a material picture. What is meant by painterly or picture-like in this sense is the effect created when every element and all the connections between all the elements make the poet's object so sensate that we are more conscious of the object itself than of the words he uses. This is called a picture because it is what brings us closest to that degree of illusion which material pictures are particularly well-adapted to producing and which can initially most easily be defined by reference to material pictures.'

Thus, even if Lessing sees poetry as the superior art form, his concept of the highest form of aesthetic sign is one that achieves the invisibility exemplified by the painterly sign. The fact that Lessing takes the creation of illusion to be the goal of art and that his ideal sign, including the poetic sign, is one that is transparent as sign, shows that he is positioning himself as a 'viewer' as do La Motte, Landois and Diderot.

Although drama is not analysed in the *Laokoon*, Lessing's remarks on the expression of bodily pain in Sophocles's *Philoctetes* are relevant to the issue of dramatic speech, particularly since the example of Philoctetes is one often mentioned in French theory. In the first and second *Entretiens*, Diderot alludes to these same scenes as a positive model for dramatic speech, as does Fénelon in his critique of the language of French tragedy.[53] Lessing's notes show that his thoughts on the cries of Philoctetes, although not included in the first draft, formed part of his thinking from very early on.[54] He introduces the example of the suffering Philoctetes to examine whether or not the representation of bodily pain is allowable in drama. Contrary to the expectation he first sets up, he concludes that it is possible to depict suffering characters on the stage in such a way as to elicit sympathy (rather than, say, horror) in the audience. Particularly interesting here is the distinction Lessing initially makes between narrative and dramatic modes, since this reveals some general assumptions he now holds about the nature of drama. He writes:

Einen andern Eindruck macht die Erzählung von jemands Geschrei; einen andern dieses Geschrei selbst. Das Drama, welches für die lebendige Malerei des Schauspielers bestimmt ist, dürfte vielleicht eben deswegen sich an die Gesetze der materiellen Malerei strenger halten müssen. In ihm glauben wir nicht bloß einen schreienden Philoktet zu sehen und zu hören; wir hören und sehen wirklich schreien. Je näher der Schauspieler der Natur kömmt, desto empfindlicher müssen unsere Augen und Ohren beleidiget werden; denn es ist unwidersprechlich, daß sie es in der Natur werden, wenn wir so laute und heftige Äußerungen des Schmerzes vernehmen.[55]

This way of differentiating drama and narrative is utterly different from the literary approach Lessing takes in the *Briefwechsel*. Gone is the distinction he draws there on the basis of the type of hero chosen and the emotional effect achieved. Here drama is defined as a form intended for 'die lebendige Malerei des Schauspielers', a phrase which echoes Mendelssohn's 'lebendige Vorstellung'; and within the space of one paragraph, Lessing

53. Diderot, *Entretiens*, DPV, x.93 and x.116-17. Fénelon, *Œuvres*, ii.1172.
54. Göpfert, vi.596.
55. Göpfert, vi.30. 'The impression made by the narration of someone's cries is one thing; the cries themselves are another. Drama, which is created for the living painting of the actor, should perhaps observe the laws of material painting even more strongly for this very reason. In drama, we do not simply believe that we see and hear Philoctetes crying out; we really do hear and see these cries. The closer the actor comes to nature, the more our eyes and ears feel hurt, for it is undeniable that they would be so in nature, if we heard such loud and vehement expressions of pain.'

makes no fewer than three references to the simultaneous reception of drama through the senses of sight and hearing. This way of describing drama, which is consistent with his presentation of painting as the art of the eye and poetry as the art of the ear throughout the *Laokoon*, corresponds to the way Diderot talks about theatrical form.

Lessing again alludes to Sophocles' play in connection with some comments concerning the length of acts in classical works. Although he agrees with French critics, who held that the Ancients did not consider it necessary for all the acts of a play to be the same length, he thinks they are wrong to cite the third act of *Philoctetes* as evidence. Lessing points out that although this act appears shorter than the first two when the play is read, in performance it lasts just about as long, because of the pauses and interruptions that are added when the text is acted.[56] This thought reverses a point made by Diderot in the second *Entretien*. When Moi complains that a certain scene in Dorval's play is too long, Dorval observes that this impression is based on Moi's reading of the play, and that the scene did not seem too long when he watched it, thanks to the liveliness and animation of the acting style.[57] In both cases, the point is that the dramatic text is an incomplete representation of the dramatic performance, which only becomes fully coherent when brought to life by the gestures and expression of the actor. This emphasis on the difference between reading and watching a play was not present in Lessing's thinking in the 1750s.

Lessing's fullest statement on the nature of dramatic language in the context of the *Laokoon* is contained in a letter sent to Nicolai in April 1769. In this letter, which was written in response to criticisms made of the *Laokoon* by Christian Garve, Lessing complains that his analysis has been misunderstood. He emphasises that he had never claimed that painting only uses natural signs and that poetry only uses arbitrary ones; both arts, says Lessing, can exploit both types of sign. He maintains, though, that painting comes closest to its perfection when it uses only natural signs and that poetry achieves its highest form when it succeeds in converting its arbitrary signs into natural ones.[58] After elaborating more fully on his point about the signs of painting, Lessing goes on to identify the means by which poetry can transform its arbitrary signs into natural ones. These are 'der Ton, die Worte, die Stellung der Worte, das Silbenmaß, Figuren und Tropen, Gleichnisse u.s.w. Alle diese Dinge bringen die willkürlichen Zeichen den natürlichen näher.'[59] But these means are not sufficient to convert the signs of poetry fully to natural ones, and consequently the genres that rely on these techniques are the lesser genres. The highest

56. Göpfert, vi.13.
57. Diderot, *Entretiens*, DPV, x.109-10.
58. Göpfert, vi.897.
59. Göpfert, vi.897-98. 'Tone, words, the position of words, metre, tropes and figures, similes etc. All these things bring the arbitrary signs closer to natural ones.'

form of poetry is the one which 'die willkürlichen Zeichen gänzlich zu natürlichen Zeichen macht. Das ist aber die dramatische; denn in dieser hören die Worte auf, willkürliche Zeichen zu sein, und werden *natürliche* Zeichen willkürlicher Dinge.'[60] Drama is the highest form of poetry because it is the only one in which words can fully become natural signs. This assertion cannot be taken to mean that the language of drama always and necessarily achieves the status of a natural sign. Only language that meets the conditions that characterise natural signs in general can be said to achieve the status of natural signs in drama. Artistic signs are natural when the beholder or reader is not conscious of the sign as sign and feels him or herself to be in the presence of the represented action or objects. Only dramatic language that successfully disguises its status as an imitation composed by a poet, and creates the illusion that the words spoken are the very words uttered by the character in the given situation could be said to meet Lessing's ideal for dramatic speech. This concept of dramatic language, as the natural signs of arbitrary things, is the one promoted by French theorists and integrated into a semiotic theory of the drama by Diderot.

In his analysis of this 1769 letter, Rudowski introduces a further dimension of Lessing's concept of dramatic language as a system of natural signs.[61] Extrapolating from an argument concerning painting sketched out in one of the *Laokoon* fragments, Rudowski explains that in order for the linguistic signs of drama to be fully natural, the dialogue in a play must also be 'contemporaneous with the dramatic action'.[62] This has implications for the function of narration within drama, and limits its use to contexts in which it serves to reveal 'character in action'. This sense of the 'present-ness' of dramatic speech is also implied in Diderot's remark about dramatic speech as a response to circumstances.

Presumably, Lessing began his semiotic analysis of the arts with painting and poetry in order to define the basic sign systems on which the various arts draw. Fragment 27 initiates a discussion of how different arts can be combined in order to achieve a mutually produced single effect ('eine gemeinschaftliche Wirkung').[63] Success depends on how harmoniously the sign systems of the arts involved can function together. Drama is not one of the combinations mentioned here, although the principle of combination is established. In one of the early numbers of the *Hamburgische Dramaturgie*, however, Lessing provides a definition of acting, which occupies, he explains, a middle position between painting and poetry.

---

60. Göpfert, vi.898. 'Fully converts the arbitrary signs into natural ones. This is the dramatic form, because in drama, words cease to be arbitrary signs and become *natural* signs of arbitrary things.' (Lessing's emphasis.)

61. Rudowski, *Lessing's 'aesthetica in nuce'*, p.74-76. Rudowski does not mention Diderot in his exposition of Lessing's thought in this letter.

62. Rudowski, *Lessing's 'aesthetica in nuce'*, p.76.

63. Göpfert, vi.651 and following.

On the one hand, it is a visible art, like painting, and must follow some of the rules pertaining to painting, but at the same time it is 'transitorisch' or consecutive, like poetry.[64] These details allow us to deduce how Lessing would have defined drama in semiotic terms. It results from the combination of consecutive natural signs that are aural (dramatic speech) with consecutive natural signs that are visible (gesture and movement in space). This is the conception of drama that the topos of the hidden spectator in French theory served to articulate. Lessing's theory of art in the *Laokoon* thus implies the same vision of dramatic form as that formulated in the prologue to *Silvie* and in Diderot's dramatic theory.

Numerous passages in the *Hamburgische Dramaturgie* offer confirmation of this. Critics often turn to this collection of practical dramatic criticism to complete the ideas of the *Laokoon*, although Lessing himself insists that the *Dramaturgie* does not set out a dramatic system ('ein dramatisches System') and he makes no apologies for the presence of any contradictions readers might find in it.[65] His commentary is largely determined by the productions in the Hamburg repertoire, itself shaped by considerations of theatrical expediency rather than ideals.[66] A recurring theme is Lessing's hostility towards French neo-classical tragedy, so wrongly held to represent a fulfilment of Aristotle's *Poetics* and the model of the Ancients.[67]

The clearest evidence of Lessing's assimilation of French theory is the presence in the *Dramaturgie* of the topoi of the invisible poet and the hidden spectator. There are a number of allusions to the invisible poet, most notably perhaps in number 36, where Lessing gives his account of the opening night of Voltaire's *Mérope* in 1743. After the performance the public called for the author, and Voltaire appeared on stage to receive their applause. Lessing condemns both the curiosity of the public and the vanity of the author who responded to it. Both reactions, he says, are proof that the play must have left too strong a sense of the presence of the writer and thus failed to create a successful aesthetic illusion. Lessing writes:

Das wahre Meisterstück, dünkt mich, erfüllet uns so ganz mit sich selbst, daß wir des Urhebers darüber vergessen; daß wir es nicht als das Produkt eines einzeln Wesens, sondern der allgemeinen Natur betrachten. [...] Die Täuschung muß sehr schwach sein, man muß wenig Natur, aber desto mehr Künstelei empfinden, wenn man so neugierig nach dem Künstler ist.[68]

---

64. Göpfert, iv.256-57.

65. See, for example, Wellbery, *Lessing's Laocoon*, p.136, and Buch, '*Ut Pictura Poesis*', p.46. Göpfert, iv.670.

66. Robertson, *Lessing's dramatic theory*, p.40. French works performed in German translation dominated the repertoire, and the best-represented dramatist was Voltaire: see p.48-49.

67. See, for example, his comments on Voltaire's *Sémiramis* in *HD* 10 (Göpfert, iv.279) and also the concluding number (Göpfert, iv.700-701).

68. Göpfert, iv.398 and iv.399. 'The true masterpiece, it seems to me, imposes itself so fully on us that we completely forget about its creator and see it not as the product of a

For Lessing, Voltaire provides an excellent example of the all-too visible dramatist. His tragedies, with their reliance on verse, rhetoric, confidants, conventional expositions, and so on, incorporate many of the features that La Motte, Landois and Diderot had attacked as exposing the hand of the writer and the artifice of form. Lessing is critical of the way in which other French dramatists have followed Voltaire's example of vanity and he praises an unnamed young dramatist who had recently refused to be drawn onto the stage by public cries for the author.[69] Lessing's attitude seems rather extreme, but the quotation above is interesting as an illustration of his acceptance of the principle. The image recurs in his discussion of *Mérope*, where he takes up the issue of ornamental language. Lessing quotes Voltaire's complaint that the public's demand for tragic speech that is unobtrusive obliged him to forgo the bold figures that Maffei was free to use. Lessing declares his support for the spectators and says that they are right to disapprove if the poet 'hier und an mehrern Stellen luxuriere, und seinen eignen Kopf durch die Tapete stecke'.[70] This vivid image of the poet's head appearing round the curtain is one of the most striking versions of the visible poet topos; Lessing has clearly made it his own. There is a similar, though less remarkable, example in the following number (*HD* 37), where Lessing directly criticises Maffei's dramatic speech.[71]

The concept of the hidden spectator also comes up more than once in the *Hamburgische Dramaturgie*. In number 48, Lessing quotes a long section from Diderot's *Discours*, where Diderot considers plot and suspense from the spectator's point of view. Diderot argues that since the spectators are 'des témoins ignorés de la chose' ('nichts als Zeugen, von welchen man nichts weiß'), there is no need for them to remain ignorant of the twists and turns in the plot, as the fictional characters must.[72] The effects on the spectators are more powerful and sustained if they are aware of the fate threatening the various characters and can 'see' the way in which their actions unwittingly contribute to their doom. Lessing supports Diderot's recommendations on this point and agrees with his claim that they represent a new approach to plot construction. He qualifies this, however, by pointing out that it is novel only in respect to recent theory; the principle itself, he stresses, derives from the model of the Ancients. He thus

particular individual but of nature in general. [...] The illusion must be very weak, the impression of artifice must be much stronger than that of nature, when people feel such curiosity about the artist.'

69. Göpfert, vi.399 and vi.880. Göpfert doubts whether this a reference to Lessing himself, as Otto Mann and others have thought (Gotthold Ephraim Lessing, *Hamburgische Dramaturgie*, ed. Otto Mann, Stuttgart 1958, p.432).

70. Göpfert, iv.423. 'Here and elsewhere is too extravagant in his expression and pokes his own head around the curtain'.

71. Göpfert, iv.425.

72. Göpfert, iv.452-55; DPV, x.368.

manages to reconcile Diderot's progressive theory with a revered tradition, a strategy Diderot himself frequently uses in promoting the new aesthetic.

Lessing's purpose in invoking Diderot here (and one of the reasons he omits Diderot's examples, which are mostly drawn from *Zaïre*) is to criticise Voltaire and his French predecessors who, Lessing claims, often deliberately devise surprise effects for the spectators. In other words, individual scenes or events are included for the sake of their immediate and transitory effect on the audience, rather than for their function within the action considered as a dramatic whole, just as an orator might seek to achieve certain responses from specific verbal effects he uses.

The topos occurs again in numbers 84 and 85 of the *Dramaturgie* in the form of the long extract, including the anecdote of the hidden spectator, from Diderot's *Bijoux indiscrets*. The significance of this passage from the novel does not need to be repeated here; Lessing's use of it shows that he considers it fundamental to the new aesthetic and sees it as an effective and concise encapsulation of its essentials. It is significant, too, that these two long sections from Diderot that Lessing decides to incorporate textually into the *Hamburgische Dramaturgie* both concern the reorientation of dramatic theory in relation to the beholder, one dealing with plot, the other with the semiotics of performance. Clearly, Lessing is endorsing this principle as one that is effective and applicable to all aspects of the dramatist's creative task.

Diderot and other like-minded French dramatists use the topoi of the invisible poet and the hidden spectator to give form to the concept of theatrical illusion. Lessing appeals to illusion on numerous occasions in the *Dramaturgie*, an effect for which he also uses the words 'Betrug' and 'Täuschung'. Here, I shall simply highlight two examples that show how Lessing's position has changed since the time of the *Briefwechsel*. Particularly interesting is his comparison of Voltaire's ghost in *Sémiramis* (1748) with the one in Shakespeare's *Hamlet* (*c*.1600) (*HD* 10-12). The difference in effect created by these two stage ghosts allows Lessing to juxtapose and contrast the concept of illusion with that of spectacle. Lessing is critical of all the ambitious novelties in Voltaire's play, which he says amount to nothing more than the spectacular effects typical of the opera, the 'Pomp und Verwandlung, als man nur immer in einer Oper gewohnt ist'.[73] The ghost itself he describes as 'eine poetische Maschine', and 'das Geschöpf eines kalten Dichters, der uns gern täuschen und schrecken möchte, ohne daß er weiß, wie er es anfangen soll'.[74] Shakespeare's ghost, on the other hand, is still capable of producing a powerful effect on any audience, and even if the spectators are not generally disposed to believe in supernatural phenomena, they cannot help being drawn into the illusion. Voltaire's

---

73. Göpfert, iv.280.

74. Göpfert, iv.283 and iv.285. 'The creature of an unfeeling poet who would like to frighten us with an illusion but does not know how to go about it'.

error is that he tries to frighten the audience directly; his ghost is intended as an apparition for them as much as for the other *dramatis personae*, despite the fact that the contemporary public no longer really believes in such things. Not so in Shakespeare's play, where the ghost does not appear primarily to the audience but to Hamlet. There the spectators are not affected by the ghost as such, but by Hamlet's reaction to it. 'Das Gespenst wirket auf uns, mehr durch ihn, als durch sich selbst. Der Eindruck, den es auf ihn macht, gehet in uns über, und die Wirkung ist zu augenscheinlich und zu stark, als daß wir an der außerordentlichen Ursache zweifeln sollten.'[75] Shakespeare here treats the audience as if they were hidden spectators, observing events from the outside. This contrast of spectacle with genuine theatrical illusion vividly illustrates the reorientation of Lessing's perspective since the dispute with Mendelssohn.[76]

Significant too is the distinction Lessing makes in this same section between narration (in this case historical narration) and dramatic representation. He stresses that the dramatic poet is not a history writer: 'er erzählt nicht, was man ehedem geglaubt, daß es geschehen, sondern er läßt es vor unsern Augen nochmals geschehen'.[77] The dramatist does not reconstruct the past; he creates the illusion of an event unfolding in the present in order to move us ('er will uns täuschen, und durch die Täuschung rühren'). The illusion is the means by which the audience is moved, and the emphasis on the action happening 'before our very eyes' draws attention to the way in which Lessing situates himself *vis-à-vis* the stage events. This emerges equally strongly in other passages in the *Dramaturgie* where Lessing discusses the differences between narration and drama. In some remarks on how the dramatist can adapt existing story material for dramatic representation, he stresses the importance of adopting the right point of view. The dramatist must be able:

sich aus dem Gesichtspunkte des Erzählers in den wahren Standort einer jeden Person versetzen können; die Leidenschaften, nicht beschreiben, sondern vor den Augen des Zuschauers entstehen, und ohne Sprung, in einer so illusorischen Stetigkeit wachsen zu lassen, daß dieser sympathisieren muß, er mag wollen oder nicht[78]

75. Göpfert, iv.284. 'The phantom affects us more through his reaction to it than for itself. The impression that it makes on him is transmitted to us and the effect itself is too vivid and too strong for us to feel doubts about its supernatural cause.'

76. Lessing invokes the creation of illusion as a measure of success in drama in a number of other contexts, for example in connection with plot (*HD* 19 and *HD* 35), overt references to theatricality (*HD* 42), the depiction of manners (*HD* 22 and *HD* 97) and the art of the actor (*HD* 5).

77. Göpfert, iv.281-82. 'He does not narrate things that we believe have taken place in the past, but allows them to happen again before our very eyes'.

78. Göpfert, iv.235. 'To abandon the viewpoint of the narrator and put himself in the position of each character; not describe the passions, but allow them to arise before the eyes of the spectator and then maintain the illusion of their constant and uninterrupted development so that the audience has to feel sympathy, whether they want to or not'.

Illusion and sympathetic effect are brought together with the same visual perspective ('vor den Augen des Zuschauers') as in the example above. The method described here could not be said to apply to Lessing's own tragedies of the fifties, which both include long narrative and descriptive speeches.

In number 77, Lessing comments on a difficult passage from Aristotle where he explains that tragedy is 'die Nachahmung einer Handlung, – die nicht vermittelst der Erzählung, sondern vermittelst des Mitleids und der Furcht, die Reinigung dieser und dergleichen Leidenschaften bewirket'.[79] Lessing interprets this to mean that it is essential for the action through which sympathy is to be aroused to be represented 'nicht als vergangen, das ist, nicht in der erzählenden Form, sondern als gegenwärtig, das ist, in der dramatischen Form'.[80] Lessing explains that the apparent disparity in the way Aristotle presents his idea is justified on the grounds that 'unser Mitleid durch die Erzählung wenig oder gar nicht, sondern fast einzig und allein durch die gegenwärtige Anschauung erreget wird'.[81] Thus only the dramatic form can truly bring about the sympathetic effect. This is a change from Lessing's position in the *Briefwechsel*, where he argues that sympathy arises from the interaction of character and plot, not from the force of dramatic representation itself. In the light of his statements in the *Dramaturgie*, the example of the beggar's tale, which he had used in the letters, is no longer a valid one, since the beggar is a narrator, relating events belonging to the past. That particular narrative situation cannot, Lessing thinks now, produce the illusion drama strives to create, nor the sympathy proper to tragedy. Other remarks Lessing makes in the *Dramaturgie* about narration and drama are consistent with this modification of his perspective.[82] These various shifts in outlook can all be seen as part of the same fundamental reorientation in Lessing's position. He no longer situates himself behind the scenes, as a poet speaking to an audience through characters, but with his audience, in front of the stage, as a beholder watching them act.

The various observations Lessing makes in the *Dramaturgie* on the nature of dramatic speech are consistent with what he has to say about illusion and dramatic representation, and again we find, in a key section, a quotation from Diderot. In number 59, Lessing discusses his own prose translations (reproduced in numbers 57 and 58) of extracts from John Banks's verse tragedy *The Earl of Essex, or the Unhappy favourite* (1682). Lessing informs his readers that he felt obliged to modify the original

79. Göpfert, iv.588. 'The imitation of an action which by means of pity and fear, and not through narration, brings about the purification of these and similar passions'.
80. Göpfert, iv.589. 'Not as past, that is, not in narrative form, but as present, that is, in dramatic form'.
81. 'Narration stimulates little or no sympathy in us; only seeing the action in present time can do this'.
82. See *HD* 22 (Göpfert, iv.340), *HD* 48 (iv.456) and *HD* 80 (iv.601).

fairly drastically, and explains why, taking advantage of the opportunity to criticise the common tendency to identify tragic speech with inflated speech, on the (incorrect) assumption that tragic heroes must speak differently from ordinary mortals simply because they are heroes. But he says nothing about his major creative decision, which was to transpose the English verse into German prose, a change that fundamentally alters the kind of text that it is. He simply quotes the line from Horace, 'Ampullae et sesquipedalia verba, Sentenzen und Blasen und ellenlange Worte', that Diderot invokes at the end of his discussion of prose tragedy in the second *Entretien*, and then quotes the paragraph that follows it.[83] This is the passage, where Diderot situates the use of verse within the context of a total theatrical system that relied on various forms of magnification (such as buskins and masks) for its effects. Lessing adds the point that the old plays were set in public spaces where personages of rank had to be mindful of their dignity and status. The formal tone imparted to their speech through the use of ornament and versification could thus be justified in terms of the principle of *vraisemblance*. In contemporary plays however, which tend to take place in private settings ('zwischen ihren vier Wänden'), this tone is no longer *vraisemblable*, so why, asks Lessing, do dramatists give their characters such decorous, studied and rhetorical speech ('eine so geziemende, so ausgesuchte, so rhetorische Sprache')?[84] He then returns to Diderot's principle, discussed in the eighty-first *Literaturbrief*, that social distinctions disappear when people are deeply moved; under the impact of emotion, they express themselves in a similar fashion. The only appropriate eloquence is that of passion itself, says Lessing, 'die in keiner Schule gelernt wird, und auf die sich der Unerzogenste so gut verstehet, als der Polierteste'.[85] Lessing goes on to insist upon the incompatibility of feeling with artful and inflated language. Such speech 'zeigt von keiner Empfindung, und kann keine hervorbringen. Aber wohl verträgt sie sich mit den simpelsten, gemeinsten, plattesten Worten und Redensarten.'[86] He quotes examples of the style of speech he gives to Elizabeth in his translation, although he expresses doubts that critics will be sympathetic to his attempts to invest this language with the qualities that give an accurate impression of the inspiration of the moment ('einen wahrern Anschein der augenblicklichen Eingebung'). This idea that dramatic speech must create the impression of being born of the moment (that it is speech happening for the first time), is constantly held up as the fundamental principle. The samples of speech that Lessing

83. Göpfert, iv.503. Diderot translates the line from Horace as 'des sentences, des bouteilles soufflées, des mots longs d'un pied et demi', DPV, x.117.

84. Göpfert, iv.504.

85. Göpfert, iv.504. 'Which is not learned in any school, and about which the least educated person knows as much as the most polished'.

86. 'Is not generated by feeling and cannot therefore call forth any in others. But feeling is compatible with the simplest and most common and ordinary words and expressions.'

gives embody the characteristics that Diderot recommends: exclamations, questions, sentence fragments, incomplete thoughts, and so on. These translations have been analysed in some detail by Schröder, who concludes that Lessing succeeds in suppressing the distancing qualities that make tragic characters seem remote, to reveal instead the universal and human dimension of the emotions.[87] In other words, he carries off the task of the dramatist as he defines it when he writes: 'wenn Pomp und Etiquette aus Menschen Maschinen mach[en], so ist es das Werk des Dichters, aus diesen Maschinen wieder Menschen zu machen. Die wahren Königinnen mögen so gesucht und affektiert sprechen, als sie wollen: seine Königinnen müssen natürlich sprechen.'[88] Or, as Diderot puts it, 'ce qu'il faut que l'artiste trouve, c'est ce que tout le monde dirait en pareil cas; ce que personne n'entendra, sans le reconnaître aussitôt en soi'.[89] This is speech as natural theatrical signs, integrated into a form of drama dedicated to the creation of illusion. Other statements in the *Dramaturgie* reiterate these principles of appropriateness, expressiveness and transparency and highlight the harmony between the views of Diderot and those of Lessing.[90]

The principles Lessing outlines in connection with the scene from Banks are obviously relevant to his own practice in *Minna* and *Emilia*, where he uses prose speech. Yet his last play, *Nathan der Weise*, is composed in verse. Comments Lessing makes elsewhere in the *Dramaturgie* shed light on how this choice too fits into his aesthetic. In a discussion of the translation of Du Belloy's *Zelmire* (transposed from French verse into German prose), Lessing makes reference to La Motte and the French debate about prose drama. Lessing declares an unambiguous preference for gritty, well-sounding prose ('eine körnichte, wohlklingende Prosa') over verse that is merely 'correct' ('matte, geradebrechte Verse').[91] But he does not endorse La Motte's wholesale rejection of verse, although he does understand why some French writers are opposed to the use of French verse, which, he says, possesses only the merit of the *difficulté vaincue*. Its metrical form serves merely to tickle the ears and adds nothing to the effectiveness of expression itself.[92] German verse, on the other hand, Lessing considers much more like Greek, 'die durch den bloßen Rhythmus ihrer Versarten

87. Schröder, *Sprache und Drama*, p.147-53.
88. Göpfert, iv.505. 'When pomp and etiquette turn people into machines, then it is the dramatist's job to make these machines humans again. True queens can speak as artificially and affectedly as they want to: his queens must speak naturally.'
89. DPV, x.100.
90. See, for example, Lessing's criticisms of Frau Gottsched's translation of Mme de Graffigny's *Cénie* in number 20 (Göpfert, iv.321-23). Schröder points out that the opinion Lessing expresses here is in complete contrast with his assessment of this same translation in a review of 1753 (Schröder, *Sprache und Drama*, p.144). The volte-face is further evidence of the shift in Lessing's overall conception of dramatic speech, attributable (the present study claims) to the influence of Diderot.
91. Göpfert, iv.319.
92. Göpfert, iv.320.

die Leidenschaften, die darin ausgedrückt werden, anzudeuten vermag'.[93] Verse, he implies, is acceptable in languages where metrical form cleaves to expression and does not stand out as a structure imposed on language by a poet. The main factor for Lessing is the overall effectiveness of the language within the framework of the play as a whole, its capacity to blend with the global illusion of the work. This is also the principle that determines the relationship between dramatic language and declamation. 'Der Ausdruck', says Lessing, 'wird sich höchstens über die alltägliche Sprache nicht weiter erheben, als sich die theatralische Deklamation über den gewöhnlichen Ton der gesellschaftlichen Unterhaltungen erheben soll.'[94] As long as the dramatist stays within the degree of magnification imposed by stage performance (clear diction, projection, and so on), and respects the need to harmonise all the theatrical signs, illusion can be achieved by diverse forms of speech. This argument rests on the concept of the theatrical code.

Thus, in the *Hamburgische Dramaturgie*, Diderot is quoted and his positions endorsed on three of the major issues that are fundamental to the reorientation of dramatic theory in relation to the beholder. Lessing evaluates plot, performance effect and dramatic speech from this perspective, with supporting reference to Diderot. The only area of divergence is the long commentary in numbers 86 to 95 where Lessing raises some important objections concerning Diderot's approach to the portrayal of character. Lessing has a number of reservations concerning Diderot's theory of *conditions* and he explicitly disagrees with his restatement of the traditional view that whilst comedy deals with types, tragedy focuses on individuals.

Diderot's theory of *conditions* is introduced as an example of a proposal that impresses upon a first reading of the *Entretiens*, but subsequently turns out to lack the solidity one might have hoped for.[95] Like Palissot, to whom he refers, Lessing asks whether it is really true to claim, as Diderot does, that the theatre has more or less exhausted the foibles of human character suitable for dramatic treatment and must turn to *conditions* for fresh inspiration. Lessing is clearly not convinced that this is the case. He then goes on to address what he sees as three weaknesses in Diderot's suggestions concerning the representation of *conditions*. He notes that Diderot sees the representation of *conditions* as being primarily the object of the *genre sérieux*, but he wonders whether it is worth investing effort in

---

93. 'Which can, simply through the rhythm of its verse forms, suggest the passions expressed in the lines'. He makes a similar argument about the expressive superiority of Greek syntax in chapter 18 of *Laokoon*, Göpfert, vi.118-19. In his *Lettre sur les sourds et muets*, Diderot offers the opinion that 'il faut parler français dans la société et dans les écoles de philosophie; et grec, latin, anglais dans les chaires et sur les théâtres', DPV, iv.165.

94. Göpfert, iv.320. 'Language should be heightened above ordinary speech only to the same extent that stage pronunciation has to be raised above the tone of normal social intercourse.'

95. Göpfert, iv.627.

the development of an autonomous aesthetic for a single genre.[96] Lessing's question implies another, namely why confine *conditions* to one genre? Secondly, Lessing anticipates the danger of creating 'perfect' (that is, totally consistent and predictable) characters, that may arise if dramatists are misled into trying to harmonise character and *condition*. He strongly disagrees with Diderot's view that Terence's play *The Brothers* needs a 'model' father to counterbalance the flaws of the other two and he offers the opinion that Diderot himself should have paid greater attention to the dangers of creating such predictable or model characters in his own plays, which are marred by this very shortcoming.[97] As both Buck and Saße point out, characters who always act exactly as you would expect them to, are inimical to the fundamental nature of drama as conflict as Lessing understands it to be from his reading of Aristotle.[98] Finally, Lessing asserts that the way in which Diderot exploits *condition* in *Le Fils naturel* amounts to a violation of his own rationale for introducing it. Diderot recommends basing plays on *conditions* in order to ensure that the spectators will identify with the characters and thus apply the lessons of the play to their own situation. Lessing points out that in the case of *Le Fils naturel*, Dorval is actually not like other people, and his *condition* together with its effect on his character are so singular that the audience can scarcely be expected to see how his situation relates to them. Diderot's practice, in Lessing's view, is therefore inconsistent with both his aims and his recommendations on how to achieve them.[99] For Lessing, then, the theory of *conditions* as Diderot formulates it is incompatible with other essential principles of drama. It is also worth noting, however, that none of the arguments Lessing advances amount to a thoroughgoing rejection of the idea that the inclusion of the dimension Diderot calls *conditions* can enrich dramatic representation; he simply focuses attention on its limitations and potential pitfalls. Moreover, in the discussion that immediately follows Lessing's observations on *conditions* (an examination of the function of names and the way these relate to the supposed universality of characters in classical drama), Lessing three times uses the phrase 'Stand und Charakter', implying that he sees both as relevant to the successful creation of *dramatis personae*. His own practice appears to confirm this and in fact, as we saw in the Introduction (p.6-8), many critics believe that his mature plays incorporate *condition* more successfully than do those of Diderot. Lessing appears to be striving for a balance between character and *condition* in which the specificities of social identity serve to enrich character portrayal by heightening illusion.

96. Göpfert, iv.630.
97. Göpfert, iv.630.
98. Buck, 'Lessing und Diderot', p.209 and p.214; Saße, 'Das Besondere und das Allgemeine', p.268.
99. Göpfert, iv.633.

Lessing's observations on Diderot's distinctions between universal and particular characters are less ambiguous. He believes Diderot's formulation to be inconsistent with what Aristotle says about dramatic characters in the *Poetics*.[100] In opposition to Diderot, he quotes from two works by the English critic Richard Hurd. The passages Lessing uses are drawn from the notes Hurd added to his translation of Horace's *Ars poetica*, and from his essay entitled 'A dissertation on the provinces of the drama'. In both these works, Hurd criticises French neo-classical tragedy and French interpretations of the theory of Antiquity, praising instead Shakespeare and his methods. His basic orientation towards the analysis of drama is that of the beholder, watching an event unfolding before him. Speaking of the representation of character, for example, he states: 'Hence every thing passing before us, as we are accustomed to see it in real life, we enter more warmly into their interests, as forgetting, that we are attentive to a *fictitious scene*' (Hurd's emphasis).[101] His general approach thus has some elements in common with that promoted by Diderot. On the issue of *dramatis personae*, however, Hurd argues that characters in both tragedy and comedy are 'general' or universal, explaining that the difference between them is one of degree and perspective. He insists, though, that even while they are universal, they must nevertheless be particular enough to reflect human experience in the world, and he comments that both Plautus and Molière sometimes failed to achieve the proper balance. In making these points, Hurd, like Diderot, often relies on analogies with the techniques of visual art, in particular portraiture. He rejects the portrayal of characters that have 'no archetype in nature' ('kein Urbild in der Natur') and he summarises the right approach to the creation of character in a quotation that exploits the vocabulary of painting.[102] Dramatists, like visual artists, must balance:

> Lights and shades, whose well-accorded strife
> Gives all the strength and colour of our life[103]

Only the proper balance of the general and the particular can lead to the successful creation of illusion. The question of the universality of dramatic characters is particularly important to Lessing because, as Hurd shows in a passage Lessing quotes, it is the riposte to Plato's unsettling condemnation of artistic representation. According to Hurd, the properly drawn dramatic character both reflects life and transcends the plane of living humanity to become 'the copy or image of truth', 'das unmittelbare

100. Göpfert, iv.641.

101. Richard Hurd, *The Works*, 8 vols (London 1811; Hildesheim 1969), ii.33.

102. Hurd, *Works*, i.255-56 and ii.48-52; Göpfert, iv.656-59.

103. Hurd, *Works*, ii.50. Lessing simply incorporates the idea expressed in these lines into his prose text with the words 'so fehlen ihr alle die Lichter und Schatten, deren richtige Verbindung allein ihr Kraft und Leben erteilen könnte'. Göpfert, iv.657.

Nachbild der Wahrheit'.[104] The effective portrayal of character is thus crucial, Lessing believes, to the justification of drama's morality, and what he criticises in Diderot's drama theory is quite specifically those recommendations that might weaken the creation of convincing *dramatis personae*. It is significant, however, that he does so in the name of the goal that Diderot himself establishes for the drama, namely the creation of illusion in order to achieve a more powerful moral effect, and that he supports his criticisms by reference to a commentator (Hurd) whose approach has affinities with that of Diderot. Moreover, Lessing concludes this entire section by finding a way to reconcile the thinking of Diderot, via Hurd, with that of Aristotle, on the grounds that 'zwei denkende Köpfe von der nämlichen Sache nicht Ja und Nein sagen'.[105] It is rare for Lessing to find such an agreeable way to disagree with someone, a tacit indication perhaps that despite certain reservations concerning Diderot's treatment of character portrayal, Lessing still felt that there was much in his theory that was sound. The representational style he adopts in *Minna von Barnhelm*, *Emilia Galotti* and *Nathan der Weise* certainly implies as much.

---

104. Göpfert, iv.664, Hurd, *Works*, i.257.
105. Göpfert, iv.669. 'Two great minds cannot say yes and no about the same thing'.

# 7. The theatrical code in Lessing's mature plays

THE three plays of Lessing's maturity belong to different genres, and their title pages indicate how Lessing himself categorised them. *Minna von Barnhelm* (1767) is a comedy in five acts ('Ein Lustspiel in fünf Aufzügen'); *Emilia Galotti* (1772) is described as a tragedy in five acts ('Ein Trauerspiel in fünf Aufzügen') and *Nathan der Weise* (1779) is called a dramatic poem in five acts ('Ein dramatisches Gedicht in fünf Aufzügen').[1] *Minna von Barnhelm* and *Emilia Galotti*, both of which treat contemporary subject matter, use prose and have a number of other technical characteristics in common, will be considered first. *Nathan der Weise*, which exploits verse, will be discussed separately at the end of this chapter (p.200-209).

In *Minna von Barnhelm*, Lessing seeks to bring about the thought-provoking, perhaps even rueful, laughter of 'true comedy' ('wahre Komödie').[2] In *Emilia Galotti*, the moral goal is to stimulate the humane empathy that Lessing sees as the object of tragedy. But despite the differences in effect, arising from the different treatments of character and plot, the theatrical code in both works is directed towards the creation of the illusion of scenes drawn from life. Both plays fulfil the semiotic goals of art as stated in the *Laokoon*, that is, they 'stellen uns abwesende Dinge als gegenwärtig, den Schein als Wirklichkeit vor'.[3] The startling improvement in the dramatic effectiveness of the speech in these plays has long attracted the attention of Lessing scholars and their commentary tends generally to confirm the explanation presented here as to how the change came about.

In his study invoked earlier (p.117-18), Böckmann demonstrates that the treatment of language in *Minna* simultaneously exploits and transcends the principle of wit that shaped the early comedies.[4] Tellheim's failing is an excess, as in traditional satirical comedy, but it is an excess of a good quality, virtue or honour, which are not anti-social characteristics in themselves. In the early scenes, dedicated to revealing his character and circumstances, Tellheim is more admirable than ridiculous, and the emphasis is on strength of character, not folly. Minna's purpose, that of winning back Tellheim by overcoming his obstinate virtue, and the playful ploy she initiates to do so, have superficial resemblances to the intrigues

---

1. Göpfert, i.605, ii.127 and ii.205.
2. Göpfert, iv.56.
3. Göpfert, vi.9. 'Represent absent things as if they were present, appearances as if they were real life'.
4. Böckmann, *Formgeschichte der deutschen Dichtung*, i.530.

of the early comedies, but differ from them in that the emotive component has much greater significance and that the outcome cannot be taken for granted. In these ways, the strategies of wit are enlisted for the more serious purpose of 'wahre Komödie'. This is true too at the level of the language. Witty exchanges, such as that between Minna and Franziska concerning Tellheim's qualities (II.i), or Franziska's conversation with Just about the Major's former employees (III.ii), do not exist for their own sake but lead the characters to emotional or ethical insights.[5] Similarly, the reiteration of the words of one character by another can be both humorous and a means of placing an aspect of character or feeling in a new light. The playfulness of the language serves not merely to entertain but to uncover important truths, and 'die Sprache des Witzes' ('the language of wit') yields place to a higher form, 'die Sprache des Herzens' ('the language of the heart') and the expression of individual feeling. Metzger agrees, arguing that the superiority of speech in *Minna* as compared with the early comedies derives from the fact that Lessing here succeeds in 'creating a characteristic pattern of language for each of the various roles he has written', even if many of the means used are the ones he exploited in the first plays.[6] Characters no longer speak and express themselves as types but as fictional individuals, responding (as Diderot proposes they should) to the circumstances of the moment.

In a review of the play, J. J. Eschenburg (one of Lessing's Wolfenbüttel friends) singles out the dialogue for special praise. He draws attention not only to the well differentiated speech of the characters, which constantly reflects background, emotions and the mood of the moment, but also to the way in which the dialogue as a whole creates the impression of everyday human exchange. He notes that the speech is everywhere characterised by 'der wahre, ungekünstelte Ton des Umgangs' and that 'alles was sie sagen, hängt ohne ängstliche Verbindung, in der verschönerten Unordnung wirklicher Gespräche, an einander'.[7] What the characters say and the way in which they say it work harmoniously to make the characters live. Although 'verschönert', 'improved upon', in accordance with its function in dramatic form, this artistic representation of dialogue successfully conceals the traces of its own production, creating an illusion for the ear.

Metzger examines in detail the precise techniques that Lessing exploits to achieve this. He finds that the dialogue in *Minna* relies on many of the same linguistic features as the early comedies (colloquial language, inversions, oaths, interjections, exclamations, anadiplosis, and interruption) but that it surpasses them in its capacity to characterise and to convey

---

5. Böckmann, *Formgeschichte der deutschen Dichtung*, i.543-44.
6. Metzger, *Lessing and the language of comedy*, p.196.
7. Göpfert, ii.673. 'The authentic, artless tone of ordinary society'; 'everything they say hangs together, free of any forced connections, in the controlled disorder of normal conversation.' (Quoted also in Metzger, *Lessing and the language of comedy*, p.190.)

tone.[8] Metzger provides an enlightening account of the discrete features typical of the speech of each of the characters and highlights the skilful way in which Lessing exploits linguistic elements to create the impression of a unique individual. Even the language of an episodic character such as Riccaut, a *tour de force* of its kind, is based on accurate observation of the difficulties French speakers generally have in mastering German pronunciation.[9] Listening to the speech we hear around us ('écouter les hommes, et s'entretenir souvent avec soi'[10]) is an essential element in Diderot's theory of dramatic speech and Lessing's achievement with Riccaut is a striking embodiment of this concept. Metzger emphasises, too, how differently Tellheim and Minna speak when compared with lovers from the early plays. They use an elevated colloquial style, but within this range their speech is differentiated from one another by a quality that Metzger considers new in Lessing's comic style, that is, tone and all its variations. He adds that Lessing directs attention to the importance of this new element by the frequency with which the word 'Ton' occurs both in the dialogue itself and in the stage directions.[11] Again, Metzger's study provides a detailed analysis of the range and variation in tone which can be traced in the speech of these two characters, and he concludes that Lessing's use of tonal nuance, in addition to the individual characterisation of each character's speech, is a major new ingredient in Lessing's mastery of dialogue. Metzger does not link this to Lessing's reading of Diderot (who is not mentioned in his study), although the new qualities that he identifies in Lessing's style appear to be a reflection of Diderot's ideas, especially his emphasis on the individualising capacity of tone. This, as we saw, is explored in his theory and exploited extensively in his stage directions.[12] Moreover, it is the idea on which the *Entretiens sur 'Le Fils naturel'* conclude.[13] The qualitative improvement that Böckmann and Metzger identify in the dialogue of *Minna* conforms both to the principles outlined by Diderot and to Lessing's definition of dramatic speech as natural signs of arbitrary things.

A similar transformation, though much more pronounced from the point of view of overall style, has been observed in the evolution of speech in Lessing's tragedies. For Staiger the language of *Emilia Galotti* marks the end of the descriptive and reflective manner of presenting the passions, typical of tragedies of the baroque age and the period immediately following (which includes *Miss Sara*) and announces the emergence of a new style for German tragedy.[14] In *Emilia*, it is only in the speech of Orsina,

8. Metzger, *Lessing and the language of comedy*, p.193.
9. Metzger, *Lessing and the language of comedy*, p.201-202.
10. DPV, x.346.
11. Metzger, *Lessing and the language of comedy*, p.215.
12. See above, p.101-102, and Whitmore, 'Two essays on *Le Père de famille*', p.144-45.
13. DPV, x.162.
14. Staiger, 'Rasende Weiber', p.53 and p.61.

the 'rasendes Weib' ('angry woman'), that traces of the reflective and descriptive style can still be found, although to nothing like the same extent as in Marwood's language. Staiger argues, in fact, that Lessing successfully domesticates these residues of the past by building the tendency to analyse into Orsina's character.[15] Marinelli draws attention to her intellectual side early on when he notes that she is burying herself in books ('Sie hat zu den Büchern ihre Zuflucht genommen'), implying it bodes no good.[16] Elsewhere, maintains Staiger, the language of the play conceals the art that Lessing applied to its creation and provides a persuasive example of naturalised speech. Other commentators agree. Lamport observes, for example, that although in *Emilia* Lessing does not exploit the linguistic idiosyncrasies associated with particular social classes or with specific dialects, the speech is nevertheless 'a precise instrument of psychological delineation'.[17] Although Staiger does not go so far as to attribute this evolution to Lessing's study of Diderot, he does point out that there are similarities between Diderot's views on dramatic speech and those Lessing articulates in the *Dramaturgie*.[18]

The differences in style between *Miss Sara* and *Emilia* are obvious on every page: speeches are far shorter than in *Miss Sara* and the exchanges between characters more rapid and immediate; for the most part, the characters give direct expression to their thoughts and feelings instead of describing and analysing them; each character has his or her unique style, with characters from the same social class differentiated from each other. Thus the Prince, Marinelli, Appiani, and Orsina, who belong to the same milieu, nevertheless speak and use language differently, as do Emilia, Claudia and Odoardo. The lifelike speech that Lessing gives these characters allows great opportunity for the kind of broad tonal range noted in *Minna*, and again, the question of tone becomes a subject of the dialogue when Claudia recalls the tone in which the dying Appiani pronounced the name of his enemy (III.viii). Appiani's tone, which Claudia cannot successfully reproduce (though her sixth speech seems to invite the actress to try), gives what he says a meaning not contained in the word itself. Meaning emerges from the utterance as a spoken whole. This oral dimension is, according to Schröder, the quality that transforms the arbitrary signs of language into 'die Sprache des Herzens'. Commenting on Claudia's remarks, he notes, 'Als Buchstabe und Abbild ist es [das Wort] unabhängig vom einzelnen Menschen; als Ton aber ist es alles, was es ist, durch den Sprecher und den einmaligen Augenblick des Sprechens.'[19]

---

15. Staiger, 'Rasende Weiber', p.58.
16. Göpfert, ii.137.
17. Lamport, *Lessing and the drama*, p.173-75.
18. Staiger, 'Rasende Weiber', p.56.
19. Schröder, *Sprache und Drama*, p.212. 'As letters of the alphabet and as representation, speech is independent of the individual; however considered as tone, it derives everything that it is from the speaker and from the unique moment in which it is uttered.'

This, precisely, was Diderot's point, and the success with which Lessing exploits this dimension of speech in *Minna* and *Emilia* shows how well he understood it.

Schröder stresses the functional character of the language of *Emilia* and Lessing's skilful shaping of the dialogue, in which the characters appear to move seamlessly from the intellectual recognition of a given state of affairs into an emotional state that produces action. He finds that the only scene in which the dialogue fails to create this effect and satisfy audience expectations is that between Emilia and her father. Here, argues, Schröder, language and psychology seem to fall apart and it is the logic of speech itself, not emotion persuasively expressed, that pushes the two characters into the tragic act. In other words, Lessing here has recourse to that 'playing with words', the apparent autonomy of language that characterised, though in a comic register, his earliest plays. Emilia and her father fall victim to the logical unfolding of the dialogue itself. Instead of making a decision based upon the circumstances, they react blindly to conventional, literary motifs, that is, the symbol of defloration expressed through Emilia's plucking of the petals from the rose, and her allusion to the classical story of Virginia.[20] Schröder attributes this failing (and here many critics agree) to the problematic story material and the difficulties of making plausible, in the modern age, a father's assassination of his daughter.[21] Lessing's modern style (in eighteenth-century terms) conflicts with his goal of creating tragedy out of classical sources.[22] This controversial passage aside, critics find that the language of the play, laconic as it surely is, permits a remarkably rich expression of the human psychology driving the action, even to the point of exposing unconscious impulses hidden from the characters themselves.[23]

20. Schröder, *Sprache und Drama*, p.207. See also Peter Horst Neumann, *Der Preis der Mündigkeit: über Lessings Dramen: Anhang über Fanny Hill* (Stuttgart 1977), p.41-42; H. Steinmetz, '*Emilia Galotti*', in *Interpretationen: Lessings Dramen* (Stuttgart 1987), p.87-137 (p.95). Gloria Flaherty, on the other hand, emphasises the rich literary tradition informing such imagery, its omnipresence in Italian writing and its relevance to the theme of seduction in Lessing's play, all of which serves to 'naturalise' these allusions. See 'Emilia Galotti's Italian heritage', *Modern language notes* 97:3 (1982), p.497-514 (p.509-12).

21. Compare Neumann, *Der Preis der Mündigkeit*, p.42. Lessing's contemporaries held the same view. Neumann quotes comments made by Nicolai, in a letter to Lessing of 7 April 1772. He wrote: 'Viele haben es nicht begreifen können, und halten es für unnatürlich, dass der Vater seine geliebte Tochter blos aus *Besorgnis der Verführung* erstechen könne' ('Many people cannot understand, and consider it quite unnatural, that a father would stab his beloved daughter, simply *for fear that she might be seduced*').

22. Francis Lamport, 'The death of Emilia Galotti – a reconsideration', *German life and letters* 44:1 (1990), p.25-34 (p.31). The fact that Lessing finished writing *Emilia Galotti* whilst it was in rehearsal may also have been a factor! Göpfert, ii.701-702.

23. See, for example, Neumann's comparison of Emilia's use of the word 'es', in her account of her experience in the church, with its role in Freudian theory (*Der Preis der Mündigkeit*, p.46). In this connection, Wolfgang Wittkowski mentions Leibniz's *Nouveaux Essais sur l'entendement humain*, published posthumously in 1760, which explore the powerful attacks made on the will by the unconscious and the senses. 'Emancipation or capitulation

If we consider the particular linguistic features that Lessing typically exploits in *Emilia Galotti*, they turn out to be the same ones that Metzger identifies in the comedies. There are numerous examples of ellipses, exclamations, oaths, interjections, questions, interruptions and anadiplosis. Pauses (which are frequent) are indicated by dashes and there are even examples of wit, and other devices typical of the comic style. In some instances, wit occurs as an expression of character. Thus, Conti expresses his frustration with Gonzaga's lack of interest in Orsina's portrait with the dry remark 'wir Maler rechnen darauf, daß das fertige Bild den Liebhaber noch eben so warm findet, als warm er es bestellte'.[24] Marinelli, in particular, is characterised by the wry humour he applies whenever the mood of those he serves, or the situation in which he finds himself, prove particularly trying. In him it is the defence mechanism of the skilled courtier. The repetition of the phrase 'eben die' ('that very one') with which he counters Gonzaga's questions as to the identity of the Emilia Galotti that Appiani is about to marry (I.vi) is the same verbal technique as Damon's 'Kleinigkeit!' (a trifle!) in *Der junge Gelehrte*; and the sentence with which Marinelli greets Emilia at Dosalo: 'Was für ein Unglück, oder vielmehr, was für ein Glück, – was für ein glückliches Unglück verschafft uns die Ehre –' is the kind of wordplay we expect to find in comedy.[25] On other occasions, Lessing uses linguistic irony to heighten our sense of the enormity of events. In act IV, scene i, when Marinelli attempts to diminish his responsibility in Appiani's death by blaming the count for shooting first, the Prince responds with heavy irony 'Wahrlich; er hätte sollen Spaß verstehen!' and 'Freilich, das ist sehr natürlich!'[26] The Prince's initial scepticism shows how well he understands Marinelli, and casts the latter's guilt and ruthlessness in clear relief, but it is the Prince's weakness that is brought out even more vividly a few speeches later, when Marinelli invokes his wounded honour and the Prince gives in, agreeing that Appiani's death was 'Zufall, bloßer Zufall' ('an accident, just an accident'). The same effect, though more intense, occurs in act V, scene v, where the ironic comments with which Odoardo greets the unfolding of Marinelli's plan for not releasing Emilia express his sense of powerlessness and, for the audience, the resignation of a desperate man. Verbal ploys typical of comedy occur at other important dramatic moments. Gonzaga's response when Orsina's arrival at Dosalo is announced – 'Die Gräfin? Was für eine Gräfin?' ('The countess? What countess?') – followed by the

---

of the middle class? The metaphor of the "long path" as a key to Lessing's political tragedy *Emilia Galotti*', *Lessing and the Enlightenment*, ed. Alexej Ugrinsky (New York 1986), p.149-63 (p.150).

24. Göpfert, ii.132-33. 'We painters count on finding the lover as passionate, when the painting is finished, as he was when he ordered it'.

25. 'To what stroke of misfortune, or rather, to what stroke of good fortune – to what fortunate stroke of misfortune must we attribute the honour –'.

26. Göpfert, ii.175. 'Yes, really; what a spoilsport!' 'Of course, it's quite natural!'

rapid assumption that Marinelli must somehow be behind this unexpected development ('Orsina? – Marinelli! – Orsina? – Marinelli!') are responses of the kind more often exploited for comic effect in a situation (the imminent arrival of the last person you would actually want to see), which is itself the stuff of comedy.[27] Similarly, Schröder sees in Emilia's initially enigmatic reply, when Claudia presses her for the identity of the man who had accosted her in the church, an example of a hackneyed but ever popular device from comedy.[28]

The reaction of Lessing's contemporaries to the exploitation of such techniques in tragedy was mixed. In a letter of 15 July 1772 Eva König gave Lessing a report on the first performance of the play in Vienna. She quotes the Kaiser, who had praised the play, but seems to have found the humour disorienting, commenting 'daß ich in meinem Leben in keiner Tragödie so viel gelacht habe. Und ich kann sagen: daß ich in meinem Leben in keiner Tragödie so viel habe lachen hören; zu weilen bei Stellen, wo, meiner Meinung nach eher hätte sollen geweinet, als gelacht werden.'[29] Others, such as Johann A. Ebert, were more enthusiastic. Describing his response to the play in a letter to Lessing of 14 March 1772, he wrote, 'daß ich durch und durch, mit Klopstock zu reden, laut gezittert habe. Selbst die komischen Szenen oder Züge haben eine ähnliche Empfindung mit der bei mir hervorgebracht, die ich einmal bei Durchlesung der ersten Szenen Ihrer Minna hatte. O Shakespear-Lessing!'[30] The powerful effects achieved by blending comedy and seriousness in this way are unthinkable in the linguistic medium Lessing uses in *Miss Sara* or *Philotas*, which do not exploit verbal humour even if, structurally, they can be seen to embody a traditional comic model.[31]

Parallels with comic technique are not confined to the use of language. Klaus Müller claims that the plot structure and character functions in *Emilia Galotti* offer a mirror image of the fundamental *commedia dell'arte* scenario, which revolves around young lovers, thwarted by an authority figure but abetted by servants whose scheming finally leads to a happy

27. Göpfert, ii.177.

28. Schröder, *Sprache und Drama*, p.388, n.34.

29. Quoted by Klaus-Detlef Müller, 'Das Erbe der Komödie im bürgerlichen Trauerspiel. Lessings "Emilia Galotti" und die commedia dell'arte', *Deutsche Vierteljahrsschrift für Literaturwissenschaft und Geistesgeschichte* 46 (1972), p.28-60 (p.28), from Lessing, *Briefe* in *Gesammelte Werke*, ed. Paul Rilla, 10 vols (Berlin 1954-1958), ix.540. 'I have never in my life laughed so much while watching a tragedy. And I can also say that I have never in my life heard so much laughing going on at a tragedy, sometimes in places where, in my opinion, there should have been tears rather than laughter.'

30. Göpfert, ii.709. 'My whole being was trembling audibly, as Klopstock puts it. Even the comic scenes, or rather elements, had the same effect on me as I felt upon reading through the first scenes of *Minna*. Oh Shakespeare-Lessing!'

31. Robert R. Heitner, 'Lessing's manipulation of a single comic theme', *Modern language quarterly* 18 (1957), p.183-98. Heitner argues that all Lessing's plays, including the tragedies, can be viewed as variations on a traditional comic pattern, though at the expense of creating 'true' tragedy or comedy (p.197).

resolution of their difficulties.[32] In Lessing's tragic adaptation of this basic plot, Marinelli becomes a male Lisette, which, for Müller, explains why so much of the situational humour is associated with his role. Müller comments little on the humour of the language itself, other than to note the ironic character of much of Marinelli's speech, and he accounts for the presence of the underlying comic structure by arguing, as Gustav Kettner earlier had, that continental domestic tragedy evolved out of comedy.[33] Both Müller and Kettner regard the comic traits in Lessing's play as evidence of the continuing impact of what they call Diderot's 'systematic realism', which itself derives, they claim, from comedy. Whilst they are no doubt right to believe that Diderot's theory is behind the change, the reason for the effect is probably the importance that Lessing now attaches to the creation of illusion, rather than anything else. When illusion becomes the goal, the traditional distinctions between genres, which formerly shaped each individual aspect of the theatrical code, spontaneously transmute, and the tragic or comic effect comes to rest largely upon subject matter (the action, in Aristotle's sense) in plays that employ similar means of imitation.

Lessing's treatment of asides provides a succinct illustration of the reorientation affecting dramatic speech. Fewer in number, they also have more of a psychological function, and the term 'bei Seite' ('aside'), which names a device that actually addresses the audience, gradually gives way to the phrase 'vor sich' ('to himself/herself'). This way of categorising such comments identifies them as a form of private thinking aloud that the spectators observe, rather than as a remark made for their benefit. Whereas in *Minna* the direction 'bei Seite' occurs four times and 'vor sich' three times, in the later play 'bei Seite' only occurs once and 'vor sich' six times. In *Minna*, five of the seven 'asides' come from the speech of Franziska, and most of them represent her mental commentary on the actions of the principals, particularly after the point where she begins to feel that Minna is pushing things too far. Werner makes one remark 'vor sich', an ironic comment on Franziska's exchange with Tellheim, and Tellheim has one remark 'bei Seite', where he makes explicit for himself the connection that Just does not, between the poodle story and his own relationship to Just.[34] Although the remark is 'for' the audience too, it appears as a spontaneous reflection on Tellheim's part. For the most part, then, this feature is concentrated in the speech of Franziska, the maid. But even her asides are not overt winks to the audience; rather, they take the form of personal reflection on what is happening. In *Emilia*, five of the asides are uttered by Marinelli in a series of scenes at the Lustschloss where events begin to slide out of control (IV.iii-vi) as, one after the

32. Müller, 'Das Erbe der Komödie', p.39 and p.43.
33. Müller, 'Das Erbe der Komödie', p.31.
34. Göpfert, i.618.

other, Claudia, Orsina and Odoardo ('Nun vollends! Der Alte! –') appear.[35] The direction 'bei Seite' is Odoardo's, in act V, scene v, where a chance remark by Gonzaga stays Odoardo's hand.[36] Again, what characterises the use of asides is restraint and motivation in the context. The change in vocabulary from 'bei Seite' to 'vor sich' suggests that Lessing is hesitating over the use of such interventions and wondering about the appropriate form and function for them within a dramatic aesthetic based on the creation of illusion.[37]

Göbel's analysis of the imagery in these plays also confirms this shift in focus. His study charts a change that is both quantitative and qualitative: there is much less linguistic imagery and the figurative language is, for the most part, colloquial rather than literary.[38] Marinelli's image of the wolf and the lamb and Claudia's reference to the mother lion in *Emilia* communicate aspects of the dramatic situation in vivid and concrete form which make them easy to grasp for the spectators. At the same time, these expressions are commonplaces of the spoken language, appropriate to the speaker and the emotion of the moment, and, argues Göbel, unobtrusive as imagery. Although in *Minna*, heart imagery still plays a role and articulates a major theme of the play, it is far less prevalent than similar language in *Miss Sara*, and not applied in a descriptive way, as a form of reflection on emotion. It is absorbed into the flow of speech and expressed directly.[39] Similarly the exploitation of the concept of 'Spiel' ('wager'), which occurs first in concrete form in the scene between Minna and Riccaut, only subsequently takes on a metaphorical force expressing Minna's approach to the resolution of the emotional tension with Tellheim.[40] More significantly though, as Göbel stresses, is the appearance of genuinely theatrical symbolism. Imagery is not developed at the level of speech because it is present visually, through objects and actions, and embedded in situations. The rings and the exchange of rooms in *Minna*, Emilia's rose, the 'dance' choreographed by Marinelli, and the figurative references to Odoardo's hand, surface in the speech of the characters but achieve their full significance only in relation to the action considered as a

---

35. Göpfert, ii.180, ii.181, ii.182, ii.183, and ii.185. ('And here, to top it all off, is the old man!')

36. Göpfert, ii.199.

37. In *Nathan*, remarks that characters make 'for themselves' are simply enclosed in parentheses, without any further stage direction. This is presumably an element of the system of punctuation Lessing said he had devised for this play, but never got around to explaining in detail. Göpfert, ii.721-22.

38. Göbel, *Bild und Sprache*, p.124 and p.141.

39. Göbel, *Bild und Sprache*, p.119.

40. See also Fritz Martini, 'Riccaut, die Sprache und das Spiel in Lessings Lustspiel *Minna von Barnhelm*', in *Gotthold Ephraim Lessing*, ed. G. and S. Bauer, p.376-426 (first published in *Formenwandel: Festschrift für Paul Böckmann*, ed. Walter Müller-Seidel and Wolfgang Preisendanz, Hamburg 1964, p.193-235).

whole. This technique is much closer to the effects created and exploited in painting.

In these different ways, Lessing's use of language in both *Minna* and *Emilia* can be seen as a successful application of Diderot's formula: 'il ne faut pas donner d'esprit à ses personnages; mais savoir les placer dans des circonstances qui leur en donnent'.[41] Diderot expresses this principle as a general one, relevant to all drama, not just one genre, and this is how Lessing applies it in his plays. The success of dramatic speech in both *Minna* and *Emilia* is largely due to the way in which it is constantly shaped by reference to character and situation; the distinctions drawn in neo-classical aesthetics between speech in tragedy and speech in comedy have disappeared. Dramatic language is no longer shaped by a theory of genres, but by the common aim of creating illusion.

In his analysis of what Lessing means by 'natural signs of arbitrary things', Rudowski takes up the question of how this relates to distinctions between narrative and dramatic modes and argues that Lessing's definition includes the idea that to be 'natural', dramatic speech must be contemporaneous with the dramatic action and reveal character in action.[42] Rudowski illustrates this by reference to statements Lessing makes on narration in the *Hamburgische Dramaturgie* and to the analysis by Stuart Atkins of the ring parable in *Nathan*. Atkins emphasises the dramatic function of this narration, which is the means whereby Nathan saves himself from 'temperamental Oriental despotic justice' and gains the friendship of Saladin.[43] It is not a narration focused on a past event that serves an informative function, but an act of narration that is itself a component of the action of the play. A closer study of Lessing's use of dramatic narrative in *Emilia Galotti* will reveal how profoundly the nature and role of speech have altered.

We have seen that narration in the traditional sense played a major role in *Miss Sara Sampson* and *Philotas*. Like the characters of neo-classical tragedy, Lessing's protagonists in these early plays are haunted by the past as the forces that have been gathering approach their catastrophic resolution. This feeling is absent from *Emilia Galotti*, a work characterised rather by a sense of rapid and sudden developments precipitated before our very eyes by the urgent emotions of the characters.[44] This change of pace is fostered by the function that narrative has in this play. In *Emilia* there are only fourteen passages of text that conform to Nina Ekstein's

41. See above, p.82 and p.157-58.

42. Rudowski, *Lessing's 'aesthetica in nuce'*, p.72-76. He refers to Lessing's discussion of narrative and dramatic modes in *HD* 53 and 77.

43. Stuart Atkins, 'The parable of the rings in Lessing's *Nathan der Weise*', *Germanic review* 26 (1951), p.259-67 (p.267). Atkins does not mention the *Arabian nights*, a widely read work in the eighteenth century, but Nathan's situation bears some resemblance to that of Scheherazade, who tells stories to a sultan in order to save her life.

44. In this connection, Pütz notes the effects of the frequent comings and goings in act II. See *Die Leistung der Form* (Frankfurt am Main 1986), p.178-79.

definition of narration that was applied earlier.[45] Of these, eight range
from a mere two and a half to four and a half lines in length and indeed
barely meet the minimum criteria Ekstein specified for a piece of dramatic
text to be considered narration at all. The longest, and most significant,
example of *récit*, Emilia's account of her experience in the church, in act
II, scene vi, amounts to a total of forty lines, divided into a passage of
twenty-three lines, followed by a further seventeen lines. This narration
far exceeds any other in the play for length; the three that come closest to
it range from only eight to eleven lines. Overall, narration amounts to less
than 4 per cent of the entire text, a low figure in comparison with the 10
to 11 per cent in *Miss Sara* or the norm for neo-classical tragedy.

It is not just the reduction in the amount of narration that is striking but
also the fact that Lessing rarely seems to use it in the way that audiences
accustomed to the neo-classical tradition would expect. Traditionally the
role of the *récit* is to relate relevant events that precede the action of the
play, or to report a contemporaneous happening that occurs in a location
that cannot be represented.[46] Quite often these events are of a kind that
would make them difficult to portray on stage, or they involve action that
would violate principles of *bienséance*, such as violent death. Generally
speaking, what is narrated is reliable as information (although this does
not apply to Marwood's long narrative in *Miss Sara*). If act III, scene i of
*Emilia* is considered with these thoughts in mind, it is apparent that
Lessing's use of dramatic narrative has changed drastically since the
tragedies of the 1750s, suggesting that the reflection to which several
numbers of the *Dramaturgie* testify has borne fruit.

Act III, scene i offers no fewer than three 'narrative opportunities',
none of which is fulfilled in the traditional manner. At the very beginning
of the scene, in the course of reporting his failed attempt to dispatch
Appiani on the fake mission to Massa, Marinelli gives an account of the
argument between himself and the count. Surprisingly perhaps, this
narrative does not relate an off-stage event but a scene the audience has
witnessed just moments before. The point is, of course, that Marinelli's
account, as we, the 'témoins ignorés de la chose', can see, is a blatant
distortion of the truth. Narration is not being used as narrative but as
character portrayal, and also as a way of suggesting something about the
relationship between language and power, an important theme of the
play. Lying, as Orsina later points out, is the lubricant Marinelli uses to
keep the wheels of power turning smoothly.[47]

Shortly after Marinelli's false account of the argument with Appiani,
the question of what happened between the Prince and Emilia at the

45. Ekstein, *Dramatic narrative*. See above, p.136, n.95.
46. This principle does justify Emilia's *récit* just mentioned, but there are other ways in
which this account differs markedly from the traditional *récit* and this will be discussed later
(p.191).
47. Göpfert, ii.180 and ii.183.

church comes up. Now, this is something that the audience would really like to know about, since the event was not represented on the stage and we have so far only heard Emilia's lengthy but nevertheless incomplete account of it in act II, scene vi. But Gonzaga denies us the satisfaction of a *récit*, dismissing the event with an ironic though vague response ('O, es ging alles nach Wunsch'; 'Sie kam meinem Verlangen, mehr als halbes Weges, entgegen'[48]) that merely stimulates curiosity.

Moments later, the discussion of how Marinelli might still be able to help Gonzaga find a way to satisfy his passions is interrupted by the sound of a gunshot. This is the signal for Marinelli to outline as a possible plan, using the future anterior as the main tense, the attack on the marriage party which is actually unfolding as he speaks. In neo-classical tragedy, the event would not, in any case, take the form of an attack on a coach, but its equivalent would be presented as *récit*, as in Théramène's account of Hippolyte's death. In terms of Diderot's theory, the attack on the coach is appropriate material for dramatic narration, since it falls into the category of actions that cannot be represented on the stage in a manner consistent with illusion.[49] But instead of having it reported by a secondary character, returning with news from the site, Lessing adapts the technique of teichoscopy to the interior setting of domestic tragedy by having Marinelli move to a window and describe the coach attack as an action *en cours*.[50] This strategy significantly increases the dramatic effect. The sound of the shot (a natural, acoustic theatrical sign) emphasises proximity, not distance, and connects the spectator directly with what is taking place. The sense of a rapidly unfolding and now incontrollable flow of events intensifies as Marinelli outlines the prepared plan, before stepping to the window where he can already see and describe the first indications of its realisation. At the beginning of the following scene, now alone in the room, he returns to his post at the window and comments, in the present tense, on the coach's slow return towards the town and the arrival of Angelo outside with news of what has happened. None of these passages can be called *récit* because they do not fulfil the basic requirement, use of the past tense. The various 'anti-narrative' strategies that Lessing exploits in this one scene suggest that he has revised his understanding of the nature of drama in such a way as to render the neo-classical conventions problematic.

This is borne out if one considers the other examples of narrative in the play. Many of the passages that technically fit Ekstein's definition of *récit* are very short and highly functional. They are plausibly motivated, in

48. Göpfert, ii.162. 'Oh, it all went according to plan'; 'She came more than halfway to meeting my desires'.

49. DPV, x.141-42. Diderot alludes to Théramène's *récit* in this passage.

50. See above, p.151, n.24. Teichoscopy will later be exploited in plays by Goethe, Schiller and Kleist. It is not used in French neo-classical tragedy.

terms of the action, by the need to communicate information. Angelo's report to Marinelli of Appiani's struggle with Nicolo (III.iii) is a good example. In two short sentences, followed by a longer one broken down into three clauses, Angelo conveys the rapid exchange of fire and the Count's lingering, but certain, death from the wound he sustained. The information is of major importance, and will have significant repercussions in the scenes to follow, as the different characters learn what the audience now knows ahead of them. Yet the space devoted to the transmission of this information is minimal, and in its very brevity the report heightens the atmosphere of urgency. It is *récit* that from all points of view (situation, character, tone, and form) meets the criterion of *vraisemblance*. The same applies to Emilia's three lines of highly succinct narration in act III, scene iv, where she tells Marinelli what she believes has happened, showing him (and the audience) that for the moment she is deceived by his scheme. Lessing usually manages to achieve additional effects from these short narrative passages. Thus, Orsina's brief statements to Marinelli in act IV which explain her presence in Dosalo (four lines in scene iii), and then reveal what she knows about the plot against Appiani and Emilia (two and a half lines and then four lines in scene v), bring home forcefully the way in which Marinelli's own plotting has been thwarted by the capricious and impulsive behaviour of Gonzaga, as well as making clear that the latter's involvement cannot be kept secret.

On the other hand, narration is not used where it would traditionally be expected, namely in the first and last acts (the exposition and the dénouement). The only piece of genuinely expository narration in act I is Marinelli's eight-and-a-half-line account to the Prince of a conversation with Orsina that took place the previous day. The information Marinelli imparts to the Prince is of course crucial from the point of view of the audience in preparation for the events of acts IV and V. Marinelli provides testimony as to Orsina's state of mind, caused by the Prince's rapidly waning interest, and Gonzaga's reaction to Marinelli's report brings out the dangerous contrast in the feelings between the two: Orsina's turbulent, repressed passion and Gonzaga's indifference. But the cause of the transformation in the Prince's feelings and the event that actually precipitates the tragic action (his meeting with Emilia at the Grimaldis') is evoked in two brief sentences delivered to Conti in act I, scene iv. The scene is not related in vivid detail, and indeed, the slight amount of attention it receives is out of all proportion to its actual significance in terms of the action, but Lessing has no need of narration here. The Prince's reticence is psychologically justifiable, since he can have no wish to divulge his real feelings to Conti, but more importantly, as in act III, scene i, Lessing has found other, more theatrical, means to show the audience what they need to know, in this case Gonzaga's reaction to the portrait. Narration has been replaced by action, and the audience grasps the importance of the meeting at the Grimaldis' through the effects of

Emilia's picture on the Prince, a scene which they witness.[51] Although not described in the first act, the Grimaldis' *vegghia* is mentioned again later, and something of what took place there is related by Claudia to her husband (II.iv) although not, strictly speaking, in the form of narration. Claudia's attempts to recount what happened, as she sees it, are constantly interrupted by Odoardo's surprised and reproachful interventions, which cast it in a different light. This makes sustained narration impossible, and the device at work here is not so much *récit* as stichomythia. Its effect is to illustrate in a most vivid manner the contrasting attitudes of Emilia's parents. Thus, the audience's desire to know what occurred at the Grimaldis' is satisfied, but in a way that simultaneously moves our understanding of the psychology of the play forward and intensifies anxiety about future developments.[52]

There are other examples of important details from the past that receive similar cursory treatment. Both the Prince's first reference to Odoardo,[53] which serves to define the power relationship between them, and the allusion to the old enmity between Appiani and Marinelli (which is never fully explained),[54] are factors that would typically have been the subject of some kind of *récit*; Lessing forfeits the clarity and detail the use of *récit* would have afforded, but gains much in terms of the dramatic pace and suspense.

The first meeting of the Prince and Emilia is not the only case where Lessing withholds the account of a significant event. The conversation between them in the entrance to the church is treated the same way. Emilia mentions it first, in the scene with Claudia, but the intensity of her feelings is still such that she cannot (or will not) recall what actually happened. This part therefore goes untold. The Prince first mentions his conversation with Emilia to Marinelli (III.i) but does not reveal what transpired. Two scenes later, he gives Marinelli a fuller account of it (III.iii), and Marinelli hears the same information (more briefly related) from Orsina in act IV, scene v. These passages tantalise, but what no one ever hears is Emilia's account of what occurred during those moments in the church porch. In a sense, this 'missing *récit*' is at the heart of much of the intense critical discussion concerning the interpretation of Emilia's death.[55]

The account that Emilia does give of the visit to the church (II.vi) stands out as different from all the others, not only because of its length but also its form. What characterises all the passages so far discussed is

51. I shall discuss the use of the portraits in this scene in more detail later (p.195-97).
52. The interruption of narration is used effectively, too, in act II, scene iii, in the conversation between Angelo and Pirro about the money.
53. Göpfert, ii.133.
54. Göpfert, ii.137.
55. Schröder emphasises the discrepancy between the Prince's description of Emilia's response and the emotional state in which she returns home: *Sprache und Drama*, p.215-16.

their concision and essential orderliness. Adapted to both situation and character, these passages are nevertheless distinguished by their clarity. The impression given by Emilia's account is radically different. It is constructed in such a way as to communicate above all the overwhelming emotional and physical effect the encounter had upon her; it is full of exclamations, pauses and sentence fragments. Sentences that convey what actually took place are interspersed with commentary upon her thoughts and reactions. Details that she can remember draw attention to the huge gaps that remain and, in the end she is no longer able to distinguish between what actually happened (her flight towards home) and what are probably the projections of her own imagination (the Prince's pursuit and his foot on the stair). The broken language and the confusion between the event itself and its reverberations in her mind and emotions signal the extent to which this entire experience remains still, in terms of Lessing's psychology, in the realm of the lower faculties, unmediated by the organising influence of symbolic cognition. Emilia is unable to give others a coherent account of what happened because she cannot provide one for herself. She does not yet know what it 'means', nor will she, until Odoardo confirms that Appiani is dead and that she is to remain in the hands of the Prince. The disorderly style of Emilia's *récit* here is in fact the exact opposite of the artful and carefully controlled linguistic distillation of emotion that characterises the *récit* in neo-classical tradition. Lessing's version relies on natural theatrical signs, not arbitrary ones.

Although the meeting itself occurred elsewhere, the intensity of its impact is brought onto the stage through Emilia's wrought-up state; she still feels intensely the emotion caused by the encounter itself, and the aftershocks flow through her attempt to relate what happened. As with the representation of the attack on the coach, the manner in which the event is made known to the spectators stresses its immediacy and draws them into its magnetic field, the opposite of the distancing of off-stage events achieved by conventional stage narratives. The impact of Emilia's account on the audience is all the more forceful for its being the only one of its kind in the play. This is a far more effective way of communicating the emotional disturbance of the character involved than the protracted telling of the dream Lessing exploited in *Miss Sara*. The dream motif recurs in *Emilia* (II.vii), where the heroine again reports a dream of the previous night. But Emilia relates the content in two sentences; its effect is concentrated in the image of the pearls, which in the dream become tears.[56] The contrast in the way that Sara and Emilia report dreams is of the same kind as that between Diderot's treatment of letters and the practice in other French plays of the period. The new approach is much more dramatically effective.[57] The possibility that Diderot's theory played

56. Göpfert, ii.155.
57. See above, p.103-106.

a role in stimulating Lessing's attempts to modify dramatic narrative seems confirmed by the fact that the concluding *tableau* of *Emilia* closely resembles the scene from La Noue's *Mahomet II* that Diderot describes in the section of the *Discours* where these matters are discussed.[58]

Dramatic narrative is treated somewhat differently in *Minna*, where there are several examples of genuine narration. These are not exploited for comic effect, however.[59] The first example is Just's account of how he came by his dog, an animal he saved from drowning. This tale presents an image in miniature of the relationship between Tellheim and Just and makes explicit the parallel between Just's devotion to his employer and the dog's loyalty to its master. This narrative serves to characterise Just by explaining and reinforcing the visual image with which the play opens: Just asleep 'in a corner', loyally awaiting Tellheim's return, and throwing out blows as he dreams of a good fight with the Innkeeper, like a sleeping dog dreaming about chasing cats. This narrative serves characterisation, offers Tellheim himself food for thought, and brings about a change in his behaviour and attitude. The other piece of narrative is the Wirt's *récit*, in act III, scene iii, of the emotional conclusion of the conversation between Minna and Tellheim at the end of act II, which, we learn from the Innkeeper, took place in the hall and stairwell. One reason for presenting this as narrative, rather than in the form of stage action, is that Lessing may have felt that the emotional intensity of it would have clashed too violently with the overall mood of the play. The narrative solution allows Lessing to break off the dialogue before it reaches this pitch and yet depict powerful feeling. The strategy he adopts, however, is also very close to Diderot's suggestion that a dramatist visualise and draft the dialogue and action of events that occur between acts, both to reinforce the coherence of the different phases of the plot and to help actors sustain the illusion of their role.[60] Diderot reproduces a fairly lengthy example of such a scene in connection with *Le Père de famille*, and in *Minna*, Lessing exploits the Innkeeper's narrative in just this kind of way. The latter's report of what he saw (which incidentally reveals that he must have been spying on his guests) is a blow-by-blow account of the actions and gestures of both characters. Some of their actual words are quoted in the form of direct speech, but without the use of verbs such as 'she said' and 'he replied'. Short and often incomplete sentences and concise turns of phrase are exploited throughout so that the passage as a whole effectively evokes the

58. DPV, x.141. See also above, p.10-11.

59. Lessing does not use dramatic narrative in his early comedies. In *Der junge Gelehrte*, there are two examples of reporting using the vivid present (II.iii; II.i), where the accent is on comic effect. These speeches represent humorous interpolations in the dialogue, rather like repartee or jokes, which simultaneously provide a snapshot of the state-of-play of the plot.

60. DPV, x.385-86. See above, p.108-109.

rapid movement and dramatic tension of the scene, an original way to exploit both narrative and Diderot's ideas about continuity.

It is apparent that both the quality of dramatic speech and the modification of its role in these two plays transform it into a theatrical sign that blends effectively with the acting style that Lessing tried to introduce, though less successfully from the point of view of speech, into *Miss Sara Sampson*. The suppression of extended narration, for example, makes it much easier for the actors to sustain the illusion created by mimetic action since long *récits* pose the problem of what other actors are going to do for minutes at a time while one character holds the floor. Both Schröder, who analyses a selection of scenes from *Minna* from the perspective of gesture, and Ritter emphasise the harmonious and effective interplay of language and gesture in *Minna*, and point to the role of Diderot's theory in this connection.[61] The general observation is equally true of the style of *Emilia*. In the *Discours*, Diderot remarks that if a play in which the dramatist has composed the dialogue whilst visualising the gestures is compared with one which does not take action into account, 'la facture sera si diverse, que celle où la pantomime aura été considérée comme partie du drame, ne se jouera pas sans pantomime; et [...] celle où la pantomime aura été négligée, ne se pourra pantomimer'.[62] *Miss Sara* and *Emilia* are both plays written with gestures in mind, but when they are compared from this perspective, it is apparent that only the second conforms to Diderot's idea of a text shaped by the dramatist simply imagining the accompanying action and allowing the speech itself, supported by appropriate stage directions not duplicated in the dialogue, to generate the gestures. In his study, Göbel reproduces a table of comparative statistics concerning stage directions in all Lessing's plays. These figures show not only a general increase in stage directions in *Minna* and *Emilia*, but also an increase in those which specifically refer to emotive gestures or vocal register.[63] Göbel relates the increase to the corresponding reduction and transformation in the nature and function of linguistic imagery, concluding that in the later plays, imagery is replaced by gesture that now performs visually tasks formerly allocated to simile and metaphor.[64] As we saw in chapter 4, this is exactly the role that Diderot ascribes to gesture and movement.[65]

The illusion created by speech and gesture is fostered by the way Lessing grounds discourse and gestural expression in everyday activities involving familiar objects (props), and by the increased visibility he gives to setting. Both these strategies figure in Diderot's theory, and his plays offer concrete examples of how these ordinary situations can be exploited

---

61. Schröder, *Sprache und Drama*, p.233-36; Ritter, 'Zur Schauspielkunst bei Diderot und Lessing', p.303.

62. DPV, x.410-11.

63. Göbel, *Bild und Sprache*, p.118.

64. Göbel, *Bild und Sprache*, p.117 and p.119.

65. See above, p.98.

in theatrically effective ways, for example the controversial scene from
*Le Fils naturel* in which Dorval takes tea, the game of tric-trac with which
*Le Père de famille* opens or the various letter scenes, all discussed above in
chapter 4.[66] Stage business of this kind provides the characters with a
focus for their exchanges and allows character and plot elements to enter
the conversation in a covert but natural-seeming way. In his mature
plays, Lessing makes creative use of such devices, often to much greater
effect than Diderot. Two of the most successful instances of this strategy
are the confrontation between Just and the Innkeeper in act I, scene ii of
*Minna*, and the conversation between Gonzaga and Conti in act I, scenes
ii and iv of *Emilia*.

Act I, scene ii of *Minna* opens with a demonstration of Just's hostility
towards the Innkeeper whose early-morning pleasantries he rejects with a
dogged and comic literal-mindedness. Unable to pacify Just's indignation
with his ingratiating commonplaces, the Innkeeper calls for aid in the
form of the Danziger liqueur. The offer and the consumption of the
liqueur do nothing to mollify Just's sense of indignation, or cloud his
judgement, but serve to reinforce, in increasingly comic fashion, the gulf
separating the two characters: Just's incorruptible loyalty to his master
and the Innkeeper's conviction that every man must have his price. Just's
genuine appreciation of the superior quality of the Innkeeper's Danziger
does not mitigate the shabbiness of the treatment his master has received
at his hands, and Just succeeds in getting his morning eye-opener without
sacrificing his principles. The Innkeeper's guilty gesture of hospitality is
an ingenious way of retaining Just despite his bitter anger, and the dialogue which takes place around the action allows the expository information concerning Tellheim's unceremonious ejection from his room to
emerge naturally. The dialogue is rooted in an activity that is a fundamental part of the Innkeeper's *condition* (serving alcohol, soothing custo-
mers) and thus fosters natural modes of expression whilst vividly revealing
character. The seamless integration of humorous action and exchanges
with exposition of character and situation demonstrates a vastly superior dramatic skill from that evident in *Die Juden*, for example, with the
comic business of the silver snuffbox. There, the action appears gratuit-
ous, grafted onto the situation for the sake of humour. In the scene between
Just and the Innkeeper, the humour is consistent with illusion, and each
character speaks or responds in his unique tone and style.[67] There are

66. The game of tric-trac, mentioned as part of the salon décor at the beginning of *Le
Fils naturel* and put to use in *Le Père de famille* became, for critics hostile to Diderot, the
symbol of his scenic innovations and of his approach to the treatment of character. See
Julie Hayes, 'Subversion du sujet et querelle du tric-trac: le théâtre de Diderot et sa
réception', *Recherches sur Diderot et sur l'Encyclopédie* 6 (1989), p.105-17 (p.113-15).
67. Goethe considered the first two acts of *Minna* a perfect model of dramatic exposition:
*Dichtung und Wahrheit*, in *Sämtliche Werke*, ed. Eduard von der Hellen, 40 vols (Stuttgart
1902-1912), xxiii.163.

several other examples of the successful exploitation of this effect in *Minna*. In act II, scene ii, the Innkeeper arrives, equipped with writing materials, and sits down at a table to take down the details of Minna's identity and her reasons for travel for his police report. Her answers to his questions supply further necessary information to the audience, whilst the situation provides entertaining satirical commentary on the wartime methods of the state. The humorous action in act IV, scene iii, where Minna ends up pouring coffee for herself because Franziska is so absorbed in what she has to say is also an illustration of Lessing's mastery of the integration of supportive stage action.

In *Emilia*, the conversation between Conti and Gonzaga, which revolves around the contemplation and discussion of the two portraits of Orsina and Emilia, is a particularly effective example of this technique. This scene presents spectators with two contrasting responses to the artistic image, an aesthetic and a non-aesthetic one. For Conti, Emilia's portrait does not represent Emilia, but the ideal of feminine beauty. His eye penetrates beyond the model to the image 'wie sich die plastische Natur, – wenn es eine gibt – das Bild dachte'.[68] Conti laments the difficulty of the challenge the artist faces in bringing this image to expression: 'Auf dem langen Wege, aus dem Auge durch den Arm in den Pinsel, wie viel geht da verloren!'[69] What makes him a great painter, he explains, is that despite his inevitable dissatisfaction with what he paints, he fully understands 'was hier verloren gegangen, und wie es verloren gegangen, und warum es verloren gehen müssen'.[70] As a 'thinking painter', Conti has a lucid grasp of the relationship between the painted image, its original in nature and the ideal form that he abstracts from nature and carries in his mind. Not so the Prince. He may consider himself a generous patron of the arts but he is a naïve viewer of portraits. He is conscious of only one dimension of the image, its 'likeness' to its original, and it is on this dimension alone that the pictures seem to affect him. He describes the portrait of Orsina as 'geschmeichelt [...] ganz unendlich geschmeichelt' ('flattering [...] enormously flattering'), whereas that of Emilia is 'wie aus dem Spiegel gestohlen' ('as if stolen from the mirror'). But his evaluation of the pictures (which he confuses with the perception of them) is largely a projection of his own emotions. The 'ideal' image that he carries within is not like that of the artist, but is a certain notion of the woman for whose beauty he has developed an obsessive passion. The painter's reaction is an aesthetic one, since contemplation of the image raises his thoughts to a

---

68. Göpfert, ii.131-32. 'As plastic nature – if it exists – imagined it'.

69. Göpfert, ii.134. 'How much is lost on the long journey from the eye, through the arm into the brush!' For Ilse Appelbaum-Graham, this statement articulates the main tragic theme of the play. She explores the significance of 'the long way' as it recurs in other situations and speeches. 'Minds without medium. Reflections on *Emilia Galotti* and *Werthers Leiden*', *Euphorion* 56 (1962), p.3-23 (p.6).

70. 'What has been lost here, why it was lost and why it must be lost'.

higher plane and allows him to perfect his knowledge of beauty itself.
Gonzaga's response is not; his reaction to the portrait is of the same kind
as his reaction to the woman herself and the portrait serves only to
intensify his erotic fantasies, trapping him in the realm of the senses:
'Hätt' ich ihn doch nicht rufen lassen! Was für einen Morgen könnt' ich
haben!', he exclaims when Marinelli is annnounced.[71] Although Conti
and Gonzaga are discussing visual art, the differences between them can
be seen to embody the contrasting responses to theatrical representation
evoked by Plato in the *Republic*, where he observes that drama 'seems to
be injurious to minds which do not possess the antidote in a knowledge of
its real nature'.[72] Conti draws attention to the differences in attitude
when he wonders whether the price the Prince is willing to pay for the
portrait is a reward for something other than art.[73] Purchasing the portrait leads the Prince's mind directly to the thought of 'purchasing' the
sitter, and the ease with which he obtains the picture makes him highly
receptive to Marinelli's proposals for 'obtaining' the woman. The stage
*tableau* at the end of the play is the shocking 'realisation' of Gonzaga's
pursuit of his ideal image of Emilia, but in his case, the 'long way' from
conception to realisation leads to the violent destruction of beauty, not its
perpetuation.[74] Conti does not appear again, but there are no superfluous
characters in this play. The painter is clearly 'involved'; I think Lessing
also wants us to ask whether or not he is in any way 'responsible'. The
play cautions us about the dual nature of the painterly sign, just as *Miss
Sara* exposes the ambivalence of the linguistic sign. Semiotic systems
can lead to truth and insight, but can equally become weapons for the
oppression of others or a path to self-delusion.[75]

The viewing and discussion of the portraits thus reveal the nature of the
prince's obsession and simultaneously allow the spectator to evaluate it by
comparison with the reactions of the artist. The use of antithetical speech
and gesture, captured in Gonzaga's spontaneous reactions to the pictures
and his attempts to constrain them (indicated in the stage directions)
demonstrates the power of his desires. Expository information about when
Gonzaga first saw Emilia, how well (or little) he knows her, details of his
relationship with Orsina, and the character of the latter emerge as if by

71. Göpfert, ii.135. 'If only I hadn't had him summoned. What a morning I could have!'
72. Plato, *The Republic*, p.324.
73. Göpfert, ii.135.
74. Graham, 'Minds without medium', p.6.
75. Lessing's sensitivity to the power of illusion, especially the illusion created by the
material of tragedy, may explain Odoardo's reference to 'eine schale Tragödie' ('a tired tragedy') at the end. Psychologically, Odoardo's remark is justified: having fulfilled his function as the 'potestas patria', he is ready to face justice, both human and divine (Neumann,
*Der Preis der Mündigkeit*, p.42-43). Lessing the dramatist worries about naïve spectators who
may be misled into acting out scenes from tragedy in their own lives. In the *Briefwechsel*,
Mendelssohn mentions a man who, inspired by the example of Cato, committed sui-
cide after watching a performance of Addison's tragedy (Göpfert, iv.181).

chance. The theme of painting and the urbane tone of the conversation are well calculated to evoke the flavour of the setting by playing on associations the audience would have with Italy as a centre of artistic excellence. Fusing these diverse elements into a conversation focused on the portraits, Lessing achieves a genuinely theatrical effect, far superior to conventional exposition. This is showing, not telling. But despite the extraordinary skill that has gone into the crafting of this scene, on the surface, and in performance, the artfulness remains hidden, content and form perfectly fused into an illusion as persuasive as Emilia's portrait.

The scenes just discussed form part of the exposition of *Minna* and *Emilia*, although they are not opening scenes. Both plays actually begin with scenes that could be described as stage *tableaux* in Diderot's sense. The humorous image of the dreaming Just and its connection with his account of his dog was mentioned above. *Emilia* also opens with a single figure on stage, the Prince seated at a desk, dealing with paperwork. He subsequently rings for his servant and a conversation ensues. According to the stage directions, Gonzaga remains seated throughout, standing only when Conti enters. Some movements (riffling through papers, skimming a letter, signing a document, ringing the bell, and so on) are explicitly prescribed; in other cases the words themselves merely imply the need for supporting gesture, such as the end of Gonzaga's second speech, with its references to lost tranquillity. Speech takes the form of short sentences with some exclamations and questions, and includes many sentence fragments and repetitions of word or phrase typical of the spoken language, and all the elements at work (décor, gesture and speech) function together to present Gonzaga from the perspective of both his *condition* and his character. The Prince's state of mind, as well as aspects of his personality, is communicated as much through his behaviour as through his words. The approach in both cases is the same as that modelled in Diderot's plays, and has equally little to do with neo-classical doctrine concerning play openings. These scenes also form a marked contrast with Lessing's earlier practice in *Miss Sara* and *Philotas*. *Miss Sara* begins with a conventional and rather wordy exchange between Sir William and his servant/confidant, Waitwell, which includes numerous items of information and *sententiae* 'planted' in the dialogue for the audience's benefit. The audience-directed nature of the long monologue with which *Philotas* opens was discussed earlier.[76] A comparison of the first scene of *Emilia* with that of *Der junge Gelehrte*, which opens in a superficially similar way (Damis at his study table, surrounded by books), also illustrates how much more effectively, in the later plays, the physical milieu is integrated into the action; it is not merely background. The differences between the two styles can most simply be characterised by saying that in the later plays, the scenes have been composed from the perspective of the spectator

76. See above, p.140-41.

(either physically in the theatre or replayed before the mind's eye) and with the assumption that some of the information is delivered visually, not through words.

Throughout both plays, these effects are reinforced by the attention given to setting. In the early comedies, as already noted, setting is conventional. It is more significant in *Miss Sara* and *Philotas*, where Lessing exploits more fully its potential to heighten the psychological tensions that inform each work: the passivity and inability to decide and act in *Miss Sara*, which is reflected in the characters' movement between different spaces and what happens in them, the isolation in *Philotas*, where the protagonist is confined in a space that offers a level of physical comfort he finds insulting for a prisoner of war. Essentially, though, the 'elendes Wirtshaus' ('miserable inn') of *Miss Sara* and the 'Zelt in dem Lager des Aridäus' ('tent in the camp of Aridäus') of *Philotas* are variants of the neo-classical approach to setting. These are poetic spaces, integrated into the theme of the play, but not conceived with a view to creating illusion.[77] It is impossible to say where and when *Philotas* is set (there is no reference to any known episode of Greek history) and only the names of the characters and the rather incongruous reference to Dover in Marwood's letter at the end evoke the 'English' milieu of *Miss Sara*. Lessing's practice in these plays corresponds to Nicolai's recommendation, mentioned earlier (p.146), to leave details of time and place vague.

However, in the later plays, his approach is radically different, and in both *Minna* and *Emilia*, he has incorporated the kind of suggestions that Diderot makes in order to intensify the effect of illusion. *Minna* is set in Berlin, in August 1763, in the period immediately following the Seven Years War. Although the play was completed in the winter of 1776 to 1777, the title page, which states 'verfertiget im Jahre 1763', emphasises its intimate connection with this period of German history. Characters, situations and numerous details are drawn from Lessing's personal experience or from known events of the time.[78] The originality of Lessing's treatment and its powerful impact on contemporary audiences is recorded by Goethe in his now famous description of Lessing's play as 'die wahrste Ausgeburt des Siebenjährigen Krieges' and 'die erste aus dem bedeutenden Leben gegriffene Theaterproduktion von spezifisch temporärem Gehalt, die deswegen auch eine nie zu berechnende Wirkung hatte'.[79] The spirit of the age is evident in all manner of ways, ranging from

77. On *Philotas*, see Burgard, 'Lessing's tragic topography'; on *Miss Sara*, see Pütz, *Die Leistung der Form*, p.120-25.

78. For details, see Gotthold Ephraim Lessing, *Minna von Barnhelm*, ed. D. Hildebrandt, *Dichtung und Wirklichkeit* 30 (Frankfurt, Berlin 1969), p.5-22, and Lamport, *Lessing and the drama*, p.29.

79. Quoted in Göpfert, ii.677. 'The most authentic product of the Seven Years War'; 'the first theatrical production to be inspired by a significant life experience and invested with specific, contemporary content and which, for these very reasons, exercised an incalculable effect'.

concrete references to the difficulties of travel, Tellheim's financial situation, the role of the Innkeeper as agent (read, spy) for the Prussian state and the various attitudes towards peace and war which come up in the course of conversations. Striking effects are achieved on stage by the visual effects of costume itself; the contrast between the military uniforms and civil clothing, for example, exploited dramatically by Lessing when Franziska suggests to Tellheim that when he comes to collect Minna, he should wear shoes (not boots) and try to look a little less 'preußisch' ('Prussian').[80] In act IV, scene vi, he appears groomed according to her instructions, but his uniform is the object of comment when Minna's Saxon uncle, the Graf von Bruchsall arrives, and acknowledging his respect for Tellheim, makes the point that it is not the uniform but the man that counts.[81] Minna has more contrasting changes of costume. She first appears in act II 'im Negligé', but at the beginning of act IV, is described as 'völlig und reich, aber mit Geschmack gekleidet', ready for her assault on Tellheim's obstinacy.[82] The costume of the widow Marloff, dressed in mourning, is a graphic reminder of the effects of war, as also Tellheim's wounded arm, which simultaneously marks him as an emotionally 'wounded' man. In addition to the rings that are pawned and exchanged, numerous other ordinary objects are required for pieces of action: Tellheim's pocketbook and documents, the Innkeeper's paper and writing-case, Minna's watch and the safety box in which she keeps her money, Werner's roll of ducats and bag of gold coins and, of course, more letters.[83]

The contemporary Italian setting of *Emilia Galotti*, although more remote for German audiences, is also evoked in tangible ways. A number of details concerning the Prince such as his name (Hettore Gonzaga), the area he governs (Guastalla), the claims of the Gonzaga family on Sabbionetta and the name of the Lustschloss (Dosalo) are inspired by historical fact.[84] The Italian ambience is heightened by other Italian names and words and the discussion of art with which the play opens. The sensuality, petulance and self-preoccupation of Gonzaga are a contemporary, if diluted, version of the tyrannical, capricious character associated with various Roman emperors. Gloria Flaherty connects other aspects of his behaviour with Castiglione's *Il Cortegiano*, a work that Lessing knew well, and she emphasises the Catholic Italian background that shapes Emilia's

80. Göpfert, i.661.

81. 'Ich bin sonst den Offizieren von dieser Farbe (*auf Tellheims Uniform weisend*) eben nicht gut. Doch Sie sind ein ehrlicher Mann, Tellheim; und ein ehrlicher Mann mag stecken, in welchem Kleide er will, man muß ihn lieben.' ('Normally, I am not well-disposed towards officers wearing this colour (*pointing at Tellheim's uniform*). But you are an honest man, Tellheim, and an honest man can dress as he will, one has no choice but to like him.') Göpfert, i.702. Although he has fought for Friedrich II, Tellheim is not himself Prussian.

82. Göpfert, i.624 and i.664.

83. Göpfert, i.616, i.627, i.624, i.633, i.653, i.699.

84. Göpfert, ii.714.

character and emotions.[85] Costume plays a role here too, where, as in *Minna*, changes of costume are built into the action, particularly Emilia's change of dress, which is the subject of an exchange between herself and Appiani in act II, scene vii, and visually underscores the tragedy of the final events in the Lustschloss. The different décor and furniture required for the scenes in the palace, in the Galottis' house and in the Lustschloss would also convey differences of class and power that do not emerge as strikingly in the dialogue.[86] It is clear that Lessing intended costumes and décor in these plays to be handled with enough attention to detail to bring about the illusion of a concrete place and time, very different from the virtual, theatrical space of the traditional genres and Lessing's earlier works. This is the type of illusion for which Diderot urges dramatists to turn to painterly models and the principle of 'le costumé' (in its broad sense); and it is this visual conception of the effect of the whole that makes *Minna* and *Emilia* (composed after the period of Lessing's intense reflection on the nature of painting for the *Laokoon*) such different plays from the earlier ones. It is this total effect, made up from the emphasis on present action, the logic of the characters, the naturalness of speech and gesture, the tone of the dialogue and the fact that everything happens 'entweder unmittelbar oder doch in seinen nächsten Folgen vor den Augen des interessierten Zuschauers' that Eschenburg praises in his review of *Emilia*.[87] The fact that both *Emilia* and *Minna* are still performed today is a testimony to the success with which Lessing fuses theme and form into works of enduring appeal.

This is true too of his final play, although its style is rather different from the two works just discussed. When *Nathan der Weise* was published in 1779, it was an immediate success and provoked a flood of reviews, as well as other plays and dramatic parodies.[88] But the scepticism that Lessing expressed in a letter to Karl Lessing (18 April 1779) about its future on the stage initially proved to be well founded, and he did not live to see his play performed.[89] It was first staged in Berlin in 1783, but it was the 1801 production of Schiller's adaptation at Goethe's Weimar theatre that established *Nathan* in the German repertoire.[90] Since that time, the play has had an extraordinary reception history, intimately entwined with the history of Germany itself. In September 1945, for example, it was

85. Flaherty, 'Emilia Galotti's Italian heritage', p.500-502 and p.504-505.

86. See also Pütz's comments on the varying rights of access to the different spaces in the play, *Die Leistung der Form*, p.152-53.

87. Göpfert ii.710. 'Either directly or through its immediate consequences before the eyes of the captivated spectators'.

88. Jo-Jacqueline Eckardt, *Lessing's 'Nathan the Wise' and the critics: 1779-1991* (Columbia, SC 1993), p.5 and p.9.

89. Göpfert, ii.723. Lessing reiterates this thought in his preface, Göpfert, ii.748-49.

90. Göpfert, ii.718; Eckardt, *'Nathan the Wise' and the critics*, p.24-25. Schiller cut the dialogue by a quarter, deleting didactic passages and eliminating 'prosaic' expressions, as well as references to money and the oriental setting.

performed at the Deutsches Theater in Berlin, where it was dubbed 'Wiedergutmachungsdrama' ('play of reconciliation'), although it has also been commandeered for various ideological purposes that would have surprised and disturbed Lessing.[91] Nevertheless, one might be justified in thinking that with this work in particular, Lessing did succeed in achieving the cultural goals towards which his earlier experiments in formal tragedy had been directed, although the success of *Nathan* may well be due to the fact that Lessing was motivated not by the intent to produce a certain kind of play, but by the intellectual needs of the moment.[92]

Lessing's awareness that *Nathan* does not readily conform to existing definitions of genre is reflected on the title page, where the sub-heading classifies it as a dramatic poem. Whilst the play can be seen to have affinities with the form and ethos of sentimental comedy, particularly in terms of its plot, it goes far beyond normal expectations for the type in both style and intent.[93] Mortier sees it as a masterful application of Diderot's vision for a philosophical drama, sketched out in the *Discours*.[94] The figure of Nathan, the wise Jew and teacher, seems to embody for Lessing many of the exemplary qualities that Diderot associates with Socrates, and Nathan's method of leading other characters such as Recha and the Tempelherr towards better insight through judicious questioning could be described as 'Socratic'. Diderot evokes 'le caractère ferme, simple, tranquille, serein, et élevé du philosophe' whose conduct 'doit amener le ris sur le bord des lèvres et les larmes aux yeux'.[95] Although inflected more strongly towards humour than Diderot's outline, and situated in a different cultural setting, Lessing's *Nathan* comes close to this formula.

Formally, Lessing's final play seems to represent a unique fusion of his love of comedy, his study of the tragic form and the reflections on illusion and the means to achieve it stimulated by Diderot's writings. Lessing brings these diverse elements together in a way that illustrates a sophisticated grasp of drama as the embodiment of a theatrical code. The salient characteristic of *Nathan* is its essential and well-conceived unity of theme, form and tone. The *invraisemblance* of the plot, another example of the 'witty' structures that characterised the early comedies, is here enlisted to convey a message intended to lift the mind of the spectator beyond a divisive present towards the possibility of genuine understanding and solidarity between people of different faiths; not the world as it is, but the world as it could be, when human beings of good will adjust their step to

91. Eckardt, '*Nathan the Wise*' *and the critics*, p.63, p.41-45 and p.56-57.

92. Göpfert, ii.717. For details of the theological dispute that precipitated the writing of the play, see also Lamport, *Lessing and the drama*, p.195-99 and Gotthold Ephraim Lessing, *Nathan der Weise*, ed. David Hill (Hull 1988), p.18-25.

93. Lessing, *Nathan der Weise*, ed. Demetz, p.126.

94. Mortier, *Diderot en Allemagne*, p.78. DPV, x.340-41 and x.412-26.

95. DPV, x.341.

the workings of Providence.[96] Lessing believed such change possible: 'die Welt, wie ich mir sie denke, ist eine eben so natürliche Welt, und es mag an der Vorsehung wohl nicht allein liegen, daß sie nicht eben so wirklich ist'.[97] This theme is brought to life through strongly drawn and varied characters, who, guided by Nathan, are able to transcend the obstacles posed by differences of race and creed and discover their shared humanity. Schlegel describes these figures as 'lebendiger gezeichnet und wärmer colorirt' ('more vividly drawn and more warmly coloured') than any in Lessing's plays.[98] Whilst they are all presented in such a way that the relationship between their religious beliefs and their conduct emerges into view, they are still individualised through traits of character that testify to Lessing's keen observation of the paradoxes of human nature. Daja's dogged attachment to articles of Christian faith is at odds with her weakness for fabrics and jewellery, on which Nathan plays; Al-Hafi's pursuit of the hermit's life is offset by his passion for the game of chess; the Tempelherr's profession of tolerance contrasts with the passionate intensity of his reactions to others and so on. The historical setting, Jerusalem at the time of the crusades, is a framework in which members of all three religions can plausibly be brought together, and yet sufficiently remote and exotic to suit what Lessing referred to as his 'anderweitige Absicht' ('larger purpose').[99] In this poetic universe, the question of what language characters of such diverse backgrounds speak to each other is, in a sense, irrelevant, and yet the fact that they do communicate and can thus all be seen to participate in human nature and human reason, reinforces Lessing's underlying conviction about the unity of humankind.[100]

In terms of a performance code appropriate to this material, Lessing seems to be striving for a delicate balance between visual illusion and symbolic form. There are four principal settings in the play: Nathan's house, Saladin's palace, the Patriarch's monastery and the palm grove near the Holy Sepulchre. The first three interior settings are each dominated by a central figure representing one of the three main religions: Nathan, Saladin and the Patriarch. The vague exterior setting of the palm grove is associated with the Tempelherr, the character whose identity and allegiances shift and change during the course of the play, until he is drawn into the family circle in Saladin's palace at the end.[101] The settings are not described in the amount of detail found in *Minna* and *Emilia*, and are evoked in the dialogue, if at all, only by a few broad strokes. Nevertheless, they are highly distinctive and reinforce audience awareness. Nathan's

96. Lamport, *Lessing and the drama*, p.201; Göpfert, ii.721.
97. *Ankündigung*, Göpfert, ii.749. 'The world as I imagine it is just as natural as the one we have, and it may not be solely the fault of providence if this world is not as real'.
98. Lessing, *Nathan der Weise*, ed. Demetz, p.220.
99. Göpfert, ii.721; Lamport, *Lessing and the drama*, p.219.
100. Pütz, *Die Leistung der Form*, p.265-66.
101. Pütz, *Die Leistung der Form*, p.261 and p.263.

house, for example, must show evidence of the recent fire, a constant visual reminder of the precipitating event that brings him and the Tempelherr together.

In various scenes action and setting are fused in a *tableau* effect, for example in act IV. In the third scene, slaves are seen carrying bags of money into Saladin's palace, tangible evidence of the wealth Nathan is putting at the disposal of the Muslim ruler. These are again visible on stage (and mentioned in the directions) at the beginning of act V.[102] In act IV, scene vi, in a scene reminiscent of the opening of act II from Diderot's *Le Père de famille*, the costly wares that Nathan has brought back from his journey are spread out, partially unpacked, and form the subject of the conversation between himself and Daja, another graphic reminder of his *condition* as a successful merchant.[103] The chess game between Saladin and Sittah at the beginning of act II also recalls a motif from the opening scene of *Le Père de famille*, the game of tric-trac in which Cécile and her uncle are engaged. But the primarily illustrative function that the game has in Diderot's play is transformed by Lessing into a means not only of revealing Saladin's distracted mental state, but also of introducing discussion of various political elements in a natural way.

Costumes are also mentioned, most notably perhaps the Tempelherr's white robe, which Recha takes to be the white wings of her guardian angel. The singed fabric visually links the Tempelherr with Nathan's fire-damaged house as well as showing his politico-religious affiliations, and the spectacle of Nathan the Jew kissing the singed robe in a gesture of gratitude is a striking image of human feeling transcending conventionally instituted boundaries between people. This impression is subsequently consolidated in the handshake of friendship between them.[104] Likewise, the first appearance of Al-Hafi, dressed not in the simple garb of a dervish, but in the magnificence befitting Saladin's treasurer, plays on the theme of the inner and the outer self, reflected in other references, for example to the tree and its bark, or to the stone of a fruit and its skin. His attitude towards his appearance is contrasted with that of the Patriarch, who, unlike Al-Hafi, derives his self-image from the splendour of his raiment and has no human depth.[105] One of the central visual gestures, indicated in the stage directions, is Saladin's grasping of Nathan's hand, at the conclusion of the story of the rings, when he asks for his friendship. Their hands remain clasped until almost the end of the scene. This gesture arises naturally from the context and yet confronts the audience with an image (a Jew and an Arab, standing with hands clasped in friendship) that challenged prejudices and assumptions of the time and,

102. Göpfert, ii.321.
103. Göpfert, ii.301 and ii.310. DPV, x.211-13.
104. Göpfert, ii.252 and ii.254.
105. Göpfert, ii.219-20; ii.250; ii.295-96; ii.304.

indeed, continues to do so. The play ends with a stage *tableau*, visually reminiscent of those with which Diderot's two plays conclude but with added metaphorical force, since the reconstituted family includes members of three religions.

The visual dimension of the play is thus clearly conceived, and the play relies on numerous, often powerful, visual effects to communicate Lessing's message. At the same time, the approach differs from that in *Minna* and *Emilia*. The settings are not so fully present in their materiality, and in *Nathan* the visual elements have both concrete and symbolic meanings. Benjamin Bennett interprets the smooth pieces belonging to the chess game, which Saladin blames for his loss, as a reference to an undesirable homogeneity of human culture, lacking true religious feeling; he sees the game as an image for the nature of drama itself.[106] In a different way, the idea of truth and wisdom is concretised in the references to money that recur throughout the play, a reflection of the idealised eighteenth-century concept of the merchant as a figure who transcends national boundaries and fosters well-being across the globe.[107] Paul Hernadi discusses the significance of the role played by economics and its terminology (much more present in *Nathan* than in any of Lessing's other plays) and the choice of a twelfth-century Jew as the embodiment of contemporary merchant values. He argues that Lessing's technique captures not just a *Bürger* but penetrates to '*die platonische Idee des Bürgers*'.[108] Thus, although Lessing is still striving to create illusion in this play, it is the illusion of a world different from the one we presently inhabit.

This overall impression is enhanced and supported by the metrical form of the speech, which is probably the work's most original feature. The decision to use blank verse in a play that superficially takes the form of a 'domestic drama' might appear surprising, and Demetz points out that Lessing's choice departs from Diderot's specific recommendations for the *genre sérieux*.[109] At the same time Lessing's disregard for many of the principles governing the use of iambic pentameters (the varying length of the lines, the shifting accent, the accumulation of single-syllable words, the pauses and the extensive use of *enjambement*) transforms it into what Demetz calls an 'Anti-Vers', that combines metrical form with ordinary turns of phrase and homespun images.[110] Demetz sees this strategy as a

106. Benjamin Bennett, *Modern drama and German classicism: renaissance from Lessing to Brecht* (Ithaca, NY 1979), p.85 and p.92.

107. See Paul Hernadi, 'Nathan der Bürger: Lessings Mythos vom aufgeklärten Kaufmann', *Lessing yearbook* 3 (1971), p.151-59 (p.156-57); and Pütz, *Die Leistung der Form*, p.267.

108. Hernadi, 'Nathan der Bürger', p.157 (Hernadi's emphasis).

109. Lessing, *Nathan der Weise*, ed. Demetz, p.129.

110. Lessing, *Nathan der Weise*, ed. Demetz, p.130-31. Lessing also uses dashes and suspension points intended to guide the actors in the use of pauses etc.; however, the explanation of how this system works never appeared. See also Göpfert, ii.721-22.

means of striking a balance between the distancing effect of the oriental setting and the familiarity of the domestic milieu.[111]

The linguistic achievement can also be interpreted as a reflection of other fundamental assumptions of Diderot's theatre theory. In the letter to Ramler, in which Lessing explains his reasons for choosing verse, he notes: 'Ich habe wirklich die Verse nicht des Wohlklanges wegen gewählt: sondern weil ich glaubte, daß der orientalische Ton, den ich doch hier und da angeben müsse, in der Prose zu sehr auffallen dürfte.'[112] His use of the word 'auffallen' ('to be conspicuous, noticeable') is an interesting variant of the invisible poet topos and shows that despite the distancing effect of the form, he is still using the argument from illusion. In this case, it is the exotic setting and the metaphysical theme that might draw too much attention to the play as artifice. By raising the tone of the language to a level commensurate with setting and theme, the internal coherence of the theatrical code is maintained and the illusion of a possible world, though not of our immediate one, is preserved. The unusual rhythms and the use of evocative proper names (Babylon, Damaskus, Euphrat, Tigris, Salomon, David, though here unburdened by the adjectives that characterised the poetic use of names in *Miss Sara*) are counterbalanced by imagery that simultaneously roots the experience of the characters in a more ordinary world of iron pots, irrigation systems, bird-catchers' whistles, sore teeth, doors waiting to open, and so on. Göbel notes that the unsophisticated images from ordinary life that characterise the speech of the servants in the early comedies now crop up in the speech of all the characters, an expression of their essential equality.[113] The broken rhythms and familiar metaphors conceal the 'poetic' form of the language, which is motivated not by the impulse to demonstrate a technical mastery of language, nor to represent the inner world of the characters in controlled verbal form, but to communicate important truths. Lessing expresses this goal in the form of a paradox, saying that his lines 'wären viel schlechter, wenn sie viel besser wären'.[114] Their role is not to attract attention as poetry but to sustain the illusion of an atmosphere appropriate to the material. David Hill describes Lessing's capacity to 'poeticise everyday speech' in this way as 'unique in German literature'.[115]

Göbel notes that imagery is much more extensive in *Nathan* than in *Minna* and *Emilia*, and is accompanied by a corresponding decrease in the

---

111. Lessing, *Nathan der Weise*, ed. Demetz, p.132.

112. Göpfert, ii.720-21. 'I did not really choose verse on account of its pleasant sound, but because I thought that the oriental tone I have to evoke in places might stand out too much in prose.'

113. Göbel, *Bild und Sprache*, p.158.

114. In a letter to his brother Karl, 7 December 1778, Göpfert, ii.720. 'Would be much worse if they were a lot better', that is, they 'wouldn't be such good lines if they were better verse'.

115. Lessing, *Nathan der Weise*, ed. Hill, p.42.

quantity of stage directions, which signals a return to a more 'epic' and 'lyrical' style.[116] He relates this readjustment to Lessing's didactic purpose, pointing to the prevalence of figurative language in his theological writings of the same period.[117] The presence of so much imagery in the play, as well as the nature of the images themselves, such as the reference to the wolf in sheep's clothing and recurring allusions to seeds and plants, evoke biblical style and enrich the oriental tone.[118] The use of a style that relies extensively on imagery and symbolism is a characteristic of the literature of spiritual wisdom in many different cultures. This kind of writing typically uses such means to communicate ideas that transcend the realm of empirical fact.

The transformation of conventional elements is apparent, too, in the role of narrative, monologues and *sententiae*. The essentially dramatic function of Nathan's narration at the centre of the play has been recognised by criticism since Atkins's article.[119] This piece of narration does not concern plot elements that fall outside the limits of time and place affecting the represented action, but has an autonomous role within it. In form, it is much closer to Lessing's theory and practice of the fable than it is to traditional dramatic *récit*, relying on simple language, a few apt adjectives, colloquial phrases ('Was zu tun?' ['What is to be done?']), questions and direct speech. The style of the speech coincides with the style and character of the speaker. Elsewhere in the play, narration is used sparingly; the fire and Recha's rescue are the subject of relatively short passages of narration in the first two scenes of act I, and the way in which Recha became Nathan's foster-daughter emerges from the brief narrative exchanges between himself and the Friar in act IV, scene vii. The economy of these, and the way they are integrated into the dramatic action, shows that Lessing is maintaining the trend visible in *Minna* and *Emilia* to subordinate narrative strictly to dramatic form. For example, Nathan uses the details of the fire at his home to challenge and revise a simplistic view of divine intervention, and these interactions reveal much about his relationship with both Daja and Recha. Similar conclusions emerge from Anne Lagny's analysis of the Tempelherr's monologues. Although, in some respects, these monologues can be seen to fulfil the traditional neo-classical functions of introspection and self-examination,

116. Göbel, *Bild und Sprache*, p.154-55.

117. Göbel, *Bild und Sprache*, p.165. In *Lessings Schwächen*, Goeze specifically attacks his style, saying that 'er scheint die Logik und gesunde Vernunft aus diesem Streite verbannet zu haben, und wil[l] schlechterdings blos durch Witz, durch Parabeln, Bilderchen und Gleichnisse den Sieg behaupten' ('he seems to have banished logic and sound reasoning from this dispute, and is determined to win the upper hand simply through the use of wit, parables, little images and similes'). Lessing, *Nathan der Weise*, ed. Demetz, p.196.

118. Göbel, *Bild und Sprache*, p.168-71.

119. In terms of both form and function, Nathan's narration can be seen as the antithesis of Marwood's 'Geschichte'.

Lessing nevertheless suppresses the lyrical effects in favour of dramatic ones. The orderliness of neo-classical or even Shakespearean treatments of monologue gives way to a style that more accurately evokes the spontaneous thought processes and emotions involved.[120] Christa Geitner makes the point that in *Nathan*, Lessing avoids the kind of 'quotable' *sententiae* so prevalent in the dramas of Goethe and Schiller.[121] She is right about *sententiae*, although *Nathan* does contain 'memorable' utterances. Here, though, they tend to be short and pithy ('Kein Mensch muß müssen'[122]), and seem to reflect Diderot's preference for the wit inspired by circumstances, that 'anyone' might express, rather than the poetic tradition of French neo-classicism or Weimar. Thus, although written in verse, the speech of *Nathan* still differs structurally from conventional verse drama and seems to be determined by its function within dramatic form, not its status as 'poetry'.

In various ways then, the poetic character of the speech is 'disguised' in order to further dramatic goals. Nevertheless, language is still central to this play, as Lessing's description of the work as a 'Gedicht' implies.[123] Schröder calls *Nathan* 'das gesprächigste aller Dramen' ('the most chatty of all plays') and points out that in most scenes, apart from the concluding one, only two, occasionally three, characters are present. Attention is often focused on the intellectual process, the way in which Nathan talks the other figures (Recha, the Tempelherr, Saladin) into new ways of seeing things. The verbal exchanges are all steps towards the moment of agreement on which the play concludes, and language itself is the instrument which brings about the important recognition.[124] Saladin realises that Nathan's friend was his brother Assad from the reference to his preference for Persian, and it is the notes (in Arabic) recorded in Wolf von Filneck's breviary (which the Friar removed from the body of the dead Conrad von Stauffen at his burial) that proves the family relationships.[125]

The importance of the precise use of language is established in the opening exchange with Daja, where Nathan questions her use of the word 'endlich' ('at last') and gently points out that the expression is not objectively justifiable, but merely a subjective projection.[126] Throughout

---

120. Anne Lagny, 'De la rhétorique des passions à la dramaturgie de la conscience: le monologue du Templier (III, 8)', *G. E. Lessing: Nathan der Weise/Die Erziehung des Menschengeschlechts*, ed. Philippe Wellnitz (Strasbourg 2000), p.73-86 (p.85).

121. Christa Geitner, ' "[...] ich dächte, sie wären viel schlechter, wenn sie viel besser wären" (Lessing à propos de ses vers dans *Nathan le sage*)', in *G. E. Lessing: Nathan der Weise/Die Erziehung des Menschengeschlechts*, p.87-102 (p.88, n.3).

122. Göpfert, ii.219. 'No one ever has to'.

123. Schröder, *Sprache und Drama*, p.251.

124. Schröder, *Sprache und Drama*, p.250.

125. Göpfert, ii.346.

126. Göpfert, ii.207.

the play, his role is constantly to guide the other characters towards a more accurate connection of their beliefs with objective circumstances through the proper use of language, as exemplified in the parable of the three rings. Nathan's well-told *Märchen* ('fairy tale') shows that Saladin's question about the 'true' or 'best' religion is the wrong way to formulate the problem and that this question cannot lead to a meaningful answer. Only when the question is posed in the right terms can an appropriate response be determined. Nathan's careful probing of positions and analysis of beliefs models how to use semiotic instruments as medicine, not poison, in the service of a rational and humane society.[127] The truth of the relationships in the play emerges when names (which typify the function of words as signs[128]) are correctly attached to the corresponding individuals, implying that when signifiers and signifieds are properly conjoined, accurate knowledge of the state of things can be achieved. In this sense, *Nathan* suggests an answer to the problems posed by the ambiguous nature of signs and the confused perceptions treated in Lessing's tragedies. In *Nathan*, language is attended to not primarily for its form, an important dimension in neo-classical tragedy, but for its meaning; not the signifier but the signified. Geitner's analysis of accent and metre shows how Lessing exploits them to serve the didactic function of the play. Nathan's use of language to guide other characters towards a greater degree of enlightenment is heightened by the way metre throws key words into relief, just as the Patriarch's abuse of language is made more apparent by the incompatibility of his professional jargon (*Apostasie, Kapitulation*) with the iambic form.[129] Expressing this in terms of Lessing's theory of the linguistic sign, one could say that in *Nathan*, the form of speech is consistent with the tone of the work as an aesthetic whole; it creates a satisfying illusion for the spectators, ready to believe that this language resembles the way in which these characters could be expected to speak, and at the same time it conveys the mind of the listener beyond the signifier to the signified, thus achieving the status of a 'natural' theatrical sign. Within the context established by the play, the language is appropriate to the characters; it is 'theirs', not Lessing's.

*Nathan* successfully achieves the internal unity and coherence which Diderot asserts to be fundamental to any theatrical work of whatever genre; language and gestures, setting and costume are mutually supporting and create an effective aesthetic illusion. Does the significant role attributed to language mean that Lessing here abandons the painterly perspective on drama established in Diderot's theory? His continuing reliance on the various visual techniques outlined here suggests that he has not, and this is confirmed in a letter of January 1779, in which he

127. Göpfert, ii.218.
128. Wellbery, *Lessing's Laocoon*, p.19-20.
129. Geitner, 'Lessing à propos de ses vers dans *Nathan le sage*', p.93-96.

evokes his creative orientation in relation to what was to be his last play in terms of a painterly metaphor. Reporting to his brother Karl on the final stages of composition, he wrote: 'Ich habe, mit den Malern zu reden, die letzten Lichterchen aufgesezt.'[130]

130. Göpfert, ii.721. 'To use the language of painters, I have just added the final touches of light.'

# Conclusion

THIS study took as its starting point Lessing's unambiguous but nevertheless puzzling assertion that the plays and theories of Diderot exercised a formative influence on his own dramatic writing. The problem of understanding exactly what he could have meant by this was tackled by first situating Diderot's dramatic writings in the context of various currents of aesthetic thought that preceded and inform them. This approach reveals that debates about the nature of painting and the painterly sign that took place in the late seventeenth and early eighteenth centuries reshaped thinking about the nature of the linguistic sign in its aesthetic function and about all the artistic signs on which theatrical representation relies. Early manifestations of the impact of the debates about painting on drama theory are to be found in the controversial essays of Houdar de La Motte and in the first French *tragédie bourgeoise*, *Silvie*, composed by the painter, Paul Landois. Their deliberate efforts to transform the nature of dramatic speech and to exploit the visual dimension of drama more effectively, which sets their work apart from that of other contemporaries such as Nivelle de La Chaussée or Mme de Graffigny, are subsequently taken up and developed by Diderot. The topoi of the invisible poet and the hidden spectator, which play an important role in formulating the kind of changes in dramatic form that La Motte and Landois envisage, recur in Diderot's theory and connect his thought directly with theirs. His theory and his plays can together be seen to represent a thorough and coherent synthesis of these earlier reflections on theatre as a medium that has the potential to exploit the kind of artistic signs eighteenth-century thinkers call 'natural' and which they saw exemplified in the artistic signs deployed by painting. Diderot's theory explores various aspects of dramatic form from the perspective of the spectator as one who simultaneously listens and watches, and his plays provide effective examples of how the artificial or arbitrary artistic signs that characterise the neoclassical theatrical code can be converted to natural ones. The form taken by dramatic speech is affected in a particularly noticeable way by this shift in perspective. In plays composed according to the new style the dialogue is not shaped by the principles that apply to literary or poetic language but by the requirement that play language create an illusion for the ear, just as the visual effects are intended to create one for the eye. One could say that in this new aesthetic, dramatic speech is construed as language that is crafted to be 'seen' as well as heard. Diderot's works also show other writers how to change their creative perspective from that of a poet working within the rhetorical framework of neo-classicism (and thus striving to produce responses in the audience through the impact that the words themselves exert upon them), to that of a dramatist who composes from a stance that more closely parallels that of the painter and communicates visually as well as aurally. This reorientation is necessary to help playwrights compose dramatic texts capable of generating for the stage the kind of illusion associated with figurative painting. Diderot believed that plays based upon experiences of a kind familiar to the spectators and simultaneously embodying this type of visual and aural dramatic illusion would restore the power of theatrical representation to shape human behaviour and social life for the good.

An interesting reflection of Diderot's dramatic theory, showing that his application of painterly concepts to stage representation and his emphasis on illusion quickly had a discernible influence on his contemporaries, can be found in Beaumarchais's *Essai sur le genre dramatique sérieux*, which was first published as a companion piece to his successful *drame, Eugénie*, in 1767.[1] Beaumarchais's enthusiasm for Diderot, his self-chosen mentor, is equal to, if not greater than, that of Lessing. In words that seem to echo those of Lessing's first preface, Beaumarchais asserts that 'Tout ce qu'on peut penser de vrai, de philosophique et d'excellent sur l'art dramatique, [Diderot] l'a renfermé dans le quart d'un in-douze. J'aimerais mieux avoir fait cet ouvrage.'[2] Throughout his essay, Beaumarchais relies on terms drawn from the vocabulary of painting such as *jeter des masses, pinceau* (instead of *plume*), *tableau, peinture, spectateur, point d'optique, coloris, illusion*. In addition to defending the non-heroic subject matter and characters which the middle genre exploits for emotional and moral effects, Beaumarchais singles out Diderot's suggestions on plot and suspense for comment. Like Lessing, who quotes the very same passage in number 48 of the *Hamburgische Dramaturgie*, Beaumarchais stresses the value of allowing the audience to know more of the developing action than the characters.[3] The spectator is more powerfully affected, he argues, when, as with the crisis in his own play, 'il l'a vue se former lentement sous ses yeux'. He also devotes long sections of his essay to a justification of the use of prose and simple language, which he supports with appeals to the idea of the invisible artist and to illusion. Like Diderot, he insists that 'le premier objet de l'auteur doit être de me transporter si loin des coulisses, et de faire si bien disparaître à mes yeux tout le badinage des acteurs, l'appareil théâtral, que leur souvenir ne puisse m'atteindre une seule fois dans tout le cours de son drame'.[4] He contrasts literary language with stage language by quoting a comment made by a friend on the dialogue of an early

1. Brian N. Morton, 'Beaumarchais's first play, *Eugénie*', *Romanic review* 57 (1966), p.81-87 (p.83). As Beaumarchais mentions in his *Essai*, he had begun work on the play some years earlier, probably in 1759.
2. Beaumarchais, *Œuvres*, p.138.
3. Beaumarchais, *Œuvres*, p.137-38.
4. Beaumarchais, *Œuvres*, p.133.

version of *Eugénie*. 'Si vous le destinez à l'impression, n'y touchez pas, il va bien; si vous voulez le faire jouer un jour, montez-moi sur cet arbre si bien taillé, si touffu, si fleuri; effeuillez, arrachez tout ce qui montre la main du jardinier.'[5] His discussion of dramatic speech also includes a detailed consideration of the individual tone appropriate to each character, an idea which, as we have seen, had a decisive impact on Lessing. In the preface he composed in 1785, to counter criticisms made of *La Folle Journée ou le Mariage de Figaro*, Beaumarchais offers further insight into how he himself continued to approach the creation of stage dialogue. Asked why his own literary style is so little in evidence in the play, Beaumarchais reasserts the principle that in drama the author's personal style should never impinge on the awareness of the audience, and he goes on to explain how he actually composes: 'Lorsque mon sujet me saisit, j'évoque tous mes personnages et les mets en situation. [...] Ce qu'ils diront, je n'en sais rien; c'est ce qu'ils feront qui m'occupe. Puis, quand ils sont bien animés, j'écris sous leur dictée rapide, sûr qu'ils ne me tromperont pas.'[6] This is the technique of visualisation described and recommended by Diderot and it is interesting to realise that we owe the brilliant dialogue of Beaumarchais's masterpiece in part, at least, to him! This brief digression into the theory of one of France's most successful eighteenth-century playwrights shows that the elements Lessing identifies as particularly important in Diderot's theatre writings are also those that impressed other contemporary dramatists. He was by no means the only writer whose theory and style were shaped in significant ways by Diderot's efforts to recast dramatic theory in terms of illusion and the use of natural artistic signs.

Previous commentators on Lessing have often emphasised the important role played in his development by his knowledge of English drama. They have drawn attention to his efforts, from very early on, to encourage interest in this and other European theatre traditions, as antidotes to the domination of the German stage by French taste.[7] It is certainly true that *Miss Sara Sampson*, Lessing's first domestic tragedy, reflects his familiarity with English theatre.[8] His conviction that the latter was more compatible with German taste than the drama of the French is forcefully expressed in the seventeenth *Literaturbrief* of February 1759, where in typical lapidary fashion Lessing condemns Gottsched for his imposition of the Gallic model and urges German writers to turn instead to Shakespeare as a source of inspiration better suited to their character and traditions and also closer to the true nature of tragedy.[9] Petersen points out that following this strongly worded declaration in favour of the English example, one would

---

5. Beaumarchais, *Œuvres*, p.139.
6. Beaumarchais, *Œuvres*, p.373.
7. Lamport, *Lessing and the drama*, p.53.
8. Lamport, *Lessing and the drama*, p.65-67. See also Kies, 'The sources and basic model of Lessing's *Miss Sara Sampson*'; and Vail, *Lessing's relation to the English language and literature*.
9. Göpfert, v.70-73.

expect to find Lessing turning to the translation or adaptation of a play by Shakespeare.[10] Instead, he translates the writings of a Frenchman, whose views on Shakespeare were somewhat less enthusiastic than his own.[11] This initially surprising step is itself an indication of the considerable importance that Lessing must immediately have seen Diderot's theatre writings to hold for the age. As Grillparzer later observed, 'sein Kultus für Shakespeare konnte ihn vor der Nachahmung Diderots nicht bewahren'.[12] It is noteworthy also that the first work in aesthetics that Lessing completed following the Diderot translation was the first part of the *Laokoon*, where he sets out to clarify once and for all the essential differences between the artistic signs employed by painting and by poetry, that is, the two sign systems that come together in drama and which Diderot systematically invokes in his theory. Lessing's rejection of the French neo-classical style (which Diderot of course shared) is thus compatible, the present study shows, with a highly receptive attitude towards progressive trends in dramatic aesthetics coming out of France. This is to accord a more important role to French influence in the development of Lessing's mature style than has traditionally been the case. But this emphasis is consistent with a statement made by Karl Lessing in his 1793 biography of his famous brother. Karl writes:

Lessing war weit entfernt, zu glauben, schon theatralische Meisterstücke gemacht zu haben, obgleich damals die seinigen zu den besten deutschen Originalen gehörten. Er wußte, was ihr Hauptfehler sei; sir hatten alle noch etwas von der Studierstube. Diderots Theater, das er noch zu Berlin übersetzt hatte, in keiner andern Absicht, als das deutsche Publicum auf edlere und richtigere Begriffe vom Theater zu bringen, veranlaßte auch selbst in ihm eine ganz andere Stimmung, und ganz neue Ideen, sogar seine Geringschätzung des französischen Theaters.[13]

But if, on the one hand, we can trace in Lessing's work evidence of a creative impulse first articulated in France, it should also be stressed that Lessing succeeded in adapting the ideas and examples of his source to

10. Petersen, ix.12-13.

11. Whilst Diderot readily recognised the genius of Shakespeare, he nevertheless considered his style unpolished and extravagant and his influence is not strongly felt in Diderot's work (Connon, *Innovation and renewal*, p.112-13). Shakespeare is barely mentioned in the works by Diderot that Lessing translated (DPV, iv.142-43, x.132 and x.404).

12. 'His devotion to Shakespeare could not keep him from imitating Diderot'. Quoted in Lessing, *Nathan der Weise*, ed. Demetz, p.122.

13. Karl G. Lessing, *Gotthold Ephraim Lessings Leben nebst seinem noch übrigen literarischen Nachlasse*, 3 vols (Berlin 1793-1795), i.236. 'Lessing was far from believing that he had created dramatic masterpieces, although at the time, his plays were among the finest of original German works. He knew what their main flaw was; there was still too much of the study about them. Diderot's theatre, which he had translated whilst he was still in Berlin with the sole purpose of giving the German public a higher and more accurate understanding of what theatre is, also brought about a change of attitude within himself, stimulating quite new ideas and even affecting his low opinion of French theatre.' I am grateful to Dr Barry Nisbet of Cambridge University for drawing my attention to this quotation.

create plays that have proved more popular and more enduring than those of Diderot. In this sense, the impact of Lessing's discovery of Diderot can be seen as an example of the active assimilation of artistically provocative material invoked by Michael Baxandall in his discussion of the relationship between Picasso and Cézanne.[14] Baxandall rejects the use of the word 'influence' as too passive a term to describe the stimulating creative effect of one artist upon another. He argues that artists approach the work of others in a purposive manner, with a consciousness of artistic problems in need of solution, and he insists that the artist whom we describe as 'influenced by' another is also an agent, transforming both the material of his source and the way in which that source is subsequently perceived by the public. Lessing read Diderot's theory and plays at a time when he was actively engaged in problems relating to the tragic form, in particular the way in which it evokes pity in the spectator. 'Moving the spectator' was the artistic challenge uppermost in Lessing's mind, and it is the central one that Diderot addresses, although from a perspective rather different from that adopted by Lessing in the correspondence of 1756-1757 with Mendelssohn and Nicolai.

When Lessing came upon Diderot's analysis of this question, he already had behind him a considerable amount of theatrical experience. He had served his dramatic apprenticeship in the comic genre, and, by the time he was twenty years old, had already written six comedies of his own and adapted into German two works by Plautus. Several of these plays were also performed. *Der junge Gelehrte* was staged in Leipzig by Caroline Neuber's theatre company in 1748; performances of both *Der Freigeist* and *Der Schatz* which took place in the 1760s are mentioned in the *Hamburgische Dramaturgie*.[15] The perhaps unexpected success of *Miss Sara Sampson* in 1755 proved that Lessing's talents were not confined to a single genre, and the composition of all these works gave him valuable experience in the construction of plot and fostered his general knowledge of stagecraft.

In addition, his study of the fable form in the period immediately following the composition of *Miss Sara* furnished further opportunity for reflection on the ways in which story or action embodies a 'message' or theme. Lessing contrasts the action of the fable as he conceives it with visual representations of moral tales, insisting that such pictures are not actually fables but merely emblems.[16] Action is essential to the fable, and its moral must arise naturally and unambiguously from 'die Folge von Veränderungen' ('the succession of changes') which constitute the story. Lessing rejects definitions of the fable which refer to its message as hidden or disguised, observing ironically that 'es muß gar keine Mühe kosten, die Lehre in der Fabel zu erkennen; es müsste vielmehr, wenn ich so reden

14. Michael Baxandall, *Patterns of intention: on the historical explanation of pictures* (New Haven, CT 1985), p.58-62.
15. Göpfert, ii.639, ii.661-62 and ii.665-66.
16. Göpfert, v.366-67.

darf, Mühe und Zwang kosten, sie darin nicht zu erkennen'.[17] Many of Lessing's own fables (from the collection published in 1759) are successful illustrations of this essential principle,[18] and his preoccupation with structure in the fable has obvious connections with the articulation of plot in drama. Invoking Lessing's metaphor from the eighty-first *Literaturbrief*, one might perhaps say that when he translated Diderot's dramatic writings he already had a firm grasp of design and that what he absorbed from Diderot was what Schiller would later expunge from the Weimar version of *Nathan*, namely colouring.[19] The new awareness of 'colouring' enriched Lessing's strong sense of dramatic conflict and structure with a vivacity and a capacity to create illusion that far surpass the effects achieved in his earlier works.

The young Diderot had felt a passion for the theatre (and for actresses!) that equalled or exceeded that of Lessing,[20] and he had also, apparently, tried his hand at verse drama.[21] But although he composed a number of philosophical dialogues, he had not (as far as we know) published any completed dramatic works nor experienced any stage successes by the time he composed *Le Fils naturel* and the *Entretiens*. He undoubtedly nurtured theatrical ambitions, but his commitment to the *Encyclopédie* made it difficult for him to pursue them, and the goals with which he contented himself in the late 1750s were actually rather modest, to judge by the quotation from Horace with which the *Discours* opens:

> Vice cotis acutum
> Reddere quae ferrum valet, exsors ipsa secandi
> HORAT., *de Arte poet.*[22]

Lessing's grateful and generous acknowledgement of Diderot's theatre writings in his 1780 preface is a testimony to the fact that his efforts had borne fruit, and Lessing's mature dramas stand as an impressive

17. Göpfert, v.370. 'It must not require any effort to recognise the moral of a fable; rather, it should, if I may put it this way, require quite considerable effort not to recognise it'.

18. Ronald M. Mazur, 'Gotthold Ephraim Lessing's fables: theory and practice', in *Lessing and the Enlightenment*, ed. Ugrinsky, p.53-57 (p.55).

19. Demetz, 'Die Folgenlosigkeit Lessings', p.739-40. Schiller's text is reproduced in *Schillers Werke*, ed. Julius Petersen *et al.*, 43 vols projected (Weimar 1943-), vol.xiii: *Bühnen-bearbeitungen*, ed. Julius Petersen and Hermann Scheider. See p.315-20 and p.416-17 for summaries of the principal changes that Schiller made. (See also p.200, n.90 above.)

20. DPV, xx.96.

21. In his 'Observations sur "Le Fils naturel"' for the *Observateur littéraire*, the abbé de La Porte quotes Desfontaines's praise of a verse play the young Diderot had shown to him. Denis Diderot, *Œuvres complètes*, ed. J. Assézat and M. Tourneux, 20 vols (Paris 1875-1879), vii.17. One wonders whether this experience is in any way related to Diderot's remarks, in the *Discours*, on the importance of preparing a complete outline of the play before embarking on the dialogue (DPV, x.347).

22. 'Horace, *Art poétique*, vers 304-305. "Faisant fonction de pierre à aiguiser, qui a la propriété de rendre le fer tranchant tout en étant elle-même incapable de couper" (Horace, "Épître aux Pisons")'. DPV, x.331.

fulfilment of Diderot's goal of revitalising contemporary theatre. Diderot must have considered the huge success of *Le Père de famille*, in Lessing's German translation, ample reward for services rendered and a gratifying confirmation of his own powers as a dramatist. Although they never met or corresponded, they both recognised their shared aims.[23] Pioneers in the reconceptualisation of theatrical illusion that was stimulated by fresh thinking about the art of painting, Diderot and Lessing together succeeded in opening up new possibilities for the theatre of their day and bequeathed to subsequent generations of dramatists a much richer appreciation for dramatic speech as language crafted to be 'seen' as well as heard.

23. Diderot had ordered a translation of *Miss Sara Sampson* for inclusion in the projected but never realised anthology of domestic dramas. See Robert R. Heitner, 'Diderot's own *Miss Sara Sampson*', *Comparative literature* 5 (1953), p.40-49, and DPV, x.546.

# Bibliography

## i. Primary sources

Addison, Joseph, and Richard Steele, *The Spectator*, ed. G. Gregory Smith, 4 vols (London 1906).

Aristotle, *The Poetics*, translation and analysis by Kenneth A. Telford (Chicago, IL 1961).

Aubignac, François Hédelin, abbé d', *La Pratique du théâtre*, ed. Pierre Martino (Paris 1927).

– *La Pratique du théâtre*, ed. Hélène Baby (Paris 2001).


Beaumarchais, Pierre-Augustin Caron de, *Œuvres*, ed. Pierre Larthomas (Paris 1988).

Boileau, Nicolas, *Œuvres complètes*, ed. Françoise Escal (Paris 1966).


Challe, Robert, *Les Illustres Françaises* (1713), ed. Frédéric Deloffre, 2 vols (Paris 1959).

–, *Les Illustres Françaises* (1713), ed. Frédéric Deloffre and Jacques Cormier, new edition (Geneva 1991).


Diderot, Denis, *Œuvres*, ed. Laurent Versini, 5 vols (Paris 1996).

–, *Œuvres complètes*, ed. J. Assézat and M. Tourneux, 20 vols (Paris 1875-1879).

–, *Œuvres complètes*, ed. Herbert Dieckmann, Jacques Proust, Jean Varloot, *et al.*, 34 vols projected (Paris 1975-).

Dubos, Jean-Baptiste, abbé, *Réflexions critiques et historiques sur la poésie et sur la peinture* (Paris 1993).

Du Fresnoy, Charles-Alphonse, *De arte graphica* (Paris 1668).


*Encyclopédie, ou Dictionnaire raisonné des sciences, des arts et des métiers par une société de gens de lettres*, 17 vols (Paris 1751-1765).


Fénelon, François de Salignac de La Mothe, *Les Aventures de Télémaque*, ed. Albert Cahen, 2 vols (Paris 1920).

–, *Œuvres*, ed. Jacques Le Brun, 2 vols (Paris 1983).

–, *Œuvres complètes*, ed. M. Gosselin, 10 vols (Paris 1851-1852; Geneva 1971).

–, *Salignac de la Mothe Fénelon's 'Dialogues on Eloquence': A translation with an introduction and notes*, ed. Wilbur Samuel Howell (Princeton, NJ 1951).

Fontenelle, Bernard Le Bovier de, *Œuvres complètes*, ed. G.-B. Depping, 3 vols (Paris 1813; Geneva 1968).


Goethe, Johann Wolfgang von, *Sämtliche Werke*, ed. Eduard von der Hellen, 40 vols (Stuttgart 1902-1912).

Gottsched, Johann Christoph, *Die deutsche Schaubühne nach den Regeln und Exempeln der Alten*, 2nd edn, 2 vols (Leipzig 1746-1750).

–, *Neuer Büchersaal der schönen Wissenschaften und freyen Künste*, 10 vols (Leipzig 1745-1754).

Grimm, Friedrich Melchior, Denis Diderot, Guillaume-Thomas Raynal, and Johann Heinrich Meister, *Correspondance littéraire, philosophique et critique*, ed. Maurice Tourneux, 16 vols (Paris 1877-1882).


Hénault, Charles-Jean-François, *Pièces de théâtre en prose* (Paris 1770).

Herder, Johann Gottfried, *Sämtliche Werke*, ed. Bernhard Suphan (Berlin 1877).

Horace, *The Satires and epistles of Horace*, translated by Smith Palmer Bovie (Chicago, IL 1996; 1959).

Hugo, Victor, *Théâtre complet*, ed. Roland Punal, J.-J. Thierry and Josette Mélèze, 2 vols (Paris 1963).

Hurd, Richard, *The Works*, 8 vols (London 1811; Hildesheim 1969).

La Chaussée, Pierre-Claude Nivelle de, *Mélanide, comédie en cinq actes en vers*, ed. W. D. Howarth (Brighton 1973).

La Mesnardière, Hippolyte Jules Pilet de, *La Poëtique* (Paris 1640; Geneva 1972).

La Motte, Antoine Houdar de, *Œuvres*, 9 vols and supplement (Paris 1753-1754).

Landois, Paul, *The First French 'tragédie bourgeoise': 'Silvie', attributed to Paul Landois*, ed. Henry Carrington Lancaster, *The Johns Hopkins studies in romance literatures and languages* 48 (Baltimore, MD 1954).

–, *Serena, ein bürgerliches Trauerspiel in Prose von einem Aufzuge. Nebst einem Vorspiel. Aus dem Französischen übersetzt*, translated by Gottlieb Konrad Pfeffel (Frankfurt and Leipzig 1764).

–, *Serena, et skuespil* (Copenhagen 1779), translated by Peder Topp Wandall.

Lessing, Gotthold Ephraim, *Das Theater des Herrn Diderot: aus dem Französischen übersetzt von Gotthold Ephraim Lessing*, ed. Klaus-Detlef Müller (Stuttgart 1986).

–, *Gesammelte Werke*, ed. Paul Rilla, 10 vols (Berlin 1954-1958).

–, *Hamburgische Dramaturgie*, ed. Otto Mann (Stuttgart 1958).

–, *Minna von Barnhelm*, ed. D. Hildebrandt, *Dichtung und Wirklichkeit* 30 (Frankfurt, Berlin 1969).

–, *Nathan der Weise*, ed. Peter Demetz, *Dichtung und Wirklichkeit* 25 (Frankfurt 1966).

–, *Nathan der Weise*, ed. David Hill (Hull 1988).

–, *Sämtliche Schriften*, ed. Karl Lachmann, 3rd edn revised by Franz Muncker, 23 vols (Stuttgart, Berlin, Leipzig 1886-1924).

–, *Lessings Werke*, ed. Julius Petersen and Waldemar von Olshausen *et al.*, 25 vols (Berlin, Vienna 1907; Hildesheim and New York 1970).

–, *Werke*, ed. Herbert G. Göpfert, 8 vols (Munich 1970-1979).

–, *Werke und Briefe in zwölf Bänden*, ed. Wilfried Barner (Frankfurt am Main 1985-2003).

–, Moses Mendelssohn and Friedrich Nicolai, *Briefwechsel über das Trauerspiel*, ed. Jochen Schulte-Sasse (Munich 1972).

Lessing, Karl G., *Gotthold Ephraim Lessings Leben nebst seinem noch übrigen literarischen Nachlasse*, 3 vols (Berlin 1793-1795).

Locke, John, *An Essay concerning human understanding*, ed. Alexander Campbell Fraser, 2 vols (New York n.d.; Oxford 1959).

Mercier, Louis-Sébastien, *De la littérature et des littératures suivi d'un nouvel examen de la tragédie française* (Yverdon 1778; Geneva 1970).

–, *Du théâtre, ou Nouvel Essai sur l'art dramatique* (Amsterdam 1773).

Molière, *Œuvres complètes*, ed. Eugène Despois and Paul Mesnard, 11 vols (Paris 1886).

Montenoy, Charles Palissot de, *Œuvres de M. Palissot*, 6 vols (Paris 1788).

Naigeon, Jacques-André, *Mémoires historiques et philosophiques sur la vie et les ouvrages de Denis Diderot* (Paris 1821; Geneva 1970).

Olivet, abbé d', 'A M. le Président Bouhier, de l'Académie Française', in *Remarques de grammaire sur Racine* (Paris 1738).

Piles, Roger de, *L'Abrégé de la vie des peintres avec un traité du peintre parfait* (Paris 1699).

– *L'Art de peinture de Charles-Alphonse Du Fresnoy, traduit en français, avec des remarques nécessaires et très amples* (Paris 1668; 2nd edn 1673).

– *Cours de peinture par principes* (Paris 1708).

– *Dialogue sur le coloris* (Paris 1673).

Plato, *The Republic of Plato*, translated by Francis MacDonald Cornford (Oxford 1945).

Pope, Alexander, *The Poems of Alexander Pope*, ed. John Butt (London 1965).

Prévost d'Exiles, Antoine-François, abbé, *Histoire du chevalier Des Grieux et de Manon Lescaut*, ed. Frédéric Deloffre and Raymond Picard (Paris 1965).

Riccoboni, Louis, *Réflexions historiques et critiques sur les différents théâtres de l'Europe* (Paris 1738).

Richardson, Jonathan, *An Essay on the theory of painting* (London 1725).

Richardson, Samuel, *The History of Sir Charles Grandison*, ed. Jocelyn Harris, 3 vols (London, New York and Toronto 1972).

Sainte-Albine, Rémond de, *Le Comédien* (Paris 1747).

Schiller, Friedrich von, *Schillers Werke*, ed. Julius Petersen *et al.*, 43 vols projected (Weimar 1943-).

Sedaine, Michel-Jean, *Maillard, ou Paris sauvé: tragédie en cinq actes en prose* (Paris 1788).

Shaftesbury, Anthony Ashley Cooper, third earl of, 'A notion of the *historical draught* or *tablature* of the judgment of Hercules', *Second characters, or the Language of forms*, ed. Benjamin Rand (1713; New York 1969).

Trublet, Nicolas Charles Joseph, *Essais sur divers sujets de littérature et de morale*, 4 vols (Paris 1760; Geneva 1968).

Voltaire, *Correspondence and related documents*, ed. Th. Besterman, in *The Complete works of Voltaire*, vol.85-135 (Geneva, Banbury, Oxford 1968-1977).

–, *Dictionnaire philosophique* in *Œuvres complètes*, ed. Louis Moland, 52 vols (Paris 1877-1885).

–, *Œdipe. Avec une préface dans laquelle on combat les sentimens de M. de la Motte sur la poësie* (Paris 1730).

–, 'Remarques sur Sertorius', *Commentaires sur Corneille*, ed. David Williams, in *The Complete works of Voltaire*, vol.53-55 (Banbury 1974-1975).

## ii. Secondary sources

Alderson, Simon, '*Ut pictura poesis* and its discontents in late seventeenth- and early eighteenth-century England and France', *Word and image* 11:3 (1995), p.256-63.

Alpers, Svetlana, 'Describe or narrate? A problem in realistic representation', *New literary history* 8:1 (1976), p.15-41.

Appelbaum-Graham, Ilse, 'Minds without medium. Reflections on *Emilia Galotti* and *Werthers Leiden*', *Euphorion* 56 (1962), p.3-23.

Atkins, Stuart, 'The parable of the rings in Lessing's *Nathan der Weise*', *Germanic review* 26 (1951), p.259-67.

Auerbach, Eric, *Mimesis: the representation of reality in western literature* (Bern 1946; Princeton, NJ 1953).

Barnett, Dene, 'The performance practice of acting: the eighteenth century', *Theatre research international*, new series 2:3 (May 1977), p.157-86, 3:1 (October 1977), p.1-19, 3:2

(February 1978), p.79-93, 5:1 (winter 1979-1980), p.1-36.

Barthes, Roland, *Sur Racine* (Paris 1960; 1963).

Baxandall, Michael, *Patterns of intention: on the historical explanation of pictures* (New Haven, CT 1985).

Bennett, Benjamin, *Modern drama and German classicism: renaissance from Lessing to Brecht* (Ithaca, NY 1979).

Bergman, Gösta M., 'Le décorateur Brunetti et les décors de la Comédie-Française au XVIII$^e$ siècle', *Theatre research* 4:1 (1962), p.6-28.

–, *Lighting in the theatre* (Stockholm, Totowa, NJ 1977).

Bérubé, Georges, 'A la recherche du malade dans *Le Mariage de Figaro*: quel(s) sens faut-il donner à l'objet-fauteuil?', *Man and nature/l'homme et la nature* 5 (1986), p.15-28.

Bloch, Haskell M., 'The concept of imitation in modern criticism', *Proceedings of the fourth congress of the International Comparative Literature Association*, ed. François Jost (The Hague 1966), p.704-20.

Böckmann, Paul, *Formgeschichte der deutschen Dichtung*, 2 vols (Hamburg 1949).

Bornkamm, Heinrich, 'Die innere Handlung in Lessings *Miss Sara Sampson*', *Euphorion* 51 (1957), p.385-96.

Braun, Theodore E. D., 'From Marivaux to Diderot: awareness of the audience in the *comédie*, the *comédie larmoyante* and the *drame*', *Diderot studies* 20 (1981), p.17-29. First published as 'La conscience de la présence des spectateurs dans la comédie larmoyante et dans le drame', *SVEC* 192 (1980), p.1527-34.

Brüggemann, Fritz, 'Lessings Bürgerdramen und der Subjektivismus als Problem', *Gotthold Ephraim Lessing*, ed. G. and S. Bauer, *Wege der Forschung* 211 (Darmstadt 1968), p.83-126. First published in *Jahrbuch des freien deutschen Hochstifts* (1926), p.69-110.

Bryson, Norman, 'Intertextuality and visual poetics', *Style* 22:2 (summer 1988), p.183-93.

– *Word and image: French painting of the ancien régime* (Cambridge 1981; 1983).

Buch, Hans Christoph, '*Ut Pictura Poesis*': *Die Beschreibungsliteratur und ihre Kritiker von Lessing bis Lukács* (Munich 1972).

Buck, Elmar, 'Lessing und Diderot – die Konditionen des Theaters', in *Schauspielkunst im 18. Jahrhundert: Grundlagen, Praxis, Autoren*, ed. Wolfgang F. Bender (Stuttgart 1992), p.205-19.

Buffat, Marc (ed.), *Diderot: l'invention du drame. Actes de la journée d'étude du 14 octobre 2000 à l'Université Paris VII – Denis Diderot* (Paris 2000).

Burgard, Peter, 'Lessing's tragic topography: the rejection of society and its spatial metaphor in *Philotas*', *Deutsche Vierteljahrsschrift für Literaturwissenschaft und Geistesgeschichte* 61:3 (1987), p.441-56.

Burwick, Frederik, *Illusion and the drama: critical theory of the Enlightenment and Romantic era* (University Park, PA 1991).

Carroll, Joseph, '*Minna von Barnhelm* and *le genre sérieux*: a reevaluation', *Lessing yearbook* 13 (1981), p.143-58.

Cerf, Steven R., '*Miss Sara Sampson* and *Clarissa*: the use of epistolary devices in Lessing's drama', in *Theatrum mundi: essays on German drama and German literature*, ed. Edward R. Haymes (Munich 1980), p.22-30.

Chatelus, Jean, *Peindre à Paris au XVIII$^e$ siècle* (Nîmes 1991).

Chouillet, Anne-Marie, 'Dossier du *Fils naturel* et du *Père de famille*', *SVEC* 208 (1982), p.73-166.

Chouillet, Jacques, *La Formation des idées esthétiques de Diderot* (Paris 1973).

–, 'Le rôle de la peinture dans les clichés stylistiques et dramatiques de

Diderot', *Europe* 661 (1984), p.150-58.

Clayton, Vista, *The Prose poem in French literature* (New York 1936).

Conisbee, Philip, *Georges de La Tour and his world* (New Haven, CT 1996).

Connon, Derek, *Innovation and renewal: a study of the theatrical works of Diderot*, *SVEC* 258 (1989).

Coulet, Henri, 'Le thème de la Madeleine repentie chez Robert Challe, Prévost et Diderot', *Saggi e ricerche di letturatura francese* 14 (1975), p.287-304.

Courville, Xavier de, *Un apôtre de l'art du théâtre au XVIIIe siècle: Luigi Riccoboni dit Lélio*, 3 vols (Paris 1943).

Critchfield, Richard, 'Lessing, Diderot, and the theatre', in *Eighteenth-century German authors and their aesthetic theories*, ed. Richard Critchfield and Wulf Koepke (Columbia, SC 1988), p.11-28.

Cronk, Nicholas, *The Classical sublime. French neoclassicism and the language of literature* (Charlottesville, VA 2002).

– (ed.), *Etudes sur 'Le Fils naturel' et les 'Entretiens sur le Fils naturel' de Diderot* (Oxford 2000).

Crow, Thomas E., *Painters and public life in eighteenth-century Paris* (New Haven, CT, London 1985).

Daemmrich, Horst S., 'Illusion: Möglichkeit und Grenzen eines Begriffs', *Lessing yearbook* 1 (1969), p.88-98.

Daunicht, Richard, *Die Entstehung des bürgerlichen Trauerspiels in Deutschland*, 2nd edn (Berlin 1965).

Demetz, Peter, 'Die Folgenlosigkeit Lessings', *Merkur. Deutsche Zeitschrift für europäisches Denken* 25:8 (1971), p.727-41.

Démoris, René, '*Ut poesis pictura?* Quelques aspects du rapport roman-peinture au siècle des Lumières', *Dilemmes du roman: essays in honor of Georges May*, ed. Catherine Lafarge, Stanford French and Italian Studies 65 (Saratoga, CA 1989).

Didier, Béatrice, 'Images du sacré chez Diderot', *Travaux de littérature* 6 (1993), p.193-209.

Duerr, Edwin, *The Length and depth of acting* (New York, Toronto, London 1962).

Dupont, P., *Un poète-philosophe au commencement du dix-huitième siècle: Houdar de La Motte* (Paris 1898).

Eckardt, Jo-Jacqueline, *Lessing's 'Nathan the Wise' and the critics: 1779-1991* (Columbia, SC 1993).

Ekstein, Nina, *Dramatic narrative: Racine's 'récits'*, (New York, Bern, Frankfurt 1986).

Fick, Monika, *Lessing-Handbuch* (Stuttgart, Weimar 2000).

Fischer-Lichte, Erika, *The Semiotics of theater*, translated by Jeremy Gaines and Doris L. Jones (Bloomington and Indianapolis, IN 1992). Originally published as *Semiotik des Theaters*, 3 vols (Tübingen 1983).

Flaherty, Gloria, 'Emilia Galotti's Italian heritage', *Modern language notes* 97:3 (1982), p.497-514.

Flax, Neil, 'From portrait to *tableau vivant*: the pictures of *Emilia Galotti*', *Eighteenth-century studies* 19 (1985), p.39-55.

Fletcher, Dennis, 'Primitivisme et peinture dans les théories dramatiques de Diderot', *Actes du colloque international Diderot* (Paris 1985), p.457-67.

–, '"Ut pictura spectaculum": Diderot and the semiotics of the stage', *Romance studies* 4 (1984), p.79-96.

Fontaine, André, *Les Doctrines d'art en France de Poussin à Diderot* (Paris 1909; Geneva 1970).

Force, Pierre, 'Peinture et poésie dans le *Télémaque* de Fénelon', *Revue de littératures française et comparée* 3 (1994), p.65-71.

Forno, Lawrence J., 'The fictional letter in the memoir novel: Robert Challe's *Illustres Françaises*', *SVEC* 81 (1971), p.149 61.

–, 'Robert Challe and the eighteenth century', *SVEC* 79 (1971), p.163-75.

France, Peter, *Rhetoric and truth in France: Descartes to Diderot* (Oxford 1972).

–, and Margaret McGowan, 'Autour du *Traité du récitatif* de Grimarest', *Dix-septième siècle* 132 (1981), p.303-17.

Frantz, Pierre, 'Jouer aujourd'hui *Le Fils naturel*: notes sur une mise en scène récente du *Fils naturel* et de *Dorval et moi* par Alain Bézu (1993)', *Diderot: l'invention du drame*, ed. Marc Buffat (Paris 2000), p.159-71.

–, *L'Esthétique du tableau dans le théâtre du XVIIIᵉ siècle* (Paris 1998).

Fricke, Gerhard, 'Bemerkungen zu Lessings *Freigeist* und *Miss Sara Sampson*', in *Festschrift für Josef Quint*, ed. Hugo Moser (Bonn 1964), p.83-120.

Fried, Michael, *Absorption and theatricality: painting and beholder in the age of Diderot* (Berkeley and Los Angeles, CA, London 1980).

Furbank, P. N., *Diderot* (London 1992; 1993).

Gabriel, André, 'Fénelon le peintre sourd', *Papers on French seventeenth-century literature* 13 (1980), p.117-34.

Gaiffe, Félix, *Le Drame en France au XVIIIᵉ siècle* (Paris 1910; 1971).

Geitner, Christa, '"[...] ich dächte, sie wären viel schlechter, wenn sie viel besser wären" (Lessing à propos de ses vers dans *Nathan le sage*)', in *G. E. Lessing: Nathan der Weise/Die Erziehung des Menschengeschlechts*, ed. Philippe Wellnitz (Strasbourg 2000), p.87-102.

Gethner, Perry, 'The role of décor in French classical comedy', *Theatre journal* 36:3 (October 1984), p.383-99.

Gilman, Margaret, *The Idea of poetry in France, from Houdar de La Motte to Baudelaire* (Cambridge 1958).

Göbel, Helmut, *Bild und Sprache bei Lessing* (Munich 1971).

Gombrich, Ernst, *Art and illusion: a study in the psychology of pictorial representation*, 2nd edn (New York, Princeton, NJ 1961).

–, 'Lessing (lecture on a master mind)', *Proceedings of the British Academy* 43 (1957), p.133-56.

Goodden, Angelica, *'Actio' and persuasion: dramatic performance in eighteenth-century France* (Oxford 1986).

–, '*Le Fils naturel*: langage du corps et discours sur le corps', in *Etudes sur 'Le Fils naturel' et les 'Entretiens sur le Fils naturel' de Diderot*, ed. Nicholas Cronk (Oxford 2000), p.53-64.

–, '"Une peinture parlante": the *tableau* and the *drame*', *French studies* 38 (1984), p.397-413.

Goulbourne, Russell, 'Diderot et Horace, ou le paradoxe du théâtre moderne', in *Etudes sur 'Le Fils naturel' et les 'Entretiens sur le Fils naturel' de Diderot*, ed. Nicholas Cronk (Oxford 2000), p.112-22.

–, 'The eighteenth-century "querelle des vers" and Jean Du Castre d'Auvigny's *La Tragédie en prose*', *SVEC* 2000:05, p.371-410.

–, 'Essai bibliographique' in *Etudes sur 'Le Fils naturel' et les 'Entretiens sur le Fils naturel' de Diderot*, ed. Nicholas Cronk (Oxford 2000), p.181-209.

Guthke, Karl S., *Das deutsche bürgerliche Trauerspiel* (Stuttgart 1972).

–, *Gotthold Ephraim Lessing* (Stuttgart 1973).

Hartung, Günter, 'Diderots *Système dramatique* und der Dramatiker Lessing', *Beiträge zur Romanischen Philologie* 24:2 (1985), p.295-99.

Hasselbeck, Otto, *Illusion und Fiktion: Lessings Beitrag zur poetologischen Diskussion über das Verhältnis von Kunst und Wirklichkeit* (Munich 1979).

Hawcroft, Michael, *Word as action: Racine, rhetoric and theatrical language* (Oxford 1992).

Hayes, Julie, 'Subversion du sujet et querelle du tric-trac: le théâtre de Diderot et sa réception', *Recherches sur Diderot et sur l'"Encyclopédie"* 6 (1989), p.105-17.

Hazard, Paul, *La Crise de la conscience européenne, 1680-1715* (Paris 1961).

Heidsieck, Arnold, 'Der Disput zwischen Lessing und Mendelssohn über das Trauerspiel', *Lessing year-book* 11 (1979), p.7-34.

Heinich, Nathalie, *Du peintre à l'artiste: artisans et académiciens à l'âge classique* (Paris 1993).

Heitner, Robert R., 'Concerning Lessing's indebtedness to Diderot', *Modern language notes* 65 (February 1950), p.82-88.

–, 'Diderot's own *Miss Sara Sampson*', *Comparative literature* 5 (1953), p.4049.

–, *German tragedy in the age of Enlightenment: a study in the development of original tragedies, 1724-1768* (Berkeley and Los Angeles, CA 1963).

–, 'Lessing's manipulation of a single comic theme', *Modern language quarterly* 18 (1957), p.183-98.

Hernadi, Paul, 'Nathan der Bürger: Lessings Mythos vom aufgeklärten Kaufmann', *Lessing yearbook* 3 (1971), p.151-59.

Herzel, Roger W., 'The décor of Molière's stage: the testimony of Brissart and Chauveau', *Publications of the Modern Languages Association* 5 (October 1978), p.925-54.

Hilgar, Marie-France, 'Théorie et pratique de la tragédie dans l'œuvre de Houdar de La Motte', *Littératures classiques* 16 (1992), p.259-67.

Hobson, Marian, *The Object of art: the theory of illusion in eighteenth-century France* (Cambridge 1982).

Homann, Renate, *Selbstreflexion der Literatur: Studien zu Dramen von G. E. Lessing und H. von Kleist* (Munich 1986).

Howard, William Guild (ed.), *Laokoon: Lessing: Goethe: Herder: selections* (New York 1910).

–, '*Ut pictura poesis*', *Publications of the Modern Languages Association* 24 (1909), p.40-123.

Ingarden, Roman, *The Literary work of art: an investigation on the borderlines of ontology, logic, and theory of literature: with an appendix on the function of language in the theater*, translated by George G. Grabowicz (Evanston, IL 1973). First published as *Das literarische Kunstwerk mit einem Anhang von den Funktionen der Sprache im Theaterschauspiel* (Tübingen 1931).

Jauss, Hans Robert, 'Diderots Paradox über das Schauspiel (*Entretiens sur le "Fils naturel"*)', *Germanische-Romanische Monatsschrift* 11 (1961), p.380-413.

Katz, Victor, J., *A History of mathematics: an introduction* (New York 1993).

Kibedi Varga, A., *Rhétorique et littérature: études de structures classiques* (Paris 1970).

Kies, Paul P., 'The sources and basic model of Lessing's *Miss Sara Sampson*', *Modern philology* 24 (1926), p.65-90.

Königsberg, Ira, *Samuel Richardson and the rise of the dramatic novel* (Ann Arbor, MI 1980).

Krieger, Murray, 'Representation in words and in drama: the illusion of the natural sign', in *Aesthetic illusion: theoretical and historical approaches*, ed. Frederick Burwick and Walter Pape (Berlin and New York 1990), p.183-216.

Ladislas, Günther, *L'Œuvre dramatique de Sedaine* (Paris 1908).

Lagny, Anne, 'De la rhétorique des passions à la dramaturgie de la conscience: le monologue du

Templier (III, 8)', *G. E. Lessing: Nathan der Weise/Die Erziehung des Menschengeschlechts*, ed. Philippe Wellnitz (Strasbourg 2000), p.73-86.

Lagrave, Henri, *Le Théâtre et le public à Paris de 1715 à 1750* (Paris 1972).

Lamport, Francis, 'The death of Emilia Galotti – a reconsideration', *German life and letters* 44:1 (1990), p.25-34.

–, 'Lessing and the "Bürgerliches Trauerspiel"', in *The Discontinuous tradition: studies in German literature in honour of Ludwig Stahl*, ed. P. F. Ganz (Oxford 1970), p.14-28.

–, *Lessing and the drama* (Oxford 1981).

–, 'Lessing traducteur et critique de Diderot', in *Etudes sur 'Le Fils naturel' et les 'Entretiens sur le Fils naturel' de Diderot*, ed. Nicholas Cronk (Oxford 2000), p.171-80.

Lancaster, Henry Carrington, *French tragedy in the time of Louis XV and Voltaire: 1715-1774*, 2 vols (Baltimore, MD 1950).

Lanson, Gustave, *Nivelle de La Chaussée et la comédie larmoyante* (Paris 1887).

Lee, Rensselaer W., '*Ut pictura poesis*: the humanistic theory of painting', *The Art bulletin* 22:4 (1940), p.196-269.

Lichtenstein, Jacqueline, *La Couleur éloquente: rhétorique et peinture à l'âge classique* (Paris 1989).

Lightbrown, R. W., 'Gaetano Giulio Zumbo', *Burlington magazine* 106 (1964), p.486-96, 563-69.

Lioure, Michel, *Le Drame* (Paris 1963).

Lote, Georges, *L'Histoire du vers français* (Aix-en-Provence 1988).

Mace, Dean Tolle, 'Transformations in classical art theory: from "poetic composition" to "picturesque composition"', *Word and image* 1 (1985), p.59-86.

Markiewicz, Henryk, '*Ut pictura poesis*: a history of the topos and the problem', *New literary history* 18:3 (spring 1987), p.535-58.

Marks, Sylvia Kasey, *Sir Charles Grandison: the compleat conduct book* (Lewisburg, PA, London, Cranbury, NJ 1986).

Martini, Fritz, 'Riccaut, die Sprache und das Spiel in Lessings Lustspiel *Minna von Barnhelm*', in *Gotthold Ephraim Lessing*, ed. G. and S. Bauer, *Wege der Forschung* 211 (Darmstadt 1968), p.376-426. First published in *Formenwandel: Festschrift für Paul Böckmann*, ed. Walter Müller-Seidel and Wolfgang Preisendanz (Hamburg 1964), p.193-235.

Maskell, David, *Racine: a theatrical reading* (Oxford 1991).

May, Gita, 'Diderot et Roger de Piles', *Publications of the Modern Languages Association* 85 (1970), p.444-55.

Mazur, Ronald M., 'Gotthold Ephraim Lessing's fables: theory and practice', in *Lessing and the Enlightenment*, ed. Alexej Ugrinsky (New York 1986), p.53-57.

Menant, Sylvain, *La Chute d'Icare: la crise de la poésie française 1700-1750* (Geneva 1981).

Ménil, Alain, *Diderot et le drame: théâtre et politique* (Paris 1995).

–, '"Ut pictura poesis erit"? Théâtre et antithéâtralité dans la théorie du drame', in *Etudes sur 'Le Fils naturel' et les 'Entretiens sur le Fils naturel' de Diderot*, ed. Nicholas Cronk (Oxford 2000), p.89-111.

Metzger, Michael M., *Lessing and the language of comedy* (The Hague, Paris 1966).

Michelsen, Peter, 'Die Erregung des Mitleids durch die Tragödie. Zu Lessings Ansichten über das Trauerspiel im Briefwechsel mit Mendelssohn und Nicolai', in *Der unruhige Bürger, Studien zu Lessing und zur Literatur des achtzehnten Jahrhunderts* (Würzburg 1990), p.107-36. An earlier version of this article was first published in the *Deutsche Vierteljahrschrift für Literaturwissenschaft und Geistesgeschichte* 40 (1966), p.548-66.

Mirot, Léon, *Roger de Piles* (Paris 1924).

Mittman, Barbara G., 'Some sources of the André scene in Diderot's *Fils naturel*', *SVEC* 116 (1973), p.211-19.

–, *Spectators on the Paris stage in the seventeenth and eighteenth centuries* (Ann Arbor, MI 1984).

Morrissey, Robert, 'La pratique du théâtre et le langage de l'illusion', *Dix-septième siècle* 146 (1985), p.17-27.

Mortier, Roland, *Diderot en Allemagne, 1750-1850* (Paris 1954).

Morton, Brian N., 'Beaumarchais's first play, *Eugénie*', *Romanic review* 57 (1966), p.81-87.

Moureau, François, 'De La Motte à Landois: le vers tragique en jugement au XVIII$^e$ siècle', *Revue d'histoire du théâtre* 2-3 (April-September 1993), p.35-48.

Müller, Klaus-Detlef, 'Das Erbe der Komödie im bürgerlichen Trauerspiel. Lessings "Emilia Galotti" und die commedia dell'arte', *Deutsche Vierteljahrsschrift für Literaturwissenschaft und Geistesgeschichte* 46 (1972), p.28-60.

Neumann, Peter Horst, *Der Preis der Mündigkeit: über Lessings Dramen: Anhang über Fanny Hill* (Stuttgart 1977).

Norton, Robert E., '"Ein bitteres Gelächter": tragic and comic elements in Lessing's *Philotas*', *Deutsche Vierteljahrsschrift für Literaturwissenschaft und Geistesgeschichte* 66:3 (1992) p.450-65.

Otto, Uwe, *Lessings Verhältnis zur französischen Darstellungstheorie* (Frankfurt, Bern 1976).

Peyronnet, Pierre, *La Mise en scène au XVIII$^e$ siècle* (Paris 1974).

Price, Lawrence Marsden, 'George Barnwell abroad', *Comparative literature* 2 (1950), p.126-56.

Proust, Jacques, 'L'initiation artistique de Diderot', *Gazette des beaux-arts* 55 (1960), p.225-32.

Pucci, Suzanne, 'The art, nature and fiction of Diderot's beholder', *Stanford French review* 8 (1984), p.273-94.

Puttfarken, Thomas, *The Discovery of pictorial composition: theories of visual order in painting 1400-1800* (New Haven, CT, London 2000).

–, *Roger de Piles' theory of art* (New Haven, CT, London 1985).

Pütz, Peter, *Die Leistung der Form: Lessings Dramen* (Frankfurt am Main 1986).

Ranscelot, Jean, 'Les manifestations du déclin poétique au début du XVIII$^e$ siècle', *Revue d'histoire littéraire* 33 (October-December 1926), p.497-520.

Rempel, Hans, *Tragödie und Komödie im dramatischen Schaffen Lessings* (Berlin 1935; Darmstadt 1967).

Ritter, Heidi, 'Zur Schauspielkunst bei Diderot und Lessing', *Beiträge zur Romanischen Philologie* 24:2 (1985), p.301-304.

Robertson, J. G., *Lessing's dramatic theory, being an introduction to and commentary on his 'Hamburgische Dramaturgie'* (Cambridge 1939; New York 1965).

–, 'Sources italiennes des paradoxes dramatiques de La Motte', *Revue de littérature comparée* 3 (1923), p.369-75.

Rosenberg, Pierre, Jacques Thuillier and Pierre Landry, *Georges de La Tour, Paris, Orangerie des Tuileries, mai-septembre* (Paris 1972).

Rothstein, Eric, '"Ideal presence" and the "non finito" in eighteenth-century aesthetics', *Eighteenth-century studies* 9 (1976), p.307-32.

Rougement, Martine de, *La Vie théâtrale en France au XVIII$^e$ siècle* (Paris and Geneva 1988).

Rudowski, Victor Anthony, *Lessing's 'aesthetica in nuce': an analysis of the May 26, 1769, letter to Nicolai* (Chapel Hill, NC 1971).

Saisselin, Rémy G., '*Ut pictura poesis*: Dubos to Diderot', *Journal of aesthetics and art criticism* (winter 1961), p.144-56.

Sambanis, Michaela, 'Mettre en scène Racine: à propos des didascalies', *Zeitschrift für Französische Sprache und Literatur* 113:1 (2003), p.27-38.

Saße, Günter, *Die aufgeklärte Familie: Untersuchungen zur Genese, Funktion und Realitätsbezogenheit des familialen Wertsystems im Drama der Aufklärung* (Tübingen 1988).

–, 'Das Besondere und das Allgemeine. Lessings Auseinandersetzung mit Diderot über Wahrheit and Wirkung des Dramas', in *Gesellige Vernunft: Zur Kultur der literarischen Aufklärung*, ed. Ortrud Gutjahr, Wilhelm Kühlman and Wolf Wucherpfennig (Würzburg 1993), p.263-76.

Schillemeit, Jost, 'Lessings und Mendelssohns Differenz. Zum Briefwechsel über das Trauerspiel', in *Digressionen: Wege zur Aufklärung: Festgabe für Peter Michelsen*, ed. Gotthardt Frühsorge, Klaus Manger and Friedrich Strack (Heidelberg 1984), p.79-92.

Schmidt, Erich, 'Diderot und Lessing', *Die Gegenwart* 9 (1882), p.133-36 and p.153-55.

–, *Lessing: Geschichte seines Lebens und seiner Schriften* 2 vols (Berlin 1923).

Schmidt, Julia Gädeke, *Lessings Philotas: Ästhetisches Experiment mit satirischer Wirkungsabsicht* (New York, Bern, Frankfurt, Paris 1988).

Schneider, Helmut, 'Aufklärung der Tragödie: Lessings *Philotas*', in *Horizonte: Festschrift für Herbert Lehnert zum 65. Geburtstag*, ed. Hannelore Mundt, Egon Schwarz and William J. Lillyman (Tübingen 1990) p.10-39.

Schröder, Jürgen, *Gotthold Ephraim Lessing: Sprache und Drama* (Munich 1972).

Schröder, Volker, '"Le langage de la peinture est le langage des muets": remarques sur un motif de l'esthétique classique', in *Hommage à Elizabeth Sophie Chéron: texte et peinture à l'âge classique*, ed. René Démoris (Paris 1992), p.95-110.

Schuppenhauer, Claus, *Der Kampf um den Reim in der deutschen Literatur des 18. Jahrhunderts* (Bonn 1970).

Scott-Prelorentzos, Alison, 'Diderot, Lessing and "Das wahre Lächerliche"', in *Momentum dramaticum. Festschrift for Eckehard Catholy*, ed. Linda Dietrick and David G. John (Waterloo 1990), p.135-48.

Seznec, Jean, *Essais sur Diderot et l'antiquité* (Oxford 1957).

Siebert, Donald T., Jr, '*Laokoon* and *Polymetis*: Lessing's treatment of Joseph Spence', *Lessing yearbook* 3 (1971), p.71-83.

Staiger, Emil, 'Rasende Weiber in der deutschen Tragödie des achtzehnten Jahrhunderts', in *Stilwandel. Studien zur Vorgeschichte der Goethezeit* (Zürich 1965), p.25-74.

Steinmetz, H., '*Emilia Galotti*', in *Interpretationen: Lessings Dramen* (Stuttgart 1987), p. 87-137.

Sterling, Charles, *La Nature morte de l'antiquité à nos jours* (Paris 1952).

Stewart, Philip, 'Diderot absconditus', in *L'Encyclopédie, Diderot, l'esthétique: mélanges en hommage à Jacques Chouillet, 1915-1990*, ed. S. Auroux, D. Bourel, and C. Porset (Paris 1991), p.149-57.

Stone, P. W. K., *The Art of poetry: 1750-1820* (London and New York 1967).

Szondi, P., '*Tableau* und *coup de théâtre*: zur Sozialpsychologie des bürgerlichen Trauerspiels bei Diderot: mit einem Exkurs über Lessing', in *Lektüren und Lektionen* (Frankfurt 1973).

Ter-Nedden, Gisbert, *Lessings Trauerspiele: der Ursprung des modernen Dramas aus dem Geist der Kritik* (Stuttgart 1986).

Teyssèdre, Bernard, *Roger de Piles et les débats sur le coloris au siècle de Louis XIV* (Paris 1957).

Todorov, Tzvetan, 'Ästhetik und Semiotik im 18. Jahrhundert: G. E.

Lessing: *Laokoon'*, *Das Laokoon-Projekt: Pläne einer semiotischen Ästhetik*, ed. Gunter Gebauer (Stuttgart 1984).

Trappen, Stefan, 'Von der persuasiven Rhetorik zur Ausdrucksprache: Beobachtungen zum Wandel der Formensprache in Lessings Trauerspielen', in *Cahiers suisses de littérature comparée* 30 (1999), p.67-87.

Tunstall, Kate E., 'Dossier', in *Etudes sur 'Le Fils naturel' et les 'Entretiens sur le Fils naturel' de Diderot*, ed. Nicholas Cronk (Oxford 2000), p.211-324.

–, 'Hieroglyph and device in Diderot's *Lettre sur les sourds et muets'*, *Diderot studies* 28 (2000), p.161-172.

Vail, Curtis C. D., *Lessing's relation to the English language and literature* (New York 1936).

Van Stockum, Theodorus, 'Lessing und Diderot', *Neophilologus* 39 (1955), p.191-202.

Verbraeken, René, 'Roger de Piles et le vocabulaire artistique', *Etudes romanes* 18 (1979), p.128-40.

Weil, Michèle, 'Du roman bourgeois au drame bourgeois', *Cahiers d'histoire des littératures romanes* 4 (1977), p.433-63.

Wellbery, David E., *Lessing's Laocoon: semiotics and aesthetics in the Age of Reason* (Cambridge 1984).

–, 'The pathos of theory: *Laokoon* revisited', in *Intertextuality: German literature and visual art from the Renaissance to the twentieth century*, ed. Ingeborg Hoesterey and Ulrich Weisstein (Columbia, SC 1993).

Whitmore, Richard Prescott, 'Two essays on *Le Père de famille'*, *SVEC* 116 (1973), p.137-209.

Wilkshire, F. M., 'Lillo and Moore in France: English influences on the dramatic theory of Diderot', *Man and nature/l'homme et la nature* 5 (1986), p.201-13.

Williams, David, 'Voltaire and the language of the gods', *SVEC* 62 (1968), p.57-81.

Wilpert, Gero von, *Sachwörterbuch der Literatur*, 4th edn (Stuttgart 1964).

Wilson, Arthur M., *Diderot* (New York 1972).

Wittkowski, Wolfgang, 'Emancipation or capitulation of the middle class? The metaphor of the "long path" as a key to Lessing's political tragedy *Emilia Galotti'*, *Lessing and the Enlightenment*, ed. Alexej Ugrinsky (New York 1986), p.149-63.

Worvill, Romira, 'Le rôle de la peinture dans l'adaptation théâtrale d'une nouvelle de Robert Challe par Paul Landois', in *Challe et/en son temps: actes du colloque de l'Université d'Ottawa, 24-26 septembre 1998*, ed. Marie-Laure Girou Swiderski and Pierre Berthiaume (Paris 2002), p.99-112.

–, 'Recherches sur Paul Landois, collaborateur de l'*Encyclopédie'*, *Recherches sur Diderot et sur l'Encyclopédie* 23 (October 1997), p.127-40.

Ziolkowski, Theodore, 'Language and mimetic action in Lessing's *Miss Sara Sampson'*, *The Germanic review* 40 (1965), p.261-76.

# Index